FROMMER'S

COMPREHENSIVE TRAVEL GUIDE

Madrid & the Costa del Sol

2nd Edition

by Darwin Porter
Assisted by Danforth Prince

MACMILLAN • USA

ABOUT THE AUTHORS

A native of North Carolina, **Darwin Porter** was a bureau chief for *The Miami Herald* when he was 21 and later worked in television advertising. A veteran travel writer, he is the author of numerous bestselling Frommer guides, notably to England, France, Germany, the Caribbean, Italy, and Spain. When not traveling (which is rare), he lives in New York City. He is assisted by **Danforth Prince**, formerly of the Paris bureau of *The New York Times*.

MACMILLAN TRAVEL

A Prentice Hall Macmillan Company
15 Columbus Circle
New York, NY 10023

Copyright 1993, 1995 by Simon & Schuster, Inc.

ISBN 0-02-860049-5
ISSN 0899-2932

Design by Michele Laseau
Maps by Geografix Inc. and Ortelius Design

SPECIAL SALES

Bulk purchases (10+ copies) of Frommer's Travel Guides are available to corporations at special discounts. The Special Sales Department can produce custom editions to be used as premiums and/or for sales promotion to suit individual needs. Existing editions can be produced with custom cover imprints such as corporate logos. For more information write to: Special Sales, Prentice Hall, 15 Columbus Circle, New York, NY 10023.

Manufactured in the United States of America

Contents

List of Maps

What the Symbols Mean

★ **FROMMER'S FAVORITES**—hotels, restaurants, attractions, and entertainments you should not miss

$ **SUPER-SPECIAL VALUES**—really exceptional values

In Hotel & Other Listings

The following symbols refer to the standard amenities available in all rooms:

A/C air conditioning
TEL telephone
TV television
MINIBAR refrigerator stocked with beverages and snacks

The following abbreviations are used for credit or charge cards:

AE	American Express	DISC	Discover
CB	Carte Blanche	MC	MasterCard
DC	Diners Club	V	Visa

Trip Planning with this Guide

Use the following features:

What Things Cost In   To help you plan your daily budget

Calendar of Events   To plan for or avoid

Suggested Itineraries   For seeing the city and environs

What's Special About Checklist   A summary of the city's highlights

Easy-to-Read Maps   Walking tours, city sights, hotel and restaurant locations—all referring to or keyed to the text

Fast Facts   All the essentials at a glance: climate, currency, embassies, emergencies, information, safety, taxes, tipping, and more

Other Special Frommer Features

Frommer's Smart Traveler Tips   Hints on how to secure the best value for your money

Cool for Kids   Hotels, restaurants, and attractions

Did You Know . . . ?   Offbeat, fun facts

Impressions   What others have said

Invitation to the Readers

While researching this book, I have come across many fine establish-ments, the best of which I have included here. I am sure that many of you will also come across appealing hotels, inns, restaurants, guesthouses, shops, and attractions. Please don't keep them to your-self. Share your experiences, especially if you want to comment on places included in this edition that have changed for the worse. You can address your letters to:

Darwin Porter
Frommer's Madrid & the Costa del Sol, 2nd Edition
c/o Macmillan Travel
15 Columbus Circle
New York, NY 10023

A Disclaimer

Readers are advised that prices fluctuate in the course of time and travel information changes under the impact of the varied and vola-tile factors that affect the travel industry. Neither the author nor the publisher can be held responsible for the experiences of readers while traveling. Readers are invited to write to the publisher with ideas, comments, and suggestions for future editions.

Safety Advisory

Whenever you're traveling in an unfamiliar city or country, stay alert. Be aware of your immediate surroundings. Wear a moneybelt and keep a close eye on your possessions. Be particularly careful with cameras, purses, and wallets—all favorite targets of thieves and pick-pockets.

1

Introducing Madrid

Tʜᴇ ᴄɪᴛʏ ᴏꜰ Mᴀᴅʀɪᴅ ʟɪᴇꜱ ʟᴀɴᴅʟᴏᴄᴋᴇᴅ ᴏɴ ᴀ ᴡɪɴᴅꜱᴡᴇᴘᴛ ᴀɴᴅ ᴏꜰᴛᴇɴ ᴀʀɪᴅ plain, beneath a sky that has been described as "Velázquez blue." Certain poets have even labeled Madrid the "gateway to the skies." It is populated by adopted sons and daughters from virtually every region of Spain, a demographic fact that adds to its cosmopolitan gloss. Despite its influence as the cultural beacon of the Spanish-speaking world and its quintessentially Spanish nature, the city lacks such all-important Iberian features as a beach, an ancient castle and cathedral, and an archbishop. To compensate for the lack of these amenities, the always-practical Madrileños long ago learned to substitute long strolls through the city's verdant parks and along its paseos. They built an airy and elegant palace (which the Spanish king and queen use mainly for ceremonial purposes) and erected countless churches, many glistening with baroque ornamentation and gilt. As for an archbishop, Madrileños are content with falling under the jurisdiction of the archbishop in nearby Toledo.

1   Background, Geography & History

Background

Madrid has been called the "Brasília of Europe," its location chosen as a national symbol rather than for any particular historic or cultural reason. Despite the city's eventual transformation into the stately capital of an immensely powerful empire, some of the most famous Spaniards in history never lived there, preferring instead the plains and hills of Andalusia or the more ancient cities of Zaragoza, Barcelona, Toledo, Segovia, and Granada. Regardless of Madrid's relative lack of cultural antecedents, the Spanish monarchs and the city's residents have vigorously overcompensated for this ever since. Rulers as diverse as the Hapsburgs, their Bourbon replacements, and Franco have poured into the city architectural bounties, priceless artworks, and the profits from many generations of businesses. An observation made by a 1644 resident is equally true today: "Each day, new houses are being built, and those that once were on the outskirts are now in the middle of the town." This unbridled building program has helped transform Madrid into a stellar capital city, home to almost 4.5 million people, and focus of the social and career ambitions of many millions more.

Known as a melting pot for individualists, which Spain seems to produce in profusion, Madrid is without question a world-class capital. Gone are the censorship, the fears, the armed guards, and the priggish morality of the years of Franco, whose influence often impelled Spain's artists, such as Picasso, to ply their crafts in neighboring countries.

Today, artists and writers gravitate to the newly revitalized Madrid, whose allures, freedoms, and promises of acclaim and fiscal recognition pull them into one of the most fertile artistic climates in the world. Whether or not you agree with its expression—artists and art

What's Special About Madrid

Museums
- The Prado, Spain's number-one attraction.
- Thyssen-Bornemisza Museum, named for the baron who collected old masters, then sold them to Spain.
- Centro de Arte Reina Sofía, a modern art museum with more than 300 works by Spanish masters (Dalí to Miró), including Picasso's powerful *Guernica.*
- Convento de las Descalzas Reales, a 16th-century royal convent with many art treasures.

Parks/Gardens
- Parque del Retiro, a verdantly landscaped refuge in the heart of Madrid.
- Mercado Puerta de Toledo, a shopping mall with 150 of Spain's most glamorous merchandisers.

Events/Festivals
- The *corrida*, a spectacle of death that has been both celebrated and condemned in Spanish art and literature.
- Fiesta de Sant' Isidro, 10 days of fairs, parades, and bullfights honoring the city's patron saint.

Cool for Kids
- Casa de Campo, a festive fun park filled with amusements.

After Dark
- Flamenco, the incomparable Spanish art form, presented at late-night clubs throughout the city.

Literary Shrine
- Casa de Lope de Vega, long-ago home (now a museum) of the 16th-century author whose work is most frequently compared to that of Shakespeare.

Architectural Highlights
- Plaza Mayor, the main square of the old town and quintessential symbol of Hapsburg Madrid.
- Palacio Real, Philip V's colossal palace, with 2,000 opulent rooms.
- The Moorish arcades of Madrid's Plaza de Toros, architectural attractions in their own right.

Shopping
- El Rastro, one of the largest open-air flea markets in Europe, best visited on a Sunday morning.

movements, like discos, come and go—Madrid is alive, passionate, and richly able to spearhead the *Movida* ("action") of a newly liberated Spanish culture. The legendary propensity of Spaniards to celebrate their nightlife is observed with something approaching passion in Madrid, as Madrileños stay awake till the wee hours, perhaps congregating in the very early morning over hot chocolate and *churros* (fried fingerlike doughnuts). Standing at the same countertop with them might be representatives of the hundreds of businesspeople and bankers whose zeal and imagination have revitalized the business landscape, transforming hypermodern office towers into well-respected and often feared entrepreneurial forces. For, despite Madrid's many pleasures, Madrileños recognize that their city is a place for work as well as for play, as evidenced by the spate of emerging industries, services, and products.

Its inhabitants are enormously proud of their well-endowed city. If you approach it with indulgence, affection, and a sense of humor, you'll be richly rewarded. The capital of the Spanish-speaking world and the object of travel fantasies for thousands of residents of Central and South America, Madrid is at the same time a monolithic big city and a tapestry of small villages that have developed individual identities throughout the various expansions of the capital. Each neighborhood offers countless subcultures that thrive within its precincts. The result is an almost inexhaustible supply of diversions and distractions, some potent enough to justify spending almost all your Spanish holiday within the confines of Madrid.

Geography

In the geographic center of the Iberian peninsula, Madrid lies amid the southern *mesetas* (tablelands) of Castilla la Nueva, close to the base of the heavily eroded Sierra de Guadarrama (maximum altitude around 8,000 feet) and the slightly more distant mountain ranges of Somosierra and Gredos.

Far from the tempering effects of the ocean, Madrid endures a hot and arid climate, but there are scattered verdant pockets thanks to the city's principal river (the Manzanares, a minor tributary of the Tagus). The terrain to the north and west of Madrid rises upward to the birch- and pine-studded rocky tablelands of the previously mentioned mountain ranges, while to the east, south, and southwest sprawl flatlands that eventually lead to the plains of Extremadura and La Mancha. (A notable exception to this dry terrain appears in the historic resort of Aranjuez, where alluvial flatlands and massive irrigation contribute to a greater verdancy.)

Madrid, as well as the entire country containing it, defines its position in relation to the Puerta del Sol. This crescent-shaped plaza has traditionally considered itself the starting point for every road and highway in Spain. A milepost in the center identifies the distance (in kilometers) to dozens of cities throughout Iberia, Europe, and the world.

Madrid is divided into three distinct geographical zones: Old Madrid, the Ensanche, and the modern sections built up since the vast expansion that began in the 1950s.

Old Madrid incorporates the compact medieval core that housed a Muslim settlement around A.D. 800. This small but historic district once contained freshwater supplies and thick fortifications.

It was much altered by later Christian monarchs, and its heart lies around the Palacio de Oriente, site of major rebuilding during the 18th century. Old Madrid also includes the city's medieval Christian neighborhoods as well as districts erected by the Hapsburgs. Originally centered around the Plaza de la Villa and the Plaza de la Paja, the population of that era eventually gravitated after about 1650 to the Plaza Mayor. Old Madrid also incorporates the grandiose 18th- and 19th-century neighborhoods of Spain's most recent royal dynasty, the Bourbons, whose most visible architectural symbol remains the neighborhoods near and along the paseo del Prado.

The areas that comprise the Ensanche developed during the 19th century after the old city ramparts were demolished to release the pressure on an urban infrastructure almost bursting at its seams. Thus developed the wide leafy boulevards of the Salamanca and Argüelles districts and the extension of the world-famous paseo de la Castellana. Populated shortly after their development with members of Spain's newly affluent bourgeoisie, they have remained ever since as symbols of the fiscal prosperity of certain segments of Spanish society.

Modern Madrid—known for its acres of angular but anonymous apartment dwellings as well as for some of the most exciting postmodern architecture anywhere—developed as the population of the city continued to burgeon after the end of the Spanish Civil War. Its boundaries have crept inexorably over such formerly independent villages as Chamartín (site of the city's largest and most modern railway station), Hortaleza, Villaverde, and many others.

In an effort to channel some of the endless traffic, which some observers consider the curse of Madrid, during the 1960s and 1970s city architects encircled all three of the city's divisions with the M-30 beltway. This super-ring-road today encloses the capital within as many as 16 lanes of endless traffic that funnel travelers and their vehicles onto the 6 superhighways, each radiating outward from its central junction at Madrid.

History

MUCH YOUNGER THAN MANY other Spanish cities—dozens of which can document their histories to before the ancient Romans—Madrid is the glittering parvenue, imposed upon the populace by autocrats and embraced ever since as the most frequently discussed and most controversial city in the country.

Despite its present-day dominance of Spanish life, Madrid (except for a small settlement first of Muslims and later of Christians, both of lackluster importance) didn't exist during most of the crucial events that defined modern Spain.

Dateline

- 800s Moors establish a fortified settlement, naming it Majrít, on the site of today's Royal Palace.
- 932 Majrít is demolished by Ramiro I but soon after is reconquered by the Moors.
- 1202 Alfonso VII grants Madrid

➤

Dateline

specific privileges, including a municipal charter.

- **1309** The Castilian Parliament (*Cortés*) chooses Madrid as its meeting place, setting a precedent for all future meetings.

- **1492** Catholic monarchs conquer the last Moorish stronghold, Granada; Columbus lands in the New World.

- **1519** Cortés seizes Mexico; Spain rushes to colonize the New World.

- **1525** François I, Renaissance king of France, is imprisoned briefly in Madrid after a humiliating military defeat.

- **1561** Philip II declares Madrid capital of the Spanish Empire.

- **1563** Philip II retires from Madrid to his monastery at El Escorial.

- **1580** Spain annexes Portugal, combining both empires into a vast landmass ruled from Madrid for 60 years.

- **1588** Sinking of the Spanish Armada by an increasingly powerful England.

- **1598** Death of Philip II; Spain is close to bankruptcy; the new monarch continues to embellish Madrid.

➤

The *Reconquista* (the wresting of the Iberian peninsula from the Moors) had ended in triumph for the Catholic monarchs long before Madrid became important. Preferring their more ancient bastions in Aragón and other parts of Castile and their newly conquered territories around Granada and Seville, Isabella and Ferdinand did not particularly favor Madrid. Columbus probably never visited it, and as a landlocked village it never played any role in the crucial voyages to the New World.

At least a century before Madrid soared into the consciousness of the world, the Pacific had been discovered, the Jews had already been expelled from Spain and scattered across North Africa and southern Europe, the Philippines had been colonized, and Buenos Aires had been founded. And at least 50 years prior to the establishment of Madrid, the Incas, Aztecs, Taínos, and many other cultures of Central and South America were well on the way to annihilation. In other words, Madrid entered late into the ongoing drama of Spanish history, but when it did it immediately became the most important character in the play.

MOORS & MEDIEVAL CHRISTIANS

The Moors first inhabited the city's site during the 800s, building thick fortifications near the Plaza de l'Oriente, on the site of today's Royal Palace. First mentioned in a historical document in 932, the settlement was demolished by the Catholic leader Ramiro II. The Moorish occupants, however, almost immediately regained control, only to be ousted again in 1083 by Alfonso VI of Castile. The settlement's Arabic name (Majrít) would, over time, become the most evocative place name in the Spanish language.

In 1202, partly to strengthen it against continuing Moorish raids, Alfonso VII granted the settlement specific privileges, as well as a *Fuero* (municipal charter). This designation encouraged the meeting there, in 1309 and again in 1478, of the fledgling Castilian Parliament (*Cortés*). In 1419, Juan II was proclaimed king of Castile there.

Three kings—Portugal's John IV, Enrique (Henry) III of Castile (famous for conquering the Canary Islands), and the weak-willed and dissolute Enrique IV of Castile—each spent prolonged periods in Madrid, perhaps setting a favorable royal precedent. Enrique IV also contributed to the town's fame by marrying Juana of Portugal there in 1464, and then again, unwittingly, by dying there in 1474. Even the very powerful and very canny French king François I (sometimes dubbed the first Renaissance king of northern Europe) was briefly imprisoned within Madrid's Torre de Los Lujanes after his army's defeat at the Battle of Pavia in 1525. Today that building is carefully preserved as one of Madrid's only surviving examples of Gothic architecture.

MADRID, CENTER OF THE SPANISH EMPIRE By the mid-1500s, however, Spain was a political entity very different from that of the previous century. Firmly in control of a united Spain, with little interference from the popes in Rome, Philip II (reigned 1556–98) developed into one of the most influential, and perhaps the most obsessive, monarchs in European history. Committed to his ambition of forever uniting the Iberian peninsula into a single political entity under a strong Catholic monarchy and surrounded by the staggering wealth produced by the New World's gold and silver mines, Philip proclaimed the unpretentious town of Madrid in 1561 as the capital of Spain. Although he cited its healthful climate and central position as his reasons, some historians have suggested he was also interested in escaping the avaricious power of the rich and solidly entrenched cities of Andalusia. Another incentive was the avoidance of the potentially dangerous archbishops in neighboring Toledo.

Many of Philip's contemporaries believed he would abandon Madrid when faced with the discomfort, inconvenience, and expense of transforming a simple Castilian village into a glittering capital,

Dateline

- **1606** Completion of the Plaza Mayor; rapid growth of Madrid's population.
- **1700** The death of Charles II provokes a dynastic battle; the War of the Spanish Succession involves most of Europe and leaves a French-born Bourbon on the Spanish throne.
- **1713** The Treaty of Utrecht sets terms for an uneasy peace; Philip V packs the government with non-Spanish administrators.
- **1734** The medieval Alcázar burns and is replaced within a few years with the neoclassical Royal Palace.
- **1760s–1800** Sewers and paved roads are built, along with other municipal improvements; many buildings are designed in the French-inspired Bourbon style.
- **1746–88** Spain is ruled by enlightened monarchs who enact liberal reforms.
- **1798** Goya paints the frescoes in the Chapel of San Antonio de la Florida.
- **1808** Forces of Napoleon invade Spain; Charles IV abdicates and is replaced by Napoleon's much-hated brother.

➤

Introducing Madrid   Background, Geography & History

Dateline

- **1808–14** War of Spanish Independence; Europe is once again deeply involved in Spain's internal problems; in 1812, aided by Wellington's English forces, Madrid evicts the French.

- **1814** Ferdinand VII rules Spain while buttressed by French troops; retracting promises of clemency, he eventually butchers hundreds of his opponents.

- **1822** Colombia is recognized as an independent nation by the United States; the loss of Spain's South and Central American colonies accelerates rapidly.

- **1833** Isabella II ascends the throne, promising libertarian reforms, but soon retracts them; riots sweep through Madrid.

- **1850** The first railroad is built within Spain.

- **1868** A revolution sends the unpopular Isabella II into exile in France; two years later a republic is established to replace the monarchy.

- **1875** The Republic collapses after five years of civil unrest; the army restores power to the ➤

although that was not to be the case. Importantly, the designation of Madrid as the empire's capital encouraged the eventual dominance of the Castilian dialect and cultural presuppositions upon all the rest of what is now known as Spain. This trend would be especially emphasized 380 years later, under the regime of Franco, when dialects and the cultural ambitions of other regions were suppressed, often brutally.

Although architectural embellishments, including the layout of the Plaza Mayor, slowly transformed Madrid's allure, Philip almost immediately chose to sequester himself within the vast somber confines of his monastery and palace, El Escorial, 30 miles west of Madrid, from which he ruled the Spanish Empire in semiascetic isolation. Ironically, his retreat began a scant two years after his designation of Madrid as his capital, ensuring he would never have to personally endure the inconvenience of ruling from a half-finished city.

Despite his other successes, his greatest was the 1580 acquisition of Portugal, the result of the 1578 disappearance of the Portuguese heir in a Moroccan battle as well as the targeted and insidious diplomacy of Philip himself and the threat of all-out war. This union, although undone by a Portuguese rebellion 60 years later, served to join—from headquarters in Madrid—the world's second-largest colonial empire in union with the largest of them all. For more than 50 years Madrid controlled the entire Iberian peninsula, including Portugal's valuable Atlantic ports, the armadas of skilled navigators for whom Portugal was at the time famous, and the infinite riches of Portugal's colony of Brazil as well.

Many of these benefits were undone by the growing tensions between Spain and England, whose officially sanctioned pirates had consistently plundered the convoys of Spanish treasure ships from the New World. England had also strewn discontent within Spain's possessions in the Netherlands and vigorously persecuted Catholics within England. All of Spain had been horrified when the British monarchs confiscated lands, buildings, and treasuries once belonging to the Catholic religious orders. Relations between Madrid and London couldn't have been worse, escalating into the showdown of 1588. Using naval techniques never before tested in large-scale battles, England utterly destroyed the largest group of warships assembled to date, the Spanish Armada, in one of naval history's most decisive battles. Its destruction was a blow from which Spain never really recovered.

Though the Armada's destruction was endlessly humiliating, a deeper malaise was already widespread within the government at Madrid. The expenses of Philip's vast empire were greater than the income produced by the gold and silver mines of Mexico and Peru, and no program of industrial or commercial development was ever promulgated to offset the deficits. As bullion flooded through Madrid into the moribund Spanish economy, hyperinflation followed, leading to virtual declarations of bankruptcy three times during Philip's reign. Inefficient and often corrupt administration of Spanish commerce and industry—which was being taxed almost out of existence—led to a staggering decline in revenues and an unwillingness of moneylenders to advance any further capital. When the influx of gold slowed substantially during the early 1700s, the result was disastrous.

Despite Philip's failures, during his reign the prodigious output of science, literature, and the arts is viewed today as partial compensation for many of his shortcomings. His tenure, in fact, is viewed as the Golden Age of Spanish literature, much of which made oblique, satirical, or honorific references to the epic scale of what was happening in Madrid.

MADRID'S EXPANSION & THE EMPIRE'S DECLINE
When Philip died in 1598, Madrileños clung desperately to their hopes that the new regime would show them the royal favor to which they

Dateline
Bourbon monarchs in the person of Alfonso XII.
- **1880** The beginning of a decade of unrest; rebellions in Cuba are suppressed by Spanish forces; Madrid expands both its borders and its population.
- **1885** Death of Alfonso XII; his heir, Alfonso XIII, is born six months later, and during his minority (1886–1902) his mother rules as Queen Regent.
- **1898** The Spanish-American War reduces the once-majestic Spanish Empire to an empty shell; Spain is once again close to fiscal ruin; Madrid continues to expand.
- **1902** Elevation of Alfonso XIII as king at age 16; every pronouncement he makes infuriates libertarians throughout Spain.
- **1914** World War I; Spain avoids direct European confrontation but finds Morocco increasingly troublesome.
- **1921** Madrid's Mayor Eduardo Dato, an influential conservative, is assassinated, leading to massive repression and

➤

Dateline

massive strikes; the Spanish army suffers a brutalizing and scandal-ridden defeat in North Africa.

- **1923–30** Dictatorship of Primo de Rivera, with full support of Alfonso XIII.

- **1931** More unpopular than ever, the king informally abdicates and goes into exile in France; only hours after his departure, the Second Republic is established.

- **1933** The right to vote is granted to Spanish women.

- **1936–39** The Spanish Civil War; on March 28, 1939, Madrid, the last Republican stronghold, falls to Franco's Nationalists.

- **1939–75** The regime of Francisco Franco.

- **1975** The liberal grandson of Alfonso XIII, Juan Carlos I, is brought back as king, although with greatly diminished powers.

- **1978** The centrist government of Adolfo Suárez adopts a new parliamentary constitution granting semiautonomy to many of Spain's dissenting regions.

had become accustomed. Strewn with muddy excavations and lofty dreams, the city was filled with adventurers, courtesans, impoverished nobility, soldiers, priests, and laborers sweating to erect buildings to house them all.

Under the subsequent ruler, Philip III (reigned 1598–1621), Madrid reinforced its role as capital of the largest power base since the fall of the Roman Empire. Despite the empire's chronic fiscal imbalances, Madrid continued to grow, often at the expense of the heavily taxed Spanish populace. (During one chapter of the new city's most intense construction, the government moved briefly and temporarily to Valladolid.) Though the city's life had originally been established around the Plaza de la Paja, and later the Plaza de la Villa, it surged northward with the 1606 completion of the new city's most visible showcase, the Plaza Mayor. Rhythmic in its gracefully repetitive classicism and large enough to conceivably cram most of the populace within its perimeter, it functioned as Madrid's nerve center and open-air living room for almost 300 years, at least until vast expansions of the city's borders diminished its crucial importance sometime in the 19th century.

BOURBON MADRID   A major era in the history of Madrid came to a violent end upon the death of Charles II (reigned 1665–1700), the last of the Spanish Hapsburgs. A disputed inheritance led to simultaneous claims upon the throne by contenders from two separate dynasties. The first was Charles of Hapsburg, the preferred candidate of England, Portugal, Holland, Austria, and some of the German states. The second candidate was Philippe of Anjou, a France-based member of the powerful Bourbon dynasty then ruling from Versailles and the grandson of the fiercely ambitious Louis XIV. Madrid almost instantly became a crucible of intense politicking as the fate of European power hung in the balance. The city was twice invaded by military forces, although the

➤

allegiance of the capital's most influential politicians with the Bourbon side (and the deathbed designation of the Bourbon candidate by the previous king as his heir) eventually helped sway the election in favor of Philippe of Anjou. Many modern historians interpret this period of Madrid's history as crucially important in defining the presuppositions of Europe's 18th- and 19th-century colonial expansions. It was also to begin a repetitive pattern that frequently designated Madrid as the fulcrum of European power politics, with its events closely watched (and often manipulated) by the other powers of Europe.

Although the war's winner, Philippe of Anjou, had made his first (aborted) triumphal entry into Madrid in 1701 as Philip V, his real reign began a dozen years later, in 1713. In that year the Treaty of Utrecht more or less rearranged the power balance of Europe, setting peace terms that would almost immediately be bitterly contested.

Dateline

- **1982** Electoral victory of Felipe González, an enlightened socialist.
- **1986** Spain joins the EC; Madrid's *Movida* (renaissance of creative thought and artistic output) gains momentum and a worldwide following.
- **1992** Madrid is designated the "cultural capital of Europe."
- **1993** Felipe González is reelected to head the government despite conservative opposition.

One act of self-preservation the new king almost immediately enacted was the promulgation of the Salic Laws of 1713, whose intention was never again to allow one of his Hapsburg rivals to gain the throne of Spain through marriage.

Impressed with the formal neoclassic architectural style then sweeping across France and the rest of Europe, Philip V initiated an energetic building program whose monuments and palaces are among the most memorable buildings in Madrid today. Although to an increasing degree he retreated from political involvement of any kind, his 33-year reign was punctuated with the construction of monuments that included the Hospicio de San Fernando, the Montserrat Church, the Cuartel del Conde-Duque, and the Toledo Bridge, all in the baroque style. For his vacation home, the French-born king commissioned a smaller version of the palace at Versailles on the fertile alluvial plain of Aranjuez, 29 miles south of Madrid, beginning in 1721.

On Christmas night of 1734, the medieval Alcázar, used for centuries as the king's residence in Madrid, was destroyed by fire, leaving a gaping hole in the city landscape that was filled in three years later by the 2,000-room Royal Palace (Palacio Real). From the 1760s up until the early 19th century, the city received such amenities as drains, paved streets, street lighting, the neoclassical brick-and-stone building that today houses the Prado (originally built as a natural science museum but converted into an art museum in 1819), the lavish but since-destroyed Palacio de Buenavista, the Botanical

Gardens (Jardín Botánico), the post office in the Puerta del Sol, the Puerta de Alcalà, and the Church of San Francisco el Grande.

Despite the architectural glories transforming the face of Madrid, the French-born monarch—a frequent victim of what his contemporaries referred to as "religious melancholia"—eventually abandoned Madrid almost completely in favor of his vast residence at La Granja. During his reign, court records recorded almost 800 executions for heresy, often by burning, and more than 14,000 imprisonments and/or tortures for religious reasons. By the time of Philip's death in 1746, Spain had been at war for 40 of the 46 years of his reign; his will was promulgated by French and Italian administrators, each of whom maintained an iron hand on Madrid politics.

During the short reign of Ferdinand VI (1746–59) and the somewhat longer and more enlightened reign of Charles III (1759–88), Spain attained peace at last as its rulers worked to improve the society at large. Artists and artisans flocked to Madrid to further embellish its monuments. Both the population of Spain and the relative importance of Madrid increased greatly. Between 1700 and 1788 the country's population increased from 5.7 million to almost 10.25 million. The brutal actions of the Inquisition were moderated greatly, and persecution of religious heresy was no longer considered an essential part of government policy. In 1773 a decree issued from Madrid ordained the distribution of large tracts of government-owned land to peasants and the colonization of many uninhabited areas of the Spanish peninsula. For this purpose, more than 6,000 Bavarians were invited to establish farms in the Sierra Morena. New industries were established, often with encouragement from Madrid and advice from foreign experts. The national lottery, today an almost inescapable sight at any Madrid streetcorner, was initiated for the first time.

DECLINE OF THE MONARCHS   During the reign of the sluggish and stupid Charles IV (1788–1808), the Plaza Mayor was reconstructed and reembellished. Goya reached some of his greatest artistic heights with the 1798 frescoes in the Chapel of San Antonio de la Florida. A series of entangling alliances and military compromises, however, soon placed Spain at the mercy of the revolutionary government of France, whose armies under Napoleon threatened to conquer all Europe.

After persuading Spain (through diplomatic and military pressure and appeals to the monarch's greed and fear) to pay large cash settlements to France, then to initiate abortive attacks against both England and Portugal, Napoleon and his French armies invaded Spain in 1808. Almost immediately the unpopular Charles IV abdicated the throne in favor of his son, Ferdinand VII. Then Charles had a change of heart and wanted his throne back. Both father and son vied for the throne and for Napoleon's backing. However, the dictator decided to send both members of the royal family into exile—with liberal pensions—and replaced them with a puppet ruler, his brother, Joseph Bonaparte.

Within a few weeks the people of Madrid rose up against the French invaders, signaling the debut of the War of Independence (1808–14). Although the revolt was suppressed and Madrid remained a captive of the French, many Madrileños joined their guerrilla counterparts in the surrounding provinces, proving themselves a serious deterrent to the French invaders. Spain proved once again a theater for the power politics of the rest of Europe.

Joseph Bonaparte fled from Madrid but was soon returned to power after his brother arrived from France to personally direct military operations. The English and the Portuguese both sent forces onto Spanish soil for operations against Napoleon's forces. Complicating matters was the support for Bonaparte of well-equipped bands of liberal Spaniards, who saw in Napoleon's revolutionary policies the hopes of ridding Spain of its traditional dynasties of despotic kings. Much aided by the English—and especially Wellington, who recaptured Madrid from the French in 1812 and has remained a hero in Spain ever since—the Spaniards eventually pushed Napoleon, who faced greater problems in Central Europe and on the Russian front, out of Spain altogether in 1813.

To power came Ferdinand VII (reigned 1814–33), who was said to have done only one thing consistently and well—persecuting and punishing liberal Spaniards. In the wake of one of the many rebellions that punctuated his reign (this one in 1823), he was captured by his subjects, who came very close to reinitiating the series of liberal reforms he had repeatedly sabotaged. Horrified at what they considered impertinent behavior toward a king, the other European monarchies opted to send a French army in to release him, which it did, ironically, under the pretext of liberal enlightenment. Once released by the embarrassed French forces, Ferdinand retracted the promises of clemency he had made and ordered the execution of many hundreds of liberal Madrileños.

Madrid's hold on its South and Central American colonies had already been severely weakened by around 1800. By 1822 Colombia was recognized as an independent nation by the United States, and Mexico and Colombia were recognized by Great Britain in 1824. Other Spanish-speaking colonies began their wars of independence in droves, drawing fertile propaganda from real and imagined stories of monarchical repressions manifested upon the people of Madrid. Upon the death of Ferdinand VII in 1833, his daughter was declared Queen Isabella II, an act that immediately provoked armed rebellions in the capital's streets. So potent were the demands of the liberals that she—partly to save her throne—called for the revision of the Spanish constitution in 1837 and the establishment of parliamentary models of government. Later she retracted these positions, an act that led to further armed conflicts.

The year 1833 is also marked by the formal beginnings of the Catalán *renaixença*, wherein a resurgence of Catalonian pride in literature, architecture, language, and politics began to whittle away at the unrivaled monolith of Madrid's supremacy in Spain.

Concrete examples of the new queen's works included the establishment of the Canal de Isabella II, which still supplies much of Madrid with its water, and the introduction of gas lighting. In 1850 the railway was introduced into Spain, connecting Madrid to the regal but not-very-distant resort of Aranjuez. A year later Isabella opened the Teatro Real, dedicated to the presentation of Spanish drama and music. A larger-than-life bronze statue in her honor still graces the park in front of the theater.

Isabella's reign was accented with endless fears on the part of both Britain and France that her political and matrimonial flirtations would upset the European balance of power. These fears proved correct when she and her younger sister, in defiance of a series of carefully orchestrated diplomatic agreements, both married French-born members of the Bourbon family in 1846 on the same day—an event that infuriated both Lord Palmerston in London and the growing numbers of Spanish liberals. The final quarter century of her reign was marked by endless changes within her ministries, countless intrigues, and continuing civil strife. It ended in defeat after an 1868 revolution sent her fleeing from Madrid over the border into France. A republic was born to replace her.

THE FIRST REPUBLIC Despite its initial euphoria caused by the departure of Spain's controversial and not-very-bright queen, the five-year life span of Spain's First Republic (1870–75) was also punctuated with repetitive bouts of civil strife. During 1870 alone, four different presidents held office in Madrid, each deposed after only a few months or weeks. It soon became very clear to all observers that only the army could restore order. Many regions of Spain during this era rejected all authority from Madrid and instituted interim governments of their own. After crushing opposition in Andalusia, the Basque country, and Catalonia, the army disbanded Madrid's Parliament and imposed military authority under General Serrano, who in 1875 restored power to the Bourbons.

THE LATER BOURBONS First of the later Bourbons was Alfonso XII (reigned 1875–85), who enjoyed almost immediate support. In 1876 he initiated a new Parliament (Cortés) based on universal suffrage and negotiated a well-intentioned peace treaty with Basque separatists in the north. With peace in effect, Madrid was able to send large armies of Spanish soldiers to quell the increasingly violent revolutions occurring in New World colonies, such as Cuba. Meanwhile, the socialist theories of Marx and the anarchist views of Bakunin gained strong footholds among workers in both Madrid and Barcelona, as disputes arose regarding which of the political philosophies would exercise ideological control. Between 1880 and 1900 Madrid endured endless and usually violent protests, each followed by harsh repression from the increasingly beleaguered government. Simultaneous with these upheavals, Madrid acquired its first tram lines, electric lights, and telephones.

Alfonso XII died in 1885, leaving two daughters and a pregnant second wife who unwittingly revived the Madrileños' traditional fears of the Hapsburgs because of her lineage as second cousin to Arch-duke Ferdinand of Austria. Six months later a son was born to the newly widowed Queen Regent, who named him Alfonso XIII.

During the time of Alfonso's infancy, much of which was spent in and around Madrid, Spain swung like a pendulum between lib-eral and conservative governments—a process that eventually bank-rupted the treasury and led to massive unrest. A misguided series of stiff import duties benefited only a handful of wealthy industrialists, throwing many laborers out of work.

Armed conflicts in the Spanish colonies of Cuba and nearby Morocco sapped Spain of both its human and fiscal resources. In 1898 the Spanish-American War stripped Spain of all but a handful of its colonies—specifically Puerto Rico, Cuba, the Philippines, the larger of the Mariana Islands, and the Sulu Islands—leaving the once-mighty Spanish Empire a ghostly shred of its former grandeur. All that remained under Madrid's control were a handful of impover-ished and sun-baked territories in north and northwest Africa, in-cluding sections of Morocco and what was referred to at the time as the Spanish Sahara. Even these were soon to prove enormously troublesome.

Alfonso XIII, a spoiled and willful child, was crowned king of Spain at the age of 16 in 1902, shortly after the population of Madrid had reached 500,000. Very much under the influences of the Catholic Church and ultra-right-wing reactionary forces, Alfonso's decisions were both conservative and controversial, often aimed at the sabotage of any hope of libertarian reform. Even his 1906 marriage to a descendant of Britain's royal family, Victoria Regina of Battenburg, caused a major political upheaval—as did his sym-bolic proclamations in defiance of libertarian models. General strikes in 1912 threatened the country with chaos.

Although Spain was spared a direct role in the horrors of World War I, civil strife and increasing hostilities in Morocco were almost as painful as the ravages suffered by the rest of Europe. All parties agreed in theory to avoid an active participation in World War I, but the country was divided further between the conservatives, who fa-vored Germany, and the liberals, who favored Britain and the Allies. As ideological walls were made ever stronger between Monarchists and Republicans, Spain grew increasingly tense and distraught as political rages swept through the corridors of power in Madrid.

During this era, the landscape of Madrid continued to grow and expand. The Gran Vía was laid out in 1910 and ultimately completed in 1931, whereupon it became the focus of much that was fashion-able and worldly. Vast new districts, including the Salamanca and Argüelles, were opened as the city's borders expanded to cope with its growing population. In 1919 the first commercial air flight was initiated between Madrid and Barcelona, and in 1921 Madrid's metro (subway) system was inaugurated. On March 8 of the same year, Eduardo Dato—mayor of Madrid and an influential mediator who had been working to achieve unity among the Conservatives of

Spain—was assassinated in Madrid, sending waves of fear through the Spanish establishment and resulting in harsh crackdowns by the government. The same year, the Spanish army—motivated by the passionate endorsement of Alfonso XIII—embarked impetuously on a course of military action against Moroccan insurgents in the Rif Mountains of North Africa. The almost-immediate result was a crushing and humiliating defeat at the Battle of Anual, as well as the loss of vast territories in eastern Morocco. The general in charge of the Spanish army, Manuel Silvestre, committed suicide; and in the wake of his death, a Republican-sponsored enquiry unearthed massive fiscal improprieties, which caused an even greater uproar.

DICTATORS VERSUS ANARCHISTS In 1923, fears of continued anarchy led to the establishment of a conservative dictatorship under military strongman Primo de Rivera, with whom Alfonso XIII closely associated himself; this dictatorship lasted until 1930. De Rivera's son, José Antonio Primo de Rivera, significantly, went on to establish the Spanish Fascist party in 1933. After the collapse of the elder Primo de Rivera's dictatorship, the king reluctantly agreed to municipal elections, which resulted in an overwhelming victory of the Republicans over the Monarchists. Bereft of supporters but refusing to formally abdicate, Alfonso XIII left Spain on April 14, 1931, for the French border to live forever in exile. On the day of his departure the provisional government of the second republic was established. Alfonso XIII had bequeathed one of the most inept monarchical records in Spanish history to the people of Madrid. His tenure had witnessed the arrival and departure of 33 finance ministers—none of whom was ever able to accumulate enough power or credibility to affect lasting change. Perhaps more important, the distrust of government that his unyielding policies engendered were to have lasting effects on Spain.

THE SECOND REPUBLIC From its base in Madrid, Spain's second attempt at democratic government did what it could to hold together the country's entrenched factions. On the right stood the Catholic Church, the army, and the landed aristocracy. On the left stood the "anarcho-syndicalists," the socialists, and the regional autonomists, who saw in the left greater chances for their eventual independence. As riots from both the left and the right disrupted the social fabric of Spanish life, the country's economy withered. In January 1933, women (who were at the time perceived as a conservative bastion within Spain) were given the right to vote, more as an incentive for the retention of power by the right, according to cynics, than as a libertarian reform.

THE CIVIL WAR Although the Spanish Civil War originated among military officers in Morocco, it was in Madrid that much of the drama unfolded. In 1936, frustrated at the fragmentation of their platforms, a wide spectrum of leftist and trade-union groups formed a unified and powerful voting block that incorporated anarchists, Republicans, Trotskyites, socialists, and Marxists into one coherent whole. Their United Front swept the 1936 elections, a victory that immediately sparked a wholesale murder of perceived capitalists; the opening of prisons throughout Spain; almost 350 labor strikes; the burning of almost 200 churches, many in Madrid; and the attempted arson of 250 other churches throughout Spain.

Spain ran wild, with the elected popular-front coalition wholly unable to cope with the trauma. On July 18, 1936, in reaction to what was perceived as a dangerous threat to law and order, an army mutiny led by Gen. Francisco Franco took command of Spanish troops stationed in Morocco. Within two days the mutiny had spread throughout the entire Spanish army, an act that sparked the Spanish Civil War and some of the 20th century's most passionately defended ideological platforms.

Franco's strongholds incorporated virtually all of Spain, except Madrid, Barcelona, and sections of the north and northwest. Some historians claim that if Madrid had capitulated, there would have been no civil war at all, only a peaceable takeover of the government. Franco and his forces labeled themselves Nationalists, claiming theirs was no mere *pronunciamiento* by a corrupt monarch but a *movimiento nacional.* In opposition were the leaders of the previously elected popular front, who at great disadvantage fought against virtually the entire armed elite of Spain. To make matters even more difficult for the popular front (thereafter known as the Republicans), their unified coalition soon began to break apart, thus losing its claim to legality and the popular vote.

Suddenly, amid massive international publicity, hordes of volunteers—many of them Communist sympathizers—came to the aid of the beleaguered Republicans, who held out in Madrid and certain cities of the east and north. Simultaneously, well-equipped and well-trained Franco-led Nationalists received massive supplies and modern weapons from Fascist-run Germany and Italy—supposedly the result of prior clandestine agreements. Contemporary participants such as Antonio Machada (a meditative and austere Spanish poet who died in the conflict in 1939) declined to label the conflict a civil war but rather condemned it as an all-out German-Italian invasion.

Some of the most notorious massacres of the 20th century were committed by members of both sides. These included priests and everyday citizens from towns as diverse as Guernica, Badajoz, Toledo, Barcelona, and Bilbao. Saved from immediate conquest because of a last-minute detour by the Nationalists to help comrades beleaguered in the Alcázar at Toledo, Madrid rallied its forces and endured 28 months of siege. The government moved from Madrid first to Valencia, then briefly to Barcelona, and eventually to the Costa Brava resort of Figueres. Madrid was left in charge of a defense council headed by Gen. José Miaja. Real power was held in siege-ridden Madrid by the unions, who adhered to Communist doctrines by banning all forms of religious worship in Madrid churches—a ban lifted only after the entry of Franco into the city three years later.

Residents of Madrid survived on two ounces of food daily, and as hundreds of city residents died of starvation, attack from Franco's forces eventually proved almost unnecessary. On March 28, 1939, Madrid, the last bastion of Republicanism, collapsed as 200,000 Nationalist troops entered the city without a struggle. The war had lasted two years and nine months, ruined Spain, and cost an esti-mated million lives.

THE FRANCO YEARS   With very few other options to choose from, France, Britain, and the United States all formally recognized Franco's government—which had set up headquarters in Madrid—before the end of 1939. Franco's Italian and German troops marched triumphantly out of Madrid during a massive parade there on May 19, 1939. Franco immediately granted strong financial credits for the reconstruction of ruined houses and public buildings. Spain be-gan rebuilding its industry, which eventually transformed Madrid into one of Europe's great industrial powers.

When World War II erupted, Franco immediately disassociated himself from the Fascists of Germany and Italy, declaring Spain at first nonbelligerent and later neutral. A few days later he signed, and later reinforced, a treaty of nonaggression with Portugal, thereby ensuring peace with one of Britain's strongest and oldest allies. The conquest of Catholic Poland by the combined efforts of Germany and the Soviet Union greatly offended the deeply Catholic Spain. Spain did, however, send troops to fight in the Ukraine in 1942, with the Nazis against the dreaded Communists. In a 1942 speech Franco reiterated a line from which he never wavered: "Yesterday, today, and tomorrow, for the countries of Europe there exists only one danger—Communism."

Throughout World War II, Franco, in one of the most amazing diplomatic feats of the 20th century, managed to avoid too close an association with Fascist Germany and Italy, despite the many phi-losophies and scandals he shared with their leaders: One of these was the almost complete suppression of most civil liberties. Although industry and the beginnings of tourism grew during the Franco years, Spain slumbered—a repressed and reactionary head of a once-great empire, dozing in the streaming Iberian sunlight. Street crime was almost nonexistent, yet so was intellectual and artistic expression as many of the country's greatest artists and scientists chose to take up residence elsewhere.

MODERN SPAIN   Franco's 1975 death has been defined as Spain's "national tragedy" coming to an end. An intricate series of events brought back to power a member of the Bourbon monarchy, Juan Carlos I, one of Franco's inner circle and grandson of the much-despised Alfonso XIII. Sensing the shift in the national mood—and

IMPRESSIONS

In winter especially she seems a capital half-frozen in the attitudes of a past generation.
—James Morris, 1964

determined to be a better spokesman than his grandfather—he has skillfully directed the path of his country along libertarian lines that have made Madrid one of the most admired capitals of Europe.

In 1978 the Centrist government of Adolfo Suárez adopted a new constitution as part of a national referendum that restored parliamentary government, with strong doses of autonomy for Spain's far-flung regions.

In 1982 the charismatic and articulate Felipe González brought new vigor to the Spanish Socialist Workers' Party (PSOE) by reviving Spain's role within Europe and by administering its membership into the EEC (European Economic Community) in 1986.

The *Movida Madrileña* (Madrid Happening) of the late 1980s was a cultural, social, and intellectual renaissance that poured a surge of creative energy into the city, making Madrid a lot of fun to be in— the envy of creative circles throughout the world.

In 1992 Madrid was named "cultural capital of Europe," a heady recognition of the rebirth of its self-confidence after the years of unhappy repression.

In 1993, despite the decline in Spain's economic growth—plus a serious challenge from the right—Felipe González was once again reelected to head the Spanish government, a hard-fought campaign victory for the Spanish socialists.

2   People & Culture

People

No city in Spain figures more prominently in the imaginations of its people than Madrid, and as such, it has always exerted a kind of magnetic lure for newcomers from the countryside. Seeking employment, the fulfillment of personal dreams, and/or freedom from the social restrictions of their villages, natives of each of the other Spanish provinces have flooded into Madrid since its original establishment in 1561.

During the past century the city's population has grown astonishingly: from 400,000 in 1880 to some 4.5 million today. This surge of newcomers (many of whom arrived since the 1940s from such relatively impoverished districts as Galicia, Castile, Extremadura, and Andalusia) has created a cosmopolitan mixture well accustomed to the assimilation of new ideas. This trend has been especially apparent in Madrid since the end of Franco's repressive regime.

The Spanish exodus from rural to urban areas presents particular ironies to anyone looking at the landscapes around Madrid: Some of the most sparsely inhabited and least productive areas of Europe lie within an hour's drive of the city limits of the Spanish capital. Today, scattered around any typical Madrileño scene, you're as likely to see tall, blue-eyed Spanish-speaking blondes, descendants of the Visigothic Celts, as olive-skinned Mediterranean types. Regardless of their looks, they indulge in the single and omnipresent Madrileño characteristic: Everyone seems to work very hard during the days and then play very hard until late into the night. Both facets of the Madrileño character exist simultaneously, a duality that sometimes baffles newcomers. It all contributes to the nickname attached to residents of Madrid: *gatos* (cats), who are best remembered for their nocturnal activities.

Madrileños are known for their friendliness and gregariousness. To citizens, the *ambiente* of a place—the amount of noise, people, visual distractions, and joy—is very important to the definition of a successful evening. City residents, especially young ones, tend to flee from calm and tranquil places, grouping instead in enclaves of often boisterous energy and noise. In the course of any ordinary night, a Madrileño might stop at four or five bars, some of them requiring some effort to reach, more on the expectation of meeting acquaintances and friends than for the drinks themselves.

Today the hard-working, hard-driving residents of Madrid seem awake with a gregarious sense of excitement, racing toward the 21st century with a freedom and abandon denied to them during the stifling Franco years.

FAMOUS SPANIARDS

Miguel de Cervantes Saavedra (1547–1616)   The reigning figure of Spanish letters led a life of more adventure than his fictional characters. A former soldier who participated in the Armada, he was later captured and sold into slavery in Algiers. In unrelated incidents, he was twice imprisoned: when accused of murder and for failure to pay his debts. During his lifetime he wrote 20 to 30 plays, only 2 of which have survived. During one of his prison sojourns, he began a tale of an idealist chasing windmills across the plains of La Mancha. Later released as *Don Quixote de La Mancha*, it reigns today as the most superlative work of literature ever produced in the Spanish language.

Salvador Dalí (1904–88)   He was the leading exponent of surrealism, depicting irrational imagery of dreams and delirium in a meticulously detailed style. Famous for his eccentricity, he was called "outrageous, talented, relentlessly self-promoting, and unfailingly quotable." Before his death at 84, he was the last survivor of the famed *enfants terribles* of Spain (García Lorca and Luis Buñuel being the other two). Dalí's partner was the Russian-born Gala, his neurotic and ambitious wife. The first volume of his autobiography was called *The Secret Life of Salvador Dalí* (1942).

El Greco (Doménikos Theotokópoulos; 1541–1614)   Born in Crete, he emigrated, as did hundreds of other artists of his era, to the Spanish Empire with its wealth of commissions. He was trained in Italy under Titian, but his greatness was not acknowledged by critics until the late 19th century. Spain's best-known adherent of Mannerist painting (a stylized evolution of the late baroque), El Greco painted his masterpiece, *The Burial of the Conde de Orgaz*, in Toledo, 42 miles southwest of Madrid. Preferring colors Philip II, among others, considered lurid, he became famous for the elongated limbs of his subjects, as well as his highly evocative pictorial depictions of mystical ecstasy. Considered insane by local residents, he was fond of publicly declaring that Michelangelo had no talent.

Francisco Paulino Hermenegildo Teódulo Franco Bahamonde (1892–1975) *El Generalísimo* or *El Caudillo,* as he was called, Franco was the Fascist dictator of Spain from the end of the Spanish Civil War until his death. A soldier from the age of 15, Franco, as all-powerful ruler of Spain, imposed rigid censorship and a stifling grip on the country's arts and commerce throughout his reign. Siding with Hitler during World War II, he declared neutrality when the tides of victory turned toward the Allies, thereby managing to retain his position during the unsettling years of the late 1940s and 1950s. Declared "Head of State for Life" in 1947, he eventually designated Juan Carlos I as his successor, passing over Juan Carlos's less malleable father, whom Franco publicly referred to as "the pretender."

Mariano José de Larra y Sánchez de Castro ("Le Figaro"; 1809–37) De Larra was the most self-destructive of the Madrileño romantics of the early 19th century. His lofty ideals and abortive imbroglios have sometimes been compared to those of Byron. Educated in France, he returned to Madrid at 17 as a drama critic and political analyst. Increasingly revered as a famous personality (whose plays, ironically, were resounding critical failures), he maintained a rigidly entrenched opposition to the absolutist kings. Mourning his unfulfilled love for a much older married woman and the frustrations of his political stalemates, he shot himself at the age of 27 in what might be the most romanticized suicide in Spanish history.

Tirso de Molina (Fray Gabriel Téllez; 1584–1648) Often compared to Shakespeare, he is considered one of the three great dramatists of the Golden Age of Spanish literature. (The other contenders are Lope de Vega and Pedro Calderón de la Barca.) Designated as the official historian of the monastic order of Mercedarians, he spent most of his time writing comedies and plays, perhaps 300 in all, although only a few have survived. His first work, *Los cigarrales de Toledo* (The Grasshopper Fields of Toledo), was published in 1621. His most famous plays were *El burlador de Sevilla* (The Bully of Seville) and *El condenado por desconfiado* (The Condemnation of the Mistrusted). In his day he was a great favorite with audiences in Madrid.

Pablo Picasso (1881–1973) He was called a "caricaturing imitator, gifted but not skillful . . . the one thing he never pulled off was a real painting." That was Salvador Dalí speaking about his fellow artist, Picasso, who became the most famous and prolific painter of the 20th century. The world did not agree with Dalí's dismal assessment. Picasso settled in Paris to explore his artistic genius with his "rose period," although by 1906 he was devoted to cubism. He is best remembered for his *Guernica,* a painting that expressed his horror of war. In 1949 he was the world's richest Communist, creating a white dove of peace for the movement.

St. Teresa of Avila (originally Teresa de Cepeda y Ahumada; 1515–82) Disgusted with what she considered the corruption of the early-16th-century church, she is known today as the most pragmatic and down-to-earth mystic in the history of the Catholic Church. Inspired to found a religious order (Las Discalced) in which the original rules of the Carmelite Order were strictly observed, she was eventually assigned to write her spiritual autobiography by her religious superiors. Until very recent times this was reputedly the third-most widely read book (after the Bible and *Don Quixote*) in Spain. Upon her death in Avila, it is said that a fragrant violet-hued oil poured forth from her tomb. She was canonized in 1622 and was made a doctor of the church in 1970.

Tomas de Torquemada (1420–98) A "name that will live in infamy," Torquemada became the inquisitor-general to Isabella and Ferdinand in 1483. An impassioned (and probably insane) fanatic, he hated everything that wasn't Catholic or Spanish. As confessor to the Catholic monarchs, he was instrumental in the expulsion of the Jews and *Moriscos* (converted Muslims) from Spain. Torquemada tried people for sorcery, witchcraft, heresy, necromancy, bigamy, blasphemy, and usury. He obtained "evidence" through torture. At least 2,000 people were executed by this man, who, legend says, never ate unless the tongue of a scorpion was placed beside his plate.

Lope Félix de Vega y Carpio ("El Fénix"; 1562–1635) The most prolific writer in the history of Spain, boasting between 1,500 and 1,800 plays (only a few hundred of which have survived), he is viewed as the creator of Spanish comedy and the greatest playwright of the Golden Age of Spanish literature. Vega led an adventurous early life and served in the Spanish Armada. Ordained as a priest after the sudden death of his son and wife, he moved to Philip II's new capital, where he spent the remaining 25 years of his life, many of them tragically. His most famous surviving plays include *El caballero de Olmedo* (The Gentleman of Olmedo), *Peribañez*, and *Fuenteovejuna*.

Diego Rodríguez de Silva Velázquez (1599–1660) Acclaimed as the greatest painter of the 17th century, this artist, who centuries later was to have great influence on Picasso, was made court painter to Philip IV at age 25. "I have found my Titian," the king declared. Velázquez was a master of atmospheric portraiture and made artistic breakthroughs in the use of color of light in painting. His masterpiece, *Las Meninas*, hangs in the Prado in Madrid.

Consuelo Vello ("La Fornarina"; 1884–1915) This turn-of-the-century darling of the *zarzuela* theaters of the Gran Vía was revered for her beauty, talent, and charm. The daughter of a washerwoman and a member of the Guardia Civil, she became the most famous Spanish actress to date. Giuseppe Verdi was numbered among her fans. After a life of much-publicized melodrama, she died at the age of 31, the result of a botched surgical procedure. Her grave at Madrid's cemetery of San Isidro is still visited by well-wishers today.

Culture

ART

By the time of Madrid's establishment in 1561, many of the great artists of the Spanish medieval age had wrought their influence upon the country's aesthetic landscape. Philip II—conscious of his status as a Hapsburg, with distinct links and possessions in faraway Flanders (Belgium)—espoused the Hispano-Flemish style of painting, with its penchant for verdant landscapes, rich depictions of fabrics and jewelry, and elevated presentation of subjects in both group and individual portraits.

Simultaneously, a strong tradition had already been established whereby Spanish artists embarked for training in heroic painting in Italy, returning with an altered sense of perspective, classical references, subtle interplays of light with shadow, and a sense of heroic grandeur. Italian Mannerism—a development of late baroque painting identified by its nervously stylized depictions of mystical events—became fashionable in Spain and was at the time of Madrid's establishment best exemplified by the works of El Greco (see "Famous Spaniards," above). Born on the island of Crete (in Greece), he emigrated with the flood of other artists and artisans to Spain, looking for the many commissions that the newly monied kingdom was prepared to pay for abundantly. Although he chose to settle in Toledo, 42 miles southwest of Madrid, his work and influence slowly affected the sense of dignity and grandeur that were associated with the newly developing capital. Unfortunately, El Greco's unusual and very strong colors and the elongated limbs of his subjects did not please Philip II, who preferred more conservative—and more Italianized—artworks to adorn the chapels and endless anterooms of El Escorial.

The construction and embellishments of Madrid coincided with what is today referred to as the Golden Age of Spanish painting (1550–1650). The Royal Collections—which later comprised the foundation of the collection in the Prado—was established during the reigns of Charles V, the previously mentioned Philip II, and Philip IV. At least some of these were acquired from the fiscally embarrassed English monarch Charles II during some of the most spectacular art sales of all time. Especially popular were works by the Venetian painter Titian, whose formal settings and mythical/heroic subject matter appealed to the empire-building Spanish monarchs.

Several talented Spaniards, most notably Juan Fernández Navarrete "El Mudo" (1526–79), rushed to emulate Titian's style, infusing Italian mannerism with a Spanish flavor. From this developed the Escorial School of *tenebrist* painters, whose style quickly spread to faraway Seville. One devoted member of this school who defined many of its terms was the Andalusia-born painter Francisco Pacheco (1564–1654), best known for his patronage of the young Velázquez who eventually married Pacheco's daughter.

Diego Rodríguez de Silva Velázquez (1599–1660), later accepted as the finest painter to emerge from Spain, is said to have prefigured certain tenets of 19th-century impressionism with his use of light to illuminate and define the space around his figures. Today entire wings in the Prado are devoted to his works, which include *Christ in the House of Martha and Mary, Musical Trio*, and an entire and very fascinating series of portraits of the royal family. Ironically, many of Velázquez's portraits were copied by talented artisans for presentation to foreign dignitaries. Today even well-trained experts are hard-pressed to tell the copies from the originals.

Meanwhile, only Seville competed with Madrid for supremacy in painting. Famous Seville artists included Francisco de Zurbarán (1589–1664), known for his dramatic use of bright light and shadow in the style of Caravaggio; and Bartolomé Esteban Murillo (1617–82), noted for the truthful yet relaxed postures of his subjects. Murillo modified baroque themes with occasional doses of sentimentality. Also important was Juan de Valdés Leal (1622–90), known for the sometimes-confusing sense of violence that often marks his works.

Meanwhile, other important painters in the School of Madrid included Juan Bautista Maino (1578–1649), Antonio Pereda (1608–78), and José Antolinez (1635–75). Painting in religious contexts, they were also known as skilled draftsmen and colorists, often emulating the Flemish style of van Dyck. The most unusual, and perhaps the most insecure, member of the school was Claudio Coello (1642–93), who spent seven laborious years on a portrait of Charles II worshiping the Sagrada Forma. Today that work hangs in the Sacristy of El Escorial.

With the takeover of the throne of Spain by the French-born Bourbon dynasties, the official tastes in Spanish art turned distinctly toward Spain's Gallic neighbor. From Paris were imported such artists as Michel-Ange Houasse, Michel Van Loo, and Jean Ranc, who were immediately feted and officially promoted as the artistic saviors of Spanish painting. Fueled by the then-prevalent French tastes, official Spanish art became increasingly preoccupied with the heroic and mythological themes popular at Versailles. Many Spanish painters simply mimicked these themes mindlessly, producing little of enduring value until a Czech-born artist, Anton Raphael Mengs (1728–79), moved to Madrid to execute a series of fine portraits whose conceptions were much emulated for years to come.

One of Mengs's most prominent students and admirers became the most famous Spanish painter of his era, the heavily politicized Francisco José de Goya y Lucientes (1746–1828). During the 14 years he spent designing cartoons (designs and themes) for wall hangings in the Royal Tapestry Factory, he was deeply influenced by the bucolic outdoor scenes of the English artist Hogarth and the Italian artist and decorator G. B. Tiepolo. Later, his portraits, usually in grays, of famous Madrileños helped him attain the rank of court painter to Charles IV. Unfortunately, the unvarnished realism of his subsequent portraits of the far-from-attractive king and members of his family caused a considerable flutter from the courtiers and gossips. The controversial portraits were followed by a satirical series of engravings depicting ignorant and licentious priests and gluttonous and unprincipled aristocrats; these earned Goya powerful enemies who would plague him all his life.

The political betrayals and bloody atrocities in Madrid during Napoleon's occupation provided subject matter for some of the most enduring paintings in the history of Europe. One of Goya's particularly graphic series, *The Disasters of War*, prefigured the scope and scale of the genocides and military horrors that would follow in the next century. These artistic, and perhaps psychic, visions occurred simultaneously with the artist's increasing deafness, which began at the age of 47. These factors probably contributed to the anguish of his world-famous "Black Paintings." Today displayed in the Prado, they are probably the best visual depiction of paranoia, rage, and despair ever created.

Goya died, a political exile, in Bordeaux, France. His body was reinterred in 1919, placed in a vault of Madrid's Church of San Antonio de la Florida, whose interior he had frescoed. Today it is a site of pilgrimage for art lovers from around the world.

The 19th century produced an array of genre, portrait, and landscape artists who catered to the demands of Madrid's growing number of newly rich capitalists. Among the most famous of these were Eduardo Rosales (1836–74), and Mariano José María Bernardo Fortuny y Carbó (1838–74), a resident of Rome and Madrid and famous for his occasionally frivolous dominance in Spanish art before the rise of impressionism. Also important was Joaquin Sorolla y Bastida (1862–1923), known for his beach scenes of the Costa Brava and for his portraits of everyday workers. A resident of Madrid from 1912 until his death, he is also closely associated with the city of Valencia.

By the end of the century, as impressionism and the roots of modern art took hold of the artistic psyche of Madrid, such artists as the cubist Juan Gris (José Victoriano González; (1887–1927) and such muralists as José María Sert y Badia (1874–1945) and Daniel Vazquez Diaz (1882–1969) made indelible impressions on the way the world looks at line and color.

Among 20th-century artists, the most incontestably famous of them all was Pablo Ruiz y Picasso (1881–1973). Long exiled from Spain for his political views and the fame of his sometimes-politicized paintings, he created his own stereotype of the brilliant Spanish artist living and working in an exiled and heroic isolation. Likewise, Joan Miró (1893–1983), whose brightly colored masterpieces helped create a poetic vision of the subconscious, moved from Madrid to the more liberalized artistic scene of Paris. Later he spent increasing amounts of time in Barcelona as well.

Finally, Barcelona native Salvador Dalí (1904–88) was the most influential surrealistic painter of all time, famous for his personal idiosyncracies and his iconoclastic ways of viewing reality. Unfortunately, many critics cite the decline of his work into sales-related gimmickry and exhibitionism toward the emotionally unbalanced end of his life.

During the late 1980s and early 1990s, Madrid reemerged as the undisputed centerpiece of all artistic production in Spain. Postmodern artists who fed (and still feed) upon the city's vivid cultural life have included painters Féderico Amet and Miguel Barcelo and such sculptors as Jorge de Oteiza, Pablo Serrano, and Miguel Ortíz Berrocal.

ARCHITECTURE

Many of the major currents in Spanish architecture were already well entrenched by the time Philip II decided to establish his capital at Madrid. What awaited him was a small provincial town with a scattering of fortifications originally laid by the Moors and an unpretentious core of Gothic buildings. The most noteworthy of these includes the Torre de los Lujanes, site of the imprisonment of François I in 1525. Much blackened by time, it still stands in the heart of Madrid's tiny Gothic neighborhood, near the Plaza de la Villa.

Inspired by lofty dreams of a capital worthy of the size and wealth of the Spanish Empire, Philip immediately approved the classical revival style whose columns, porticoes, and proportions emulated the grandeur of ancient Rome. One of his preferred architects, Herrera, designed parts of the new capital, as well as the somber majesty of the king's semimonastic retreat at El Escorial, 30 miles west of Madrid. Inspired by these precedents, royal architect Juan Gómez de Mora laid out the dignified symmetry of the era's most visible remaining landmark, the Plaza Mayor, completed in 1606.

The Bourbons, whose first member ascended the throne after much bloodshed in 1700, opted for a graceful neoclassicism of the type then sweeping through their homeland in France. Today many of the monumental buildings that line the showcase boulevards of Madrid, including those near the Prado Museum and the Alcala Gate, are derivatives of the Bourbon taste for the symmetry and restrained opulence of the French aesthetic. Ample use was made at this time, incidentally, of the rose-pink brick the region produced in such abundance.

Surprisingly, although many of the buildings from these eras are dignified and, at their best, even graceful, Madrid possesses relatively few monuments erected to the glories of Spain's imperial empire. Considering the size of that empire, and the wealth produced by it, the city's architecture—though splendid—is relatively unpretentious. (London, Paris, and Vienna, also seats of empire, have many more grandiose monuments than Madrid, for example.) At least part of Madrid's human scale is because of the many political upheavals that punctuated the city's 19th-century history. Much of this is probably also because of the Spanish appreciation of street life on an intimate and personalized scale. The combined effect seems to divide Madrid's vast precincts into a series of well-defined, and often very charming, villagelike neighborhoods.

After around 1850, the wealth and growing power of the newly prosperous Madrileño bourgeoisie called for the construction of hundreds of new villas, town houses, and elegant apartment buildings. The result was the knocking down of the 17th-century ramparts that ringed the city's core and the creation of several new districts, which are today collectively referred to as the Ensanche. These districts incorporated each of the different styles of Iberia, including mudéjar/Neo-Andalusian, neoclassical, Neo-Gothic, art nouveau, Neo-Renaissance, and a scattering of the iconoclastic and organic styles then springing up in Catalonia. These districts are among the most architecturally interesting in Madrid. Specific neighborhoods that are still considered upscale embodiments of 19th-century capitalistic wealth include the Salamanca and Argüelles districts, set to the northwest and northeast, respectively, of the city's 16th- and 17th-century core.

Since the end of World War II, Madrid's population has grown so rapidly the city has almost split its architectural seams. In response, vast new neighborhoods bristling with all descriptions of modern buildings have sprung up. Their design ranges from insipid and angular blocks of low-cost apartment buildings erected during the Franco years to recently completed examples of some of the most dramatic modern and postmodern design in Europe.

LITERATURE

One of Spain's most worthwhile by-products has been its fertile outpouring of literature. Roots of the art form were already flourishing long before Madrid was established, although, significantly, the city's foundation and subsequent population explosion coincided almost exactly with what is considered the Golden Age of Spanish literature.

The cultural streams that contributed to Madrid's eventual dominance of Spanish literature began with the ancient Romans. Ancient writers who composed on what is now Spanish soil included Seneca the Elder (54 B.C.–A.D. 39), Seneca the Stoic (4 B.C.–A.D. 65), the epic poet Lucan (A.D. 39–65), and the epigrammist Martial (A.D. 42–104).

The next surge of literary output in Spain came from Muslim, not Christian, sources. By 800 the Hispano-Arabic homeland of Al Andalus was considered one of the Mediterranean's most brilliant beacons of culture. Astronomy, medicine, architecture, and literature flourished as Córdoba became the largest city in Europe (with an estimated population of 500,000), with both Seville and Granada following close behind. Notable poets included Yosef the Scribe (ca. 1000), Ibn Quzman (ca. 1100), Muccadam bon Muafa (ca. 900), Ibn Rushd (Averröes; 1126–1198), and the Jewish mystic Maimonides (1135–1204). Considered among the most brilliant philosophers of their era, both Averröes and Maimonides (writing, ironically, in Arabic) forged landmark reconciliations of Aristotelian logic with the tenets of their respective faiths.

By the 1200s, Christian Spain was beginning to assert its own literary identity. In Barcelona, whose merchants flourished as competitors of Venice, Catalán poetry fed richly off Provençale models in neighboring France. In the heartland of Spain (Castile, the then-independent province that contains what is now Madrid) Alfonso X the Wise (1252–84) repressed the use of Latin, favoring instead the vernacular dialect of Castilian. This preference had been established during the mid-1100s by the fame of the epic poem *El cantar del mio Cid* (The Song of My Cid), set down in writing from what might have been a long-standing oral tradition. Its subject, dear to the hearts of the Catholic monarchs, involved the reconquest of Iberia from the Moors. A noted poet and scholar in his own right, Alfonso gathered the literary traditions of ancient Rome, the Arabic world, medieval Christianity, and mystical Judaism into his Castilian court.

The almost-immediate result was a surge of original literary creativity. Around 1300 Juan Ruiz, a prominent archbishop (ca. 1283–1351), compiled *The Book of Spiritual Love*, a semi-satirical/semi-mystical tract exposing ecclesiastic corruption, set in the context of both lyrical and narrative verse.

By the time Madrid was selected as the center of the Spanish Empire, Castilian had entrenched itself as the literary language of a united Spain. Bartolomé de las Casas (1474–1566) defended the dignity of the New World's native peoples in his tract *The Tears of the Indians*. Late in the 1400s, a religiously motivated mystery play, *Misteri d'Elch*, offered hordes of Christian pilgrims an insight into Catholic spiritualism.

The real artistry of the era's literary output, however, dealt with secular rather than religious themes. One of the earliest of these was the raucous and earthy novel *The Comedy of Calixto and Melibea* (*La Celestina*) by Fernando de Rojas (1465–1541). Even more prominent was a particularly prolific playwright, Lope Félix de Vega y Carpio (see "Famous Spaniards," above). A participant in the humiliating defeat of the Spanish Armada in 1588 and an adventurer in both the romantic and military sense of the word, he produced more than 1,800 plays, 400 of which have survived. Flawed by their sometimes hasty execution, they are nonetheless considered seminal to the beginnings of a purely Madrileño repertoire of plays.

Lope de Vega shares his literary stardom with two other famous Madrileños: Tirso de Molina (1584–1648) and Pedro Calderón de la Barca (1600–81). Tirso de Molina, in one of the 300 plays he wrote, was the original creator of the amorous character of Don Juan, whose fame spread instantly throughout Europe, assisted greatly by the musical efforts, a century later, of Mozart.

The Golden Age, fueled by the excitement and wealth of Spain's expanding colonial empire, produced such disparate writers as St. Teresa of Avila (1515–82) and her follower, St. John of the Cross (1542–91); and a series of poets who included Luis de Góngora y Argote (1561–1627), whose Castilian verse adopted the poetic models of the ancient Romans. Also noteworthy was the bitterly satirical social critic Francisco Gómez de Quevedo y Villegas (1580–1645).

Each of these writers paved the way for the greatest author in Spanish history, Miguel de Cervantes Saavedra (1547–1616). His *Don Quixote de la Mancha* remains one of the most enduring classics of world-class literature, avidly read by contemporaries who included Shakespeare, and by such modern novelists as Marcel Proust, Vladimir Nabokov, James Joyce, and virtually every notable author of the Hispanic world today.

With the arrival of the French-derived Bourbon dynasty on the throne of Spain, authors drew more and more of their inspiration from the neoclassical models then popular in the literary salons of Paris and in such power centers as Versailles. Leandro Fernández de Moratín (1760–1828), chief librarian to Joseph Bonaparte, the puppet ruler placed on the throne by French intervention, produced plays and poems based without apology on French precedents. Gaspar Melchor de Jovellanos (1744–1811), poet, economist, and politician, kept his finger on the pulse of the Enlightenment through his frequent experiments with French models.

A contemporary, however, who broke the elevated tone of the salon-inspired writing of his day, was Ramón Francisco de la Cruz (1731–94); his characters elevated Madrid's working classes to the status of cultural heroes. An avowed enemy of the materialistic and social-climbing bourgeoisie, he penned one of his era's most famous satirical works, *The Tertulias of Madrid.*

During the 19th century Spanish Romanticism led to the development of many dozens of dashingly theatrical literary heroes—flamboyant in their personal lives and endlessly controversial in the then-prevalent climate of monarchical absolutism. Spanish writers—in trends which paralleled those in the rest of Europe—rejected the reason and objectivity of neoclassicism and embraced instead the emotionalism and subjectivity of Romanticism.

The beginning of the Romantic movement in Spanish art and literature is today defined as the accession to the Spanish throne of Isabella II in 1833. The brief period of freedom that preceded her eventual, and much-resented, autocratic crackdown permitted the return from exile of many politically active writers and politicians. The art of satire became increasingly fine-tuned, exemplified by such writers as Mariano José de Larra (see "Famous Spaniards," above), José Zorilla y Moral (1817–93), and the pugnacious political dissident José de Espronceda y Delgado (1808–42). Despite the beauty of Espronceda's poetry, his most famous work was a novel, *El estudiante de Salamanca* (The Student of Salamanca), which was based, as were many other literary works of the Romantic age, on the inexhaustible implications of the Don Juan legend.

In 1904 post-Romantic dramatist José Echegaray y Eizaguirre (1832–1916) was the first Spaniard to win the Nobel Prize for literature. Other famous Spanish writers—many of whom returned to the cultural wellsprings of Madrid—included Vicente Blasco Ibáñez (1867–1928), author of *La barraca* (The Cabin), *Blood and Sand,* and *The Four Horsemen of the Apocalypse.* Also important (and prolific) was Benito Pérez Galdós (1843–1920), whose vast output (46 volumes of historical romances) led to frequent comparisons with both Honoré de Balzac and Charles Dickens.

The loss of power, money, and prestige caused by Spain's defeat during the Spanish-American War of 1898 led to a loose coalition of writers known as the Generation of 1898. Well-respected members of this group included Ramón del Valle Inclán (1866–1936), author of four novellas (called *Sonatas*), each named after one of the seasons; the Basque-born philosopher Miguel de Unamuno y Jugo (1864–1936), winner of the 1922 Nobel Prize for literature; and Jacinto Benavente y Martínez (1866–1954), author of *Los intereses creados* (Bonds of Interest). Two other major figures included Federico García Lorca (1898–1936), author of some of the most hauntingly beautiful drama, prose, and poetry in the history of Spain, and Antonio Buero Vallejo (b. 1916). Although many writers and poets were killed on active duty during the Spanish Civil War, the bludgeoning to death of García Lorca by Franco supporters in an Andalusian graveyard was particularly horrible.

Since the end of the Civil War, one of Madrid's most prevalent literary movements was *modernismo*. Two winners of the Nobel Prize (in 1956 and 1977, respectively) were Juan Ramón Jiménez (1881–1958), author of *Platero y yo*, and Vicente Aleixandre (1898–1984). Also important was José Ortega y Gasset (1883–1955), author of *La rebelión de las masas* (Revolt of the Masses; 1930). A more recent winner of the coveted prize, this time in 1989, was Camilo José Cela (b. 1916), author of *La colmena* (The Hive), who evocatively described Madrid during the artistic bleakness of the Franco years.

Since the 1975 death of Franco, new writers have cropped up on the literary landscape of Spain. They are often preoccupied with the advancement of their native regions (examples include Catalonian authors Miguel Delibes, Carmen Laforet, and Monserrat Roig). Despite the attraction of these authors for themes relating to their specific regions, they nonetheless continue to look toward the omnipresent *Movida* of Madrid for their publishing contacts and at least part of their artistic inspiration.

MUSIC

Easy to recognize, Spanish music is passionate, moody, and rhythmical; and although each region of Spain produced its own distinctive variety of music, they can all be unearthed in Madrid's richly diverse nightclubs, concert halls, and theaters.

A common thread that seems to run through the country's music is its shimmering nationalism, pride of place, and subliminal expression of Spain's proud and richly nuanced national identity. Spanish music is a composite of more than two millennia of cultural influences, incorporating elements from the Phoenicians, Greeks, Romans, Visigoths, Moors, Jews, Aryan gypsies, and residents of the former Spanish colonies in the Americas and Asia.

Today many of the country's musical forms are inseparable from the dance forms meant to accompany them. Joyful, exuberant, or disturbingly evocative of either collective or personal anguish, Spanish dances and the music that accompanies them are archetypically Spanish—and one of the country's most famous cultural exports.

The first written music of Spain sprang from the early Christian era, when church liturgies evolved into Visigothic chants. Before the Arab invasion, church music flourished in such population centers as Toledo, Zaragoza, and Seville, and it continued as Christian Spain developed hymns and liturgical chants in its dozens of cloistered convents and monasteries.

To this rich tapestry were added the chants and love poetry of the Arabs. From their North African kingdoms they brought with them many interesting instruments, which included the square tambourine (*adufe* in Spanish), standard tambourine (*panderete*), drum (*atabal*), and metal castanets (*sonajas de azófar*).

During the Renaissance—whose first glimmerings arrived in Spain during the late 1400s—instrumental music became an important art form. This was especially true of pieces written for an early six-string guitar called the *vihuela*, which was later replaced by the five-string guitar during the 17th century, and eventually by the six-string Spanish guitar that is famous today.

Shortly after the 1561 establishment of Madrid, the capital began to dominate the musical life of Spain. Opera—brought to Spain from Italy during the 17th century—was encouraged by the Portuguese-born Queen Barbara of Braganza, wife of Ferdinand VI; the queen organized major operatic performances for her courtiers. Domenico Scarlatti, son of the better-known Alessandro Scarlatti, benefited from the royal patronage of the Bourbon monarchs. Living in Madrid from 1728 to 1757, he composed some of his 500 harpsichord sonatas there and taught his operatic techniques to new generations of Spanish musicians. Another composer who enjoyed Bourbon patronage was Luigi Boccherini (1743–1805), who composed part of his vast repertoire of string quartets and quintets—more than 230 in all—in Madrid beginning in 1768.

From the formal contexts of opera—which many Spaniards justifiably considered a cultural imposition from France and Italy—came the *zarzuela*. Light and sometimes sentimental musical entertainments similar to Gilbert and Sullivan operettas, they richly fulfilled the 19th-century Madrileño penchant for singing, dancing, social satire, and inconsequential romantic imbroglios. Later, zarzuelas developed into a type of variety show, where plots of any kind were abandoned in favor of singing and dancing for their own sake. The art form was greatly encouraged when the Teatro de Zarzuela opened in 1856.

Shortly afterward, Isabella II opened the Teatro Real for serious opera, and the Sociedad de Conciertos, established in 1865, welcomed visiting orchestras from around the world. Despite the civil unrest and general strikes that continued to plague Madrid during the late 19th century, an array of theaters catering to zarzuela and popular taste flourished—holding such foreign visitors as Friedrich

Nietzsche, Camille Saint-Saëns, and Giuseppe Verdi in thrall during their occasional visits to the Spanish capital.

Meanwhile, flamenco, a musical expression of the collective despair of Andalusia, reached widespread prominence as Spain's growing sense of nationalism embraced it as a national art form. Famous throughout the world, but with diminishing numbers of skilled performers, it incorporates rhythmic hand clapping with guitar playing, shrill and not very melodious singing, and—at its best—a cathartic form of dancing. Incorporating a mixture of Jewish liturgical chanting, the calls to prayer of the Muslim *muezzin*, and Byzantine Christian rituals, it has been called a seductive blend of fierce personal passion and technical discipline. The art form's most renowned dancers have included personalities as famous as any of the country's legendary bullfighters, including La Niña de los Peines, Antonio Mairena, Antonio Chacón, and Antonio Gades.

Into this rich cultural stewpot stepped some of Spain's most enduring classical musicians, whose efforts used the above-mentioned musical forms in new and dramatic orchestral modes. Foremost among them was Manuel de Falla (1876–1946), who achieved international fame with such compositions as *El amor brujo* (Love, the Magician), *Nights in the Gardens of Spain*, and *El sombrero de tres picos* (The Three-Cornered Hat). Some of Falla's works were composed expressly for Spanish guitarist Andrés Segovia; their joint efforts set a world-class level of acceptance of the classical guitar on the concert-hall circuit.

Other important classical composers include Joaquin Turina (1882–1949), best defined as a musical nationalist. His most famous works include *Mujeres españolas* (Spanish Women), *Danzas gitanas* (Gypsy Dances), and *La procesión del Rocio* (The Procession at Rocio). Isaac Albéniz (1860–1909) carried the zeal of Spanish nationalism even further during the three years it took to compose his *Iberia Suite*. Comprised of a dozen piano pieces derived from the ancient musical idioms of Spain, they are among the most original piano works of the late 19th century. Simultaneously, Enrique Granados (1867–1916), composer of the piano suite *Goyescos*, derived his inspiration from works of the quintessentially Spanish painter Francisco Goya.

The musical scene in Madrid continues to flourish, showing a healthy respect for the past but moving rapidly ahead into the electronic present. The works of two composers—Frederic Mompou (1893–1987) and Joaquin Rodrigo (b. 1902)—are occasionally presented. Two composers, Lluis de Pablo (b. 1930) and Cristóbal Halffter (b. 1930), the latter a musical disciple and former protégé of Falla, are also presented in Madrid. Both these artists grew up in the turbulent political atmosphere of 1930s Madrid.

The tradition of the Spanish guitar has been handed down from the previously mentioned Andrés Segovia to such new musical stars as Narcisco Yepes (b. 1927), although the position of premier cellist is today in dispute since the 1973 demise of Spanish-born Pau (Pablo) Casals. As for singers, Spain has produced such world-class stars as soprano Montserrat Caballé and tenor José Carreras. Madrid has enjoyed an especially strong link to the legendary tenor Plácido Domingo, who traces his birth to an address in the Spanish capital: calle Ibiza 34, which seems on the verge of becoming an impromptu site of musical pilgrimage.

DANCE

From Madrid's lowliest *taberna* (tavern) to its poshest nightclub, you are likely to hear heel clicking, foot stamping, castanet rattling, hand clapping, and sultry guitar strumming. This is *flamenco*. Its origins lie deep in Asia, but the Spanish gypsy has given it an original and unique style of its own. It is a dance dramatizing inner conflict and pain. Performed by a great artist, flamenco can tear your heart out.

Flamenco has no story line. The leader sets the pace, drawing each of the performers forward. He or she lurks behind and around the group at all times, trying to infuse them with rhythm and the moody passions of the art form. It can be contagious, so don't be surprised if you end up with the castanets yourself.

Other regional dances you're likely to see in Madrid include the *sardana* of Catalonia; the *muineira* of Galicia; and the fiery, colorful dances of León, Castile, and Valencia. The *jota* of Aragón is also renowned. When this dance is presented in a more sensuous Arabic fashion, it is transformed into the fandango. The *seguidilla* has much in common with the jota and fandango. Described by Cervantes as "the quicksilver of all senses," the seguidilla gave birth to the music and dancing of the *bolero*, popular in the taverns of the 18th and 19th centuries. The exoticism of many of these dances has been amplified by such non-Spanish composers as Georges Bizet and with such classical Spanish composers as Ibañez and Falla, who infused their orchestral music with the passions and rhythms of these native music and dance forms.

Today the most popular dance, especially in Madrid, is the *sevillana*. In the classic tradition, music and rhythm would be provided exclusively by either one or two flamenco guitars to accompany the dancers. Today, however, as part of the expanding horizons of a Spain eager to assimilate its cultural classics with new input from abroad, the dancers might perform to the music of mariachi-derived brass band and/or conga drums. Regardless of their degree of historic accuracy, and irrespective of their formality, all these dances can appropriately end with *Olé!*

BULLFIGHTS—THE SPECTACLE OF DEATH

Many consider bullfighting to be cruel and shocking; others consider it a cathartic representative of the mystery of life and death. As Ernest Hemingway pointed out in *Death in the Afternoon*, "The bullfight is not a sport in the Anglo-Saxon sense of the word, that is, it is not an equal contest or an attempt at an equal contest between a bull and a man. Rather, it is a tragedy; the death of the bull, which is played, more or less well, by the bull and the man involved and in which there is danger for the man but certain death for the bull." Hemingway, of course, was an aficionado.

When the symbolic drama of the bullfight is acted out, some think that both its actors and its observers can reach a higher emotional (and sometimes spiritual) plane. Some people argue that it is not a public exhibition of cruelty at all, but rather a highly skilled art form requiring great human qualities: survival, courage, showmanship, and gallantry.

Regardless of your viewpoint, this spectacle is an authentically Spanish experience, and as such it has much to reveal about the character of the land and its people.

The season of the *corridas* (bullfights) lasts from early spring until mid-October, or earlier. Fights are held in a *plaza de toros* (bullring). The oldest ring in Spain lies in Andalusia's remote town of Ronda, although many of those in Spain's larger cities are stadium-size architectural wonders, often built (as in the case of Madrid) in a richly embellished mudéjar/Andalusian style. Unless you happen to arrive during a bullfighting festival (as in the case of Madrid's Festival of San Isidro, when fights are held every day during a three-week period in late springtime), fights are usually held every Sunday afternoon. Madrid, however, because of its size and the devotion of its fans, often holds corridas on Thursday as well.

Tickets fall into three classifications: *sol* (sun), the cheapest and sometimes the most stiflingly hot; *sombra* (shade), the most expensive; *sol y sombra* (a mixture of sun and shade), the medium-price range.

The corrida begins with a parade. For many viewers, this may be the high point of the afternoon's festivities, since all the bullfighters are clad in their *trajes de luce*, or "suits of light."

Bullfights are divided into *tercios* (thirds). The first is the *tercio de capa* (cape), during which the matador tests the bull with various passes and gets acquainted with him. The second portion, the *tercio de varas* (sticks), begins with the lance-carrying *picadores* on horseback, who weaken, or "punish," the bull by jabbing him in the shoulder area. The horses are sometimes gored, even though they wear protective padding, or the horse and rider may be tossed into the air by the now-infuriated bull. The picadores are followed by the *banderilleros*, whose job it is to puncture the bull with pairs of boldly colored darts.

In the final *tercio de muleta*, the action narrows down to the lone fighter and the bull. Gone are the fancy capes. Instead, the matador uses a small red cloth known as a *muleta*, which, to be effective, requires a bull with lowered head. The picadores and banderilleros have already worked, through the wounds inflicted upon the animal, to

IMPRESSIONS

It may truly be affirmed that as God worked six days, and rested on the seventh, Madrileños rest the six and on the seventh . . . go to the bull-fight.
—H. O'Shea, 1865

achieve this. Using the muleta as a lure, the matador wraps the bull around himself in various passes, the most dangerous of which is the *natural;* here, the matador holds the muleta in his left hand, the sword in his right. Right-hand passes pose less of a threat, since the sword can be used to spread out the muleta, making a larger target for the bull. After a number of passes, the time comes for the kill, the "moment of truth." In a moment that, depending on your reaction, might be a moment of deeply emotional high tragedy, a truly skilled fighter may dispatch the bull in one thrust, traditionally aiming to sever the animal's spinal cord just behind its skull.

After the bull dies, the highest official at the ring may award the matador an ear from the dead bull, or perhaps both ears, or ears and tail. For a really extraordinary performance, the hoof is sometimes added. The bullfighter may be carried away as a hero, or if he has displeased the crowd, be chased out of the ring by an angry mob. At a major fight, six bulls are usually killed by three matadors in one afternoon.

RELIGION

With the exception of Poland, and perhaps Italy and Portugal, Spain has been the most staunchly and unwaveringly Catholic country in all of Europe. The Catholic Church has vastly influenced world events through its cooperation with the Spanish monarchs, who dubbed themselves *Los Reyes Católicos* (the Catholic Monarchs) as proof of their devotion. Much of the passion for cultural and political expansion and the inspiration for Spain's greatest buildings were derived from the country's often-unquestioned acceptance of the tenets of the Catholic Church.

The history of Spanish liberalism has usually included opposition to Church presuppositions and power. Much of the social history of 19th-century Madrid reads like a series of liberal reforms with their subsequent retraction by the absolutist monarchs. Major inroads were made against Church power during constitutional reforms of 1868–74 and 1931, although many of the Church prerogatives and privileges were reinstated by Franco after his victory in the Civil War and his subsequent 36-year stranglehold on organized dissent within Spain. In 1953 an official concordat between the Roman Catholic Church and the Franco regime reinforced many of the Church's rights in exchange for its declaration of fealty and allegiance to the Spanish state.

Today Roman Catholicism is the country's established religion, with 10 metropolitan and 64 suffragan sees. The primate of all Spain is the archbishop of Toledo. Since the liberal reforms that followed the death of Franco, church authority is no longer as ironbound as before, and many otherwise devoted Catholics are openly challenging such Church tenets as restrictions concerning divorce, among others.

FOLKLORE

Drawing richly on the dim prehistory of its Celtiberian past, Spain is practically awash with folkloric festivals whose mystical significance lies deep within the country's collective unconscious. Some religious historians cite the cult of bull worship as one of the most enduring mystical rituals in the Mediterranean world. Although Spain long ago embraced Catholicism with something approaching passion, the folkloric significance of the bullfight is much older, sociologists claim, than the Christian tradition.

Additionally, the Spanish folklore associated with rituals involving flamenco, cult worship of the Virgin, wedding or funeral ceremonies, and the legendary frenzies of religious processions in such places as Rocio, has preoccupied psychologists and sociologists for many years.

Despite its relatively late arrival in 1561 onto the landscape of Spain, many of the country's most famous legends revolve around the city of Madrid. One of them concerns the Virgen de la Almudena, one of the city's patron saints, a likeness of whom was concealed in a niche of the city's medieval fortifications during the 9th century, just before the city's capture by the Moors. Two hundred years later, the legend goes, just prior to Madrid's Christian reconquest, a local beauty of impeccable character named María (*La Beata*) recited stories told by local gossips that the long-forgotten statue had requested liberation from the masonry that surrounded it. King Alfonso immediately organized a massive religious procession around the periphery of the walls and announced his intention of demolishing the city's fortifications so that the supposed image would be released.

Terrified that her information might have been false, but believing nonetheless in the existence of such a statue, María La Beata offered her life to the Virgin in exchange for a rescue of the statue. The next day, during the procession, an avalanche of stones fell from the wall, revealing the image of the Virgin. María La Beata, struck dead on the spot by the intensity of her religious ecstasy, was found in a position of prayer, near the newly exposed niche, from which the statue of the Virgin seemed to be smiling at her. Since then, November 9 has been reserved as a special Madrid-based celebration of the Virgen of Almudena, whose legend is a particular favorite of impressionable teenage girls.

Madrid's other patron saint was a humble servant and farmhand, San Isidro, who was happily married (the legend goes) to an endlessly patient peasant woman named María de la Cabeza. A historical resident of a house opposite the Church of San Miguel, on calle del Doctor Letamendi in Madrid, Isidro is credited with the ability to perform such miracles as making water gush from barren rocks, healing the blind and the sick, and convincing a team of angels to descend from heaven to plow his master's fields while he was either absorbed in prayer or sleeping (the stories differ). Not without mystical powers of her own, María de la Cabeza performed her best-publicized miracle after throwing her cloak upon the raging currents of the Jarama River; instantly transformed into a bridge, it permitted her and Isidro an easy passage across.

Today Madrid's most famous annual event involves parties, processions, and an almost continuous run of bullfights, all of which are collectively known as the Festival of San Isidro. Scheduled to fall during a three-week period beginning on or around May 15, the day which the Catholic Church specifically designates in honor of San Isidro, it includes an array of almost obsessive taurine activities that are considered among the most skilled and elegant in the entire world.

The celebrations of both Christmas (Navidad) and New Year's (Año Nuevo) are observed with both public and private parties throughout Madrid. At midnight on New Year's Eve, the Puerta del Sol is the site of a gathering of thousands of celebrants, each of whom amusedly pops a grape into his or her mouth with each midnight chime of the plaza's main clock. The Christmas season culminates in parties on the night of January 5 and the Procession of the Three Kings (Cabalgata de los Reyes Magos). Winding through the streets of Madrid, replete with Middle Eastern costumes of long ago, it especially appeals to children.

In January, during the fiesta of San Antón, lovers of animals lead their pets to the San Antonio Abad church, where a priest blesses them in honor of the patron saint of animals, San Antón.

Madrid offers its own distinctive version of Carnival. Replete with parades, elaborate costumes, and lots of civic brouhaha, it ends on the Tuesday before Ash Wednesday, just before the enforced piety of Semana Santa, or Holy Week, the seven days before Easter. Modern Madrid seems about equally divided between those observers who spend long hours in church or on religious pilgrimages, and those who use the holidays to depart for long and very secular vacations.

Many other folkloric celebrations occur at annual intervals in Madrid, some of which are concerned with past military victories. Most important of these is the 2 de Mayo (May 2), an observation of the 1802 revolt of the Madrileños against the French forces of Napoleon. Naturally, the bulk of Madrid's parties, parades, and celebrations emanate outward from the Plaza 2 de Mayo.

3 Food & Drink

Madrid manages to incorporate within its borders a gastronomic sampling of each of the country's best-loved dishes. The city's highly varied cuisine seems to hold one thing in common: The portions are immense, and though the prices are not as moderate as in recent years, they can still be moderate by North American standards. Whenever possible, try to sample some of Spain's regional specialties, abundantly offered at restaurants throughout the city. Many of these, such as Andalusian gazpacho and Valencian paella, have transcended their region and are now considered great dishes of the world.

MEALS • Breakfast In Madrid, the day starts with a continental breakfast of hot coffee, hot chocolate, or tea, with assorted rolls, butter, and jam. A typical Spanish breakfast often includes *churros* (fried fingerlike doughnuts) and a hot chocolate that's very sweet and thick. The coffee is usually strong and black, served with hot milk. Some people consider it too strong and bitter for their tastes and therefore ask for instant coffee instead.

• **Lunch**   An important meal in Spain, lunch here is comparable to the farm-style noonday "dinner" in America. It usually includes three or four courses, beginning with a choice of soup or several dishes of hors d'oeuvres called *entremeses*. Often a fish or egg dish is served after this, then a meat course with vegetables. Wine is always on the table. Dessert usually consists of pastry, custard, or assorted fruit; this is followed by coffee. Lunch is served from 1 to 3:30pm, with "rush hour" at 2pm.

• **Tapas**   After an early-evening promenade, many Spaniards head for their favorite *tascas*, or bars, where they drink wine and sample assorted *tapas* such as bits of fish, eggs in mayonnaise, or olives.

• **Dinner**   Another extravaganza. A typical meal starts with a bowl of soup, followed by a second course, often a fish dish, and by another main course, usually veal, beef, or pork, which is accompanied by vegetables. Again, desserts tend to be fruit, custard, or pastries.

Wine is always available. Afterward, you might have a demitasse and a fragrant Spanish brandy. The chic dining hour, even in one-donkey towns, is 10 or 10:30pm. In Madrid's popular tourist districts, as well as in hard-working Catalonia, you can usually dine by 8pm. In most middle-class establishments, people dine no later than 9:30pm. Your choice.

THE CUISINE • **Soups & Appetizers**   Soups are usually served in big bowls. Cream soups, such as asparagus and potato, can be fine; sadly, however, they are too often made from powdered ingredients in foil packets from such companies as Knorr and Liebig. The chilled gazpacho, on the other hand, is tasty and usually made fresh. Served year round, it's particularly refreshing during the hot months. The combination of ingredients is pleasant: olive oil, garlic, ground cucumbers, and raw tomatoes with a sprinkling of croutons. Madrid also offers a sampling of the many varieties of fish soup (*sopa de pescado*) that seem to derive from each of Spain's many provinces, and many of these are superb.

In Madrid's top restaurants, as many as 15 tempting hors d'oeuvres might be offered, often among the best of their kind anywhere. In lesser-known places, including restaurants without an active turnover of clients or inventories, avoid these entremeses, which often consist of last year's sardines and shards of sausage left over from the Moorish conquest.

• **Eggs**   These are served in countless ways. A Spanish omelet, *tortilla española*, is made with potatoes. A simple omelet is called a *tortilla francesa*. A *tortilla portugésa* is similar to the American version of a Spanish omelet.

• **Fish**   Madrid gathers into its periphery both the raw ingredients and the regional recipes for some of the finest fish dishes in Spain. One of the most common varieties is hake (*merluza*), sweet and white. *Langosta*, a variety of small-clawed lobster, is seen everywhere, particularly on ice or in refrigerated display cases. Although it's a treat, it's also terribly expensive. The Portuguese in particular, but some Spaniards, too, go into raptures at the mention of barnacles. Gourmets relish their seawater taste; others find them tasteless. *Rape* is the Spanish name for monkfish, a sweet, wide-boned ocean fish with a texture like that of scallops. Also try a few dozen half-inch baby eels. They rely heavily on olive oil and garlic for their flavor, but they're great tasting. Squid cooked in its own ink is suggested for those who want to go native. The city's frequent offerings of charcoal-broiled sardines, a particular treat in the Basque provinces but occasionally available in Madrid, however, are a culinary delight. Trout Navarre is one of the capital's most popular fish dishes, carefully deboned and usually stuffed with bacon or ham.

• **Paella**   You can't go to Madrid without sampling what might be the most famous dish to ever emerge from Spain. Originally a specialty of the seacoast city of Valencia and now considered the property of Spaniards around the world, it's an aromatic rice-and-saffron dish usually topped with shellfish, chicken, sausage, peppers, and local spices. Served authentically, it comes steaming hot from the kitchen in a metal pan called a *paellera*. (Incidentally, what is known in America as Spanish rice isn't Spanish at all. If you ask an English-speaking waiter for your Spanish rice, he'll probably serve you paella.)

• **Meats**   Don't expect Kansas City steak, but do try the spit-roasted suckling pig, so sweet and tender it can often be cut with a fork. The veal is also good, and the Spanish *lomo de cerdo* (loin of pork) is unmatched anywhere. As for chicken, it will sometimes qualify for the Olympics in that it's stringy and muscular. Spit-roasted chicken, however, can often be flavorful.

• **Vegetables & Salads**   Such treats as vine-ripened tomatoes—available in summer—are excellent, but in winter some of the cheaper restaurants often serve canned vegetables instead of fresh. String beans, peas, and artichokes are among the most popular vegetables in Madrid, and potatoes are a staple. Salads in the 1990s have more variety in choice of lettuce and appear more frequently on menus than in days of yore.

• **Desserts**   The Spanish don't emphasize dessert. Flan, a home-cooked egg custard, appears on all menus—sometimes with a burnt-caramel sauce. Ice cream appears on nearly all menus as well. The best bet is to ask for a basket of fresh fruit, which you can wash at your table in the bowl of water that's usually provided. Homemade pastries are usually moist and not too sweet. As a dining oddity, many restaurants serve fresh orange juice for dessert. Madrileños love it!

• **Olive Oil & Garlic**   Olive oil is used lavishly in Madrid and throughout Spain. Despite its well-documented health effects, you may not want it in all dishes. If, for example, you prefer your fish fried in butter, the word for butter is *mantequilla* (in some instances you'll be charged extra for the butter). Garlic is also an integral part of the Spanish diet, and even if you love it, you may find the Spaniard loves it more than you do and uses it in the oddest dishes.

NONALCOHOLIC BEVERAGES • Water   Tap water is usually considered safe to drink in Madrid and in tourist resorts along the Costa del Sol. Despite that, many frequent travelers opt for drinking bottled water instead, simply because it usually tastes better. If you'd like your water with a little kick, then ask for *agua mineral con gas*. Note that in some remote hamlets, bottled water transported from a faraway district of Spain sometimes costs more than the locally bottled regional wine.

• Soft Drinks   In general, avoid the carbonated citrus drinks on sale everywhere—most of them never saw an orange, much less a lemon. If you want a citrus drink, order old, reliable Schweppes. An excellent noncarbonated drink for the summer is Tri-Naranjus, which comes in lemon and orange flavors. Your cheapest bet is a liter bottle of *gaseosa*, which comes in various flavors. In summer you should also try a drink I've never seen outside Spain, *horchata*, a nutty, sweet milklike beverage made of tubers called *chufas*. Its flavor is vaguely reminiscent of liquefied almonds.

• Coffee   Even if you're a dedicated coffee drinker, you may find the *café con leche* (coffee with milk) a little too strong. I suggest *leche manchada*, a little bit of strong, freshly brewed coffee in a glass, filled with lots of frothy hot milk.

• Milk   Even though some old-time aficionados in rural districts claim that some of milk's flavor is lost during the pasteurization process, always avoid untreated milk and milk by-products. Most of the milk sold in Madrid, fortunately, is bottled and properly sterilized. One of the city's popular brands of fresh and pasteurized milk is Lauki, sold in food stores throughout the city.

ALCOHOLIC BEVERAGES • Beer   Although not native to Spain, beer (*cerveza*) is now drunk everywhere. Domestic brands include San Miguel, Mahou, Aguila, and Cruz Blanca.

• Wine   Sherry (*vino de Jerez*) has been called the "wine with a hundred souls." Drink it before dinner (try the topaz-colored *finos*, a very pale sherry) or whenever you drop in to some old inn or bodega for refreshment; many of them have rows of brimming kegs with spigots. Manzanilla, a golden-colored, medium-dry sherry, is extremely popular. The sweet cream sherries (Harvey's Bristol Cream, for example) are favorite after-dinner wines (called *olorosos*). While the French may be disdainful of Spanish table wines, they can be truly noble, especially two leading varieties, Valdepeñas and Rioja, both from Castile. If you're fairly adventurous and not too demanding in your tastes, you can always ask for the *vino de la casa* (wine of the house) wherever you dine. The Ampurdan of Catalonia is a heavy and somewhat coarse, but flavorful wine. From Andalusia comes the fruity Montilla. There are also some good Spain-derived champagnes (*cavas*) widely available in Madrid, such as Freixenet. One brand, Benjamin, also comes in individual-size bottles.

• **Sangría**   This is the all-time favorite refreshing drink in Spain. It's red-wine punch that combines wine with oranges, lemons, seltzer, and sugar.

• **Whisky & Brandy**   Imported whiskies are available at most Madrileño bars, but at a high price. If you're a drinker, switch to brandies and cognacs, where the Spanish reign supreme. Try Fundador, made by the Pedro Domecq family in Jerez de la Frontera. If you're seeking a smooth cognac, ask for "103" white label.

4   Recommended Books, Films & Recordings

BOOKS   Historically, Spain's Golden Age lasted from the late 15th to the early 17th century; this era is well surveyed in J. H. Elliot's *Imperial Spain 1469–1716* (New American Library, 1977).

Most accounts of the Spanish Armada's defeat are written from the English point of view. For a change of perspective, try David Howarth's *The Voyage of the Armada* (Penguin, 1981).

One of the best accounts of Spain's earlier history is found in Joseph F. O'Callaghan's *History of Medieval Spain* (Cornell University Press, 1983).

In the 20th century, the historical focus was almost dominated by the tragedies of the Spanish Civil War, recounted in the classic by Hugh Thomas, *The Spanish Civil War* (Harper & Row, 1977). For a personal account of the war, read George Orwell's *Homage to Catalonia* (Harcourt Brace Jovanovich, 1969). The poet García Lorca was murdered during the Civil War; the best account of the brutality of his death is found in Ian Gibson's *The Assassination of Federico García Lorca* (Penguin, 1983).

If you like more contemporary history, read John Hooper's *The Spaniards* (Penguin, 1987). Hooper provides insight into the events of the post-Franco era.

The Moors contributed much to Spanish culture, leaving Spain with a distinct legacy that's documented in Titus Burckhardt's *Moorish Culture in Spain* (McGraw-Hill, 1972).

Antoni Gaudí is the Spanish architect who most excites many first-time visitors. Among the many illustrated books on his work, *Gaudí* (Escudo de Oro's "Collection of Art in Spain," 1990) contains 150 photographs of some of the most unusual early-20th-century architecture in Europe.

For the first time in English, *Juan de Herrera: Architect to Philip II of Spain* by Catherine Williamson Zerner (Yale University Press, 1994), describes the remarkable three-decade partnership between Herrara (1530–97) and his royal patron. Richly illustrated.

Spain's most famous artist was Pablo Picasso. The most controversial recent book about the late painter is *Picasso, Creator and*

Destroyer by Arianna Stassinopoulos Huffington (Simon & Schuster, 1988).

Spain's other headline-grabbing artist was Salvador Dalí. In *Salvador Dalí: A Biography* (E. P. Dutton, 1986), author Meryle Secrest asks: Was he a mad genius or a cunning manipulator?

Andrés Segovia: An Autobiography of the Years 1893–1920 (Macmillan, 1976), translated by W. F. O'Brien, is useful for understanding the demands placed upon professionals in the world of Spanish classical music.

Passed over by some as superficial, James A. Michener's *Iberia* (Random House, 1968) remains the classic travelogue on Spain.

The most famous Spanish novel of all time is *Don Quixote de La Mancha* by Miguel de Cervantes. Exploring the conflict between the ideal and the real in human nature, it has been one of the most artistically influential novels in literary history.

The collected works of the famous dramatist of Spain's Golden Age, Pedro Calderón de la Barca, can be read in *Plays* (University Press of Kentucky, 1985).

The major works of one of the most lyrically evocative authors in pre–Civil War Spain, Federico García Lorca, can be enjoyed in *Five Plays: Comedies and Tragicomedies* (New Directions, 1964).

Ernest Hemingway, an avid Hispanophile, completed many works on Spain, none more notable than his novels of 1926 and 1940, respectively, *The Sun Also Rises* (Macmillan, 1987) and *For Whom the Bell Tolls* (Macmillan, 1988), the latter based on his experiences in the Spanish Civil War. Don Ernesto's *Death in the Afternoon* (various editions) remains the English-language classic on bullfighting.

The Life of Saint Teresa of Avila by Herself (Penguin, 1987) is reputedly the third most widely read book in Spain, after the Bible and *Don Quixote*. The translation is by J. M. Cohen.

FILM One of the biggest names in Spanish cinema is Luis Buñuel, whom some regard as the ultimate genius of Spanish cinema. In 1928, Salvador Dalí and Buñuel cooperated on the director's first movie, *Un chien andalou* (An Andalusian Dog), considered the most important surrealist film ever made. Two years later, sadistic scenes in *L'Age d'Or* (The Golden Age)—again written with Dalí's help—led to riots in some movie houses. Buñuel also directed *La mort en ce jardin* (Death in This Garden) with Simone Signoret (1957). In 1960 he made *Viridiana*, which won the prize for best picture at Cannes, even though Franco banned the film in Spain.

Today's *enfant terrible* is Pedro Almódovar, whose *Women on the Verge of a Nervous Breakdown* won an Academy Award nomination in 1990. Ostensibly the film is the story of a woman's abandonment, but its madcap proceedings deal with everything from spiked gazpacho to Shiite terrorists. An iconoclast like Almódovar, who has publicly declared his homosexuality, flourishes in the contemporary liberalized Spain, which abolished censorship in 1977, two years after the death of Franco.

Another Almódovar international hit, *High Heels* (1991), is a soap opera involving a highly theatrical and emotional film diva who returns to Madrid and the daughter she abandoned years before. Praised by critics for "spanking his favorite ideas until they turn red with pleasure," Almódovar plays with what has been defined as "the theatricality of the real and the authenticity of the theatrical—all in an engagingly funny combination of high and low camp." He continued his glitz with *Kika* (1994), which he both wrote and directed. His eponymous heroine, Verónica Forqué, a beautician, is full of surprises. For example, she meets her lover-to-be, Ramón, when she's making up his presumably dead corpse. He wakes up and they fall in love, but that's only the beginning of twists and turns in this crazed soap opera.

In 1982, José Luís Garci became the first Spaniard to win an Oscar for best foreign-language film, with *Volver a empezar* (To Begin Again).

One of the biggest box-office hits in Spanish film history, and still available in video, is *El crimen de Cuenca* (The Crime in Cuenca), directed by Pilar Miró, who went on to become "chief of state of Spanish television." The film, which details Civil Guard torture, caused a furor when it was released. It was suppressed until the coup attempt of 1981.

Hailed by some critics as a variation of the farmer's daughter tale, *Belle Epoque*, directed by Fernando Trueba and written by Rafael Azcona (in Spanish with English subtitles), won the 1993 Oscar as best foreign-language film. It is a hot-blooded human comedy of a handsome innocent, a deserter from the Spanish army in the winter of 1930–31, who is seduced by the four flirtatious daughters of a droll old painter.

RECORDINGS As residents of the premier cultural bastion of Spain, Madrileños cultivate their tastes in a wide variety of music. Here is a list of recordings that the city's critics consider important.

Don Odilo Cunill directs the Cor Monastic de Abadia de Montserrat in *Cantos Gregorians de la Missa Per Els Fidels Missa orbis Factor*, Gregorian chants recorded in the chapel of the monastery at Montserrat.

In the album *Andrés Segovia, España*, the late master plays guitar versions of fandangos and *tonadillas*. In a more classical vein the same artist plays Bach, Scarlatti, and music by the Czech composer Benda (1722–95) in *Recital Intímo*.

The Orquesta de Conciertos de Madrid performs Falla's *El amor brujo* and *El sombrero de tres picos*. The same group, conducted by Enrique Jorda, can be heard in Albéniz's *Suite española* and *Dos piezas españoles*.

Isabel Pantoja, widow of the late bullfighter, sings soulful interpretations of Andalusian ballads in *Se me enamora el alma*. Rocio Jurado renders them smolderingly in *Punto de partida* and *Canciones de españa*.

Carlos Cana performs popular interpretations of Spanish Argentinian tangos, habañeras, and sevillanas on *Luna de Abril*. In *Canalla,*

Antonio Cortés Chiquetete is heard performing 19th-century folk melodies. Felipe Campuzano gives piano interpretations of Andalusian folk music in *Cadiz: Andalucia espiritual.*

Pasodobles famosos, performed by the Gran Banda Taurina, is popular with older Spaniards, partly for its nostalgic value. This was the music played until very recently at every Spanish gathering, from bullfights to weddings to christenings.

In *Siroca,* Paco de Lucía combines traditional flamenco guitar in its purest form with modern influences, including tangos, *bulerías,* and *tanquillos.* You can also hear Paco de Lucía on *Fantasía flamenca,* interpreting authentic flamencas in a traditional manner. One of his most recent releases, *Zyryab,* is named for the 8th-century Persian musician who brought new musical techniques to Córdoba, including (probably) the basis for the modern guitar.

The brilliance of the late virtuoso Narcisco Yepes can be heard on *Musica española para guitarra,* performing traditional favorites.

The Spanish beauty Ana Belén sings contemporary love ballads in *A la sombra de un León.* She is married to the somewhat less popular singer Victor Manuel, known for his collection of contemporary ballads, *Tiempo de cerezas.*

In Madrid, an outstanding local band is called Radio Futura. They have been called the "Einsteins of Spanish rock music." Reviewers usually cite the Mecano, a Madrid band, as "pretty boys" who sell records by the ton. Borrowing a name from a famous old German movie, the Gabinete Caligari, in the words of one reviewer, is a band that represents "macho Hispano-pop." From Catalonia comes a duo with a unique sound, a band recording rock music as El Ultimo de la Fila.

One of the biggest record sellers in Spain is Joan Manual Serrat, a singer/songwriter recording more traditional popular music in both Catalán and Castilian.

In Madrid, traditional Spanish music is also offered by singer/songwriter Luis Eduardo Aute, who has thousands of fans throughout the Spanish-speaking world.

In current Spanish jazz, Tete Montoliu's recordings represent some of the best the country has to offer. All, or most, of these records are available at Spanish music stores in the United States. They are available in Madrid and throughout Spain as well.

2

Planning a Trip to Madrid

THIS CHAPTER IS DEVOTED TO THE WHERE, WHEN, AND HOW OF YOUR TRIP—
the advance-planning issues required to get it together and take
it on the road. After deciding where to go, most people have two
fundamental questions: What will it cost? and How do I get there?
This chapter will answer both of those questions, and resolve other
important issues, such as when to go, what insurance coverage is
necessary, and where to obtain more information about Madrid.

1 Information, Entry Requirements & Money

Sources of Information

IN THE U.S.   For information before you go, contact the **Tourist
Office of Spain,** 665 Fifth Ave., New York, NY 10022
(☎ **212/759-8822**). Other information offices are the Spanish
Tourist Office, 8383 Wilshire Blvd., Suite 960, Beverly Hills, CA
90211 (☎ **213/658-7188**); Tourist Office of Spain, Water Tower
Place, Suite 915 East, 845 N. Michigan Ave., Chicago, IL 60611
(☎ **312/642-1992**); and Tourist Office of Spain, 1221 Brickell
Ave., Miami, FL 33131 (☎ **305/358-8223**).

OUTSIDE THE U.S.   Tourist offices include the Spanish Tourist Information, 203 Castlereagh St., Suite 21A (P.O. Box 675),
NSW 2000 Sydney, South Australia (☎ **612/264-7966**); Tourist
Office of Spain, 102 Bloor St. W., 14th Floor, Toronto, ON M5S
1M8, Canada (☎ **416/961-3131**), and Spanish Tourist Office,
57–58 St. James's St., London SW1(☎ **0171/499-0901**).

OTHER SOURCES   Other useful sources are **newspapers** and
magazines. To find the latest articles that have been published on
your destination, go to your library, ask for the *Readers' Guide to
Periodical Literature,* and look under the city/country for listings.

You may also want to contact the U.S. State Department for its
background bulletins. Contact the Superintendent of Documents,
U.S. Government Printing Office, Washington, DC 20402
(☎ **202/783-3238**).

A **travel agent** can also be a good source of information. If you
use one, make sure he or she is a member of the American Society of
Travel Agents (ASTA). If you get poor service from a travel agent,
contact ASTA's Consumer Affairs Department, 1101 King St.,
Alexandria, VA 22314 (☎ **703/739-2782**).

And finally, we come to the best source of all—**friends** and **other
travelers** who have just returned from your destination.

Entry Requirements

PASSPORTS   A valid passport is all an American, a British, a Canadian, or a New Zealand citizen needs to enter Spain. (Australians
need a visa—see below.) You don't need an international driver's
license if you're renting a car; your local license from back home
should suffice.

VISAS For visits to Spain of less than three months, visas are not required by citizens of the United States, Canada, the United Kingdom, and New Zealand. Australians, however, need a visa and should apply in advance at the Spanish Consulate in their home country.

CUSTOMS Spain permits you to bring in most personal effects and the following items duty free: two still cameras with 10 rolls of film each, one movie or video camera, tobacco for personal use, one bottle of wine and one bottle of liquor per person, a portable radio, a tape recorder, a typewriter, a bicycle, golf clubs, tennis racquets, fishing gear, two hunting weapons with 100 cartridges each, skis, and other sports equipment.

In the U.S. Returning to the United States from Spain, American citizens may bring in $400 worth of merchandise duty free, provided they have not made a similar claim within the past 30 days. Remember to keep receipts for purchases made in Spain. For more specific guidance, request the free pamphlet "Know Before You Go" by writing to the **U.S. Customs Service,** P.O. Box 7407, Washington, DC 20044.

In Canada For total clarification, Canadians can write for the booklet "I Declare," issued by **Revenue Canada Customs Department,** Communications Branch, Mackenzie Avenue, Ottawa, ON K1A OL5. Canada allows its citizens a $300 exemption, and they can bring back duty free 200 cigarettes, 2.2 pounds of tobacco, 40 ounces of liquor, and 50 cigars. In addition, they are allowed to mail unsolicited gifts (but *not* alcohol or tobacco) into Canada from abroad at the rate of $40 (Canadian) a day. On the package, mark "UNSOLICITED GIFT, UNDER $40 VALUE." All valuables you own and take with you should be declared before departure from Canada on the Y-38 form, including serial numbers. **Note:** The $300 exemption can be used only once a year and then only after an absence of seven days.

In the U.K. & Ireland Members of EC countries do not necessarily have to go through Customs when returning home, providing all their travel was within EC countries. Of course, Customs agents reserve the right to search if they are suspicious. However, there are certain EC guidelines for returning passengers, who can bring in 400 cigarillos, 200 cigars, 800 cigarettes, and 1 kilogram of smoking tobacco. They can also bring in 20 liters of fortified wine, 90 liters of wine, and 110 liters of beer. Persons exceeding these limits may be asked to prove that the excess is either for one's personal use or gifts for friends. For further details, contact **HM Customs and Excise,** Excise and Inland Customs Advice Centre, Dorset House, Stamford Street, London SE1 9NG (☎ **071/202-4227**).

In Australia The duty-free allowance in Australia is A$400 or A$200 for those under 18. Personal property mailed back from Spain should be marked "AUSTRALIAN GOODS RETURNED" to avoid payment of duty. Upon returning to Australia, citizens can bring in 200 cigarettes or 250 grams of loose tobacco and 1 liter of alcohol. If you're returning with valuable goods you already own, such as foreign-made cameras, you should file form B263. A helpful brochure, available from Australian consulates or Customs offices, is *Customs Information for All Travellers.*

In New Zealand   The duty-free allowance is $NZ500. Citizens over 16 can bring in 200 cigarettes or 250 grams of loose tobacco or 50 cigars, 4.5 liters of wine or beer, or 1.125 liters of liquor. New Zealand currency does not carry restrictions regarding import or export. A Certificate of Export listing valuables taken out of the country allows you to bring them back without paying duty. Most questions are answered in a free pamphlet, *New Zealand Customs Guide for Travellers,* available at New Zealand Consulates and Customs offices.

Money

To give you an idea of what Madrid costs, consult the "What Things Cost" chart on page 50.

CASH & CURRENCY   The basic unit of Spanish currency is the **peseta (pta.),** currently worth about $7/10$ of a cent in U.S. currency. One U.S. dollar is worth about 140 pesetas. (**Warning:** This is subject to change, of course, because the dollar and the peseta fluctuate on the world market. Check with your bank for up-to-date quotations.)

Pesetas are distributed in coin denominations of 1, 2, 5, 10, 25, 50, 100, and 200 pesetas. Paper money comes in bills of 100, 200, 500, 1,000, 5,000, and 10,000 pesetas.

Hotels usually offer the worst rate of exchange, while banks generally offer the best. But even banks charge a commission for the service, often $2 or $3, depending on the transaction.

TRAVELER'S CHECKS   Traveler's checks are the safest way to carry cash while traveling. Before leaving home, purchase traveler's checks and arrange to carry some ready cash (usually about $250, depending on your habits and needs). In the event of theft, if the checks are properly documented, the value of your checks will be refunded. Most large banks sell traveler's checks, charging fees that average between 1% and 2% of the value of the checks you buy, although some out-of-the-way banks, in rare instances, charge as much as 7%. If your bank wants more than a 2% commission, it sometimes pays to call the traveler's check issuers directly for the address of outlets where this commission will be less.

Issuers sometimes have agreements with groups to sell checks commission free. For example, the Automobile Association of America (AAA) sells American Express checks in several currencies without commission.

American Express   (☎ toll free **800/221-7282** in the U.S. and Canada) is one of the largest and most immediately recognized issuers of traveler's checks. No commission is charged, as mentioned above, to AAA members and holders of certain types of American

Express charge cards. The company issues checks denominated in U.S. or Canadian dollars, British pounds sterling, Swiss or French francs, German marks, and Japanese yen. The vast majority of checks sold in North America are denominated in U.S. dollars. For questions or problems that arise outside the U.S. or Canada, contact any of the company's many regional representatives.

Citicorp (☎ toll free **800/645-6556** in the U.S. and Canada, or **813/623-1709,** collect, from anywhere else), issues checks in U.S. dollars, British pounds, German marks, and Japanese yen.

Thomas Cook (☎ toll free **800/223-9920** in the U.S., or **609/987-7300,** collect, from anywhere else) issues MasterCard traveler's checks denominated in U.S. dollars, French francs, German marks, Dutch guilders, Spanish pesetas, Australian dollars, Japanese yen, and Hong Kong dollars. Depending on individual banking laws in each of the various states, some of the above-mentioned currencies might not be available in every outlet.

The Spanish Peseta

For U.S. Readers At this writing $1 = approximately 140 ptas. (or 1 pta. = 0.71¢), and this was the rate of exchange used to calculate the approximate dollar values given in the table below and throughout this edition.

For U.K. Readers At this writing £1 = approximately 200 ptas. (or 1 pta. = 0.5p), and this was the rate of exchange used to calculate the pound values in the table below.

Note International exchange rates fluctuate from time to time according to a complicated series of politicoeconomic factors and may not be the same when you travel to Spain. Therefore, this table should be used only as a guide for approximate values.

Pesetas	U.S.$	U.K. £	Pesetas	U.S.$	U.K. £
5	0.04	0.03	1,000	7.10	5.00
10	0.07	0.05	2,500	17.75	12.50
25	0.18	0.13	5,000	35.50	25.00
50	0.36	0.25	7,500	53.25	37.50
75	0.53	0.38	10,000	71.00	50.00
100	0.71	0.50	12,500	88.75	62.50
200	1.42	1.00	15,000	106.50	75.00
300	2.13	1.50	17,500	124.25	87.50
400	2.84	2.00	20,000	142.00	100.00
500	3.55	2.50	25,000	177.50	125.00
600	4.26	3.00	27,500	195.25	137.50
700	4.97	3.50	30,000	213.00	150.00
800	5.68	4.00	50,000	355.00	250.00
900	6.39	4.50	100,000	710.00	500.00

Planning a Trip to Madrid Information, Entry Requirements & Money

What Things Cost in Madrid	U.S. $
Taxi from airport to Puerta del Sol	17.80
Public transportation within the city	.90
Local telephone call	.15
Double room at the Palace (very expensive)	227.20
Double room at Hotel Carlos V (moderate)	71.00
Double room at Hostal Principado (budget)	41.20
Lunch for one, without wine, at Alkalde (expensive)	25.50
Lunch for one, without wine, at Foster's Hollywood (budget)	14.00
Dinner for one, without wine, at El Cabo Mayor (expensive)	32.70
Dinner for one, without wine, at Sobrino de Botín (moderate)	19.90
Dinner for one, without wine, at Gran Café de Gijón (budget)	9.90
Coca-Cola in restaurant	1.95
Cup of coffee	1.95
Glass of wine or beer	1.80
Roll of ASA 100 color film, 36 exposures	7.90
Admission to the Prado	3.20
Movie ticket	6.50
Theater ticket	6.00

Interpayment Services (☎ toll free **800/221-2426** in the U.S. or Canada, or **800/453-4284** from most anywhere else) sells Visa checks sponsored by Barclays Bank and/or Bank of America at selected branches around North America. Traveler's checks are denominated in U.S. or Canadian dollars, British pounds, Swiss or French francs, German marks, and Japanese yen.

CREDIT & CHARGE CARDS   You'll find that carrying credit and charge cards is useful in Spain. **American Express, Visa,** and **Diners Club** are widely recognized. If you see the Eurocard or Access sign on an establishment, that means it accepts **MasterCard.**

Credit and charge cards can save your life when you're abroad. With American Express and Visa, for example, not only can you charge purchases in shops and restaurants that take the card, but you can also withdraw pesetas from bank cash machines at many locations in Spain. Check with your card company before leaving home.

Keep in mind that the price of purchases is not converted into your national currency until notification is received in your home country, so the price is subject to fluctuation. If your national currency—be it dollars, pounds, or whatever—declines by the time your bill arrives, you'll pay more for an item than you expected. But those are the rules of the game. It can also work in your favor if your national currency should rise against the Spanish peseta.

CURRENCY EXCHANGE   Many Madrid hotels will simply not accept a dollar- or pound-denominated check, and if they do, they'll almost certainly charge for the conversion. In some cases, they'll accept countersigned traveler's checks or a credit card, but if you're prepaying a deposit on hotel reservations, it's cheaper and easier to pay with a check drawn on a Spanish bank.

This can be arranged by a large commercial bank or by a specialist such as **Ruesch International,** 825 14th St. NW, Washington, DC, 20005 (☎ **202/408-1200,** or toll free **800/424-2923**), which performs a wide variety of conversion-related tasks, usually for only $2 U.S. per transaction.

If you need a check payable in pesetas, call Ruesch's toll-free number, describe what you need, and note the transaction number given to you. Mail your dollar-denominated personal check (payable to Ruesch International) to the office in Washington, DC. Upon receiving this, the company will mail a check denominated in pesetas for the financial equivalent, minus the $2 charge. The company can also help you with many kinds of wire transfers and conversions of VAT (value-added tax, which is known as IVA in Spain), refund checks, and also will mail brochures and information packets on request. Britishers can go to **Ruesch International Ltd.,** 18 Saville Row, London W1X 2AD (☎ **0171/734-2300**).

Mutual of Omaha/Travelex, 1225 Franklin Ave., Garden City, NY 11530 (☎ toll free **800/377-0051** in the U.S.) provides foreign currency exchange at 30 U.S. airport locations or through the mail. With exchanges of $500 or more, they will guarantee to exchange back up to 30% at the same rate you originally exchanged with no service fee. Annual or short-term flight insurance policies are available starting at $5.

2   When to Go—Climate, Holidays & Events

CLIMATE   In Madrid, climate is subject to rapid change. July and August are the most uncomfortable months—in fact, the government virtually shuts down in August, except for a skeleton crew, and goes into "exile" at the northeast Atlantic resort of San Sebastian. The temperature can often reach a high of 91° Fahrenheit in July, 76° in September. In winter, it can plunge to 34°F, although it averages around 46°.

In October (average temperature: 58°F), Madrid enjoys its "season." Hotel space is at a premium. Every bullfighter, doll manufacturer, Galician hotelier, Andalusian olive grower, or Santander vineyard keeper having business with the government descends on Madrid at this time. In the same month, wealthy Spanish aristocrats flock here from secluded ducal palaces in Andalusia and Castile to savor the capital's attractions, opera, theater, and endless rounds of parties and dinners. The air is clear, the sun kind; the restaurants and *tascas* (bars) overflow with Iberian *joie de vivre.*

In my view, however, the balmy month of May (average temperature: 61°F) is the best time for making your own descent on the capital.

Madrid's Average Daytime Temperature & Rainfall

	Jan	Feb	Mar	Apr	May	June	July	Aug	Sept	Oct	Nov	Dec
Temp. (°F)	43	45	49	54	61	68	75	74	68	58	48	43
Rainfall (in.)	2	2	1.6	2	1.5	1.2	0.4	0.3	1.3	2	2.4	2

HOLIDAYS   National holidays in Spain include January 1 (New Year's Day), January 6 (Epiphany), March 19 (Day of St. Joseph), Good Friday, Easter Monday, May 1 (May Day), June 10 (Corpus Christi), June 29 (Day of St. Peter and St. Paul), July 25 (Day of St. James), August 15 (Feast of the Assumption), October 12 (Spain's National Day), November 1 (All Saints' Day), December 8 (Immaculate Conception), and December 25 (Christmas).

No matter how large or small, every city or town in Spain also celebrates its local saint's days. In Madrid, it's on May 15 (Saint Isidro).

Madrid Calendar of Events

February

- **ARCO**   Madrid's International Contemporary Art Fair is one of the biggest draws in Spain's cultural calendar, bringing the best in contemporary art from Europe and America. At the Crystal Pavilion of the Casa de Campo, the exhibition presents both regional and international known artists. Dates vary.
- **Madrid Carnival**   The carnival kicks off with a big parade along paseo de la Castellana, culminating in a masked ball at the Círculo de Belles Artes the following night. Fancy-dress competitions last until Ash Wednesday, when the festivities end with a tear-jerking "burial of a sardine" at the Fuente de los Pajaritos in the Casa de Campo; the evening is topped off with a concert in the Plaza Mayor. Dates vary.

May

✪ Fiestas de San Isidro

Madrileños run wild with a 10-day celebration honoring their patron saint. Food fairs, Castilian folkloric events, street parades, parties, music, dances, bullfights, and other festivities mark the occasion.

Where: Madrid. **When:** May 12–21. **How:** Make hotel reservations early. Expect crowds and traffic (beware of pickpockets). For information, write the Oficina Municipal de Informacion y Turismo, Plaza Mayor 3, 28014 Madrid.

- **Veranos de la Villa**   Called "the summer binge" of Madrid, this summer-long program presents folkloric dancing, pop music, classical music, zarzuelas, and flamenco at various venues throughout the city. Open-air cinema is a feature in the Parque del Retiro. Ask at the various tourist offices for complete details (which change every summer). Sometimes admission is charged, but often these events are free.

- **Fiestas of Lavapíes and La Paloma**   These two fiestas— the most traditional in Madrid—begin with the Lavapies on August 1 and continue through the hectic La Paloma celebration on August 15, the day of the Virgen de la Paloma. Tens of thousands of residents and visitors race through the narrow streets. Apartment dwellers above hurl buckets of cold water onto the crowds below to cool them off. Children's games, floats, music, flamenco, and zarzuelas, along with street fairs, mark the occasion. Aug 1–15.

⭐ Autumn Festival

Both Spanish and international artists participate in this cultural program, with a series of operatic, ballet, dance, music, and theatrical performances. From Strasbourg to Tokyo, this event is a premier attraction, yet tickets are reasonable.

Where: Madrid. **When:** Mid-Sept to mid-Nov. **How:** Make hotel reservations early and write for tickets to the Festival de Otoño, Plaza de España 8, 28008 Madrid (☎ **34-1/580-25-65**).

3   Health & Insurance

Health

Madrid should not pose any major health hazards. Many travelers suffer from diarrhea, generally caused by the overly rich cuisine— garlic, olive oil, and wine. Take along some antidiarrhea medicine, moderate your eating habits, and—even though the water in most parts of Madrid is considered safe—consume mineral water only. Milk and milk products are pasteurized and generally considered safe. The Mediterranean, a horrendously polluted sea, washes up on Spain's shores, and fish and shellfish from it should only be eaten cooked. Try to make sure it's fresh; sometimes inadequate refrigeration of fish and shellfish—especially in the hot summer months—

can lead to what some foreign visitors to Spain call the "Toledo trot," the equivalent of Mexico's "Montezuma's revenge."

Sometimes travelers find that the change of diet in Madrid leads to constipation. If this occurs, eat a high-fiber diet and drink plenty of mineral water. Avoid large lunches and dinners with wine. Consult your doctor before you go about taking Colace, a stool softener, or Metamucil.

DOCTOR   If you need a doctor, ask your hotel to locate one for you. You can also obtain a list of English-speaking doctors in Spain from the **International Association for Medical Assistance to Travelers (IAMAT),** in the United States at 417 Center St., Lewiston, NY 14092 (☎ **716/754-4883**); in Canada, at 40 Regal Rd., Guelph, ON N1K 1B5 (☎ **519/836-0102**). Getting medical help in Spain is relatively easy, compared to many countries, and competent English-speaking doctors are found in each of the country's widely scattered regions.

CHRONIC ILLNESS   If your medical condition is chronic, always talk to your doctor before taking an international trip. He or she may have specific advice to give you. For conditions such as epilepsy, a heart condition, diabetes, and some other afflictions, wear a Medic Alert Identification Tag, which will immediately alert any doctor to the nature of your condition. It also provides the number of Medic Alert's 24-hour hotline, so a foreign doctor can obtain your medical records. A lifetime membership costs $35, $45, or $60, depending on your choice of identification. Contact the **Medic Alert Foundation,** P.O. Box 1009, Turlock, CA 95381-1009 (☎ toll free **800/432-5378**).

PRESCRIPTION DRUGS   Take along an adequate supply of any prescription drugs you need and prescriptions with the generic name—not the brand name—of the drugs as well. Carry all vital medicines and drugs (the legal kind only) with you in your carry-on luggage, in case your checked luggage is lost.

Also, take your own personal medical kit. Include first-aid cream, insect repellent, aspirin, nose drops, and Band-Aids. If you're subject to motion sickness on a plane or train, remember to bring along motion-sickness medicine as well.

It's also a good idea to take along a good sunscreen, one that has a protection factor high enough to block out most of the dangerous ultraviolet rays, which can be intense in Madrid and along the Costa del Sol. In case you do find yourself overexposed to the sun, have some liquid solution of the aloe plant with you for soothing relief.

VACCINATIONS   You aren't required to have any particular inoculations to enter Spain (except for yellow fever if you're arriving from an infected area).

Insurance

Before purchasing any additional insurance, check your homeowner, automobile, and medical-insurance policies. Also check the membership contracts issued by automobile and travel clubs and by credit-card companies. If, after close examination, you feel you still need insurance, consider the following.

HEALTH/ACCIDENT   Many credit-card companies insure their users in case of a travel accident, provided a ticket was purchased with their card. Sometimes fraternal organizations have policies that protect members in case of sickness or accidents abroad. The best policies provide advances in cash or transfers of funds so that you won't have to dip into your travel funds to settle any medical bills you might incur while away from home. To submit a claim, you'll need documentation from a medical authority.

Another option is **Travel Assistance International** by Worldwide Assistance Services, Inc., 1133 15th St. NW, Suite 400, Washington, DC 20005 (☎ **202/331-1596,** or toll free **800/821-2828**), which offers on-the-spot medical payment coverage up to $15,000, $30,000, $60,000, or $90,000 for emergency care practically anywhere in the world, as well as unlimited medical evacuation/ repatriation coverage back to the United States if necessary. For an additional fee, you can be covered for trip cancellation/disruption, lost/delayed luggage, and accidental death and dismemberment. Fees are based on the length of your trip and the coverage you select. Prices begin at $52 per person ($72 per family) for a one- to eight-day trip.

LOSS/THEFT   Many homeowner insurance policies cover theft of luggage during foreign travel and loss of documents—your Eurailpass, your passport, or your airline ticket, for instance. Coverage is usually limited to about $500. To submit a claim on your insurance, you'll need police reports; such claims can be filed only when you return from Spain.

CANCELLATION   If you've booked a charter flight, you'll probably have to pay a cancellation fee if you cancel a trip suddenly, even if it's due to an unforeseen crisis. It's possible to get insurance against such a possibility; some travel agencies provide this coverage. Often flight insurance against a canceled trip is provided by credit-card companies when you use the card to pay for the ticket. Most tour operators or insurance agents can provide cancellation insurance.

Travel Guard Internationale, 1145 Clarke St., Stevens Point, WI 54481 (☎ **715/345-0505,** or toll free **800/826-1300**), offers a comprehensive travel insurance policy that includes coverage and service ranging from trip cancellation and interruption to medical and 24-hour emergency assistance.

You can also contact **Travelers Insurance Company,** Travel Insurance Division, One Tower Square, 10NB, Hartford, CT 06183-5040 (☎ toll free **800/243-3174** in the U.S.). Travel accident and illness coverage starts at $10 for 6 to 10 days; $500 worth of coverage for lost, damaged, or delayed baggage costs $20 for 6 to 10 days; and trip cancellation goes for $5.50 per $100 worth of coverage (written approval is necessary for cancellation coverage above $10,000).

Mutual of Omaha, Mutual of Omaha Plaza, Omaha, NE 68175 (☎ toll free **800/228-9792**), offers insurance packages beginning at from $113 for a three-week trip. Included in the packages are travel-assistance services and financial protection against trip cancellation, trip interruption, flight and baggage delays, accident-related medical costs, accidental death and dismemberment, and medical evacuation coverages. Applications for insurance can be taken over the phone for holders of major credit or charge card.

Healthcare Abroad (MEDEX), Wallach & Co., 107 Federal St. (P.O. Box 480), Middleburg, VA 22117-0480 (☎ **703-687-3166,** or toll free **800/237-6615**), offers a policy good for 10 to 120 days costing $3 per day; it includes accident and sickness coverage (to the tune of $100,000), medical evacuation, and $25,000 accidental death and dismemberment compensation. Trip-cancellation and lost or stolen luggage coverage can also be written into this policy at a nominal cost.

Access America, 6600 W. Broad St., Richmond, VA 23230 (☎ **804/285-3300,** or toll free **800/284-8300**), has a 24-hour emergency hotline. It offers a comprehensive travel insurance and assistance package, including medical expenses, on-the-spot hospital payments, medical transportation, baggage insurance, trip-cancellation/interruption insurance, and collision-damage insurance for a car rental. Its 24-hour hotline connects you to multilingual coordinators who can offer advice and help on medical, legal, and travel problems. Packages begin at $27.

Insurance for U.K. Travelers   Most big travel agents offer their own insurance and will probably try to sell you their package when you book a holiday. Think before you sign. Britain's Consumers' Association recommends you insist on seeing the policy and reading the fine print before buying travel insurance.

You should also shop around for better deals. You might contact **Columbus Travel Insurance Ltd.** (☎ **0171/375-0011** in London), or, if you're a student, **Campus Travel** (☎ **0171/730-3402** in London). If you're unsure about who provides what kind of insurance and the best deal, contact the **Association of British Insurers,** 51 Gresham St., London EC2V 7HQ (☎ **0171/600-333**).

4 **What to Pack**

Always pack as light as possible. Sometimes it's hard to get a porter or a baggage cart at rail and air terminals. And airlines are increasingly strict about how much luggage you can take along, not only as carry-on but also as checked baggage.

It depends on where you're going in Spain and at what time of year, but as a general rule, pack the same clothes you might wear in the southeastern United States. That is, dress as if you were visiting Virginia or the Carolinas at the same time of year as your trip to Spain.

Buildings in Spain tend not to be very well heated, so you might want to take an extra sweater.

Dress is casual in Madrid. A jacket and tie are required in only first-class establishments. For special occasions, men should pack a suit. For women, skirts and sweaters, suits, simple dresses, and dress slacks are never out of place.

For sightseeing, casual clothes and comfortable shoes (two pairs) are best. When touring churches and cathedrals, dress appropriately: Head coverings are not required, but you'll be denied entry if you're wearing shorts or a revealing top. After sunning at the beach, both men and women should wear a cover-up over their bathing suits when on the street. If you plan to visit a casino or nightclub, dress up—casual but chic is best.

Finally, pack only items that travel well. Don't count on being able to get your clothes pressed at hotels, especially budget hotels. Take clothes you can wash in your bathroom sink and hang up to dry overnight. Pack a plastic bag for clothes that are still damp when you move on to your next destination.

5 Tips for the Disabled, Seniors, Families, Singles & Students

FOR THE DISABLED   Because of its many hills and endless flights of stairs, getting around Spain can be difficult for the disabled. Despite the lack of adequate services, more and more disabled travelers are taking on the challenge of Spain, and conditions are slowly improving.

The newer hotels are more sensitive to the needs of the disabled, and in general, the more expensive restaurants are wheelchair accessible. However, since most places have very limited, if any, facilities for the disabled, it would be best to consider an organized tour especially designed to accommodate the disabled.

Before you go, there are several agencies that can provide advance-planning information. For example, contact **MossRehab,** 1200 W. Tabor Rd., Philadelphia, PA 19141 (☎ **215/456-9603**), for assistance with your travel needs, though this service is not a travel agent. MossRehab provides information to telephone callers only. To receive an information package through the mail, contact **Mobility International USA,** P.O. Box 10767, Eugene, OR 97440 (☎ **503/343-1284**).

You may also want to consider joining a tour for visitors with disabilities. Names and addresses of such tour operators can be obtained by writing to the **Society for the Advancement of Travel for the Handicapped,** 347 Fifth Ave., New York, NY 10016 (☎ **212/447-7248**). Annual membership dues are $45 or $25 for senior citizens and students. Send a self-addressed stamped envelope.

FEDCAP Rehabilitation Services (formerly known as the Federation of the Handicapped), 211 W. 14th St., New York, NY 10011

(☎ **212/727-4268**), operates summer tours to Europe and elsewhere for its members. Membership costs $6 yearly.

You can also obtain a copy of **Air Transportation of Handicapped Persons,** published by the U.S. Department of Transportation. The copy is sent free by writing for Free Advisory Circular No. AC12032, Distribution Unit U.S. Department of Transportation, Publications Division, M-4332, Washington, DC 20590.

For the blind, the best source is the **American Foundation for the Blind,** 15 W. 16th St., New York, NY 10011 (☎ **212/620-2000,** or toll free **800/232-5463**).

Note: There's a museum in Madrid that will be of interest to persons both with and without sight. The **Tiflological Museum,** calle la Coruña (☎ **91/571-1236**), was designed for blind or sight-impaired visitors and contains exhibits meant to be touched. Maintained by the Spanish National Organization for the Blind, it's one of the few museums in the world that has a kind of bipolar emphasis on both visual appeal for the sighted and tactile appeal for the blind. Exhibits are accessorized with audiotapes in both English and Spanish that guide the visitors' hands over the exhibits, while pamphlets are offered with text in large type and also in Braille. One section features small-scale replicas of such architectural wonders as the Mayan and Aztec pyramids of Central America, the Eiffel Tower, and the Statue of Liberty. Another area contains painting and sculpture crafted by such blind artists as Miguel Detrel and José Antonio Braña. A final section contains a historical overview of the status of blind people throughout history, with a focus on the sociology and technology that led to the development of Braille during the 19th century.

The museum is open Monday through Friday from 10:30am to 2:30pm. Admission is free.

Tips for Disabled U.K. Travelers   RADAR (Royal Association for Disability and Rehabilitation), 25 Mortimer St., London W1N 8AB (☎ **0171/637-5400**), publishes an annual holiday guide for the disabled, "Holidays and Travel Abroad" (£3.50 in the U.K., £5.26 in Europe, £7 in other destinations). RADAR also provides a number of holiday fact sheets on such subjects as sports and outdoor holidays, insurance, financial arrangements, and accommodations with nursing care for groups or for the elderly. There is a nominal charge for all these publications.

Another good resource is the **Holiday Care Service,** 2 Old Bank Chambers, Station Road, Horley, Surrey RH6 9HW (☎ **01293/774-535;** fax 01293/784-647), a national charity that advises on accommodations accessible for elderly and disabled people. It provides a free reservations service offering discounted rates. The service's Holiday Care Awards recognize those in the tourism industry who provide excellent service for people with disabilities.

If you're flying around Europe, the airline and ground staff will help you on and off planes and reserve seats for you with sufficient leg room, but it is essential to arrange for this assistance *in advance* by contacting your airline.

The **Airport Transport Users Council,** 2/F Kingsway House, 103 Kingsway, London WC2B 6QX (☎ **0171/242-3883**), publishes two free pamphlets: "Flight Plan—A Passenger's Guide to Planning and Using Air Travel," packed with information, and "Care in the Air," specifically designed to help the disabled traveler.

FOR SENIORS   Many discounts are available for seniors, but often you need to be a member of an association to obtain them.

For information before you go, write for a free booklet called "101 Tips for the Mature Traveler," available from **Grand Circle Travel,** 347 Congress St., Suite 3A, Boston, MA 02210 (☎ **617-350-7500,** or toll free **800/248-3737**).

One of the most dynamic travel organizations for seniors is **Elderhostel,** 75 Federal St., Boston, MA (☎ **617/426-7788**). Established in 1975, it operates an array of programs throughout Europe, including Spain. Most courses last around three weeks and are a good value, since they include airfare, accommodations in student dormitories or modest inns, all meals, and tuition. Courses involve no homework, are ungraded, and are often liberal arts–oriented. These are not luxury vacations, but they are fun and fulfilling. Participants must be at least 60 years old. A companion or spouse must be at least 50 years old.

SAGA International Holidays, 222 Berkeley St., Boston, MA 02116 (☎ toll free **800/343-0273**), runs all-inclusive tours for seniors, preferably for those 60 years or older. Insurance is included in the net price.

In the United States, the best organization to belong to is the **American Association of Retired Persons (AARP),** 601 E St. NW, Washington, DC 20049 (☎ **202/434-AARP**). Members are offered discounts on car rentals, hotels, and airfares. The association's group travel is provided by the AARP Travel Experience from American Express. Tours may be purchased through any American Express office or travel agent or by calling toll free **800/927-0111.** Flights to the various destinations are handled by the toll-free number as part of land arrangements.

Information is also available from the **National Council of Senior Citizens,** 1331 F St. NW, Washington, DC 20005-1171 (☎ **202/347-8800**), which charges $12 per person or per couple. You receive a monthly newsletter, part of which is devoted to travel tips, and reduced discounts on hotel and auto rentals are available.

If you're between 45 and 89 and need a travel companion, **Golden Companions,** P.O. Box 754, Pullman WA 99163 (☎ **208/858-2183**), might provide the answer. A research economist, Joanne R. Buteau, founded this helpful service and is quick to point out that it's not a dating service. Travelers meet potential companions through a confidential mail network. Members, once they have "connected," make their own travel arrangements. Created in 1987, this organization draws members from many walks of life. Members also receive a bimonthly travel newsletter, *The Golden Gateways*. Membership for a full year costs $85 per person.

Another company that caters to solo seniors 50 years or older seeking compatible traveling companions is **Tempo Travelers,** 938 N. 70th #125, Lincoln, NE 68605. Appealing to single, widowed, or divorced travelers, it responds to requests for written information.

Uniworld, 16000 Ventura Blvd., Encino, CA 91436 (☎ **818/382-7820,** or toll free **800/733-7820** in the U.S.), features single tours for the mature person. Its staff either arranges for you to share an accommodation with another single person or gets you a low-price single supplement. Uniworld specializes in travel to certain districts of England, France, Spain, Italy, or Scandinavia.

Tips for U.K. Seniors   Wasteels, Victoria Station, opposite platform 2, London SW1V 1JY (☎ **0171/836-8541**), currently provides an over-60s Rail Europe Senior Card. Its price is £5 to any British person with government-issued proof of his or her age and £19 to anyone with a certificate of age not issued by the British government. With this card, discounts are sometimes available on certain trains within Britain and throughout the rest of Europe.

FOR FAMILIES   Advance planning is the key to a successful overseas family vacation.

*   If you have very small children, discuss your vacation plans with your family doctor and take along such standard supplies as children's aspirin, a thermometer, Band-Aids, and the like.
*   On airlines, a special menu for children must be requested at least 24 hours in advance, but if baby food is required, bring your own and ask a flight attendant to warm it to the right temperature.
*   Take along a "security blanket" for your child (a pacifier, a favorite toy or book) or, for older children, something to make them feel at home in different surroundings (a baseball cap, a favorite T-shirt, or some good-luck charm).
*   Make advance arrangements for cribs, bottle warmers, and car seats if you're driving anywhere.
*   Ask the hotel if it stocks baby food, and if not, take some with you and plan to buy the rest in local supermarkets.
*   Draw up guidelines on bedtime, eating, keeping tidy, being in the sun, even shopping and spending—they'll make the vacation more enjoyable.
*   Babysitters can be found for you at most hotels, but you should always insist, if possible, that you secure a babysitter with at least a rudimentary knowledge of English.

Family Travel Times, a newsletter about traveling with children, costs $55 for 10 issues. Subscribers can also call in with travel questions, but only on Wednesdays from 10am to 1pm eastern standard time. Contact TWYCH, which stands for Travel With Your Children, 45 W. 18th St., New York, NY 10011 (☎ **212/206-0688**).

Tips for U.K. Families   The best deals for families are often package tours put together by some of the giants of the British travel industry. Foremost among these is **Thomsons Tour Operators.** Through its subsidiary, **Skytours** (☎ **0181/200-8733**), Thomsons offers dozens of air/land packages to Spain where a predesignated number of airline seats are reserved for the free use of children under 18 who accompany their parents. To qualify, parents must book airfare and hotel accommodations lasting two weeks or more and do so as far in advance as possible. Savings for families with children can be substantial.

FOR SINGLES   It's no secret the travel industry caters to people who are not traveling alone. Double rooms, for example, are usually much more reasonably priced than singles. One company has made heroic efforts to match single travelers with like-minded companions. Founder Jens Jurgen charges $36 to $66 for a six-month listing in his well-publicized records. New applicants desiring a travel companion fill out a form stating their preferences and needs. They then receive a list of people who might be suitable. Companions of the same or opposite sex can be requested. A bimonthly newsletter averaging 34 large pages also gives numerous money-saving travel tips of special interest to solo travelers. A sample copy is available for $4. For an application and more information, write to **Jens Jurgen, Travel Companion,** P.O. Box P-833, Amityville, NY 11701 (☎ **516/454-0880;** fax 516/454-0170).

   Singleworld, 401 Theodore Fremd Ave., Rye, NY 10580 (☎ **914/967-3334,** or toll free **800/223-6490**), is a travel agency that operates tours for solo travelers. Some, but not all, are for people in their 20s and 30s. Annual dues are $25.

   Another agency to check is **Grand Circle Travel,** 347 Congress St., Boston, MA 02110 (☎ **617/350-7500,** or toll free **800/248-3737**), which offers escorted tours and cruises for retired people, including singles.

   Since single supplements on tours usually carry a hefty price, a way to get around paying the supplement is to find a tour company that allows you to share a room with a hitherto-unknown fellow traveler. One company offering a "guaranteed-share plan" for their tours within Spain is **Cosmos** (an affiliate of Globus Tours). Upon your arrival in Spain, a suitable roommate will be assigned from among the tour's other participants. The company maintains offices at 5301 S. Federal Circle, Littleton, CO 80123. Its tour information can be obtained through any travel agency.

Tips for U.K. Singles   Single people sometimes feel comfortable traveling with groups composed mostly of other singles. One tour operator whose groups are usually composed of at least 50% unattached persons is **Explore, Ltd.** (☎ **01252/344-161**), with a well-justified reputation for offering offbeat tours. Groups rarely include more than 16 participants, and children under 14 are not allowed.

Dedicated independent travelers may want to check out **The Globetrotters Club,** BCM/Roving, London WCIN 3XX, which enables members to exchange information and generally assist one another in traveling as cheaply as possible. Persons wishing to join in the United Kingdom for one year pay £12 for the first year, then £9 for each year's renewal.

FOR STUDENTS   Council Travel is America's largest student, youth, and budget travel group, with more than 60 offices world-wide. It also sells a number of publications for young people consid-ering traveling abroad. For a copy of *Student Travels* magazine, providing information on all of Council Travel's services and CIEE's programs and publications, send $1 in postage.

Council Travel has offices throughout the United States, with its main office at 205 E. 42nd St., New York, NY 10017 (☎ **212/661-1450**). Call that number to find the location nearest you.

The most commonly accepted form of identification is also an "open sesame" to bargains. An **International Student Identity Card (ISIC)** gets you such benefits as special student airfares to Europe, medical insurance, and many special discounts. In Spain the card secures you free entrance into state museums, monuments, and archeological sights. Domestic train fares in Spain are also reduced for students. The card, which costs only $16, is available at Council Travel offices nationwide, as well as on hundreds of college/university campuses across the country. Proof of student status and a passport-size (2 in. by 2 in.) photograph are necessary. For information on the nearest ISIC-issuing office near you, contact the **Council on International Educational Exchange,** 205 E. 42nd St., New York, NY 10017 (☎ toll free **800/GET AN ID**).

The **IYHF (International Youth Hostel Federation)** was de-signed to provide bare-bones overnight accommodations for serious budget-conscious travelers. For information, contact HI-AYH (Hostelling/International/American Youth Hostels), 733 15th St. NW, Suite 840, Washington, DC 20005 (☎ **202/783-6161**). Membership costs $25 annually; those under 18 pay $10, and those 54 or more pay $15.

Tips for U.K. Students   Campus Travel, 52 Grosvenor Gardens, London SW1W OAG (☎ **0171/730-3402**), provides a wealth of information and offers for the student traveler, ranging from route planning to flight insurance, including railcards.

The **International Student Identity Card (ISIC)** is an inter-nationally recognized proof of student status that will entitle you to savings on flights, sightseeing, food, and accommodations. It costs only £5 and is well worth the price. Always show your ISIC when booking a trip—you may not get a discount without it.

Youth hostels are the place to stay if you're a student. You'll need an **International Youth Hostels Association** card, which you can purchase from the youth hostel store at 14 Southampton St., London WC23 7HY (☎ **0171/836-8541**), or **Campus Travel** (☎ **0171/730-3402**). Take both your passport and some passport-size photos of yourself, plus your membership fee. In England and Wales, this is £3 (for those under 18) or £9 (for those over 18). In Scotland, the fee is slightly less: £2.50 for those under 18 and £6 for everyone else.

The Youth Hostel Association puts together *The Hostelling International Budget Guide,* listing every youth hostel in 31 European countries. It costs £5.99 when purchased at the Southampton Street store in London; add 61p postage if it is being delivered within the United Kingdom.

If you're traveling in summer, you'll find many youth hostels full. To avoid disappointment, it's best to book ahead. In London, you can make advance reservations at the membership department at 14 Southampton St. (see above).

6 Alternative/Adventure Travel

Offbeat, alternative modes of travel often cost less and can be an enriching way to travel to Madrid.

U.S. Specialists

EDUCATIONAL TRAVEL   An international series of programs for those over 50 who are interested in combining travel and learning is offered by **Interhostel,** developed by the University of New Hampshire. Each two-week program is led by a university faculty or staff member and arranged in conjunction with a host college, university, or cultural institution. Participants may stay longer if they wish. Programs in Spain include field trips to museums and other centers of interest. For information, contact the **University of New Hampshire,** Division of Continuing Education, 6 Garrison Ave., Durham, NH 03824 (☎ **603/862-1147,** or toll free **800/733-9753**).

A good source of information about courses in Spain is the **American Institute for Foreign Study (AIFS),** 102 Greenwich Ave., Greenwich, CT 06830 (☎ **203/869-9090,** or toll free **800/727-2437**). This organization can set up transportation and arrange for summer courses, with bed and board included.

The biggest organization dealing with higher education in Europe is the **Institute of International Education,** 809 United Nations Plaza, New York, NY 10017 (☎ **212/883-8200**). A few of its booklets are free, but for $36.95 (plus $4 postage) you can purchase the more definitive *Vacation Study Abroad.* Visitors to New York may use the resources at the institute's information center, which is open to the public Monday through Friday from 10am to 4pm. The institute is closed on major holidays.

One well-recommended clearinghouse for academic programs throughout the world is the Milwaukee-based **National Registration Center for Study Abroad (NRCSA),** 823 N. 2nd St. (P.O. Box 1393), Milwaukee, WI 53201 (☎ **414/278-0631**). The organization maintains language-study programs in Madrid and about nine other cities in Spain. With lodgings in private homes included as part of the price and part of the experience, tuition begins at around $800 for an intensive two-week language course. Courses of six weeks, eight weeks, a semester, and a full academic year are also available. (Some colleges do accept successful completion of the curriculums as independent studies.) Courses accept participants over age 17 (many are senior citizens).

A clearinghouse to contact for information on Spain-based language schools is **Lingua Service Worldwide,** 2 W. 45th St., Suite 500, New York, NY 10036 (☎ toll free **800/394-5327**). It represents organizations devoted to the teaching of Spanish in 11 cities of Spain, including one in Madrid.

The **Education Office of Spain,** 150 Fifth Ave., Suite 918, New York, NY 10011 (☎ **212/741-5144**), whose funding comes from the Spanish Ministry of Education, offers information on language schools in the universities and privately funded schools of Spain, including Madrid. Information is provided free.

For more information about study abroad, contact the **Council on International Educational Exchange (CIEE),** 205 E. 42nd St., New York, NY 10017 (☎ **212/661-1450**).

HOMESTAYS   The **Friendship Force,** 575 South Tower, 57 Forsyth St. NW, Suite 900, Atlanta, GA 30303 (☎ **404/522-9490,** or toll free **800/688-6777**), is a nonprofit organization existing for the sole purpose of fostering and encouraging friendship among people around the world. Group visits are arranged to a given host country, where each participant is required to spend two weeks—one with a family.

Servas, 11 John St., New York, NY 10038 (☎ **212/267-0252**)—the name means "to serve" in Esperanto—is a nonprofit, nongovernmental, international, interfaith network of travelers and hosts whose goal is to help promote world peace, goodwill, and understanding. Servas travelers stay at people's homes without charge for up to two days. Visitors pay a $55 annual fee, fill out an application, and undergo an interview for suitability. They then receive a directory listing the names and addresses of Servas hosts.

HOME EXCHANGES   One of the most exciting breakthroughs in modern tourism is the home exchange, whereby the Diego family of Madrid can exchange their home with the Brier family in North Carolina. Sometimes the family automobile is included. Of course, you must be comfortable with the idea of having relative strangers in your home and be content to spend your vacation in one place.

Home exchanges cut costs. You don't pay hotel bills, and you can also save money by shopping in markets and eating in.

Intervac U.S., P.O. Box 590504, San Francisco, CA 94159 (☎ toll free **800/756-HOME**), is part of the world's largest home-exchange network. It publishes three catalogs a year containing listings of more than 9,000 homes in more than 36 countries. Members contact one another directly. The $62 cost buys all three of the company's catalogs (excluding mailing costs) and provides a listing of your home in one of the three catalogs. Seniors over 62 pay $55. Photos cost $11.

The Invented City, 41 Sutter St., Suite 1090, San Francisco, CA 94104 (☎ **415/673-0347,** or toll free 800/788 CITY), is another international home-exchange agency. Home-exchange listings are published three times a year: February, May, and November. The $50 membership fee allows you to supply a descriptive summary of your home-exchange offer for publication in the listings.

Vacation Exchange Club, P.O. Box 650, Key West, FL 33041 (☎ **305/294-1448,** or toll free **800/638-3841**), will send you four directories a year—in one of which you're listed—for $60.

COOKING SCHOOLS   Thanks to Spain's colonies in the New World, Spanish cuisine may have been more widely diffused than that of any other country. One organization devoted to training Hispanophiles in the fine art of the nation's cuisine is the **Escuela de Cocina Juan Altimiras,** 2 Plaza de la Incarnación, Madrid (☎ **91/547-88-27**). Established by Clara María González de Amezúa in 1973, it offers a series of lectures and demonstrations that benefit even professional chefs.

U.K. Specialists

ADVENTURE TRAVEL   Cycling tours are a good way to see Spain at your own pace. **Alternative Travel Group Ltd.,** 69–71 Banbury Rd., Oxford OX2 6PE (☎ **01865/310399**), organizes walking and cycling holidays, plus wine tours in Italy, Spain, and France through the scenic countryside and medieval towns.

The **Cyclists' Tourist Club,** 69 Meadrow, Godalming, Surrey GU7 3HS (☎ **01483/417-217**), charges £24 a year for membership, part of which includes information and suggested cycling routes through Spain and dozens of other countries.

The appeal of hill climbing and hiking, especially in areas of scenic or historic interest, is almost universal. **Waymark Holidays,** 44 Windsor Rd., Slough SL1 2EJ (☎ **01753/516-477**) is known for its walking tours in Europe, some lasting as long as two weeks.

The oldest travel agency in Britain, **Cox & Kings,** 45 Buckingham Gate, St. James's Court, London SW1E 6AF (☎ **0171/873-5006**) was established in 1758 as the paymasters and transport directors for the British armed forces in India. The company continues to send large numbers of travelers from Britain throughout the rest of the world, specializing in unusual, if pricey, holidays. Its offerings in Spain include organized tours through the country's sites of historic or aesthetic interest; pilgrimage-style visits to sites of religious interest; and visits to the country's most legendary horse stables, stud farms, and racetracks. The company's staff is noted for their interest in tours of ecological and environmental interest.

There's one final possibility if your interests are more varied than those mentioned above. Ringing the London headquarters of **IATA (International Association of Travel Agencies)** at **0181/744-9280** can provide names and addresses of tour operators specializing in travel relating to your particular interest. This organization will soon change its name to AITO (Association of Independent Tour Operators); its address is 133A St. Margaret's Rd. Twickenham, Middlesex TN1 1RG.

7   Getting There

By Plane

Flights to Madrid from the U.S. East Coast take six to seven hours, depending on the season and prevailing winds. Any information about fares or even flights in the highly volatile airline industry is not writ in stone; even travel agencies with banks of computers have a hard time keeping abreast. For last-minute conditions, including a list of the carriers that fly to Madrid, check with a travel agent or the individual airlines. Here is a rundown on the current status.

FROM NORTH AMERICA

The national carrier of Spain, **Iberia Airlines** (☎ toll free **800/772-4642**) offers more routes into and within Spain than any other airline, with daily nonstop service to Madrid from both New York and Miami. From Miami, Iberia takes off for at least six destinations in Mexico and Central America, and, in cooperation with its air partner, Ladeco (a well-maintained airline based in Chile), to dozens of destinations throughout South America as well. Iberia also flies every day to Madrid from Los Angeles, on flights which touch down briefly in Miami before continuing nonstop to Madrid. Canadians appreciate Iberia's service from Toronto, through Montréal, to Madrid, which is provided between two and three times a week, depending on the season. Also available are attractive rates on fly/drive programs within Iberia and Europe that can substantially reduce the cost of what you would have paid had you booked an air ticket and a car rental as separate transactions.

Iberia's fares are cheapest if you reserve an APEX (advance-purchase excursion) ticket at least 21 days in advance, schedule your return 7 to 30 days after your departure, and leave and return between Monday and Thursday. From June 1 to September 15, round-trip tickets from New York to Madrid cost $778 midweek ($838 if you travel between Friday and Sunday), plus $23 tax. Round-trip flights from Los Angeles to Madrid during the same season cost $1,018 midweek and $1,078 on weekends, plus tax. Fares, which are subject to change, are lower during off-season. Most transatlantic flights are on carefully maintained 747s and DC-10s, and in-flight services reflect an interpretation of Spanish traditions, values, and cuisine.

A noteworthy cost-cutting option involves Iberia's Europass. Available only to passengers who simultaneously arrange for transatlantic passage on Iberia, it allows passage on any flight within Iberia's European or Mediterranean dominion for $250 for the first two flights, $125 for each additional flight. This is especially attractive for passengers wishing to combine trips to Spain with, for example, visits to such far-flung destinations as Cairo, Tel Aviv, Istanbul, Moscow, and/or Munich. For details, ask Iberia's phone representative.

Iberia's leading competitor is employee-owned **Trans World Airlines** (☎ toll free **800/221-2000**), whose transatlantic service into Spain has flourished since 1946. TWA operates separate daily nonstop flights to both Barcelona and Madrid from New York's Kennedy Airport. TWA's cheapest APEX ticket requires a 21-day advance purchase and a delay of between 7 and 30 days before activating the return portion of your flight. Depending on the day of flight (Monday through Thursday is least expensive), round-trip passages during high season cost from $778 to $838 from JFK to either Madrid or Barcelona. Changes are permitted in departure dates for $150 each.

TWA also offers a limited number of youth fares, which must be arranged three days or less before any particular flight. Available only for passengers 12 to 24 who insist on a minimum of restrictions, youth fares are from $389 to $419 each way, depending on the day of flight. Note that at TWA, as at each of its competitors, youth fares do not represent any noteworthy financial savings over the price of the APEX ticket described above; they do, however, allow a prolonged sojourn in Spain without the penalties sometimes associated with long-term stays abroad and are therefore ideal for anyone studying or traveling without fixed itineraries. Like its competitors, TWA offers access to its trip-planning service (in this case, the Getaway Vacation desk) and can arrange fly/drive holidays, land packages at Madrid hotels, and/or escorted motorcoach tours, depending on a client's needs and priorities.

American Airlines (☎ toll free **800/433-7300**) offers daily non-stop service to Madrid from its massive hub in Miami, with excellent connections from there to the rest of the airline's impressive North and South American network. With a 21-day advance purchase and a scheduled return between 7 and 30 days after your departure, American's least expensive round-trip ticket during high season from Miami to Madrid costs $868 Monday through Thursday and $928 Friday through Sunday. Imposing restrictions that are more flexible than in years gone by, American charges a $150 penalty for any changes in itinerary once you've used the outbound portion of your ticket. American offers a wide choice of fly/drive programs and escorted motorcoach tours as well as a youth fare for travelers 12 to 24. Priced at $525 each way Monday through Thursday and $550 each way Friday through Sunday, it is not substantially less expensive than the APEX fare described above. It does, however, favor last-minute departures, since its restrictions bypass the usual 21-day advance-booking requirements. The youth fare cannot be reserved more than three days before departure in either direction, and it's always issued with an open (unscheduled) return, allowing maximum flexibility for travelers whose plans and projects might change during the course of their trips.

Delta (☎ toll free **800/241-4141**) maintains daily nonstop service from Atlanta (centerpiece of its worldwide network) to Madrid, with ongoing service (with no change of equipment) into Barcelona. The cheapest tickets require 21-day advance booking, a stay abroad of between 7 and 30 days, and cost—depending on the day of the week—between $848 and $908 round-trip to either Madrid or Barcelona. (Many travelers use Delta as a cost-conscious means of landing in one city and departing from the other at the end of their trip.) Delta's Dream Vacation department maintains access to flydrive programs, land packages, and escorted bus tours through the Iberian peninsula.

Another possibility for transatlantic flights into Spain comes from **United Airlines** (☎ toll free **800/538-2929**). Inaugurated in 1991, these routes fly passengers nonstop daily from Washington, DC's Dulles Airport into Madrid. With a 21-day advance purchase and a stay abroad of between 7 and 30 days, United charges high-season rates of between $828 and $888 round-trip during midsummer, depending on flight dates. United also offers fly/drive programs; escorted motorcoach tours; and youth fares similar to those of its competitors, charging between $414 and $444 each way for travelers 12 to 24. These are bookable only three days or less prior to departure.

Frommer's Smart Traveler: Airfares

1. Shop all the airlines that fly to your destination.

2. Always ask for the lowest fare, not just for a discount fare.

3. Keep calling the airline—availability of cheap seats changes daily. Airlines would rather sell a seat than have it fly empty. As the departure date nears, additional low-cost seats become available.

4. Ask about frequent-flyer programs when you book a flight.

5. Check bucket shops for last-minute discounts even greater than their advertised slashed fares.

6. Ask about discounted land arrangements. Sometimes they're cheaper when booked with an air ticket.

7. Ask if standby fares are offered.

8. Fly for free (rarely) or at a heavy discount (usually) as a courier.

9. Look for special promotional fares offered by major carriers or airlines struggling to gain a foothold in the market.

Continental Airlines (☎ toll free **800/231-0856**) offers between six and seven nonstop flights per week, depending on the season, to Madrid from Newark, NJ, an airport many New York residents prefer more than any other departure point. Round-trip APEX fares during high season, with restrictions similar to those at the competitors listed above, range from $778 to $838, plus tax, depending on the days of travel. A youth fare, available to travelers 12 to 25 with a valid student ID, costs between $491 and $516 each way, depending on the day of travel; they must be arranged within three days or less of any departing flight. Likewise, Continental offers 10% discounts on most of its fares to anyone 62 or older, as well as to a senior citizen's companion, regardless of his or her age. Continental also offers regularly scheduled sales promotions that come and go with the seasons. A recent example cost $299 each way between Newark and Madrid and required reservations and payment before mid-May for flights that then could be taken throughout the summer. Although that particular promotion ended just before press time, watch for equivalent Continental bargains that might be in effect at the time of your trip.

FROM GREAT BRITAIN

British Airways (☎ **0171/897-4000** in London) and **Iberia** (☎ **0171/437-5622** in London) are the two major carriers flying between the United Kingdom and Spain. In spite of the frequency of their routes, however, we suspect most vacationing Brits fly charter (see below).

More than a dozen daily flights, on either BA or Iberia, depart from both London's Heathrow and Gatwick Airports. The Midlands is served by flights from Manchester and Birmingham, two major airports that can also be used by Scots flying to Spain. About seven flights a day go between London and Madrid, with at least six to Barcelona (trip time: 2 to 2$^{1}/_{2}$ hours). From either the Madrid airport or the Barcelona airport, you can tap into Iberia's domestic network—flying, for example, to Seville or the Costa del Sol (centered at the Málaga airport). The best air deals on scheduled flights from the United Kingdom are those requiring a Saturday night stopover.

As mentioned, most vacationing Brits go charter, at least those looking for air-flight bargains. Delays are frequent (some last two whole days and nights), and departures are often at inconvenient hours. Booking conditions can also be severe, and one must read the fine print carefully and deal with only a reputable travel agent. Stays rarely last a month, and booking must sometimes be made at least a month in advance, although a two-week period is sometimes possible.

Charter flights leave from most British regional airports for various destinations (for example, Málaga), bypassing the congestion at the Madrid airports. Figure on saving approximately 10% to 15% off regularly scheduled flight tickets. But check carefully. British Sunday papers are full of charter deals, and a travel agent can always advise what the best values are at the time of your intended departure.

STANDARD FARES

Most airlines divide their year roughly into seasonal slots, with the least expensive fares between November 1 and March 14. The shoulder season (spring and early fall) is only slightly more expensive—and includes October, which many western tourists consider the ideal time to visit Madrid. Summer, of course, is the most expensive time.

SPECIAL PROMOTIONAL FARES   Since the airlines are now deregulated, expect announcements of promotional fares to Europe. This means you'll have to have a good travel agent or do a lot of shopping around yourself to learn what's available at the time of your intended trip.

REGULAR FARES   If your schedule doesn't permit you one of the options discussed above, you can opt for a regular fare. **Economy class** is the lowest regular fare, followed by **business class,** and then by **first class,** the most expensive ticket. In first class, increased amenities are the rule: The food is better, the seats extend backward into something resembling a bed, and drinks are free. You'll also get free drinks and better meals in business class, but in economy class you pay for alcoholic beverages. All three of these fares have one thing in common: You can book them at the last minute and can depart and return when you wish. Of course, you'll pay more for the lack of restrictions.

OTHER GOOD-VALUE CHOICES

CHARTER FLIGHTS   A charter flight is one reserved months in advance for a one-time-only transit to a predetermined destination. For reasons of economy, some travelers choose this option.

Before paying for a charter, check the restrictions on your ticket or contract. You may be asked to purchase a tour package and pay far in advance. You'll pay a stiff penalty (or forfeit the ticket entirely) if you cancel. Charters are sometimes canceled if the tickets don't sell out. In some cases the charter-ticket seller will offer you an insurance policy for your own legitimate cancellation (hospital stay or death in the family, for example).

There's no way to predict whether a charter flight or a bucket-shop (see below) flight will be cheaper. You'll have to investigate this at the time of your trip. Charter operators and bucket shops used to perform separate functions, but today many perform both functions.

Among charter-flight operators is **Council Charter,** a subsidiary of the Council on International Educational Exchange, 205 E. 42nd St., New York, NY 10017 (☎ **212/661-0311,** or toll free **800/800-8222**). This outfit can arrange charter seats to most major European cities, including Madrid, on regularly scheduled aircraft.

One of the biggest New York charter operators is **Travac,** 989 Sixth Ave., New York, NY 10018 (☎ **212/563-3303,** or toll free **800/TRAV-800**).

Be warned that some charter companies have proved unreliable in the past.

BUCKET SHOPS Sometimes referred to as "consolidators," bucket shops exist in many shapes and forms. In their purest form they act as clearinghouses for blocks of tickets that airlines discount and consign during normally slow periods of air travel. Ticket prices vary, sometimes going for as much as 35% off full fare. Terms of payment can be anywhere from 45 days before departure to the last minute.

Bucket shops abound from coast to coast, but just to get you started, here are some recommendations (look also for ads in your local newspaper's travel section):

In New York, try **TFI Tours International,** 34 W. 32nd St., 12th Floor, New York, NY 10001 (☎ **212/736-1140** in New York State, or toll free **800/745-8000** elsewhere in the U.S.).

For the Midwest, explore the possibilities of **Travel Avenue,** 10 S. Riverside Plaza, Suite 1404, Chicago, IL 60606 (☎ toll free **800/333-3335**), a national agency whose headquarters are here. Its tickets are often cheaper than those at most shops, and it charges the customer only $25 on international tickets, rather than taking the usual commission from an airline. Travel Avenue rebates most of that back to the customers—hence, the lower fares.

In New England, a possibility is **TMI (Travel Management International),** 39 JFK St. (Harvard Square), 3rd Floor, Cambridge, MA 02138 (☎ toll free **800/245-3672**), which offers a wide variety of discounts, including youth fares, student fares, and access to other kinds of air-related discounts as well. Among others its destinations include Madrid.

One of the biggest U.S. consolidators is **Travac,** 989 Sixth Ave., New York, NY 10018 (☎ **212/563-3303,** or toll free **800/TRAV-800**), which offers discounted seats throughout the United States to most cities in Europe, including Madrid, on airlines that include TWA, United, and Delta.

UniTravel, 1177 N. Warson Rd., St. Louis, MO 63132 (☎ toll free **800/325-2222**), offers tickets to Madrid and elsewhere in Europe at prices that may or may not be reduced from the price a client would get if he or she had phoned the airlines directly. UniTravel is best suited to providing discounts for passengers who decide (or need) to get to Europe on short notice.

One final option—suitable only for clients with supremely flexible travel plans—is available through **Airhitch,** 2790 Broadway, Suite 100, New York, NY 10025 (☎ toll free **800/326-2009**). Prospective travelers inform Airhitch of any five consecutive days in which they're available to fly to Europe. Airhitch agrees to fly its passengers within those five days from any of three U.S. regions (the East Coast, West Coast, and Midwest/Southeast). Attempts will be made to fly passengers to and from the cities of their choice, but no guarantees are made.

STANDBYS A favorite with spontaneous travelers who have absolutely no scheduled demands on their time, a standby fare leaves them dependent on the whims of fortune—and hoping that a seat will be open at the last minute. Not all airlines offer standbys. In fact, most airlines are phasing out standbys—so this option is now becoming increasingly rare.

GOING AS A COURIER   This cost-cutting technique has lots of restrictions, and tickets may be hard to come by, so it's not for everybody. Couriers are hired by overnight air-freight firms hoping to skirt the often tedious Customs hassles and delays that face regular cargo on the other end. With a courier, the checked freight sails through Customs just as quickly as the passenger's luggage. Don't worry—the courier service is absolutely legal; you won't be asked to haul in illegal drugs, for example. For performing this service, the courier gets a great discount on airfare, and sometimes even flies for free. You're allowed one piece of carry-on luggage only (your usual baggage allowance is used by the courier firm to transport its cargo). As a courier, you don't actually handle the merchandise you're "transporting" to Europe; you just carry a manifest to present to Customs. Upon arrival, an employee of the courier service will reclaim the company's cargo.

Incidentally, as a courier you fly alone; a friend may be able to arrange a flight as a courier on a consecutive day, but don't count on it. Most courier services operate from Los Angeles or New York, but some operate out of other cities, such as Chicago or Miami.

Courier services are often listed in the *Yellow Pages* or in advertisements in travel sections of newspapers. One such firm is **Halbart Express,** 147-05 176th St., Jamaica, NY 11434 (☎ **718/656-8189** daily from 10am to 3pm). Another is **Now Voyager,** 74 Varick St., Suite 307, New York, NY 10013 (☎ **212/431-1616**). Call to speak with someone from 10am to 6pm daily; at other times you'll get a recorded message.

For an annual $35 membership the **International Association of Air Travel Couriers,** P.O. Box 1349, Lake Worth, FL 33460 (☎ **407/582-8320**), will send you six issues of its newsletter, "Shoestring Traveler," plus about half a dozen issues of "Air Courier Bulletin," a directory of air-courier bargains around the world. The fee also includes access to a 24-hour FAX-ON-DEMAND update of last-minute courier flights available for people willing to travel on short notice. One typical recent offering was a $159 round-trip airfare from the U.S. East Coast to Madrid. Most last-minute flights usually go out the same day in which they're posted, so you have to have your bag packed.

REBATORS   To confuse the situation even more, rebators also compete in the low-cost air-travel market. Most rebators offer discounts that run 10% to 25% (but this could vary from place to place), plus a $25 handling charge. They're not the same as travel agents, although they sometimes offer similar services, including discounted land arrangements and car rentals.

Some rebators include **Travel Avenue,** 641 W. Lake St., Suite 201, Chicago, IL 60606-3691 (☎ **312/876-6866,** or toll free **800/333-3335**); and **The Smart Traveller,** 3111 SW 27th Ave. (P.O. Box

330010), Miami, FL 33133 (☎ **305/448-3338,** or toll free **800/ 448-3338**). The Smart Traveller also offers discount tours, hotel packages, and fly/drive packages.

TRAVEL CLUBS   Another possibility for low-cost air travel is the travel club, which supplies an unsold inventory of tickets offering discounts in the usual range of 20% to 60%.

After you pay an annual fee, you are given a hotline number to call to find out what discounts are available. Many of these discounts become available several days in advance of actual departure, sometimes as long as a week and sometimes as much as a month. Of course, you're limited to what's available, so you have to be fairly flexible.

Some of the best of these clubs include the following: **Discount Travel International,** Ives Building, 114 Forrest Ave., Suite 203, Narberth, PA 19072 (☎ **215/668-7184**), charges an annual membership of $45. **Moment's Notice,** 425 Madison Ave., New York, NY 10017 (☎ **212/486-0500**), has a 24-hour members' hotline (regular toll charges) and a yearly fee of $45 per family.

Sears Discount Travel Club, 3033 S. Parker Rd., Suite 1000, Aurora, CO 80014 (☎ toll free **800/255-1487**), offers members, for $49, a catalog (issued four times a year), maps, discounts at select hotels, and a 5% cash bonus on purchases.

Encore Travel Club, 4501 Forbes Blvd., Lanham, MD 20706 (☎ toll free **800/638-8976**), charges $49 per year for membership in a club that offers 50% discounts at well-recognized hotels, sometimes during off-peak periods. It also offers substantial discounts on airfare, cruises, and car rentals through its volume-purchase plans. Membership includes a travel package outlining the company's many services, plus use of a toll-free number for advice and information.

A Note for U.K. Travelers   A regular fare from the United Kingdom to Spain is considered extremely high, so savvy Brits usually call a travel agent for a "deal"—either a charter flight or some special air-travel promotion. These so-called deals are always available, because of great interest in Spain as a tourist destination. If one is not possible for you, then an APEX (advance-purchase excursion) ticket might be the way to keep costs trimmed. However, a PEX (public excursion fare) ticket offers a discount without the usual booking restrictions. You might also ask the airlines about a Eurobudget ticket, which requires restrictions or length-of-stay requirements.

British newspapers are always full of classified advertisements touting "slashed" fares to Spain. One good source is *Time Out,* a magazine published in London. London's *Evening Standard* has a daily travel section, and the Sunday editions of almost any newspaper will run many ads. Recommended companies include **Trailfinders** (☎ **0171/937-5400** in London) and **Avro Tours** (☎ **0181/543-0000** in London), which operate charters.

There are many London bucket shops around Victoria Station and Earl's Court that offer cheap fares. Make sure the company you deal with is a member of the IATA, ABTA, or ATOL. These umbrella organizations will help you out if anything goes wrong.

CEEFAX, a British TV information service included on many home and hotel TVs, runs details of package holidays and flights to Europe and beyond. Just switch to your CEEFAX channel to find a menu of listings that includes travel information.

Make sure you understand the bottom line on any special deal you purchase—that is, ask if all surcharges, including airport taxes and other hidden costs—are cited before committing yourself to purchase. Upon investigation, some of these "deals" are not as attractive as advertised. Also, make sure you understand what the penalties are if you're forced to cancel at the last minute.

By Train

If you're already in Europe, you may want to go to Spain by train, especially if you have a Eurailpass. Even if you don't, the cost is moderate, depending on where you are. Rail passengers who visit from Britain or France should make couchette and sleeper reservations as far in advance as possible, especially during the peak summer season.

Since Spain's rail tracks are of a wider gauge than those used for French trains (except for the TALGO and Trans-Europe-Express trains), it's therefore often necessary to change trains at the border unless you're on an express (see below). For long journeys on Spanish rails, seat and sleeper reservations are mandatory.

The most comfortable and the fastest trains in Spain are the TER, TALGO, and Electrotren. However, you pay a supplement to ride on these fast trains. Both first- and second-class travel is available on Spanish trains. Tickets can be purchased in either the United States or Canada at the nearest office of French Rail, Inc., or from any reputable travel agent. Confirmation of your reservation will take about a week.

If you want your car carried, you must travel Auto-Expreso in Spain. This type of auto transport can be booked only through travel agents or rail offices once you arrive in Europe.

To go from London to Spain by rail, you'll need to change not only the train but also the rail terminus in Paris. In Paris, it's worth the extra bucks to purchase a TALGO express or a "Puerta del Sol" express—that way, you can avoid having to change trains once again at the Spanish border. Trip time from London to Paris is about 6 hours; from Paris to Madrid, about 15 hours or so, which includes 2 hours spent in Paris changing trains and stations. Many rail passes are available in the United Kingdom for travel in Europe. Stop in at the **International Rail Centre,** Victoria Station, London SW1V 1JY (☎ **0171/834-2345**), or **Wasteels,** 121 Wilton Rd., London SW1V 1JZ (☎ **0171/834-7066**). They can help you find the best option for the trip you're planning.

In addition to the regular ferry service across the English Channel, connecting England and France, visitors can take the Chunnel, inaugurated in 1994. A train transports passengers along the 31-mile journey beneath the Channel in just 35 minutes. Called "Le Shuttle," the train accommodates passenger cars, charter buses, taxis, and motorcycles through a tunnel from Calais, France, to Folkestone, England (or vice versa). Service is all year, 24 hours a day.

By Bus

Bus travel to Spain is possible but not popular—it's slow. Coach services do operate regularly from major capitals of Western Europe to Madrid and Barcelona. The busiest routes are from London and are run by **Eurolines Limited,** 23 Crawley Rd., Luton LU1 1HX in Bedfordshire (☎ **01582/404511**). The journey from London's Victoria Station to Madrid is provided by two services: Service 180 is an express from Victoria Station to Madrid, departing London daily at 9pm, arriving in Madrid the following day at 9:30pm. Service 181 leaves London at 9pm on the first day, arriving in Madrid at 12:30am on the third day.

By Car

FROM EUROPE Motor approaches from Europe to Spain are across France on expressways. The most popular border crossing into Spain is east of Biarritz. To Madrid, the best route to take is the E70 west to Bilbao; then cut south on the E804 to the junction with the E05, which heads southwest to Burgos. Bypass Burgos and continue south on the route to Madrid, which is also known as the N-I.

FROM BARCELONA If you're driving from Barcelona to Madrid, connect with the E90 heading west to Zaragoza; from there continue west to Madrid along the E90 via Guadalajara.

Package Tours

Some people prefer that a tour operator take care of all their travel arrangements. There are many such companies, each offering transportation to and around Spain, prearranged hotel space, and such extras as a bilingual tour guide and lectures. Often these tours to Spain include excursions to Morocco or Portugal.

American Express Vacations, 300 Pinnacle Way, Norcross, GA 30071 (☎ **404/368-5100,** or toll free **800/241-1700**), offers some of the most comprehensive programs available to Spain, including Madrid as the major stopover.

Sun Holidays, 26 Sixth St., Suite 603, Stamford, CT 06905 (☎ **203/323-1166,** or toll free **800/678-4787**), has been specializing in extended vacations for senior citizens since 1980. The company regularly features fully escorted motorcoach tours of Spain and Portugal and pays special attention to retired Americans. Its Florida office is at 7280 W. Palmetto Park Rd., Ste. 301, Boca Raton, FL 33433 (☎ **407/243-2057,** or toll free **800/243-2057**).

As noted in the section on airlines (see above), virtually every airline flying transatlantic into Spain can offer some kind of a fly/drive program whereby rental cars are discounted if airfare into Spain is arranged simultaneously. One of several recommendable companies is **Kemwel Car Rental,** 106 Calvert St., Harrison, NY 10528-3199 (☎ **914/835-5555,** or toll free **800/678-0678**). At press time, if you buy a round-trip ticket to Spain from Iberia Airlines, you'll receive a three-day free use of a small rental car (an Opel Corsa) that otherwise would rent for around $59 per day. Unlimited mileage, all taxes, and a collision-damage waiver are included. There are no hidden extras—you pay only for the gasoline you use. The offer is based on at least two passengers traveling together; single travelers pay a supplement of $35. For additional information, you can call either Iberia Airlines (☎ toll free **800/772-4642**) or Kemwel. If you're shopping around for fly/drives, don't overlook the package deals and options offered by other airlines, such as Delta, American, and Continental.

Welcome Tours Hispanidad, 99 Tulip Ave., Floral Park, NY 11001 (☎ **516/488-4700,** or toll free **800/274-4400**), offers a number of attractive features on its tours. These include car rentals, accommodations at *paradores* (deserted castles, monasteries, and the like that have been converted into state-owned inns), prepackaged and independent travel options, and "stay-put" land/air vacations at resort areas. It offers escorted motorcoach tours as well. Its fly/drive program—called "A la Carte"—allows travel to anywhere in Spain for those wishing to make their own itineraries. Compact budget cars are included in the program. Hotels or apartments can be arranged along the Costa del Sol (see Chapter 11).

3

Getting to Know Madrid

In *THE SUN ALSO RISES*, HEMINGWAY DESCRIBED MADRID AS "A WHITE sky-line on the top of a little cliff away off across the sun-hardened country." Papa would not know the city today. The little pueblo that was Madrid continues to grow at a dramatic rate, expanding rapidly in land area and industrial development, sprouting suburbs of apartment houses for the burgeoning population.

On a plateau of the Sierra de Guadarrama, the capital of Spain is the highest in Europe, reaching a peak of 2,373 feet above sea level at its loftiest point. The sierra air is dry, almost crystal pure, the sky cerulean as if painted by Velázquez.

As Spanish cities go, Madrid is still young. *Don Quixote de La Mancha* was already known throughout the world when in 1561 Philip II decided to make Madrid the capital of Spain. The location was apt: Geographically, it was the heart of the Iberian peninsula.

On your way into Madrid from Barajas Airport, you're likely to see an aging *dueña* shrouded in black—perhaps mourning for her husband who died in the Spanish Civil War in the late 1930s. This scene is one of many *tableaux vivants*, frozen in time and space.

As you near the center of the city, however, skyscrapers herald tomorrow's world. Flashy billboards implore everybody to "*BEBE* COCA-COLA" or to wear Yankee-style Levi's for greater sex appeal.

It's impossible to separate Madrid or Castile from the saga of the nation as a whole. It was from the barren, undulating plains of the country's heartland that the proud, sometimes arrogant, Castilians emerged. They were destined not only to unify the country, but to dominate it—and to go even further, carving out an empire that was to embrace the Aztecs and Incas, even the far-away Philippines.

In Castile you'll meet a survival-sharpened people. One scholar put it this way: "The Spaniards are a fierce, idealistic, generous people, capable of great sacrifice and heroism when driven by their proud and burning passions, but they are also intolerant, dogmatic, and individualistic." Regardless, know that Madrileños—whatever their backgrounds—are generally friendly, especially to their well-behaved guests. As hosts, they have great style and graciousness, and Madrid today is among the most hospitable capitals in Europe.

1   Orientation

No one ever claimed that knowing or getting around Madrid was easy. Many taxi drivers (usually from the provinces) are unfamiliar with the city as well, once they branch off the main boulevards.

Everything in the Spanish capital is spread out, and this may cause you difficulty until you get the feel of it. For example, on one typical night you may want to sample the *tapas* (hors d'oeuvres) at a *tasca* on the Ventura de la Vega, dine at a restaurant that opens onto the fairly far-off Plaza Mayor, witness an evening of flamenco near the Ritz Hotel, then head for your hotel at the gateway to Toledo. The easiest, most sensible and practical means of getting around to all these widely scattered places is by taxi (see "Getting Around," later in this chapter).

Arriving & Departing

BY PLANE   The international airport for Madrid is **Barajas,** and it's divided into two separate terminals—one for international flights, the other for domestic. Conveyors transport passengers between the two. For Barajas Airport information, telephone **305-43-72.**

Air-conditioned yellow buses take you from right outside the arrivals terminal at Barajas to the underground bus depot under the Plaza Colón. You can also get off at several points along the way, provided you don't have your suitcases stored in the hold. The fare is 325 ptas. ($2.30), and buses leave about every 15 minutes, either to or from the airport.

If you go by taxi into town, the fare will run about 2,500 ptas. ($17.80), depending on traffic. The driver is entitled to assess a surcharge (in either direction) not only for the trip but also for baggage handling. If you should step into a nonmetered limousine, it's important to negotiate the price in advance.

BY TRAIN   Madrid has three major railway stations: **Atocha,** avenida Ciudad de Barcelona (☎ **527-31-60;** Metro: Atocha RENFE), for trains to Lisbon, Toledo, Andalusia, and Extremadura; **Chamartín** (☎ **323-21-21;** Metro: Chamartín), in the northern suburbs at Agustín de Foxa, for trains to and from Barcelona, Asturias, Cantabria, Castile-León, the Basque country, Aragón, Catalonia, Levante (Valencia), Murcia, and the French frontier; and **Estación Príncipe Pío,** or Norte, Po. del Rey 30 (☎ **247-00-00;** Metro: Norte), for trains to and from northwest Spain (Salamanca and Galicia).

Warning: When leaving Madrid or taking an excursion, don't wait to buy your rail ticket or to make a reservation at the train stations. There may be no tickets left. Go to the principal RENFE office at Alcalá 44 (☎ **563-02-02;** Metro: Banco de España). The office is open Monday through Friday from 9:30am to 8pm.

BY BUS   Madrid has at least eight major bus terminals, including the large **Estación Sur de Autobuses,** calle Canarias 17 (☎ **468-45-11;** Metro: Palos de la Frontera). Buses to the environs of Madrid, such as Toledo and Segovia, leave from numerous other stations; it's best to call **580-19-80** for current departure information.

BY CAR   The following are the major highways leading into Madrid.

Route	From	Distance to Madrid
N-I	Irún	315 miles (505 km)
N-II	Barcelona	389 miles (622 km)
N-III	Valencia	217 miles (347 km)
N-IV	Cádiz	388 miles (625 km)
N-V	Badajoz	254 miles (409 km)
N-VI	Galicia	374 miles (598 km)

Madrid Orientation

Tourist Information

The most convenient tourist office is on the ground floor of the 40-story **Torre de Madrid,** Plaza de España (☎ **91/541-23-25;** Metro: Plaza de España). It's open Monday through Friday from 9am to 7pm and Saturday from 9:30am to 1:30pm. The staff here can give you a list of hotels and hostales but cannot recommend any particular establishment.

If you're heading on to another city after your visit to Madrid, ask for a street map of the next destination on your itinerary, especially if you're driving.

City Layout

The Spanish capital, as mentioned, is a fast-growing city, its development sporadic and largely haphazard. It can be described in many ways and from many points of view.

If you're interested in "Royal Madrid," you'll want to explore the **Palacio Real,** which fronts the handsome **Plaza de Oriente,** with its Velázquez-inspired equestrian statue of Philip IV. The gardens, parks, and wide avenues—all appropriate for state receptions and parades—took new significance with the restoration of the Spanish monarchy.

If you're a romanticist nostalgic for the 19th century, you'll watch in sadness as the mansions along the **paseo de la Castellana** and its satellite streets are torn down to make way for modern offices and shops, deluxe hotels, and apartment buildings. Thankfully, a few are still preserved and used today by foreign embassies.

If you're an artist or a devotee of art, you'll spend most of your time at the great old **Prado,** the treasure house of Spanish masterpieces that shelters a once-royal collection of European art.

If you're on a shopping spree, you'll gravitate to the **Gran Vía,** called the avenida José Antonio during the long dictatorship of Franco. The Gran Vía is the main street of Madrid, with its stores, cinemas, and hotels—the latter both luxury and budget. The wide avenue—flanked with sidewalk cafes—ends at the **Plaza de España** with its Edificio España, one of the tallest skyscrapers in Europe. Or you'll wander past the multitude of shops, boutiques, coffeehouses, and couturiers' salons of the more prestigious **calle de Serrano.**

If medieval Madrid intrigues you, you'll seek out the Moorish towers of the old quarter, looking for the *mudéjar* style of architecture. You'll photograph (in your mind, if not with your camera) the **Plaza de la Villa** and focus especially on the **Torre de los Lujanes.** According to tradition, François I of France was held captive at the tower after he was taken prisoner in Pavia, Italy.

The colonnaded and rectangular **Plaza Mayor,** one of the most harmoniously designed squares in Europe, recalls 17th-century Madrid. The scene of many an *auto-da-fé* (burning of a heretic), bullfight, or execution of a traitor, it is today one of the best spots in the city for a *paseo* (stroll), especially if you take time out from your outing to explore the adjoining shops, some of which sell sombreros.

Later you can select a restaurant, perhaps one with tables set right on the square.

If you walk through one of the vaulted porticoes of the Plaza Mayor to the south, down the street of *típico* restaurants and taverns—**calle de Cuchilleros**—you'll reach the **calle de Toledo.** Then you'll be entering a special world of Old Madrid, still preserved. Known as the *barrios bajos*, it is home to the Madrileño lowest on the economic scale. In some cities it would be called a ghetto or slum. But in Madrid the area abounds with such style—screaming gypsy *niños*, arcaded markets stuffed with meats and vegetables, shops, *tascas, cuevas*—that it retains great punch.

THE CITY CENTER & MAIN AVENUES   The real center of the city is the **Puerta del Sol** (the Gateway of the Sun). Despite its grand appellation, it's a dull terminus of considerable traffic congestion and crime. Beginning at the Puerta del Sol, **calle de Alcalá** is Madrid's most traffic-choked artery, running more than $2^1/_2$ miles. It's the avenue of Spanish bankers and houses the Escuela y Museo de la Real Academia de Bellas Artes de San Fernando.

Madrid's greatest boulevard, its Champs-Elysées, begins at Atocha Railway Station. Heading north, it's called the **paseo del Prado** and passes on its right the Botanical Gardens and the Prado. It doesn't end, but changes its name at the **Plaza de la Cibeles,** dominated by the "cathedral of post offices" and a fountain honoring Cybele, "the great mother of the gods."

At Cibeles, the boulevard is henceforth the **paseo de Carvo Sotelo** and leads into the **Plaza de Colón.** At Colón, the **paseo de la Castellana** begins. Seemingly endless, paseo de la Castellana stretches through a posh area spreading out on both sides and featuring apartment houses, restaurants, department stores, and hotels; it continues past the public ministries, up to the flourishing **Plaza de Castilla,** then on to the huge La Paz hospital complex.

FINDING AN ADDRESS   In Madrid this can be a problem: The city is noted for its long boulevards—one stretching for $2^1/_2$ miles— so knowing the street number and cross street is very important. The rule about street numbers is that there is no rule. Most streets begin their numbering on one side, running in order until the end, then running back in the opposite direction on the other side. Therefore, no. 50 could be opposite no. 308. But there are many exceptions to this, so be prepared.

STREET MAPS   Arm yourself with a good map before setting out. The best, published by **Falk,** is available at most newsstands and kiosks in Madrid. Those given away free by tourist offices and hotels aren't adequate, because they don't show the maze of little streets.

Neighborhoods in Brief

Madrid can be divided into three principal districts—Old Madrid, which holds the most tourist interest; Ensanche, the new district, often with the best shops and hotels; and the periphery, which is of little interest to visitors.

Plaza Mayor/Puerta del Sol   This is the heart of Old Madrid, often called "the tourist zone." Filled with taverns and bars, it is bounded by carrera de San Jerónimo, calle Mayor, cava de San Miguel, cava Baja, and calle de la Cruz. From the Plaza Mayor, the arco de Cuchilleros is filled with Castilian restaurants and taverns; more cuevas (wine bars) lie along cava de San Miguel, cava Alta, and cava Baja. To the west of this old district is the Manzanares River. Muslim Madrid centers on the present-day Palacio de Oriente and Las Vistillas. What is now the Plaza de la Paja was the heart of Madrid and its main marketplace during the medieval and Christian period. In 1617 the Plaza Mayor became the hub of Madrid, and it remains the nighttime center of tourist activity, more so than the Puerta del Sol.

The Salamanca Quarter   Ever since Madrid's city walls came tumbling down in the 1860s, the district of Salamanca to the north has been a fashionable address. Calle de Serrano, lined with stores and boutiques, cuts through it. The U.S. Embassy is also here.

Gran Vía/Plaza de España   Gran Vía is the city's main street, lined with cinemas, department stores, and the headquarters of banks and corporations. It begins at the Plaza de España, with its bronze figures of Don Quixote and his faithful Sancho Panza.

Argüelles/Moncloa   The university area is bounded by Pintor Rosales, Cea Bermúdez, Bravo Murillo, San Bernardo, and Conde Duque. Students haunt its famous ale houses.

Chueca   This is an old and decaying area north of the Gran Vía. Its main streets are Hortaleza, Infantas, Barquillo, and San Lucas. It's the center of gay and lesbian nightlife, with many clubs and cheap restaurants. It can be dangerous at night, however, although more police are evident then.

Castellana/Recoletos/Paseo del Prado   Not really a city district, this is Madrid's north-south axis, its name changing along the way. The Museo del Prado and some of the city's more expensive hotels are found here. Many restaurants and other hotels are located along its side streets. In summer the several open-air terraces are filled with animated crowds. The most famous cafe is the Gran Café Gijon.

2   Getting Around

BY PUBLIC TRANSPORTATION • Discount Passes   You can save money on public transportation by purchasing a 10-trip ticket—known as a *bonos*—for the Metro (subway) for 600 ptas. ($4.30) at any Metro station. The center of the system is the Puerta del Sol; call **552-49-00** for more information.

For 600 ptas. ($4.30) you can also purchase a 10-trip ticket (but without transfers) for Madrid's bus system. It's sold at Empresa Municipal de Transportes, Plaza de la Cibeles (☎ **401-99-00**), where you can also purchase a guide to the bus routes. It's open daily from 8am to 8:30pm.

• **Subway (Metro)**   The Metro system, first installed in 1919, is quite easy to learn, and you can travel if not comfortably at least without any congestion or crushing as in former years.

Line 7 is completely different from the rest and as modern as some of Europe's newest subway systems. The future lines under construction will be the same type as no. 7.

The central converging point of the Metro is at the Puerta del Sol. The subways begin their runs at 6am and shut down at 1:30am. It's best to try to avoid traveling on the subways during the rush hours, of course. The fare is 125 ptas. (90¢). For information, call **552-49-00**.

• **Bus**   A network of buses traverses the city, fanning out to the suburbs. The route of each bus is clearly marked at each stop on a schematic diagram. Buses are fast and efficient and travel down special lanes made for them all over the city. Both red and yellow buses charge 125 ptas. (90¢) per ride—and most of the yellow buses have the advantage of being air-conditioned. (For information on buses from the airport into Madrid, see "Arriving/Departing" under "Orientation," above.)

Madrid has at least eight principal bus terminals, including the large **Estación Sur de Autobuses,** calle Canarias 17 (☎ **468-45-11;** Metro: Palos de la Frontera). Buses to the environs of Madrid, such as Toledo and Segovia, leave from numerous stations.

BY TAXI   Even though fares have risen recently, taxis are still so reasonable that I can recommend them. When you flag down a taxi, the meter should register 155 ptas. ($1.10), then it's 70 ptas. (50¢) per kilometer. A supplement is charged for trips to the railway station or the bullring, as well as on Sundays and holidays. The ride to Barajas Airport carries a 325-ptas. ($2.30) surcharge, and a 160-ptas. ($1.10) supplement from railway stations. In addition, there is a 150-ptas. ($1.10) supplement on Sundays and holidays, plus a 150 ptas. ($1.10) supplement at night. It's customary to tip at least 10% of the fare.

A ride is usually an adventure, since Madrileño drivers go fast, occasionally (but not always) stopping at red lights.

Taxi-riding has some minor traps that visitors will do well to avoid. There are two major types of taxis: black with horizontal red bands and white with diagonal red bands. Their rates are usually the same. However, many unmetered, unbanded taxis also abound in Madrid; the drivers rent their services as guides for the day or half day. But when business is slow, these guides sometimes operate as "gypsy" cabs and pick up unsuspecting passengers, take them to their destinations, and charge them whatever they think the market will bear. Beyond that pitfall, you must be careful to require that your driver start the meter when you enter the cab. Otherwise, the driver may "assess" the cost of the ride to your disadvantage.

To call a taxi, dial **445-90-08** or **447-51-80**.

BY CAR • **Rentals**   You won't want to drive in Madrid; it's too congested. But if you're touring the environs, you'll find a rented car will come in handy, allowing you to stop off at that *tipico* roadside tavern for *tapas* or to make that side detour to a medieval village. You'll be your own guide, exploring at your leisure places not covered—or covered too hurriedly—on an organized tour.

Many of North America's biggest car-rental companies—including **Avis** (☎ toll free **800/331-2112** in the U.S.), **Budget** (☎ toll free **800/427-3325** in the U.S.), and **Hertz** (☎ toll free **800/654-3001** in the U.S.)—maintain offices throughout Spain. Though several Spain-based car-rental companies will try to entice you to their facilities, letters from readers have shown that the resolution of billing irregularities and insurance claims tends to be less complicated with the U.S.-based car-rental firms.

To qualify for the best rates, you should reserve a car at least two weeks prior to your departure from North America.

• **Insurance** Insurance options at each of the companies are complicated; some companies will, for a higher net rate, include the insurance and taxes in a car's weekly rental fee. Others, such as Budget, prefer to quote the insurance as a separate add-on fee. A collision-damage waiver (CDW) costs around $13 per day for most small and medium-size cars. Unless you're covered through independent insurance (such as that offered by some credit-card companies), it's usually an excellent idea to take the extra insurance.

• **Gas** Gas is easily obtainable and is the usual fuel for rented cars in Spain. The average Spanish vehicle—predominantly Seats or Fiats—gets close to 45 miles per gallon. At time of press, a liter of gas costs about 98 pesetas—this works out to about $4 per U.S. gallon.

• **Parking** This is a nightmare! Street parking is not readily available. As spaces become free, motorists often compete fiercely for the vacancy. If you're driving into Madrid—the only time you should use your car, really—you should call your hotel and ask if it offers a space. If not, ask the location of the nearest garage. Stop first at your hotel, unload your luggage, and then follow directions to the nearest parking garage. Parking prices depend on the neighborhood. Those in the very center of Madrid are the most expensive, of course.

Warning: Do not expect many hotels in Madrid to have private garages. Many were built before the invention of the automobile, and even those that weren't often didn't have room for a garage in congested Madrid.

• **Driving Rules** Madrileños drive on the right side of the road. Drivers should pass on the left; local drivers sound their horns when passing another car. Autos coming from the right have the right-of-way.

If you must drive in Madrid, try to do so between 3 and 5pm, when many motorists are having a siesta. Never park your car facing oncoming traffic, because that's against the law. If you're fined by the highway patrol (Guardia Civil de Tráfico), you must pay on the spot. Penalties for drinking and driving are very stiff. The speed limit is 35 mph (55 kmph).

Madrid Metro

BY BICYCLE Ever wonder why you see so few people riding bicycles in Madrid? Those who tried were overcome by the traffic pollution. It's better to walk.

ON FOOT   Walking is the perfect way to see Madrid, especially the ancient narrow streets of the old town. If you're coming to the old town from another district—and chances are that your hotel will be outside the old town—you can take the bus or Metro. For such a large city, Madrid can be covered amazingly well on foot, because so much of what will interest a visitor lies in various clusters.

BY HITCHHIKING   This is no longer smiled upon as much as it used to be. Although it's technically legal, I don't recommend that you stick out your thumb in the presence of the Civil Guard. More important, hitchhiking is an increasingly dubious and unsafe way to travel, with the inherent danger of simply not knowing what maniac is likely to pick you up. Take the bus or train—it's safer, easier, and faster.

Fast Facts: Madrid

How do you find what you're seeking quickly and conveniently? In an emergency, of course, your hotel is your best bet. But some of the smaller hotels aren't staffed with personnel entirely fluent in English; and sometimes—even if they are—the person at the desk can be apathetic about something of vital interest to you.

American Express   For your mail or banking needs, try the American Express office at the corner of the Marqués de Cubas and Plaza de las Cortés 2 (☎ **322-55-00**; Metro: Gran Vía), across from the Palace Hotel. The office is open Monday through Friday from 9am to 5:30pm and on Saturday from 9am to noon.

Area Codes   The telephone area code for Madrid is 91 if you are calling from within Spain. If you're dialing Spain from North America, the country code for Spain is 34 and the area code for Madrid is 1. (Don't dial 91 when calling Madrid from the United States.)

Babysitters   Nearly all major hotels in Madrid can arrange for babysitters, called *canguros* in Spanish. Usually the concierge keeps a list of reliable sitters and will put you in touch with one of them, provided you give adequate notice. Rates vary considerably, but tend to be reasonable. More and more babysitters in Madrid speak English, but don't count on it. Chances are yours won't—although you can request it, of course.

Bookstores   Turner's, Genova 3 & 5 (☎ **319-28-67**; Metro: Alonso Martínez), has one of the largest collections of English-language books in the city, as well as a good selection of Spanish CDs. It's open Monday through Friday from 10am to 8pm and Saturday from 10am to 2pm.

Business Hours   Banks are open Monday through Friday from 9:30am to 2pm and Saturday from 9:30am to 1pm. Most **offices** are open Monday through Friday from 9am to 5 or 5:30pm; the longtime practice of early closings in summer seems to be dying out.

In **restaurants,** lunch is usually served from 1 to 4pm and dinner is 9 to 11:30pm or midnight. There are no set rules for the hours of **bars** and **taverns:** Many open at 8am, others at noon; most stay open until 1:30am or later. Major **stores** are open Monday through Saturday from 9:30am to 8pm; smaller establishments, however, often take a siesta, doing business from 9:30am to 1:30pm and 4:30 to 8pm. Hours can vary from store to store.

Currency Exchange   For the best rate when changing your money from dollars/pounds into pesetas, you should go to a bank. Banks are open Monday through Friday from 9:30am to 2pm; it's best to go after 10am. Many banks are also open on Saturday from 9:30am to 1pm. The currency exchange at Chamartín railway station (Metro: Chamartín) is open 24 hours a day.

Dentist/Doctor   For an English-speaking dentist or doctor, contact the U.S. Embassy, calle Serrano 75 (☎ **577-40-00;** Metro: Núñez de Balboa), which maintains a list of dentists and doctors who have offered their services to Americans abroad. For doctor or dental services you can also consult Unidad Médica Anglo-Americana, Conde de Arandá 1 (☎ **435-18-23;** Metro: Usera), behind the Plaza de Colón. Office hours are Monday through Friday from 9am to 8pm and Saturday from 10am to 2pm, although there is a 24-hour daily answering service.

Drugstores   Drugstores are scattered all over Madrid. One of the most central is Farmacia Gayoso, Arenal 2 (☎ **521-28-60;** Metro: Puerta del Sol). If you're trying to locate one at an odd hour, look for a list of open pharmacies posted outside the door of any closed drugstore. The Spanish government requires drugstores to operate on the rotating system of hours—thereby assuring you that some will be open at all times, even on Sunday at midnight.

Electricity   Many North Americans find that the plugs of their hairdryers and razors won't fit into the sockets in Madrid, where the electricity is 200 volts AC, 50 cycles. In the unlikely event you manage to force the plug of your appliance into the outlet, you will destroy your appliance, upset the hotel management, and possibly cause a fire, so don't try. Many hardware stores in North America sell the appropriate transformers (often called converters), and the concierge desks of most hotels will either lend you a transformer and an adapter for your plugs or tell you where you can buy them nearby. If you have any doubt about whether you have the appropriate transformer, ask questions at your hotel desk.

Embassies   If you lose your passport, fall seriously ill, get into legal trouble, or have some urgently serious problem, your embassy located in Madrid will probably have a mechanism to help you. The **U.S. Embassy,** calle Serrano 75 (☎ **577-40-00;** Metro: Núñez de Balboa), is open Monday through Friday from 9:30am to 1pm and 2:30 to 5pm. The **Canadian Embassy,** Núñez de Balboa 35 (☎ **431-43-00;** Metro: Velázquez) is open Monday through Friday from 8:30am to 5pm. The **U.K. Embassy,** Fernando el Santo 16

(☎ 319-02-00; Metro: Colón), is open Monday through Friday from 9am to 2pm and 3:30 to 6pm. The **Republic of Ireland Embassy**, calle Claudio Coello 73 (☎ 576-35-00; Metro: Serrano), is open Monday through Friday from 10am to 2pm. The **Australian Embassy**, paseo de la Castellana 143 (☎ 579-04-28; Metro: Cuzco), is open Monday through Thursday from 8:30am to 1:30pm and 2:30 to 5pm and Friday from 8:30am to 2pm. New Zealand citizens should contact the U.K. Embassy for assistance or advice (see address above).

Emergencies   If you need the police, call **091.** In case of fire, dial **080.** For an ambulance, as in the case of an accident, telephone **734-25-54.**

Etiquette   Women often kiss one another once on both cheeks when they meet. Men extend a hand when introduced; if they are good friends, they will often embrace. In general, women (except young moderns) expect men to open doors for them and to rise when they enter a room. The elderly are often treated with great respect and courtesy. When it comes to lining up for something—say, for a bus—you should step forward or you may find yourself the last one on. As a foreign guest, avoid all unfavorable references to Spain; Spanish nationalist pride often asserts itself vigorously in the face of criticism by a foreigner.

Eyeglasses   Glasses can be sold or repaired at one of several branches of Optica 2000, the most central of which is at El Corte Inglés, Princesa 56 (☎ 541-63-14; Metro: Callao); contact lenses also are available.

Film   Negra makes both black-and-white and color film. Valca is another popular brand. Also see "Photographic Needs," below.

Hairdressers/Barbers   A good salon for women or men is Galico, Velázquez 89 (☎ 563-47-63; Metro: Núñez de Balboa), open Monday through Saturday from 10am to 6pm; call for an appointment. For men, a fine choice is Jacques Dessange, O'Donnell 9 (☎ 435-32-20; Metro: Principe de Vergara), open Monday through Saturday from 10am to 6:30pm. All the El Corte Inglés department stores have good barbershops (see "Department Stores" under "Shopping A to Z" in Chapter 8).

Hospitals/Clinics   Unidad Médica Anglo-Americana, Conde de Arandá 1 (☎ 435-18-23; Metro: Usera), is not a hospital but a private outpatient clinic offering the services of various specialists. This is not an emergency clinic, although someone is available on the staff all the time. Office hours are Monday through Friday from 9am to 8pm and Saturday from 10am to 2pm; there is a 24-hour daily answering service. For a real medical emergency, call **734-25-54** for an ambulance.

Language   Spanish is the official language of the land, of course, and French is also widely spoken in parts. In Madrid, more and more people, especially the younger ones, are learning English. Nearly all major hotels and top restaurants are staffed with English-speakers. However, out in the country it will help a lot if you were a language major in school. The best phrase book is *Spanish for Travellers* by Berlitz; this pocket dictionary has a menu supplement and a 12,500-word glossary of both English and Spanish.

Another way of communicating if you don't speak Spanish is through *Quickpoint*, a visual translator allowing you to point at pictures to communicate. This three-panel brochure contains some 400 color illustrations of such everyday items as a pay phone and gasoline. Single copies cost $6 and can be ordered by calling **703/548-8794** in the U.S. or writing Gaia Communications Inc., Dept. 102, P.O. Box 239, Alexandria, VA 22313-0239.

Laundry/Dry Cleaning   A self-service facility, Lavandería Donoso Cortés, Donoso Cortés 17 (☎ **446-96-90;** Metro: Quevedo), is open Monday through Friday from 9am to 7pm and Saturday from 9am to 1pm. A good dry-cleaning service is provided by the El Corte Inglés department store at calle Preciados 3 (☎ **532-18-00;** Metro: Callao), where the staff speaks English.

Libraries   A large selection of American magazines and other material is available at the Washington Irving Center, Marqués de Villamagna 8 (☎ **435-6922;** Metro: Rubén Darío), open Monday through Friday from 2 to 6pm. The British Cultural Center, Almagro 5 (☎ **337-35-001;** Metro: Alonso Martínez), also has a large selection of English-language reading material; hours are Monday through Friday from 9am to 1pm and 3 to 6pm (in winter, Monday through Thursday from 9am to 7pm and Friday from 9am to 3pm).

Liquor Laws   The legal drinking age is 18. Bars, taverns, and cafeterias usually open at 8am, and many serve alcohol until around 1:30am or later. Generally, you can purchase alcoholic beverages in almost any grocery.

Lost Property   If you've lost something on a Madrid bus, go to the municipal office at Alcántara 26 (☎ **401-31-00;** Metro: Goya), open Monday through Friday from 9am to 2pm. If you've lost something on the Metro, go at any time to the Cuatro Caminos station (☎ **552-49-00**). For objects lost in taxis, go to Plaza de Chamberí (☎ **448-79-26;** Metro: Chamberí), open Monday through Friday from 9am to 2pm and Saturday from 9am to 1pm. For objects lost anywhere else, go to the Palacio de Communicaciones at the Plaza de la Cibeles (☎ **532-93-52;** Metro: Banco de España), open Monday through Friday from 9am to 2pm and Saturday from 9am to 1pm. Don't call—show up in person.

Luggage Storage/Lockers   These can be found at both the Atocha and Chamartín railway terminals, as well as at the major bus station, the Estación Sur de Autobuses, calle Canarias 17 (☎ **468-45-11;** Metro: Palos de la Frontera). Storage is also provided at the air terminal underneath the Plaza de Colón.

Mail   To send airmail letters to the United States or Canada costs 83 ptas. (60¢) for up to 15 grams; letters to the United Kingdom and other EU countries cost 45 ptas. (30¢) up to 20 grams, and letters within Spain cost 35 ptas. (20¢). Postcards cost the same rate as letters. Allow about a week for delivery to North America, generally less to the United Kingdom; in some cases letters take two weeks to reach North America. Rates change frequently, so check at your hotel before mailing anything. As for surface mail, forget it. Chances are you'll be home before your letter arrives.

Newspapers/Magazines   Most newsstands along the Gran Vía or kiosks at the major hotels carry the latest edition of the *International Herald Tribune* or *USA Today*. If you're traveling south, look for *Lookout* magazine, a quality production in English with stories focused primarily on Spain's Costa del Sol along with some articles of general interest to the traveler to Spain.

Pets   It's best to leave them at home. If you don't, you must bring any licenses and proof of vaccinations to your nearest Spanish consulate before you leave. Normally pets aren't welcome in public places; certain hotels will accept them, however—but these arrangements should be made in advance. Don't forget to check quarantine regulations affecting your animal upon your return. Guide dogs, however, are always excluded from such rigid rules. For the pamphlet "Pets," write the U.S. Customs Service, P.O. Box 7407, Washington, DC 20044; or call **202/566-8195** for a recorded message concerning Customs rules about pets.

Photographic Needs   Film is expensive in Spain; take in as much as Customs will allow. I suggest that you wait to process it until you return home. However, if you can't wait, you can take your undeveloped film to the leading department store, El Corte Inglés calle Precíados 3 (☎ **532-18-00;** Metro: Puerta del Sol).

Police   Dial **091.**

Post Office   If you don't want to receive your mail at your hotel or the American Express office, direct it to *Lista de Correos* ("General Delivery") at the central post office in Madrid. To pick up mail, go to the window marked LISTA, where you'll be asked to show your passport. Madrid's central post office is in "the cathedral of the post offices" at the Plaza de la Cibeles (☎ **536-01-11;** Metro: Cibeles).

Radio/TV   During the day on shortwave radio you can hear the Voice of America and the BBC. An English-language radio program in Madrid called "*Buenos Días*" (Good Morning) airs many useful hints for visitors; it's broadcast Monday through Friday from 6 to 8am on 657 MegaHertz. Radio 80 broadcasts news in English Monday through Saturday from 7 to 8am on 89 FM. Some TV programs are broadcast in English in summer. Many hotels—but, regrettably, not most of our budget ones—also bring in satellite TV programs in English.

Religious Services   Most churches in Madrid are Catholic, and they're all over the city. Catholic masses in English, however, are given at Alfonso XIII no. 165; for information, call **233-20-32** in the morning. The British Embassy Church of St. George, an Anglican/ Episcopalian church, is at Núñez de Balboa 43 (call **576-51-09** for worship hours; Metro: Velázquez). The interdenominational Protestant Community Church offers weekly services in the Colegio El Porvenir, Bravo Murillo 85 (☎ **858-55-57;** Metro: Quevedo), while the Immanuel Baptist Church offers English-speaking services at Hernández de Tejada 4 (☎ **407-43-47;** Metro: Concepcion). A Christian Science Church is at Pinilla del Valle 5 (☎ **259-21-25;** Metro: Prosperidad). You'll find a Jewish synagogue at Balmes 3 (☎ **445-98-35;** Metro: Iglesia); services are on Friday at 7:30pm and Saturday at 9:30am.

Restrooms Some are available, including those in Retiro Park in Madrid and on the Plaza del Oriente across from the Royal Palace. Otherwise, you can always go into a bar or *tasca*, but you really should order something—perhaps a small glass of beer or even a bag of peanuts.

The Spanish designations for restrooms are *aseos* or *servicios*. *Caballeros* are for men and *damas* are for women.

Safety Because of increased thefts in Madrid, the U.S. Embassy urges visitors to leave valuables in a hotel safe or other secure place while exploring the city's sights. Purse-snatching is prevalent, with the criminals working in pairs, grabbing purses from pedestrians, cyclists, and even cars. If your car is standing still, a thief may open the door or break a window in order to snatch a purse or package, even from under the seat. A popular scam against tourists in Madrid involves one miscreant's smearing the back of the clothing of the victim, perhaps with mustard or chocolate; an accomplice pretends to help the victim clean off the mess, meanwhile picking all pockets of valuables. The embassy statement advises: Don't carry a purse; keep your valuables in front pockets; carry only enough cash for the day's needs; be aware of who is around you; and keep a separate record of your passport number, traveler's check numbers, and credit-card numbers.

In the wake of so many robberies, visitors have taken to leaving their passports back at the hotel. But here's a Catch-22 situation: Identification checks are common by Spanish police who are actually cracking down on illegal immigrants. Police or plainclothes agents can stop you at any time of the day or night and demand to see your passport. You can be arrested, as many visitors are, when you can't produce one. Carry your passport with you but carefully conceal it on your body, perhaps in a moneybelt.

Every car can be a target, parked or just stopped at a light. Don't leave anything in sight in your car. Place valuables in the trunk when you park and always assume someone is watching you to see whether you're putting something away for safekeeping. Keep the car locked while you're driving and even for a one-minute stop.

Whenever you're traveling in an unfamiliar city or country, stay alert. Be aware of your immediate surroundings. Wear a moneybelt and keep a close eye on your possessions. Be particularly careful with cameras, purses, and wallets—all favorite targets of thieves and pickpockets. It's your responsibility to be aware and be alert, even in the most heavily touristed areas.

Shoe Repairs   In an emergency, go to one of the "Mister Minit" shoe-repair centers at any El Corte Inglés department store. The flagship store of this chain is at calle Precíados 3 (☎ **532-18-00;** Metro: Puerta del Sol); it's open Monday through Saturday from 10am to 9pm.

Smoking   In Spain virtually everyone smokes—on buses, in the Metro, everywhere. NO FUMA signs are often ignored.

Taxes   Since Spain joined the Common Market (EC; now known as the European Union, or EU) on January 1, 1986, it committed itself to gradually eliminating most tariff barriers between itself and the rest of Europe. In consequence, internal sales taxes (value-added tax, known in Spain as IVA) were immediately adjusted upward to between 6% and 33%, depending on the commodity being sold. Most of the basic necessities of the Spaniard's life, including food and most wines, are taxed at 6%. The majority of goods and services, as well as rental cars, are taxed at the "ordinary" rate of 12%. Luxury goods such as jewelry, furs, motor yachts, and private airplanes also carry a 12% tax. The rental of rooms in hotels with government ratings of four or five stars is subject to a 12% tax; rooms in hotels rated three stars or fewer are levied a 6% tax. These taxes are usually (but not always) quoted as part of the hotel rates.

For drinkers and smokers, all imported liquors and all tobaccos (whether Spanish or foreign) are taxed at 6% or 12% (depending on the store), making the prices of vices just a little bit higher. Most drinkers solve the problem by switching from scotch to Spanish wines, Spanish beers, or Spanish brandies with soda.

If you buy goods worth a total of more than 82,400 ptas. ($585), you're eligible for a tax rebate of 6% or 12%, depending on the type of purchase. Major department stores will deduct the tax from your bill if you present your passport. Small stores may provide you with a form to fill out that you must show with your purchase to the Spanish Customs IVA desk at your departure point. If a shop does not have a form, save your receipts to show at the IVA desk. The government will refund by mail the amount due in pesetas. Refunds take between two and three months.

Telegrams/Telex/Fax   Cables may be sent from the central post office building in Madrid on the Plaza de la Cibeles (☎ **536-01-11;** Metro: Cibeles). To send a telegram by phone, dial **522-20-00.** In Spain it's cheaper to telephone within the country than to send a telegram. You can send telex and fax messages from the same central post office and from all major hotels.

Telephones   If you don't speak Spanish, you'll find telephoning from your hotel the easiest. Know, however, that this is often very expensive, since hotels impose a surcharge on every operator-assisted call. If you're more adventurous, you'll find street phone booths, known as *cabinas*, with dialing instructions in English. A three-minute local call can be made by inserting three coins of 5 ptas. (5¢) each. For long-distance calls—especially transatlantic ones—it may be best to go to the main telephone exchange, Locutorio Gran Vía, Gran Vía 30, or Locutorio Recoletos, paseo Recoletos 37–41. However, you may not be lucky enough to find an English-speaking operator. You'll have to fill out a simple form that will facilitate placing your call.

Time   Spain is six hours ahead of eastern standard time in the U.S. Daylight saving time (one hour ahead of standard time) is in effect from the last Sunday in March to the last Sunday in September.

Tipping   Don't overtip. The government requires that restaurants and hotels add their service charges (usually 15%) to the bill. However, that doesn't mean you should skip out of a place without dispensing some extra pesetas. Following are some guidelines:

In **hotels,** tip the porter 50 ptas. (40¢) per bag, but never less than 100 ptas. (70¢), even if you have only one suitcase; for the maid, 100 ptas. (70¢) per day; the doorman, 100 ptas. (70¢) for assisting with baggage and 25 ptas. (20¢) for calling a cab. In a top-ranking hotel the concierge will often submit a separate bill, showing charges for newspapers and other services; if he or she has been particularly helpful, tip extra.

For **cab drivers,** add about 10% to 15% to the fare shown on the meter. However, if the driver personally unloads or loads your luggage, add 25 ptas. (20¢) per bag.

At **airports** such as Barajas in Madrid and major terminals, the porter who handles your luggage will present you with a fixed-charge bill, usually from 75 to 100 ptas. (50¢ to 70¢).

In both **restaurants** and **nightclubs,** a 15% service charge is added to the bill. To that, add another 3% to 5%, depending on the quality of the service. Waiters in deluxe restaurants and nightclubs are accustomed to the extra 5%, which means you'll end up tipping 20%. If that seems excessive, you must remember that the initial service charge reflected in the fixed price is distributed among all the help.

In addition, **barbers** and **hairdressers** expect 10% to 15%; **tour guides** expect 200 ptas. ($1.40), although it's not mandatory; and **theater/bullfight ushers** get 25 to 50 ptas. (20¢ to 40¢).

Transit Information   For Metro information, call **552-49-00.**

Useful Telephone Numbers   For telegrams by phone, dial **522-20-00;** for Iberia Airlines information, call **563-99-66.**

Water   It's generally safe to drink the tap water in Madrid; however, if you have a delicate stomach, it's better to switch to mineral water instead.

Weather   Dial **094** for the latest reports.

3 Networks & Resources

FOR STUDENTS   Contact **TIVE,** calle José Ortega y Gasset 71 (☎ 347-77-00; Metro: Lista), which provides data on low-cost transportation in Spain and also Europe. Always check their discounts against those of other airlines to see just how great a reduction you're getting.

FOR GAY MEN & LESBIANS   Before you go to Spain, you can order the international gay guide *Spartacus* ($29.95) from **Giovanni's Room,** 1145 Pine St., Philadelphia, PA 19107 (☎ 215/923-2960). Gay men headed only for Spain—and not the rest of Europe—might purchase instead *Spartacus International: España Edition* for $19.95. Lesbians, for whom neither of the *Spartacus* guides is appropriate, might be interested in *Ferrari's Places for Women* at $12.

Madrid is now one of the gay capitals in Europe. Besides Madrid, the major gay and lesbian centers in Spain are Barcelona, Sitges, and Torremolinos on the Costa del Sol (although that resort attracts a mixed crowd). Madrid's gay life centers on the **Chueca district,** north of the Gran Vía, where the bar life begins around 11pm and often lasts until dawn.

In Madrid, **Librería El Galeón,** calle Sagasta 7 (☎ 445-57-38; Metro: Bilbao), is a gay bookshop where you can purchase the annual version of *Guía Gay Visado,* containing the most complete list of gay and lesbian entertainment in the country. Hours are Monday through Friday from 9:30am to 1:30pm.

Lesbian life remains much more underground in Spain than does gay male life. The best source of information is the **Librería de Mujeres** (see below), a feminist bookshop with much useful data. The best women's entertainment center in Madrid (attracting men, too) is **No Sé les Digas a Nadie** ("Don't Tell Mama"), which will be recommended in Chapter 9.

FOR WOMEN   The **Women's Medical Hotline** in Madrid is **730-49-01,** receiving calls Monday through Friday from 3:30 to 6:30 pm. A women's center is the **Librería de Mujeres,** calle San Cristóbal 17 (☎ 521-70-43), near the Plaza Mayor (Metro: Puerta del Sol). Poetry readings, concerts, talks, and a good international bookstore with some English-language editions are part of the activities and offerings of this group. It's open Monday through Saturday from 10am to 2pm and 5 to 8pm.

4

Madrid Accommodations

MADRID'S HOTEL BOOM HAS BEEN SPECTACULAR: THREE-QUARTERS OF MY recommendations are modern. Yet many guests prefer the landmarks of yesteryear, including those grand old establishments the Ritz and the Palace (ca. 1910–12). However, many other older hostelries in Madrid haven't kept abreast of the times. A handful haven't added improvements or overhauled bedrooms substantially since the 1960s.

Traditionally, hotels in Madrid were clustered around the Atocha Railway Station and the Gran Vía. In my search for the most outstanding hotels in the upper brackets, I've almost ignored these two popular but noisy districts. The newer hotels have been erected away from the center, especially on residential streets jutting off from paseo de la Castellana. However, bargain-seekers will still find great pickings along the Gran Vía and around the Atocha station.

RESERVATIONS   Most hotels require at least a day's deposit before they will reserve a room for you. Preferably, this can be accomplished with an international money order; a credit or charge-card number; or, if agreed to in advance, a personal check. You can usually cancel a room reservation one week ahead of time and get a full refund. A few hotelkeepers will return your money three days before the reservation date, but some will take your deposit and never return it, even if you cancel far in advance. Many budget hotel owners operate on such a narrow margin of profit they find just buying stamps for airmail replies too expensive by their standards. Therefore, it's most important that you enclose a prepaid International Reply Coupon with your payment, especially if you're writing to a budget hotel. Better yet, call and speak to the hotel of your choice or send a fax.

If you're booking into a chain hotel, such as Hyatt or Forte, you can call toll free in North America and easily make reservations over the phone. Toll-free 800 numbers, when available, are indicated in the individual hotel recommendations in this guide.

If you arrive without a reservation, begin your search for a room as early in the day as possible. If you arrive late at night, you may have to take what you can get, often in a much higher price range than you'd like to pay.

PRICE CLASSIFICATIONS   The following prices are for double rooms with private baths. Hotels rated **very expensive** charge from 30,000 ptas. ($213) for a double, although some establishments in this bracket—including the Villa Magna, Santo Mauro, and Ritz—can ask twice that price. Hotels judged **expensive** ask from 17,000 to 30,000 ptas. ($120.70 to $213) for a double, and **moderate** hotels—at least moderate in the sense of Madrid's hotel price scale—want from a low of 10,000 ptas. ($71) to a high of 17,000 ptas. ($120.70) for a double. Hotels considered **inexpensive**—again, by Madrid's pricing standards—ask for 6,000 ptas. ($42.60) up to 10,000 ptas. ($71) for a double. Any double under 6,000 ptas. ($42.60) is definitely **budget** in today's high-priced Madrid.

Note: All hotels in the very expensive and expensive categories include private baths with their guest rooms unless otherwise specified. Hotels in the other categories may or may not include baths; however, assume private baths are offered unless otherwise specified. Also, breakfast is not included in the quoted rates unless otherwise specified.

A 6% government room tax is added to all rates.

THE STAR SYSTEM Spain officially rates its hotels by star designation. Five stars is the highest rating in Spain, signaling a deluxe establishment complete with all the amenities and high tariffs associated with such accommodations.

Most of the establishments recommended in this guide are three- and four-star hotels falling into that vague "middle-bracket" category. Hotels granted one and two stars, as well as pensions (guesthouses), are far less comfortable, although they may be perfectly clean and decent places, but with limited plumbing and other physical facilities. The latter category is strictly for dedicated budgeteers.

Reminder: The telephone area code for Madrid is 91 if you're calling from within Spain. If you're dialing from North America, the country code is 34 and Madrid's area code is 1.

PARKING This is a serious problem because so few hotels have garages; many buildings turned into hotels were constructed before the invention of the automobile. Street parking is rarely available, and, even if it is, you run the risk of having your car broken into. If you're driving into Madrid, most hotels (or most police) will allow you to park in front of the hotel long enough to unload your luggage. Someone on the staff will pinpoint the location of the nearest garage, often giving you a map showing the way. In instances where a hotel has its own parking, charges are given.

---

1 Near the Plaza de las Cortés

Very Expensive

Hotel Villa Real, Plaza de las Cortés 10, 28014 Madrid.
☎ **91/420-37-67.** Fax 91/420-25-47. 115 rms, 19 suites.
A/C MINIBAR TV TEL **Metro:** Plaza de la Cibeles.
Rates: 24,000 ptas. ($170.40) single; 31,000 ptas. ($220.10) double; 55,000–65,000 ptas. ($390.50–$461.50) suite. Breakfast 1,350 ptas. ($9.60) extra. AE, DC, MC, V. **Parking:** 1,600 ptas. ($11.40).

Until 1989, the Villa Real was little more than a run-down 19th-century apartment house auspiciously located across a three-sided park from the Spanish Parliament (Congreso de los Diputados), between the Puerta del Sol and the paseo del Prado. Its developers poured billions of pesetas into renovations to produce a stylish hotel that's now patronized by Spain's cognoscenti. The eclectic facade boasts an odd mix of neoclassical and Aztec motifs, and in front of it wait footmen and doormen in uniforms of buff and forest green. The interior contains a scattering of modern paintings amid neoclassical moldings and details.

Each accommodation offers a TV with video movies and satellite reception, a safe for valuables, soundproofing, a sunken salon filled with leather-upholstered furniture, and built-in burlwood-inlaid furniture.

Dining/Entertainment: The social center is the high-ceilinged formal bar. The hotel's formal Restaurant Europa serves Spanish and international cuisine at both lunch and dinner, with meals beginning at 5,500 ptas. ($39.10).

Services: 24-hour room service, laundry/valet, babysitting, express checkout, foreign currency exchange.

Facilities: Sauna, business center.

★ **The Palace,** Plaza de las Cortés 7, 28014 Madrid.
☎ **91/429-75-51,** or toll free **800/221-2340,** in the U.S., **800/955-2442** in Canada. Fax 91/429-86-55. 487 rms, 31 suites. A/C MINIBAR TV TEL **Metro:** Banco de España or Antón Martín.
Rates: 25,000–32,000 ptas. ($177.50–$227.20) single; 32,000–38,000 ptas. ($227.20–$269.80) double; from 90,000 ptas. ($639) suite. Breakfast 2,400 ptas. ($17). AE, DC, MC, V. **Parking:** 1,600 ptas. ($11.40).

The Palace is known as "the grand *dueña*" of Spanish hotels. The establishment had an auspicious beginning, inaugurated by the late Alfonso XIII in 1912. Covering a city block, it is superbly located, facing the Prado and Neptune Fountain, in the historical and artistic area, within walking distance of the main shopping center and the best antiques shops. Some of the city's most intriguing tascas and restaurants are only a short stroll away.

Architecturally, it captures the elegant pre–World War I "Grand Hotel" style, with an emphasis on space and comfort. Even though it's one of the largest hotels in Madrid, it retains a personal atmosphere. The hotel is fully air-conditioned, with an impressive lobby. The rooms are conservatively traditional, with plenty of space for leisurely living and large baths boasting lots of extra amenities.

Dining/Entertainment: The elegant dining choice is La Cupola, decorated in the style of Venice. It serves Italian specialties along with some of the more famous dishes of Spanish cuisine, with meals costing from 6,500 ptas. ($46.20). The Ambigu offers a full buffet starting at 3,950 ptas. ($28) per person and is open daily from 12:30pm to 1:30am. Piano music and other entertainment are featured.

Services: 24-hour room service, laundry/valet, babysitting, express checkout, foreign currency exchange.

Facilities: Business center.

Inexpensive

$ **Hostal Cervantes,** Cervantes 34, 28014 Madrid.
☎ **91/429-27-45.** 12 rms. **Metro:** Banco de España.
Rates: 5,000 ptas. ($35.50) single; 6,000 ptas. ($42.60) double. No credit cards.

One of Madrid's most pleasant family-run hotels, the Cervantes has been widely appreciated by our readers for years. Take a tiny birdcage-style elevator to the immaculately maintained second floor of this stone-and-brick building. Each accommodation contains a bed, spartan furniture, and a private bath. No breakfast is served, but the Alfonsos will direct you to a nearby cafe. The establishment is convenient to the Prado, Retiro Park, and the older sections of Madrid.

2 Near the Plaza de España

Expensive

Plaza Hotel, Plaza de España 8, 28013 Madrid. ☎ **91/547-12-00.**
Fax 91/548-23-89. 266 rms, 40 suites. A/C MINIBAR TV TEL
Metro: Plaza de España.
Rates: 15,200 ptas. ($107.90) single; 19,000 ptas. ($134.90) double; from 24,000 ptas. ($170.40) suite. Breakfast 1,300 ptas. ($9.20) extra. AE, DC, MC, V. **Parking:** 2,500 ptas. ($17.80).

The Plaza, built in 1953, could be called the Waldorf-Astoria of Spain. A massive rose-and-white structure, the hotel soars upward to a central tower 26 stories high, making it a landmark visible for miles around and one of the tallest skyscrapers in Europe.

The accommodations include conventional singles and doubles as well as luxurious suites, each of which contains a sitting room and abundant amenities. Each accommodation, regardless of size, contains an expansive marble-covered bath. Furniture is usually a standardized modern style, in harmonized colors.

Dining/Entertainment: The hotel has a traditional restaurant, the Toledo, and a smaller, somewhat less expensive eatery, the Acelea. There's also a piano bar.

Services: 24-hour room service, laundry/valet, concierge, babysitting.

Facilities: Top-floor pool and sun terrace with sweeping views over the architectural symmetry of Plaza de España.

Moderate

$ Casón del Tormes, calle Rió 7, 28013 Madrid.
☎ **91/541-97-46.** Fax 91/541-18-52. 63 rms. A/C MINIBAR
TV TEL **Metro:** Plaza de España.
Rates: 7,900 ptas. ($56.10) single; 11,000 ptas. ($78.10) double; 13,900 ptas. ($98.70) triple. Breakfast 600 ptas. ($4.30) extra. MC, V.
Parking: 1,200 ptas. ($8.50).

The attractive three-star Casón del Tormes is around the corner from the Royal Palace and the Plaza de España. Set behind a four-story red-brick facade with stone-trimmed windows, it overlooks a quiet one-way street. The long, narrow lobby contains vertical wooden paneling, a marble floor, and a bar opening into a separate room. Motorists appreciate the public parking lot near the hotel. Laundry service is provided.

Accommodations In Central Madrid

3 On or Near the Gran Vía

Moderate

Hostal Buenos Aires, Gran Vía 61, 28013 Madrid. ☎ **542-01-02.**
Fax 91/542-28-69. 25 rms. TEL **Metro:** Plaza de España. **Bus:** 1, 2,
or 44.

Metro ◈ Church ╬ Post Office ⊠ Information ⓘ

Rates: 5,000 ptas. ($35.50) single; 7,000 ptas. ($49.70) double. Breakfast 500 ptas. ($3.60) extra. AE, DC, MC, V.

To reach this place, you pass through a street-floor marble lobby within a 1955 building, then take the elevator to the second floor. The hostal occupies two floors. One of its best features is a wood-sheathed cafe/bar that's open 24 hours daily. The guest rooms are comfortable, modern, and clean, each with a safety deposit box, balcony, and hairdryer.

Hotel Atlàntico, Gran Vía 38, 28013 Madrid. ☎ **91/522-64-80,** or toll free **800/528-1234** in the U.S. and Canada. Fax 91/531-02-10. 80 rms. A/C MINIBAR TEL **Metro:** Gran Vía.

Rates (including continental breakfast): 8,150 ptas. ($57.90) single; 11,350 ptas. ($80.60) double. AE, DC, MC, V.

Refurbished in stages between the late 1980s and 1994, this hotel occupies five floors of a grand turn-of-the-century building on a corner of one of Madrid's most impressive avenues. Established in 1989 as a Best Western affiliate, it offers security boxes in well-furnished guest rooms. Near the reception area is an English-inspired bar serving drinks and snacks 24 hours a day.

Residencia Liabeny, Salud 3, 28013 Madrid. ☎ **91/532-53-06.** Fax 91/532-74-21. 219 rms. A/C MINIBAR TV TEL **Metro:** Puerta del Sol, Callao, or Gran Vía.

Rates: 10,000 ptas. ($71) single; 15,000 ptas. ($106.50) double; 19,300 ptas. ($137) triple. Breakfast 900 ptas. ($6.40) extra. AE, MC, V. **Parking:** 1,200 ptas. ($8.50).

Behind a stone-sheathed rectangular facade, this hotel is in a prime location midway between the tourist highlights of the Gran Vía and the Puerta del Sol. Named after the original owner of the hotel, it contains seven floors of comfortably contemporary guest rooms.

Inexpensive

Anaco, Tres Cruces 3, 28013 Madrid. ☎ **91/522-46-04.** Fax 91/531-64-84. 39 rms. A/C TV TEL **Metro:** Gran Vía, Callao, or Puerta del Sol.

Rates: 5,500–6,500 ptas. ($39.10–$46.20) single; 8,500–9,500 ptas. ($60.40–$67.50) double; 11,475–12,825 ptas. ($81.50–$91.10) triple. Breakfast 500 ptas. ($3.60) extra. AE, DC, MC, V.

A modestly modern hotel, the Anaco is just off the shopping thoroughfare, the Gran Vía. Opening onto a tree-shaded plaza, it attracts those seeking a resting place featuring contemporary appurtenances and cleanliness. The guest rooms are compact, with built-in headboards, reading lamps, and lounge chairs. Useful tip: Ask for one of the five terraced rooms on the top floor, which rent at no extra charge. The hotel has a bar/cafeteria/restaurant that's open daily from 7:30am to 2:30am. English is spoken here. Nearby is a municipally operated garage.

Hostal Nuevo Gaos, calle Mesonero Romanos 14, 28013 Madrid. ☎ **91/532-71-07.** Fax 91/522-70-98. 23 rms. A/C MINIBAR TV TEL **Metro:** Callao. **Bus:** 1, 2, or 44.

Rates: 6,200–8,200 ptas. ($44–$58.20) single or double. AE, DC, MC, V.

On the second, third, and fourth floors of a 1930s building just off the Gran Vía, this residencia offers guests the chance to enjoy a comfortable standard of living at moderate rates. The place lies directly north of the Puerta del Sol, across from the popular flamenco club Torre Bermejas. Breakfast can be taken at a nearby cafe.

Hotel Nuria, Fuencarral 52, 28004 Madrid. ☎ **91/531-92-08.**
Fax 91/532-90-05. 80 rms. TV TEL **Metro:** Gran Vía or Tribunal.
Bus: 3, 7, or 40.
Rates (including breakfast): 3,600–4,750 ptas. ($25.60–$33.70) single; 6,250 ptas. ($44.40) double. AE, DC, MC, V.

Hotel Nuria, three blocks from the Gran Vía, has some guest rooms with especially interesting views of the capital. Furnishings are simple and functional. A bar, restaurant, and TV lounge are available to guests. The hotel was renovated in 1986.

Budget

 Hostal-Residencia Continental, Gran Vía 44, 28013 Madrid.
☎ **91/521-46-40.** 29 rms. TEL **Metro:** Callao. **Bus:** 1, 2, 36, or 46.
Rates: 3,600 ptas. ($25.60) single; 4,900 ptas. ($34.80) double.
Breakfast 500 ptas. ($3.60) extra. AE, DC, MC, V.

Sprawling handsomely over the third and fourth floors of Gran Vía 44, this hostal is a bit more expensive than the other accommodations in the building, but the rooms are comfortable, tidy, and renovated. The desk clerk speaks English. The Continental is in a virtual "casa of budget hotels," a 19th-century building filled exclusively with small

---

Frommer's Smart Traveler: Hotels

Value-Conscious Travelers Should Take Advantage of the Following:

1. Reductions in rates for rooms without private bath. Usually a room with a shower is cheaper than a room with a private bath, and even cheaper is a room with a basin only.

2. Reductions in some hotels if you pay cash instead of with a credit card.

3. Long-term discounts if you're planning to spend more than one week in Madrid.

Questions to Ask If You're on a Budget:

1. If there's a garage, what's the parking charge?

2. Is there a surcharge for local or long-distance telephone calls? Usually there is, and it can be as high as 40%; in that case, make your calls at the nearest post office.

3. Is service included or will it be added to your final bill? Likewise, are all taxes included, or will you be billed extra?

4. Is a continental breakfast included in the rate? After a stay of three or four days, the cost of breakfast alone can make a big difference in your final bill.

hotels and pensions. If no room is available here, you can ring the doorbells of the other establishments.

Hotel Alcázar Regis, Gran Vía 61, 28013 Madrid.
☎ **91/547-93-17.** 25 rms (none with bath). **Metro:** Plaza de España or Santo Domingo.
Rates: 2,300 ptas. ($16.30) single; 4,000 ptas. ($28.40) double. Breakfast 350 ptas. ($2.50) extra. AE.

Conveniently perched on a corner in the midst of Madrid's best shops is this post–World War II building, complete with a Greek-style circular temple as its crown. On the building's fifth floor you'll find long and pleasant public rooms; wood paneling; leaded-glass windows; parquet floors; crystal chandeliers; and high-ceilinged guest rooms, each with hot and cold running water.

4 Near the Puerta del Sol

Expensive

Gran Hotel Reina Victoria, Plaza Santa Ana 14, 28012 Madrid.
☎ **91/531-45-00.** Fax 91/522-03-07. 187 rms, 9 suites.
A/C MINIBAR TV TEL **Metro:** Tirso de Molina or Puerta del Sol.
Rates (including breakfast): 17,000 ptas. ($120.70) single; 22,000 ptas. ($156.20) double; from 28,200 ptas. ($200.20) suite. AE, DC, V.
Parking: 1,600 ptas. ($11.40).

This establishment is about as important to the legends of Madrid as the famous bullfighter Manolete himself. He used to stay here, giving lavish parties in one of the reception rooms and attracting mobs in the square below when he went out on his balcony for morning coffee. Since the renovation and upgrading of this property by Spain's Tryp Hotel Group, it's less staid and more impressive than ever.

Originally built in 1923 and named after the grandmother of the present king of Spain, Juan Carlos, the hotel sits behind an ornately eclectic stone facade the Spanish government protects as a historic monument. Although it's located in a congested neighborhood in the center of town, it opens onto its own verdant and sloping plaza, rich in tradition as a meeting place of intellectuals during the 17th century. Each guest room contains sound-resistant insulation, a safe for valuables, and a private bath with many amenities.

Dining/Entertainment: At the popular lobby bar, the Manuel González Manolete, bullfighting memorabilia and potent drinks add another attraction to an already memorable hotel. The in-house restaurant is El Ruedo.

Services: 24-hour room service, concierge, babysitting.

Moderate

Hotel Carlos V, Maestro Vitoria 5, 28013 Madrid. ☎ **91/531-41-00,** or toll free **800/528-1234** in the U.S. and Canada.
Fax 91/531-37-61. 67 rms. A/C TV TEL **Metro:** Puerta del Sol or Callao.

Rates: 8,900 ptas. ($63.20) single; 11,200 ptas. ($79.50) double. Breakfast 750 ptas. ($5.30) extra. AE, DC, MC, V.

Hotel Carlos V has long been a Frommer favorite—many faithful readers discovered it in 1967 when they used the guide *Spain on $5 a Day*. Some have been returning ever since those less expensive days. The seven-story art nouveau building dating from 1904 has been altered over the years. Rooms have been upgraded and now contain such amenities as music and personal safes; baths have been modernized. What hasn't changed is the unbeatable location: around the corner from the Galerías Preciados and just a short walk from the Gran Vía and the Puerta del Sol. The lobby retains its air of elegance.

Hotel Francisco I, Arenal 15, 28013 Madrid. ☎ **91/548-43-14.** Fax 91/542-28-99. 58 rms. TEL **Metro:** Puerta del Sol or Ópera.

Rates: (including breakfast): 6,300 ptas. ($44.70) single; 8,700 ptas. ($61.80) double. MC, V.

Here you can rent modern, clean rooms. There's a pleasant lounge/bar, and on the sixth floor you'll find a comfortable, rustically decorated restaurant where a fixed-price meal costs around 2,000 ptas. ($14.20). The hotel was considerably modernized in 1993, with the addition of new baths as well as air-conditioning in most of the rooms. The hotel provides 24-hour room service and laundry/valet service.

$ Hostal Inglés, calle Echegaray 8, 28014 Madrid. ☎ **91/429-65-51.** Fax 91/420-24-23. 50 rms, 8 suites. TEL **Metro:** Puerta del Sol or Sevilla.

Rates: 6,500 ptas. ($46.20) single; 9,500 ptas. ($67.50) double; 13,000 ptas. ($92.30) suite. Breakfast 1,100 ptas. ($7.80) extra. AE, DC, MC, V. **Parking:** 1,100 ptas. ($7.80).

You'll find the Inglés on a central street lined with tascas, which you might not need to visit since the hotel operates its own 24-hour cafeteria. Now it's perhaps more modern and impersonal than when Virginia Woolf made it her address in Madrid. Behind its red-brick facade you'll find unpretentious and contemporary rooms, each well maintained. The comfortable armchairs in the TV lounge are likely to be filled with avid soccer fans. The lobby is air-conditioned, but the rooms are not. Guests who have to open the windows at night are likely to hear noise coming from the enclosed courtyard, so light sleepers should be aware of this.

Hotel Residencia Santander, calle Echegaray 1, 28014 Madrid. ☎ **91/429-95-51.** 38 rms. TEL **Metro:** Puerta del Sol.

Rates: 5,600 ptas. ($39.80) single; 7,000 ptas. ($49.70) double. Breakfast 400 ptas. ($2.80) extra. No credit cards.

A snug little hotel just off the Puerta del Sol, the Santander is a refurbished 1930 house containing adequate rooms, some with TVs. Although it's on a teeming street, you might appreciate the nonstop local atmosphere. Restaurants and bars in the area are active day and night.

Budget

$ **Hostal la Macarena**, cava de San Miguel 8, 28005 Madrid.
☎ **91/365-92-21.** Fax 91/364-27-57. 18 rms. **Metro:** Puerta del Sol, Ópera, or La Latina.

Rates: 3,800 ptas. ($27) single; 6,000 ptas. ($42.60) double; 7,500 ptas. ($53.30) triple; 8,000 ptas. ($56.80) quad. Breakfast 500 ptas. ($3.60) extra. AE, MC, V.

Known for its reasonable prices and praised by readers for the warmth of its reception, this unpretentious, clean hostal is run by the Ricardo González family. Its 19th-century facade ornamented with Bell Epoque patterns offers an ornate contrast to the chiseled simplicity of the ancient buildings facing it. The location is one of the hostal's assets, on a street (admittedly noisy) immediately behind the Plaza Mayor, near one of the best clusters of tascas (bars) in Madrid. Windows facing the street have double panes.

Hostal la Perla Asturiana, Plaza de Santa Cruz 3, 28012 Madrid.
☎ **91/366-46-00.** 32 rms. **Metro:** Puerta del Sol.

Rates: 3,600 ptas. ($25.60) single; 4,900 ptas. ($34.80) double. Breakfast 500 ptas. ($3.60) extra. AE, DC, MC, V.

Ideal for those who want to stay in the heart of Old Madrid (one block from the Plaza Mayor and two blocks from the Puerta del Sol), this small family-run establishment has a courteous staff member at the desk 24 hours a day for security convenience. You can socialize in the small, comfortable lobby adjacent to the reception desk. The guest rooms are clean, with fresh towels supplied daily. Many inexpensive restaurants and tapas bars are nearby.

Hostal Residencia Americano, Puerta del Sol 11, 28013 Madrid.
☎ **91/522-28-22.** 43 rms. TEL **Metro:** Puerta del Sol.

Rates: 3,300 ptas. ($23.40) single; 4,700 ptas. ($33.40) double; 7,000 ptas. ($49.70) triple; 8,000 ptas. ($56.80) quad. No credit cards.

The Americano, on the third floor of a five-story building, is suitable for those who want to be in the Puerta del Sol area. Owner/manager A. V. Franceschi has refurbished all the rooms, most of them outside chambers with balconies facing the street. Mr. Franceschi promises hot and cold running water 24 hours a day. No breakfast is served.

Hotel Residencia Lisboa, Ventura de la Vega 17, 28014 Madrid.
☎ **91/429-98-94.** Fax 91/369-41-96. 23 rms. **Metro:** Puerta del Sol.

Rates: 4,000 ptas. ($28.40) single; 6,000 ptas. ($42.60) double. AE, DC, MC, V.

The Lisboa, on Madrid's most famous restaurant street, can be a bit noisy, but that's my only complaint. It occupies a neat, modernized town house with compact rooms and central heating in the cooler months. The staff speaks five languages. The Lisboa does not serve breakfast, but it's surrounded by budget dining rooms, cafes, and tascas (bars).

Hostal-Residencia Principado, Zorilla 7, 28014 Madrid.
☎ **91/420-81-87.** 15 rms. **Metro:** Puerta del Sol, Sevilla, or Banco de España. **Bus:** 5, 9, or 53.
Rates: 4,000 ptas. ($28.40) single; 5,800 ptas. ($41.20) double. AE, MC, V.

The two-star Principado is a real find. Located in a well-kept town house, it is run by a gracious owner who keeps everything clean and inviting. New tiles, attractive bedspreads, and curtains give the guest rooms a fresh look. Safety boxes are provided. For breakfast, you can go to a nearby cafe. English is spoken.

---

5 Near Atocha Station

Moderate

Hotel Mercátor, calle Atocha 123, 28012 Madrid. ☎ **91/429-05-00.**
Fax 91/369-12-52. 89 rms. 3 suites. MINIBAR TV TEL
Metro: Atocha or Antón Martín.
Rates: 8,000 ptas. ($56.80) single; 11,250 ptas. ($79.90) double; 12,500 ptas. ($88.80) suite. AE, DC, MC, V. **Parking:** 1,320 ptas. ($9.40).

Only a three-minute walk from the Prado, Centro de Arte Reina Sofía, and the Thyssen-Bornemisza Museum, the Mercátor draws a clientele seeking a good hotel—orderly, well run, and clean, with enough comforts and conveniences to please the weary traveler. The public rooms are simple, outfitted in a vaguely modern type of minimalism. Some of the guest rooms are more inviting than others, especially those with desks and armchairs. Twenty-one units are air-conditioned. The Mercátor is a *residencia*—that is, it offers breakfast only and doesn't have a formal restaurant for lunch and dinner. However, it has a bar/cafeteria serving light meals such as *platos combinados* (combination plates). The hotel has a garage and is within walking distance of the American Express office. Laundry service is provided, plus room service daily from 7am to 10pm.

Hotel Residencia Cortezo, Doctor Cortezo 3, 28012 Madrid.
☎ **91/369-01-01.** Fax 91/369-37-74. 90 rms. A/C MINIBAR TV TEL **Metro:** Tirso de Molina.
Rates: 7,950 ptas. ($56.40) single; 11,225 ptas. ($79.70) double. Breakfast 800 ptas. ($5.70) extra. AE, MC, V. **Parking:** 1,000 ptas. ($7.10).

Just off calle de Atocha, which leads to the railroad station of the same name, the hotel is a short walk from the Plaza Mayor and the Puerta del Sol. The accommodations are comfortable and attractive, with contemporary baths. The beds are springy, the colors are well chosen, the furniture is pleasantly modern; often there is a sitting area with a desk and armchair. The public rooms match the guest rooms in freshness. The hotel was built in 1959 and last renovated in 1989.

Frommer's Cool for Kids: Hotels

Novotel Madrid   (see p. 113) Children under 16 stay free in their parents' room, where the sofa converts into a comfortable bed. Kids delight in the open-air pool and the offerings of the bountiful breakfast buffet.

Plaza Hotel   (see p. 101) Kids like the rooftop pool and sun terrace so much it might be hard to get them to leave for the Prado. The Plaza is a landmark, a skyscraper for Madrid.

Tirol   (see p. 121) This centrally located three-star hotel is a favorite of families seeking good comfort at moderate prices. Kids enjoy the cafeteria.

---

6   Near Retiro/Salamanca

Very Expensive

⭐ **Park Hyatt Villa Magna**, Paseo de la Castellana 22, 28046 Madrid. ☎ **91/576-75-00**, or toll free **800/228-9000** in the U.S. and Canada. Fax 91/575-95-04. 166 rms, 16 suites. A/C MINIBAR TV TEL **Metro:** Rubén Darío.

Rates: 34,000 ptas. ($241.40) single; 40,000 ptas. ($284) double; from 69,500 ptas. ($493.50) suite. Weekend packages: Two nights in a single or double room 40,000 ptas. ($284). Breakfast 2,750 ptas. ($19.50) extra. AE, DC, MC, V. **Parking:** 2,000 ptas. ($14.20).

Considered one of the finest hotels in Europe, the Park Hyatt is faced with slabs of rose-colored granite and set behind a bank of pines and laurels on the city's most fashionable boulevard. It was already a supremely comfortable and elegant modern hotel when Hyatt International took over its management in 1990.

The hotel was conceived when a handful of Spain's elite teamed up to create a setting in which their special friends, along with an array of discriminating international visitors, would be pleased to live and dine. They hired an architect, imported a French decorator (whose style has been described as a contemporary version of neoclassicism), planted gardens, and put the staff through an intensive training program.

Separated from the busy boulevard by a parklike garden, its facade has contemporary lines. In contrast, its interior recaptures the style of Carlos IV, with paneled walls, marble floors, and bouquets of fresh flowers. Through the lobby and drawing rooms passes almost every film star shooting on location in Spain.

This luxury palace offers plush but dignified guest rooms decorated in Louis XVI, English Regency, or Italian provincial style. Each has fresh flowers and a TV with video movies and satellite reception (including news broadcasts beamed in from the United States).

Dining/Entertainment: In the lobby-level champagne bar, the bartender can mix any drink you might fancy, while a pianist provides entertainment. The in-house restaurant, Berceo, serves international food in a glamorous setting. The hotel is known for its summer terraces, Calalú and Berceo, set in gardens; Calalú is the only terrace in Madrid where you can enjoy live jazz performed from Tuesday through Saturday.

Services: 24-hour room service, concierge, car rental, same-day laundry/dry cleaning, limousine service, babysitting.

Facilities: Business center; barber and beauty shop; Villa Magna boutique; tennis and golf available 15 and 25 minutes from hotel, respectively.

★ **The Ritz**, Plaza de la Lealtad 5, 28014 Madrid. ☎ **91/521-28-57,** or toll free **800/435-4542** in the U.S. and Canada.
Fax 91/532-87-76. 158 rms, 24 suites. A/C MINIBAR TV TEL
Metro: Banco de España.
Rates: 33,000–38,000 ptas. ($234.30–$269.80) single; 43,000–44,000 ptas. ($305.30–$312.40) double; from 77,500 ptas. ($550.30) suite. Breakfast 2,000 ptas. ($14.20) extra. AE, DC, MC, V. **Parking:** 2,000 ptas. ($14.20).

This is an international rendezvous of legendary renown, one of the two most famous hotels in Spain. Its name has appeared in countless pages of Spanish-language tabloids that have documented the comings and goings of its glamorous guests. Encased in a turn-of-the-century shell of soaring ceilings and graceful columns, it contains all the luxuries and special attentions world travelers have come to expect of a grand hotel. Billions of pesetas have been spent on renovations since its 1980s acquisition by the British-based Forte chain. The result is a bastion of glamour where, despite modernization, great effort was expended to retain the hotel's Belle Epoque character and architectural details.

No other hotel, except perhaps the Palace, has a more varied history. One of *Les Grand Hotels Européens,* the Ritz was built at the command of Alfonso XIII, with the aid of César Ritz, in 1908. It looks out onto the big circular Plaza de la Lealtad in the center of town, near the 300-acre Retiro Park, facing the Prado museum and its extension, the Palacio de Villahermosa, and the Stock Exchange. The Ritz was constructed when costs were relatively low, and when spaciousness, luxury, and comfort were the order of the day. The facade of the hotel is classed as a historic monument. The new hotels going up in Madrid simply can't match its elegance.

The guest rooms contain fresh flowers, well-accessorized marble baths, and TVs with video movies and satellite reception.

Dining/Entertainment: The hotel maintains a formal dining room decorated in shades of cream, blue, and gold and lined with mirrors and 16th-century Flemish tapestries. Its chefs present an international menu featuring a paella said to be one of the most elaborate in Madrid. In time-honored Spanish tradition, guests tend to dress up here, sometimes even for breakfast. (Management stresses that this is not a resort hotel.) Guests looking for a more casual eatery usually head for the Terraza Ritz.

Services: 24-hour room service, laundry/valet, express checkout, foreign currency exchange.

Facilities: Car-rental kiosk, business center.

Wellington, Velázquez 8, 28001 Madrid. ☎ **91/575-44-00.**
Fax 91/576-41-64. 280 rms, 10 suites. A/C MINIBAR TV TEL
Metro: Retiro or Velázquez.

Rates: 19,520 ptas. ($138.60) single; 30,500 ptas. ($216.60) double; from 53,500 ptas. ($379.90) suite. Breakfast 2,100 ptas. ($14.90) extra. AE, DC, MC, V. **Parking:** 2,000 ptas. ($14.20).

The Wellington, with its impressive antique-tapestried entrance, is one of Madrid's more sedate deluxe hotels, built in the mid-1950s but substantially remodeled since. Set within the Salamanca residential area near Retiro Park, the Wellington offers redecorated rooms, each with cable TV and movie channels, music, two phones (one in the bath), and a guest-operated combination safe. Units are furnished in English-inspired mahogany reproductions, and the baths are modern and immaculate, with marble sheathing and fixtures. Doubles with private terraces (at no extra charge) are the most-sought-after accommodations.

Dining/Entertainment: An added bonus here is El Fogón grill room, styled like a 19th-century tavern, where many of the provisions for the typically Spanish dishes are shipped in from the hotel's own ranch. The pub-style Bar Inglés is a hospitable rendezvous. Lighter meals are served in Las Llaves de Oro (Golden Keys) cafeteria.

Services: 24-hour room service, same-day dry cleaning/laundry.

Facilities: Outdoor pool in summer, garage, beauty parlor.

Expensive

Emperatriz, López de Hoyos 4, 28006 Madrid. ☎ **91/563-80-88.**
Fax 91/563-98-04. 158 rms, 4 suites. MINIBAR TV TEL
Metro: Rubén Darío.

Rates: 19,200 ptas. ($136.30) single; 24,000 ptas. ($170.40) double; 40,000 ptas. ($284) suite. Breakfast 1,200 ptas. ($8.50) extra. AE, DC, MC, V. **Parking:** 1,500 ptas. ($10.70) nearby.

This hotel lies just off the wide paseo de Castellana, only a short walk from some of Madrid's most deluxe hotels, but it charges relatively reasonable rates. Built in the 1970s, it was last renovated in 1994. It contains comfortably unpretentious guest rooms, each with a TV receiving many European channels, and a mixture of both traditional and modern furniture. If one is available, ask for a room on the eighth floor, where you'll get a private terrace at no extra charge.

Dining/Entertainment: Well-upholstered lounges attract globe-trotting Americans, among others, who often have predinner drinks here before patronizing the hotel restaurant, also called Emperatriz, which serves international cuisine.

Services: Room service (daily 6:30am–midnight); concierge arranges business services, car rentals, translators, city tours.

Facilities: Barber/hairdresser, beauty shop.

Grand Hotel Velázquez, calle de Velázquez 62, 28001 Madrid.
☎ **91/575-28-00.** Fax 91/575-28-09. 71 rms, 75 suites.
A/C MINIBAR TV TEL **Metro:** Retiro.
Rates: 15,900 ptas. ($112.90) single; 19,925 ptas. ($141.50) double;
from 21,160 ptas. ($150.20) suite. Breakfast 1,200 ptas. ($8.50) extra.
AE, DC, MC, V. **Parking:** 1,700 ptas. ($12.10).

Opened in 1947 on an affluent residential street near the center of
town, this hotel has a 1930s-style art-deco facade and a 1940s interior
filled with well-upholstered furniture and richly grained paneling.
Several public rooms lead off a central oval area; one includes a bar
area. As in many hotels of its era, the guest rooms vary—some are
large enough for entertaining, with a small but separate sitting area
for reading or watching TV. All receive piped-in music. This is one
of the most attractive medium-size hotels in Madrid with plenty of
comfort and convenience.

   Dining/Entertainment: The in-house restaurant, Las Lanzas,
open for both lunch and dinner, features international cuisine. Guests
often meet one another before dinner in the hotel's Maxwell Bar.

   Services: Room service (daily 7:30am–10:30pm); concierge
arranges car rentals, tours.

   Facilities: Beauty shop, hairdresser.

Hotel Alcalá, Alcalá 66, 28009 Madrid. ☎ **91/435-10-60.**
Fax 91/435-11-05. 153 rms. A/C MINIBAR TV TEL
Metro: Príncipe de Vergara.
Rates: 13,000 ptas. ($95.90) single; 17,900 ptas. ($127.10) double.
Breakfast 1,000 ptas. ($7.10) extra. AE, DC, MC, V. **Parking:** 1,400 ptas.
($9.90).

The Alcalá enjoys an enviable position on a busy boulevard near the
northern edge of Retiro Park, close to the "Golden Triangle" of art
museums, including the Prado. It has tastefully modern guest rooms,
each with voluminous draperies, tile-and-wooden headboards,
coordinated color schemes, and a TV broadcasting many European
channels.

   Dining Entertainment: The ornately decorated Restaurant
Basque serves not only Basque regional dishes but also dishes from
throughout Spain and Europe. In addition, a lower-level coffee shop
is ideal for drinks and light meals. The American Bar, painted a bright
Toledo red, opens off the bilevel lounge.

   Services: Room service (daily 7am–1pm).

   Facilities: Underground garage.

Novotel Madrid, calle Albacete 1, 28027 Madrid. ☎ **91/405-46-00,**
or toll free **800/221-4542** in the U.S. and Canada.
Fax 91/404-11-05. 236 rms. A/C MINIBAR TV TEL
Metro: Concepción. **Directions:** Exit from the M-30 at Barrio de la
Concepción/Parque de las Avenidas, just before reaching the city
limits of central Madrid; then look for the chain's trademark electric-
blue signs.
Rates: 15,794 ptas. ($112.10) single; 18,550 ptas. ($131.70) double.
Children under 16 stay free in parents' room. Weekend rate: 11,130 ptas.

($79) single or double. Breakfast 1,272 ptas. ($9) extra. AE, DC, MC, V. **Parking:** Free.

Novotel was originally intended to serve the hotel needs of a cluster of multinational corporations with headquarters 1¹/₂ miles east of the center of Madrid, but its guest rooms are so comfortable that tourists have begun using it as well. Opened in 1986, it has a position on the highway, away from the maze of sometimes confusing inner-city streets, that makes it attractive to motorists.

The guest rooms are designed in a standardized format whose popularity in Europe has made it one of the hotel industry's most notable success stories. Each contains a well-designed bath, in-house movies, radio, TV, and soundproofing. The sofa, once bolster pillows are removed, can be transformed into a comfortable bed where children can sleep. The English-speaking staff is well versed in both sightseeing attractions and solutions to most business-related problems.

Dining/Entertainment: Beginning at 6am for early risers, the hotel restaurant offers a bountiful buffet breakfast. It also serves lunch and dinner, with both Spanish and international dishes. Clients in Madrid on business often patronize the hotel bar.

Services: Room service (daily 6am–10pm); reception staff arranges car rentals, translators, city tours.

Facilities: Open-air pool.

Moderate

Gran Hotel Colón, Pez Volador 11, 28007 Madrid.
 ☎ **91/573-59-00.** Fax 91/573-08-09. 274 rms, 16 suites.
A/C MINIBAR TV TEL **Metro:** Sainz de Baranda.
Rates: 11,000–13,000 ptas. ($78.10–$92.30) single; 16,000 ptas. ($113.60) double; from 22,000 ptas. ($156.20) suite. Breakfast 900 ptas. ($6.40) extra. AE, DC, MC, V. **Parking:** 1,500 ptas. ($10.70).

The Gran Hotel Colón, west of Retiro Park, is a few minutes from the city center of Metro. Built in 1966, it offers comfortable yet moderately priced accommodations in one of the city's modern hotel structures. More than half the rooms have private balconies, and each contains comfortably traditional furniture, much of it built-in.

To literally top everything off, there's a pool on the roof, 11 stories up, where you can sunbathe with a view of the skyline of Madrid. Other assets include two dining rooms, a covered garage, and Bingo games. One of the Colón's founders was an accomplished interior designer, which accounts for the unusual stained-glass windows and murals in the public rooms and the paintings by Spanish artists in the lounge.

Hotel Claridge, Plaza Condo de Casal 6, 28007 Madrid.
 ☎ **91/551-94-00.** Fax 91/501-03-85. 150 rms. A/C TV TEL
Metro: Conde Casal.
Rates: 9,950 ptas. ($70.60) single; 12,990 ptas. ($92.20) double. Breakfast 700 ptas. ($5) extra. AE, MC, V. **Parking:** 1,700 ptas. ($12.10) in nearby garage.

This contemporary building, last renovated in 1994, is beyond Retiro Park, about five minutes from the Prado by taxi or Metro. The guest rooms are well organized and styled: small, compact, with coordinated furnishings and colors. You can take your meals in the hotel's cafeteria or just relax in the modern lounge.

7   Chamberí

Very Expensive

Castellana Inter-Continental Hotel, paseo de la Castellana 49, 28046 Madrid. ☎ **91/310-02-00,** or toll free **800/327-0200** in the U.S. Fax 91/319-58-53. 270 rms, 35 suites. A/C MINIBAR TV TEL **Metro:** Rubén Darío.

Rates: 29,500–33,000 ptas. ($209.50–$234.30) single; 37,000–41,000 ptas. ($262.70–$291.10) double; from 70,000 ptas. ($497) suite. Breakfast 1,700 ptas. ($12.10). AE, DC, MC, V. **Parking:** 1,600 ptas. ($11.40).

Solid, spacious, and conservatively modern, this is one of the more reliable hotels in Madrid. Built in 1963 as the then-most-prestigious hotel on this famous boulevard, the Castellana Inter-Continental lies behind a barrier of trees within a neighborhood of apartment houses and luxury hotels. Its high-ceilinged public rooms provide a welcome refuge from the Madrileño heat. They're considered a tribute to the art of Spanish masonry, with terrazzo floors and a large-scale collection of angular abstract murals pieced together from multicolored stones and tiles. Most of the accommodations have private balconies and traditional furniture; all have color TVs with in-house videos and many channels beamed in from across Europe.

Dining/Entertainment: La Ronda Bar offers drinks near the elegant Los Continentes Restaurant, serving both a creative and Mediterranean cuisine. In addition, El Jardín is a retreat in summer, with candlelit dinners and soft live background music. Good cookery and thrifty prices are found at El Sarracín.

Services: Concierge; travel agent who books theater tickets, rental cars, airline connections; 24-hour room service; laundry; babysitting.

Facilities: Kiosks and boutiques, hairdresser/barbershop, business center, top-floor gym with sauna and outdoor solarium.

★ **Santo Mauro Hotel,** calle Zurbano 36, 28010 Madrid. ☎ **91/319-69-00.** Fax 91/308-54-17. 31 rms, 6 suites. A/C MINIBAR TV TEL **Metro:** Rubén Darío or Alonso Martínez.

Rates: 27,000 ptas. ($191.70) single; 52,000 ptas. ($369.20) double; from 60,500 ptas. ($429.60) suite. Breakfast 1,950 ptas. ($13.80) extra. AE, DC, MC, V. **Parking:** 1,950 ptas. ($13.80).

This hotel opened in 1991 within the once-decrepit neoclassical walls of a villa built in 1894 for the duke of Santo Mauro. Set within a garden and reminiscent of the kind of architecture you'd expect to find in France, it contains a mixture of rich fabrics, art deco objets and furnishings, and an impressive number of staff members who exceed the number of accommodations by two to one. Each guest room contains an audio system with a wide choice of tapes and CDs as well as many coordinated decor notes, which might include raw-silk curtains, Persian carpets, and jewel-toned colors.

Dining/Entertainment: The Belagua Restaurant is recommended superiorly (see Chapter 5). There's also an elegant bar located off the main lobby, plus tables set up beneath the garden's large trees for drinks and snacks.

Services: 24-hour room service, laundry/valet, reception staff trained in the procurement of practically anything.

Facilities: Indoor pool, health club with sauna and massage.

Expensive

Conde Duque, Plaza Conde Valle de Súchil 5, 28015 Madrid. ☎ **91/447-70-00.** Fax 91/448-35-69. 136 rms, 7 suites. TEL **Metro:** San Bernardo.

Rates (including breakfast): 19,780 ptas. ($140.40) single; 25,850 ptas. ($183.50) double; 30,600 ptas. ($217.30) suite. AE, DC, MC, V.

The modern three-star Conde Duque, near a branch of the Galerías Preciados department store, opens onto a tree-filled plaza in a residential neighborhood near the Glorieta Quevado. The hotel is 12 blocks north of the Plaza de España, off calle de San Bernardo, which starts at the Gran Vía—too long a walk, but a subway stop is nearby. The furnishings include modern built-in headboards and reproductions of 19th-century English pieces. There are bedside lights and telephones.

Dining/Entertainment: The hotel's restaurant, also called Conde Duque, serves both Spanish and international cuisine. For lighter meals or drinks, there is the Bar/Cafeteria Conde Duque.

Services: 24-hour room service, concierge who arranges car rentals, translators, city tours.

Hotel Escultor, Miguel Angel 3, 28010 Madrid. ☎ **91/310-42-03.** Fax 91/319-25-84. 17 rms, 38 suites. A/C MINIBAR TV TEL **Metro:** Rubén Darío.

Rates: Mon–Thurs, 11,775 ptas. ($83.60) single, 18,200 ptas. ($129.20) double or suite. Fri–Sun, 7,975 ptas. ($56.60) single, 9,950 ptas. ($70.60) double or suite. Breakfast 1,100 ptas. ($7.80) extra. AE, DC, MC, V. **Parking:** 1,800 ptas. ($12.80) nearby.

Built in 1975, this comfortably furnished hotel provides fewer services and offers fewer facilities than others in its category, but compensates with larger accommodations. Each unit has its own charm and contemporary styling, with video films and a layout that's well organized, efficient, and logical. The hotel is fully air-conditioned, and the staff provides information about facilities in the surrounding neighborhood.

Dining/Entertainment: The hotel has a small but comfortable bar, open nightly from 7pm to 1am, and a traditional restaurant, the Señorio de Erazu, which closes on Saturday at lunch and all day on Sunday.

Services: Room service at breakfast only (7–11am).

Miguel Angel, Miguel Angel 29–31, 28010 Madrid.
☎ **91/442-81-99.** Fax 91/442-53-20. 278 rms. 26 suites.
A/C MINIBAR TV TEL **Metro:** Rubén Darío.

Rates: Mon–Thurs, 27,350 ptas. ($194.20) single or double. Breakfast 1,800 ptas. ($12.80). Fri–Sun (including breakfast), 13,125 ptas. ($93.20) single, 16,600 ptas. ($117.90) double. Suites from 51,000 ptas. ($362.10) all week. AE, DC, MC, V. **Parking:** 1,800 ptas. ($12.80).

Just off paseo de la Castellana, Miguel Angel, sleekly modern, opened its doors in 1975 and has been renovated and kept up-to-date periodically ever since. It has much going for it—ideal location, contemporary styling, good furnishings and art objects, an efficient staff, and plenty of comfort. Behind its facade is an expansive sun terrace on several levels, with clusters of garden furniture that are surrounded by semitropical paintings.

The guest rooms contain color-coordinated fabrics and carpets and, in many cases, reproductions of classic Iberian furniture. Each is soundproof and has a radio and TV. Art exhibitions are sponsored in the arcade of boutiques.

Dining/Entertainment: The Farnesio bar is decorated in a Spanish Victorian style, and piano music is played from 8pm. A well-managed restaurant on the premises is the Florencia, which serves a set lunch or dinner for 6,000 ptas. ($42.60). Dinner is also served until around 3 am in the Zacarias boîte restaurant, where you can dine while watching an occasional cabaret or musical performance.

Services: 24-hour room service, same-day laundry/valet.

Facilities: Indoor heated pool, saunas, hairdressers, drugstore, boutiques.

Residencia Bréton, Bréton de los Herreros 29, 28003 Madrid.
☎ **91/442-83-00.** Fax 91/441-38-16. 56 rms. A/C MINIBAR TV TEL **Metro:** Ríos Rosas.

Rates: 13,500 ptas. ($95.90) single; 18,550 ptas. ($131.70) double. Breakfast 1,000 ptas. ($7.10) extra. AE, DC, MC, V. **Parking:** 1,200 ptas. ($8.50) nearby.

You'll find this modern hotel on a side street several blocks from paseo de la Castellana. It's well furnished with reproductions of Iberian pieces. As a residencia it doesn't offer a major dining room, but it does have a little bar and breakfast room adjoining the reception lounge. All the guest rooms have wooden beds, wrought-iron electrical fixtures, wall-to-wall curtains, comfortable chairs, and tilework painted with ornate designs in the baths.

Inexpensive

Hostal Residencia Don Diego, calle de Velázquez 45, 28001 Madrid. ☎ **91/435-07-60.** Fax 91/431-42-63. 58 rms. A/C TEL **Metro:** Velázquez.

Rates: 5,800 ptas. ($41.20) single; 7,500 ptas. ($53.30) double; 10,125 ptas. ($71.90) triple. Breakfast 600 ptas. ($4.30) extra. MC, V.

On the fifth floor of a building with an elevator, Don Diego is in a combination residential/commercial neighborhood that's relatively convenient to many of the city monuments. The vestibule contains an elegant winding staircase accented with iron griffin heads supporting its balustrade. The hotel is warmly inviting, filled with leather couches and a kind of comfortable, no-nonsense style of angular but attractive furniture. A bar stands at the far end of the main sitting room. The hotel's cafeteria serves breakfast starting at 8am and remains open for drinks and snacks until 4 pm. From 8pm to midnight daily you can also order drinks and snacks, especially sandwiches and omelets. Laundry service is provided, and room service is available daily from 8 am to midnight.

8   Chamartín

Very Expensive

Eurobuilding, calle Padre Damián 23, 28036 Madrid.
☎ **91/345-45-00.** Fax 91/345-45-76. 420 rms, 100 suites.
A/C MINIBAR TV TEL **Metro:** Cuzco.
Rates: 25,000 ptas. ($177.50) single; 32,000 ptas. ($227.20) double; from 40,000 ptas. ($284) suite. Breakfast 1,900 ptas. ($13.50) extra. AE, DC, MC, V. **Parking:** 1,800 ptas. ($12.80).

Even while it was on the drawing boards, the rumor was that this five-star sensation of white marble would provide, in the architect's words, "a new concept in deluxe hotels." The Eurobuilding long ago lived up to its advance billing, reflecting a high level in taste and design. It's two hotels linked by a courtyard, away from the city center but right in the midst of apartment houses, boutiques, nightclubs, first-class restaurants, tree-shaded squares, and the heart of the modern Madrid business world.

The more glamorous of the twin buildings—called Las Estencias de Eurobuilding—contains only suites decorated in pastel shades. These suites were renovated in various stages in the early 1990s. Drinks await you in the refrigerator. Ornately carved gold-and-white beds, background music, a roomwide terrace for breakfast and cocktail entertaining—all are tastefully coordinated. Across the courtyard, the companion Eurobuilding contains less impressive— yet still very comfortable—single and double rooms, many with views from private balconies of the formal garden and pool below. All the accommodations have TVs with video movies and satellite reception, security doors, and individual safes.

Dining/Entertainment: Le Relais Coffee Shop is suitable for a quick bite, and Le Relais Restaurant offers buffets at both breakfast and lunch. For more formal dining at lunch and dinner, La Taberna features a selection of Spanish and international cuisine, specializing in seafood and various paella dishes.

Services: Laundry/valet, concierge, 24-hour room service, babysitting.

Facilities: Health club with sauna, outdoor pool.

Melía Castilla, calle Capitán Haya 43, 28020 Madrid.

☎ **91/571-22-11,** or toll free **800/336-3542** in the U.S.
Fax 91/571-2210. 896 rms, 14 suites. A/C MINIBAR TV TEL
Metro: Cuzco.

Rates: 25,000–30,500 ptas. ($177.50–$216.60) single; 31,000–36,000
ptas. ($220.10–$255.60) double; from 63,000 ptas. ($447.30) suite.
Breakfast 1,950 ptas. ($13.80) extra. AE, DC, MC, V. **Parking:** 1,850
ptas. ($13.10).

This mammoth hotel qualifies, along with the Palace, as one of the
largest hotels in Europe. Loaded with facilities and built primarily
to accommodate huge conventions, the Melía Castilla also caters to
the needs of the individual traveler. Everything is larger than life here:
You need a floor plan to direct yourself around its precincts. The
lounges and corridors of pristine marble are vast—there are even a
landscaped garden and a showroom full of the latest-model cars.

Each of the twin-bedded rooms comes equipped with a radio, a
color TV, and modern furniture. The Melía Castilla is in the north
of Madrid, about a block west of paseo de la Castellana, a short drive
from the Chamartín railway station.

Dining/Entertainment: The hotel has a coffee shop, a seafood
restaurant, a restaurant specializing in paella and other rice dishes,
cocktail lounges, and the Trinidad nightclub. In addition, there's the
restaurant/show, Scala Melía Castilla.

Services: 24-hour room service, hairdresser/barber, concierge,
babysitting, laundry/valet.

Facilities: Pool, shopping arcade with souvenir shops and
bookstore, saunas, gymnasium, parking garage.

Expensive

Cuzco, paseo de la Castellana 133, 28046 Madrid. ☎ **91/556-06-00.**
Fax 91/556-03-72. 320 rms, 10 suites. A/C MINIBAR TV TEL
Metro: Cuzco.

Rates: 15,440 ptas. ($109.60) single; 20,550 ptas. ($145.90) double;
from 26,000 ptas. ($184.60) suite. Breakfast 1,190 ptas. ($8.40) extra.
AE, DC, MC, V. **Parking:** 1,500 ptas. ($10.70).

Popular with businesspeople and tour groups, Cuzco lies in a
commercial neighborhood of big buildings, government ministries,
spacious avenues, and the main Congress Hall. The Chamartín
railway station is a 10-minute walk north, so it's a popular and
convenient address. This 15-floor structure, set back from Madrid's
longest boulevard, has been redecorated and modernized many times
since it was completed in 1967. The architect of the Cuzco allowed
for spacious guest rooms, each with a separate sitting area and video
movies.

Dining/Entertainment: There are a bilevel snack bar/cafeteria and
a cocktail bar. The lounge is a forest of marble pillars and leather
armchairs, the ambience enhanced by contemporary oil paintings and
tapestries.

Facilities: Beauty parlor, sauna, massage, gymnasium.

Hotel Chamartín, Agustín de Foxa, Estacíon de Chamartín, 28036
Madrid. ☎ **91/323-30-87.** Fax 91/733-02-14. 378 rms, 18 suites.
A/C MINIBAR TV TEL **Metro:** Chamartín. **Bus:** 5.
Rates: 12,500 ptas. ($88.80) single; 17,300 ptas. ($122.80) double;
from 28,000 ptas. ($198.80) suite. Breakfast 1,000 ptas. ($7.10) extra.
AE, DC, MC, V. **Parking:** 1,200 ptas. ($8.50) in nearby garage.

This brick-sided hotel soars nine stories above the northern periphery
of Madrid. It's part of the massive modern shopping complex attached
to the Chamartín railway station, although once you're inside your
soundproofed room, the noise of the railway station will seem far
away. The owner of the building is RENFE, Spain's government
railway system, but the nationwide chain that administers it is HUSA
Hotels. The hotel is 15 minutes by taxi from both the airport and
the historic core of Madrid, and it's conveniently close to one of the
capital's busiest Metro stops. Especially oriented to the business
traveler, the Chamartín offers a video screen in the lobby that posts
the arrival and departure of all trains.

　Dining/Entertainment: The hotel restaurant, Cota 13, serves an
international cuisine. A coffee bar serves breakfast daily.

　Services: Room service (7am–midnight).

　Facilities: Currency-exchange kiosk, travel agency, car-rental
office. A short walk from the hotel lobby, in the railway-station
complex, are a handful of shops and movie theaters, a roller-skating
rink, a disco, and ample parking.

Moderate

Aristos, avenida Pío XII 34, 28016 Madrid. ☎ **91/345-04-50.**
Fax 91/345-10-23. 24 rms. A/C TV TEL **Metro:** Pío XII.
Rates: 12,000 ptas. ($85.20) single; 16,000 ptas. ($113.60) double.
Breakfast 750 ptas. ($5.30) extra. AE, DC, MC, V. **Parking:** 1,500 ptas.
($10.70).

This three-star hotel is in an up-and-coming residential area of Madrid, not far from the Eurobuilding (see above). Its main advantage
is a garden in front, where you can lounge, have a drink, or order a
complete meal. The hotel's restaurant, El Chaflán, is frequented by
residents of the neighborhood in addition to hotel visitors. Each guest
room has a small terrace and an uncomplicated collection of modern
furniture.

9　Argüelles/Moncloa

Very Expensive

Husa Princesa, Serrano Jover 3, 28015 Madrid. ☎ **91/542-35-00.**
Fax 91/559-46-65. 320 rms, 38 suites. A/C TV TEL
Metro: Argüelles.
Rates: 24,800 ptas. ($176.10) single; 31,200 ptas. ($221.50) double;
from 61,000 ptas. ($433.10) suite. Breakfast 1,950 ptas. ($13.80)
extra. AE, DC, MC, V. **Parking:** 2,500 ptas. ($17.80).

Built during the mid-1970s and renovated after its 1991 takeover by the Spanish HUSA chain, the Princesa is a sprawling hotel designed like a series of massive rectangular solids clustered into an angular whole. The concrete-and-glass facade overlooks busy boulevards in the city center. The Princesa is well patronized by both businesspeople and groups of tourists. Each guest room contains comfortable contemporary furniture and a modernized bath.

Dining/Entertainment: The hotel's restaurant is called Rincón de Argüelles. There is also the Bar Royal.

Services: 24-hour room service, concierge, babysitting.

Facilities: Large assortment of conference rooms, underground garage, hairdressing salon.

Expensive

Melía Madrid, Princesa 17, 28008 Madrid. ☎ **91/541-8200,** or toll free **800/336-3542** in the U.S. Fax 91/541-19-05. 260 rms, 5 suites. A/C MINIBAR TV TEL **Metro:** Rodríguez.

Rates: 25,000 ptas. ($177.50) single; 26,000 ptas. ($184.60) double; from 45,000 ptas. ($319.50) suite. Breakfast 1,200 ptas. ($8.50) extra. AE, DC, MC, V. **Parking:** 1,600 ptas. ($11.40).

Here you'll find one of the most modern yet uniquely Spanish hotels in the country. Its 23 floors of wide picture windows have taken a permanent position in the capital's skyline. Each guest room is comfortable, spacious, and filled with contemporary furnishings, plus a TV broadcasting video movies and many channels from across Europe. Most offer views over the Madrid skyline. The chalk-white walls dramatize the flamboyant use of color accents; the baths are sheathed in marble.

Dining/Entertainment: Restaurant Princesa is elegant and restful; equally popular is the Don Pepe Grill. The cuisine in both restaurants is international and includes an array of Japanese and Indian dishes. There are also three bars and a coffee shop.

Services: 24-hour room service, concierge, babysitting, hairdresser/barber, laundry.

Facilities: A gallery that includes souvenir shops and bookstores; health club with sauna and massage.

Moderate

Tirol, Marqués de Urquijo 4, 28008 Madrid. ☎ **91/548-19-00.** Fax 91/541-39-58. 97 rms, 4 suites. A/C TEL **Metro:** Argüelles. **Bus:** 2 or 21.

Rates: 7,300 ptas. ($51.80) single; 10,325 ptas. ($73.30) double; 14,390 ptas. ($102.20) suite. Breakfast 535 ptas. ($3.80) extra. MC, V. **Parking:** 1,710 ptas. ($12.10).

A short walk from the Plaza de España and the Melía Madrid Hotel (see above) is a good choice for clean, unpretentious comfort. A three-star hotel, the Tirol offers only nine singles and eight of the hotel's accommodations have private terraces. Furnishings are simple and functional. There are a cafeteria and a parking garage in the hotel.

5

Madrid Dining

IT'S THE CUSTOM IN MADRID TO CONSUME THE BIG MEAL OF THE DAY BETWEEN 2 and 4pm. After a recuperative siesta, Madrileños then enjoy *tapas* (snacks) in hundreds of *tascas* (bars) scattered throughout the capital.

All this nibbling is then followed by dinner—more likely a light supper—in a restaurant, usually beginning about 9:30pm to as late as midnight. Many restaurants, however, start serving dinner at 8pm to accommodate visitors from other countries.

Madrid restaurant prices shock first-time visitors—that is, those who don't live in such expensive cities as Tokyo, Oslo, London, and Paris. Restaurants listed in this chapter as **Very Expensive** charge 6,000 ptas. ($42.60) and up per person for a meal. Meals include service and tax (ranging from 6% to 12% depending on the restaurant), but this doesn't include drinks, which add to the tab considerably. Restaurants rated **Expensive** charge 4,000 to 6,000 ptas. ($28.40 to $42.60) per person for a meal; **Moderate** establishments ask 2,000 to 4,000 ptas. ($14.20 to $28.40); and **Inexpensive** eateries offer meals under 2,000 ptas. ($14.20) per person.

BUDGET DINING   If you can't afford the prices charged by most first-class restaurants in Madrid, you'll find a variety of budget dining options to keep the bill down.

Menu del Día & Cubierto   Order the *menu del día* (menu of the day) or *cubierto*, both of which are fixed-price menus based on what's fresh at the market that day. They're the finest dining bargains in Madrid. Usually, each will include a first course, such as fish soup or hors d'oeuvres, followed by a main dish, plus bread, dessert, and the house wine. Though you won't have a large choice, you'll never get the most expensive ingredients, of course.

Menu Turístico   The *menu turístico* is a similar fixed-price menu, but for many it's too large, especially at lunch. Only those with enormous appetites find it the best bargain.

Cafeterias   These are not self-service establishments but restaurants serving light, often American, cuisine. Go to one for breakfast instead of dining at your hotel, unless breakfast is included in the room price. Some cafeterias offer no hot meals, but many feature combined plates of fried eggs, french fries, veal, lettuce-and-tomato salads, or light fare like hot dogs and hamburgers.

Tapas   An option is to dine well at lunch and then stop by a tasca (local tavern) for an evening meal of appetizer-size tapas, which might be eggs in mayonnaise, potato omelets, codfish salad, cured ham, Russian salad, octopus in garlic-mayonnaise sauce, grilled mushrooms, stuffed peppers, potato croquettes, and other such fare.

Don't overtip. Follow the local custom. Theoretically, service is included in the price of your meal, but it's customary to leave 10% additional.

For more details on dining (such as when and what to eat) see "Food and Drink" in Chapter 1.

1   Near the Plaza de las Cortés

Expensive

El Espejo, paseo de Recoletos 31. ☎ 308-23-47.

> **Cuisine:** INTERNATIONAL. **Reservations:** Required. **Metro:** Banco de España or Colón. **Bus:** 27.
>
> **Prices:** Appetizers 950–1,400 ptas. ($6.70–$9.90); main courses 1,650–2,700 ptas. ($11.70–$19.20); *menu del día* 3,500 ptas. ($24.90). AE, DC, MC, V.
>
> **Open:** Lunch Sun–Fri 1–4pm; dinner daily 9pm–midnight.

Here you'll find good-tasting food and one of the most perfectly crafted art nouveau decors in Madrid. If the weather is good, you can choose one of the establishment's outdoor tables, served by a battery of uniformed waiters who carry food across the busy street to a green area flanked with trees and strolling pedestrians. I personally prefer a table inside, within view of the tile maidens with vines and flowers entwined in their hair. You'll pass through a charming cafe/bar, where many visitors linger before walking down a hallway toward the spacious dining room. Dishes include grouper ragoût with clams, steak tartare, guinea fowl with Armagnac, and lean duck meat with pineapple. Profiteroles with cream and chocolate sauce make a delectable dessert.

Moderate

Edelweiss, calle Jovellanos 7. ☎ 521-03-26.

> **Cuisine:** GERMAN. **Reservations:** Not accepted. **Metro:** Sevilla. **Bus:** 5.
>
> **Prices:** Appetizers 800–1,200 ptas. ($5.70–$8.50); main courses 1,200–2,600 ptas. ($8.50–$18.50); fixed-price menu 1,900 ptas. ($13.50). AE, MC, V.
>
> **Open:** Lunch daily 12:30–4pm; dinner Mon–Sat 8:30pm–midnight. **Closed:** Aug.

Edelweiss is a German standby that has provided good-quality food and service at moderate prices since World War II. During peak dining hours the bar is likely to be full of clients waiting for tables. You are served hearty portions of food, mugs of draft beer, and fluffy pastries; that's why there's always a wait. *Tip:* To beat the crowds, go for dinner at un-Spanish hours, say around 9pm. But even when it's jammed, service is almost always courteous. You can start with Bismarck herring, then dive into goulash with spaetzle or Eisbein (pigs' knuckles) with sauerkraut and mashed potatoes, the most popular dish. Finish with homemade apple tart. The decor is vaguely German, with travel posters and wood-paneled walls. Edelweiss is air-conditioned in summer.

Inexpensive

La Trucha, Manuel Fernández González 3. ☎ 492-58-33.

> **Cuisine:** SPANISH/SEAFOOD. **Reservations:** Recommended. **Metro:** Sevilla.
> **Prices:** Appetizers 350–2,600 ptas. ($2.50–$18.50); main courses 950–3,200 ptas. ($6.70–$22.70), *menu del día* 2,800 ptas. ($19.90). No credit cards.
> **Open:** Lunch Mon–Sat 1–4pm; dinner Mon–Sat 8pm–midnight.
> **Closed:** Aug.

With its Andalusian tavern ambience, La Trucha boasts a street-level bar and small dining room—the arched ceiling and whitewashed walls festive with hanging braids of garlic, dried peppers, and onions. On the lower level the walls of a second bustling area are covered with antiques, bullfight notices, and bric-a-brac. The specialty is fish, and there's a complete à la carte menu including *truchas* (trout); *verbenas de ahumados* (literally a "street party" of smoked delicacies); a stew called *fabada* ("glorious"—made with beans, Galician ham, black sausage, and smoked bacon); and *comida casera rabo de toro* (homestyle oxtail). No one should miss nibbling on the *tapas variadas* in the bar. If this Trucha turns out to be too crowded, there's another at Núñez de Arce 6 (☎ 532-08-82).

Frommer's Smart Traveler: Restaurants

Value-Conscious Travelers Should Consider the Following:

1. Most budget restaurants offer a *cubierto* or *menu del día*. It's not very adventurous, and limited in selections, but in most cases it's at least 30% cheaper than ordering à la carte.

2. Often, major restaurants will offer a *menu del día* at lunch (the Madrid equivalent of a businessperson's lunch) but will revert to expensive à la carte listings in the evening. Check the menu offerings posted outside the restaurant.

3. Patronize the *tascas* (local taverns), and order two or three *tapas* (hors d'oeuvres). Most portions are generous, and you can dine for a quarter of the price you'd pay in most restaurants.

4. Look for the *platas del día* (daily specials). They're invariably fresh, and usually carry a much lower price tag than regular à la carte listings.

5. Ask for the *vino de la casa* (house wine); it's served in a carafe and is only a fraction of the cost of bottled wine.

6. Anything consumed standing up at a counter or sitting on a bar stool is cheaper than at a table.

7. Patronize the famous budget restaurant streets of Madrid: calle del Barco, Ventura de la Vega, and calle Echegaray.

2   Near the Plaza de España

Expensive

Bajamar, Gran Vía 78. ☎ 559-59-03.

Cuisine: SEAFOOD. **Reservations:** Recommended. **Metro:** Plaza de España.
Prices: Appetizers 850–3,600 ptas. ($6–$25.60); main courses 1,750–4,500 ptas. ($12.40–$32). AE, DC, MC, V.
Open: Lunch daily 1–4pm; dinner daily 8pm–midnight.

Bajamar is one of the best fish houses in Spain, and it's right in the heart of the city, near the Plaza de España. Both fish and shellfish are shipped in fresh daily by air from their points of origin. Lobster, king crab, prawns, soft-shell crabs, and the like are all priced according to weight. There's a large array of reasonably priced dishes as well. The setting is contemporary and attractive, and the service smooth and professional. The menu is in English. For an appetizer, I'd recommend half a dozen giant oysters or rover crayfish. The special seafood soup is a most satisfying selection, a meal in itself. Try also the lobster bisque. Some of the more recommendable main courses include turbot Gallego style, the special seafood paella, even baby squid cooked in its ink. Desserts are simple, including the chef's custard.

Moderate

Las Cuevas del Duque, calle de la Princesa 16. ☎ 559-50-37.

Cuisine: SPANISH. **Reservations:** Required. **Metro:** Ventura Rodríguez. **Bus:** 1, 2, or 42.
Prices: Appetizers 800–3,000 ptas. ($5.70–$21.30); main courses 1,875–3,000 ptas. ($13.30–$21.30). AE, DC, MC, V.
Open: Lunch daily 1–4pm; dinner daily 8pm–midnight.

In front of the duke of Alba's palace, a short walk from the Plaza de España, is Las Cuevas del Duque, with an underground bar and a small, 10-table *mesón* that serves such simple Spanish fare as roast suckling pig, sirloin, lamb cutlets, and a few seafood dishes, including fish cooked in a sheathing of salt. In fair weather a few tables are set outside, beside a tiny triangular garden. Other tables line calle de la Princesa and make an enjoyable roost for an afternoon drink.

Budget

 Vera Cruz, San Leonardo 5. ☎ 547-11-50.

Cuisine: SPANISH. **Reservations:** Not required. **Metro:** Plaza de España.
Prices: Appetizers 350–550 ptas. ($2.50–$3.90); main courses 550–950 ptas. ($3.90–$6.70); fixed-price menu 950 ptas. ($6.70). No credit cards.
Open: Lunch daily 1–5pm; dinner daily 8pm–midnight.

Behind the Plaza de España, a short walk from the soaring Edificio España, you'll find this old standby for hungry budget-minded diners.

It's a simple *económico*, but the food is acceptable and the service polite. The *menu del día* usually includes soup or hors d'oeuvres, followed by a meat or fish dish, then cheese or fruit, plus bread and wine. The Vera Cruz also has daily specials like paella and *cocido* (a typical Madrid dish of chickpeas, sausage, cabbage, and potatoes).

3   On or Near the Gran Vía

Moderate

Arce, Augusto Figueroa 32. ☎ **522-59-13.**

> **Cuisine:** BASQUE. **Reservations:** Recommended. **Metro:** Colón.
> **Prices:** Appetizers 1,100–2,850 ptas. ($7.80–$20.20); main courses 2,150–2,850 ptas. ($15.30–$20.20). AE, DC, MC, V.
> **Open:** Lunch Mon–Fri 1:30–4pm; dinner Mon–Sat 9pm–midnight.
> **Closed:** Week before Easter, Aug 15–31.

Arce has brought some of the best modern interpretations of Basque cuisine to the palates of Madrid, thanks to the enthusiasm of owner/ chef Inaki Camba and his wife, Theresa. In a comfortably decorated dining room designed for the unabashed enjoyment of food without unnecessary decorative frills, you can enjoy simple preparations of the finest available ingredients, where the natural flavors are designed to dominate your taste buds. Examples include a salad of fresh scallops, an oven-baked casserole of fresh boletus mushrooms with few seasonings other than the woodsy taste of the original ingredients, unusual preparations of hake, and seasonal variations of game dishes such as pheasant and woodcock.

La Barraca, Reina 29–31. ☎ **532-71-54.**

> **Cuisine:** VALENCIAN. **Reservations:** Recommended. **Metro:** Gran Vía or Sevilla. **Bus:** 1, 2, or 74.
> **Prices:** Appetizers 650–4,000 ptas ($4.60–$28.40); main courses 1,800– 5,000 ptas. ($12.80–$35.50); fixed-price menu 2,800 ptas. ($19.90). AE, DC, MC, V.
> **Open:** Lunch daily 1–4pm; dinner daily 8:30pm–midnight.

La Barraca is like a country inn—right off the Gran Vía. This Valencian-style restaurant is well-managed and recommendable for its tasty provincial cooking. There are four dining rooms, three of which lie one flight above street level, and they're colorfully cluttered with ceramics, paintings, photographs, Spanish lanterns, flowers, and local artifacts. The house specialty is paella à la valenciana, made with fresh shellfish. The portions are enormous—only the most ravenous will clean out the skillet. Specialties in the appetizer category include *desgarrat* (a salad made with codfish and red peppers), Barraca mussels, and shrimp Orly. In addition to the paella, you can select from at least 16 other rice dishes, including rice with duck and rice with conger eel. Main-dish specialties include angler fish and prawns brochette and rabbit with fines herbes. Lemon-and-vodka sorbet makes a good finish.

Dining In Central Madrid

Alkalde
El Amparo
El Anciano Rey de los Vinos
Antonio Sánchez
Arce
La Argentina
Bajamar
La Barraca
La Bola
Café de Oriente
Casa Alberto
Casablanca
Casa Ciriaco
Casa Lucio
Casa Mingo
Casa Paco
El Cenador del Prado
Cervecería Alemania
Cervecería Santa Bárbara
La Chata
El Cuchi
Las Cuevas del Duque
Las Cuevas de Luís Candelas
Edelweiss
El Espejo
Los Galayos
La Galetta
La Gamella
Gran Café de Gijón
Gur-Etxea (Restaurant Vasco)
Horcher
Hylogui
El Inca
Jockey
Lhardy
El Mentidero de la Villa
Mesón Las Descalzas
Nabucco
Paellería Valenciana
Platerías Comedor
La Plaza
Ríofrío
El Schotis
Sobrino de Botín
Taberna Carmencita
Taberna del Alabardero
Taberna Toscana
Tienda de Vinos
La Trucha
V.I.P.
Vera Cruz
Viridiana

Casablanca, calle del Barquillo 27. ☎ 521-1568.

Cuisine: SPANISH/CONTINENTAL/AMERICAN. **Reservations:** Required. **Metro:** Alonso Martínez.

Prices: Appetizers 475–1,200 ptas. ($3.40–$8.50); main courses 1,250–2,200 ptas. ($8.90–$15.60). AE, DC, MC, V.

Open: Lunch daily 1:30–4pm; dinner daily 9pm–1am.

Information ℹ

Post Office ✉

Church ✝■

The theme here, of course, is the famous movie, and memorabilia (such as posters of Bogart and Bergman) are scattered over the two levels of its premises. The cuisine served at the umbrella-covered tables is a combination of Spanish, French, Italian, and American. You might begin with leeks in pastry. The chef's specialties include red peppers with smoked salmon, raw salmon marinated in champagne, filet mignon Bogart, and spaghetti vongole prepared with cream and shellfish. Selections from the American cuisine include Maryland-style fried chicken, barbecue spareribs, and chili con carne made Western style (hot). The owner is Dick Angstadt, an American. Casablanca also has a tapas bar.

El Mentidero de la Villa, Santo Tomé 6. ☎ **308-12-85.**

Cuisine: JAPANESE/SPANISH. **Reservations:** Required. **Metro:** Alonso Martínez, Colón, or Gran Vía. **Bus:** 37.
Prices: Appetizers 950–1,700 ptas. ($6.70–$12.10); main courses 2,200–2,900 ptas. ($15.60–$20.60). AE, DC, MC, V.
Open: Lunch Mon–Fri 1:30–4pm; dinner Mon–Sat 9pm–midnight.
Closed: Last two weeks of Aug.

This restaurant is certainly a multicultural experience. The owner describes the cuisine as "modern Spanish with Japanese influence; the cooking technique is French." Regardless of how confusing that may sound, the end result is usually a graceful achievement; each ingredient in every dish manages to retain its natural flavor. The kitchen staff prepare such dishes as veal liver in sage sauce, a version of spring rolls filled with fresh shrimp and leeks, noisettes of veal with tarragon, filet steak with a sauce of mustard and brown sugar, medallions of venison with chestnut and celery purées, and desserts like sherry trifle. The postmodern decor includes softly trimmed tromp-l'oeil ceilings, exposed wine racks, ornate columns with unusual lighting, and a handful of antique carved horses from long-defunct merry-go-rounds.

Inexpensive

 Paellería Valenciana, Caballero de Gracia 12. ☎ **531-17-35.**

Cuisine: SPANISH. **Reservations:** Recommended. **Metro:** Gran Vía.
Prices: Appetizers 600–700 ptas. ($4.30–$5); main courses 900–1,200 ptas. ($6.40–$8.50); fixed-price menus 1,250–1,600 ptas. ($8.90–$11.40). AE, MC, V.
Open: Lunch only, Mon–Fri 1:30–4:30pm.

This lunch-only restaurant ranks as one of the best in the city for value. The specialty is paella, which you must order by phone in advance. Once you arrive, you might begin with a homemade soup or the house salad, then follow with the paella, served in an iron skillet. At least two diners must order this rib-sticking fare. The choice of desserts includes the chef's special pride: razor-thin orange slices flavored with rum, coconut, sugar, honey, and raspberry sauce. A carafe of house wine comes with the fixed-price menu, and after lunch the owner comes around dispensing free cognac.

4 Near the Puerta del Sol

Expensive

 El Cenador del Prado, calle del Prado 4. ☎ **429-15-61.**

Cuisine: INTERNATIONAL. **Reservations:** Recommended. **Metro:** Puerta del Sol.

Prices: Appetizers 900–1,500 ptas. ($6.40–$10.70); main courses 1,750–2,000 ptas. ($12.40–$14.20); fixed-price menu 13,200 ptas. ($93.70). AE, DC, MC, V.
Open: Lunch Mon–Fri 1:45–4pm; dinner Mon–Sat 9pm–midnight.
Closed: Aug 15–31.

This restaurant is deceptively elegant. In the simple anteroom an attendant will check your coat and packages in an elaborately carved armoire, and you'll be graciously ushered into one of a trio of rooms. Two of the rooms, done in rich tones of peach and sepia, have thick cove moldings and English furniture in addition to floor-to-ceiling gilded mirrors. A third room, perhaps the most popular, is ringed with lattices and floods of sun from a skylight.

You can enjoy such well-flavored specialties as house-style crêpes with salmon and Iranian caviar and many other succulent dishes, including a salad of crimson peppers and salted anchovies, a casserole of snails and oysters with mushrooms, a ceviche of salmon and shellfish, soup studded with tidbits of hake and clams in a potato-and-leek base, and sea bass with candied lemons. Jackets and ties for men are recommended.

Lhardy, carrera de San Jéronimo 8. ☎ **521-33-85.**

Cuisine: SPANISH. **Reservations:** Recommended for the upstairs dining room. **Metro:** Puerta del Sol.
Prices: Appetizers 1,100–2,100 ptas. ($7.80–$14.90); main dishes 3,000–5,000 ptas. ($21.30–$35.50). AE, DC, MC, V.
Open: Lunch Mon–Sat 1–3:30pm; dinner Mon–Sat 9–11:30pm.
Closed: Late July to early Sept.

Lhardy has been a Madrileño legend since it opened in 1839 as a gathering place for the city's literati and political leaders. In 1846, it entertained the playwright/novelist Alexandre Dumas père. Its street level contains what might be the most elegant snack bar in Spain. Within a dignified antique setting of marble and varnished hardwoods, cups of steaming consommé are dispensed from silver samovars into delicate porcelain cups and rows of croquettes, tapas, and sandwiches are served.

Customers pay for their food at a cashier's kiosk near the entrance and then stand at counters or take their food elsewhere. Cups of consommé cost 119 ptas. (80¢) each, while virtually anything else you select (tapas, sandwiches, or pastries) usually costs around 80 ptas. (60¢) each. The ground-floor deli/takeout service is open Monday through Saturday from 9am to 9pm and Sunday from 9am to 2:30pm.

The real culinary skill of the place, however, is visible on Lhardy's second floor, where you'll find a formal restaurant decorated in the ornate Belle Epoque style of *Isabel Segunda*. Specialties of the house include fish; pork; veal; tripe in garlicky tomato-and-onion wine sauce; and *cocido*, the celebrated chickpea stew of Madrid. *Soufflé sorpresa* (baked Alaska) is the dessert specialty.

Platerías Comedor, Plaza de Santa Ana 11, ☎ **429-70-48.**

Cuisine: SPANISH. **Reservations:** Required. **Metro:** Puerta del Sol.

Prices: Appetizers 1,200–1,800 ptas. ($8.50–$12.80); main courses 4,000–4,500 ptas. ($28.40–$32). AE, DC, MC, V.
Open: Lunch Mon–Fri 1:30–4pm; dinner Mon–Sat 9pm–midnight.

One of the most charming dining rooms in Madrid, Platerías Comedor has richly brocaded walls evocative of 19th-century Spain. Despite the busy socializing on the famous plaza outside, this serene oasis makes few concessions to the new generation in its food, decor, or formally attired waiters. Specialties include beans with clams, stuffed partridge with cabbage and sausage, magret of duckling with pomegranates, duck liver with white grapes, veal stew with snails and mushrooms, and guinea hen with figs and plums. You might follow with passionfruit sorbet.

Moderate

Casa Paco, Puerta Cerrada 11. ☎ **366-31-66.**

Cuisine: STEAK. **Reservations:** Required. **Metro:** Puerta del Sol, Ópera, or La Latina. **Bus:** 3, 21, or 65.
Prices: Appetizers 1,000–1,200 ptas. ($7.10–$8.50); main courses 2,500–3,500 ptas. ($17.80–$24.90); fixed-price menu 3,000 ptas. ($21.30). DC.
Open: Lunch Mon–Sat 1:30–4pm; dinner Mon–Sat 8:30pm–midnight.
Closed: Aug.

Madrileños defiantly name Casa Paco, just beside the Plaza Mayor, when someone has the "nerve" to put down Spanish steaks. They know here you can get the thickest, juiciest, most flavorsome steaks in Spain. The steaks are priced according to weight. Señor Paco was the first Madrid restaurant to seal steaks in boiling oil before serving them on plates so hot the almost-raw meat continues to cook, preserving the natural juices.

Located in the old town, this two-story restaurant offers three dining rooms, where reservations are imperative. Otherwise you face a long wait, which you can while away sampling the tapas (hors d'oeuvres) in the tasca in front.

Casa Paco isn't just a steakhouse. You can start with a fish soup and proceed to such dishes as grilled sole, baby lamb, Casa Paco *cocido*, or *callos a la madrileña*. You might top it off with one of the luscious desserts, but you can't have coffee here—Paco won't serve it, not necessarily for health reasons but because customers used to be inclined to linger too long over their cups.

Inexpensive

Casa Alberto, calle de las Huertas 18. ☎ **429-93-56.**

Cuisine: CASTILIAN. **Reservations:** Recommended. **Metro:** Antón Martín.
Prices: Appetizers 750–1,250 ptas. ($5.30–$8.90); main courses 850–2,250 ptas. ($6–$16). AE, V.
Open: Lunch Tues–Sun 1–4pm; dinner Tues–Sat 8:30–midnight.

One of the oldest tascas in the neighborhood was established in 1827 and has thrived through the many regimes and governments since.

Occupying the street level of the house where Miguel de Cervantes lived briefly in 1614, it contains an appealing mixture of bullfighting memorabilia, engravings, and reproductions of Old Masters. Many visitors opt only for some of the tapas, which are continually replenished from platters on the bartop, but there's also a sit-down dining area for more substantial meals. Specialties include fried squid; shellfish in vinaigrette; chorizo in cider sauce; and several versions of baked or roasted lamb.

Mesón las Descalzas, Postigo San Martín 3. ☎ 522-72-17.

> **Cuisine:** SPANISH. **Reservations:** Recommended. **Metro:** Callao.
> **Prices:** Appetizers 550–700 ptas. ($3.90–$5); main courses 1,600–1,800 ptas. ($11.40–$12.80); fixed-price menu 1,200 ptas. ($8.50). AE, DC, MC, V.
> **Open:** Lunch daily noon–4pm; dinner daily 8pm–midnight.

Las Descalzas, a tavern-style restaurant, sits behind a red facade accented with a black-metal sign. Inside you'll be greeted with a massive tapas bar, often crowded at night. Behind a glass-and-wood screen is the restaurant section, where the specialties include kidneys with sherry, *sopa castellana*, seafood soup, Basque-style hake, crayfish, shrimp, oysters, clams, and paella with shellfish. For entertainment, there's folk music sometimes.

---

5 Retiro/Salamanca

Very Expensive

⭐ **La Gamella,** calle Alfonso XII 4. ☎ 532-45-09.

> **Cuisine:** CALIFORNIAN/CASTILIAN. **Reservations:** Required. **Metro:** Retiro. **Bus:** 19.
> **Prices:** Appetizers 1,050–2,200 ptas. ($7.50–$15.60); main courses 2,300–4,200 ptas. ($16.30–$29.80). AE, DC, MC, V.
> **Open:** Lunch Tues–Sat 1:30–4pm; dinner Tues–Sat 9pm–midnight.
> **Closed:** Mid-Aug to mid-Sept.

La Gamella established its gastronomic reputation shortly after it opened several years ago in less imposing quarters in another part of town. In 1988 its Illinois-born owner, former choreographer Dick Stephens, moved into the 19th-century building where the Spanish philosopher Ortega y Gasset was born. The prestigious and legendary Horcher (see below) is just across the street (the food at La Gamella is better). The design and decor of La Gamella invite customers to relax in high-ceilinged russet-colored warmth. Mr. Stephens has prepared his delicate and light-textured specialties for the king and queen of Spain as well as for many of Madrid's most talked about artists and merchants, many of whom he knows and greets personally between sessions in his kitchen.

Typical menu items include ceviche of Mediterranean fish; sliced duck liver in truffle sauce; Caesar salad with strips of marinated anchovies; a dollop of goat cheese served over caramelized endives; duck breast with peppers; and an array of well-prepared desserts, among which is an all-American cheesecake. Such traditional Spanish dishes as chicken with garlic have been added to the menu, plus what has been called "the only edible hamburger in Madrid."

Horcher, calle Alfonso XII 6. ☎ **532-35-96.**

Cuisine: GERMAN/INTERNATIONAL. **Reservations:** Required. **Metro:** Retiro.

Prices: Appetizers 1,100–2,300 ptas. ($7.80–$16.30); main courses 2,500–7,200 ptas. ($17.80–$51.10). AE, DC, V.

Open: Lunch Mon–Sat 1:30–4pm; dinner Mon–Sat 8:30pm–midnight.

Horcher originated in Berlin in 1904. In a sudden move—prompted by a tip from a high-ranking German officer that Germany was losing the war—Herr Horcher brought his restaurant to Madrid in 1943. The restaurant has continued its grand European traditions, including excellent service, ever since.

You might try the seafood mousse. Wild-duck salad also attains distinction. Both the venison stew in green pepper with orange peel and the crayfish with parsley and cucumber are excellent. For dessert, the house specialty is crêpes Sir Holden, prepared at your table, with fresh raspberries, cream, and nuts; or you may prefer a Sachertorte.

Your best chance of getting a seat is to go early. Jackets and ties are imperative for men.

Expensive

Alkalde, Jorge Juan 10. ☎ **576-33-59.**

Cuisine: BASQUE. **Reservations:** Required. **Metro:** Retiro or Serrano. **Bus:** 8, 20, 21, or 53.

Prices: Appetizers 1,000–2,800 ptas. ($7.10–$19.90); main courses 1,800–5,000 ptas. ($12.80–$35.50); fixed-price menu 4,900 ptas. ($34.80). AE, DC, MC, V.

Open: Lunch daily 1–4:30pm; dinner daily 8:30pm–midnight. **Closed:** Sun in July–Aug.

Alkalde has been known for decades for serving top-quality Spanish food in an old tavern setting. It's decorated like a Basque inn, with beamed ceilings and hams hanging from the rafters. Upstairs is a large *típico* tavern; downstairs is a maze of stone-sided cellars, pleasantly cool in the summer, although the whole place is air-conditioned.

You might begin with the cream of crabmeat soup, followed by *gambas a la plancha* (grilled shrimp) or *cigalas* (crayfish). Other well-recommended dishes include *mero salsa verde* (brill in a green sauce), trout Alkalde, stuffed peppers, and chicken steak Alkalde. The dessert specialty is copa Cardinal, an ice-cream sundae.

★ **El Amparo,** callejón de Pulgcerdá 8, at the corner of Jorge Juan. ☎ 431-64-56.

Cuisine: BASQUE. **Reservations:** Required. **Metro:** Goya. **Bus:** 21 or 53.

Prices: Appetizers 1,500–2,500 ptas. ($10.70–$17.80); main courses 2,900–3,500 ptas. ($20.60–$24.90). AE, MC, V.

Open: Lunch Mon–Fri 1:30–3:30pm; dinner Mon–Sat 9–11:30pm. **Closed:** Week before Easter, Aug.

El Amparo, behind the cascading vines of its facade, is one of the most elegant gastronomic enclaves of Madrid. It sits beside a quiet alleyway close to a bustling commercial section of the city center. Inside, three tiers of roughly hewn wooden beams surround elegantly appointed tables where pink napery and glistening silver add cosmopolitan touches of glamour. A sloping skylight floods the interior with sunlight by day, and at night pinpoints of light from the high-tech hanging lanterns create intimate shadows. A battalion of polite uniformed waiters serves well-prepared versions of cold marinated salmon with tomato sorbet, cold cream of vegetable-and-shrimp soup, bisque of shellfish with Armagnac, seafood-stuffed ravioli, ragoût of sole, steamed fish of the day, roulades of lobster with soy sauce, and steamed hake with pepper sauce.

El Pescador, José Ortega y Gasset 75. ☎ **402-12-90.**

> **Cuisine:** SEAFOOD. **Reservations:** Required. **Metro:** Lista.
> **Prices:** Appetizers 1,200–3,000 ptas. ($8.50–$21.30); main courses 2,200–4,500 ptas. ($15.60–$32). MC, V.
> **Open:** Lunch Mon–Sat 1:30–4pm; dinner Mon–Sat 8:30pm–midnight.
> **Closed:** Aug.

El Pescador is a fish restaurant that has become a favorite of the Madrileños who appreciate the more than 30 kinds of fish prominently displayed in a glass case. Many of these are unknown in North America, and some originate off the coast of Galicia. Management air-freights them in and prefers to serve them *a la plancha* (grilled).

You might precede your main course with a spicy fish soup and accompany it with one of the many good wines from northeastern Spain. If you're not sure what to order—even the English translations might sound unfamiliar—try one of the many varieties and sizes of shrimp. These go under the name of *langostinos, cigalas, santiaguinos,* and *carabineros.* Many are expensive and priced by the gram, so be careful when you order.

Viridiana, Juan de Mena 14. ☎ **523-44-78.**

> **Cuisine:** INTERNATIONAL. **Reservations:** Recommended. **Metro:** Banco.
> **Prices:** Appetizers 1,800–3,000 ptas. ($12.80–$21.30); main courses 2,400–3,600 ptas. ($17–$25.60). No credit cards.
> **Open:** Lunch Mon–Sat 1:30pm–4pm; dinner Mon–Sat 9pm–midnight.
> **Closed:** Aug.

Viridiana, praised as one of Madrid's up-and-coming restaurants, is known for the creative imagination of its chef and part owner, Abraham Garcia. Menu specialties are usually contemporary adaptations of traditional recipes and change frequently according to the availability of the ingredients. Examples include a salad of exotic lettuces served with smoked salmon; guinea fowl stuffed with herbs and wild mushrooms; baby squid with curry served on a bed of lentils; roasted lamb served in puff pastry with fresh basil; carpaccio of beef with white-truffle mousseline; and a dessert specialty of apple tart flambéed in Calvados.

Inexpensive

Gran Café de Gijón, paseo de Recoletos, 21. ☎ 521-54-25.

> **Cuisine:** SPANISH. **Reservations:** Required for the restaurant. **Metro:** Banco de Espana, Colon, or Recoletos.
>
> **Prices:** Appetizers 390–1,020 ptas. ($2.80–$7.20); main courses 870–3,000 ptas. ($6.20–$21.30); fixed-price menu 1,400 ptas. ($9.90). No credit cards.
>
> **Open:** Daily 9am–1am (lunch Mon–Sat 1–4pm; dinner Mon–Sat 9am–midnight).

Each of the old European capitals has a coffeehouse that has traditionally attracted the literati—in Madrid it's the Gijón, which opened in 1888 in the heyday of the city's Belle Epoque. Artists and writers still patronize this venerated old cafe, many of them spending hours over one cup of coffee. Ernest Hemingway made the place famous for Americans, and in his footsteps in the 1950s followed such notables as Ava Gardner and Truman Capote. The place has open windows looking out onto the wide paseo, as well as a large terrace for sun worshipers and birdwatchers. Along one side of the cafe is a stand-up bar, and on the lower level is a restaurant. A fixed-price menu consists of two dishes, bread, wine or beer, and dessert, with main dishes varying daily. In summer you can sit in the garden enjoying a *blanco y negro* (black coffee with ice cream) or mixed drinks.

---

6 Chamberí

Very Expensive

★ **Las Cuatro Estaciones,** General Ibéñez Ibero 5. ☎ 553-63-05.

> **Cuisine:** INTERNATIONAL. **Reservations:** Required. **Metro:** Guzmán el Bueno.
>
> **Prices:** Appetizers 1,200–2,800 ptas. ($8.50–$19.90); main courses 2,200–4,500 ptas. ($15.60–$32); fixed-price dinner 6,000 ptas. ($42.60). AE, DC, MC, V.
>
> **Open:** Lunch Mon–Fri 1–4pm; dinner Mon–Sat 9pm–midnight. **Closed:** Aug.

Las Cuatro Estaciones is placed by gastronomes and horticulturists alike among their favorite dining spots of Madrid. In addition to superb food, the establishment prides itself on the masses of flowers that change with the season, plus a modern and softly inviting decor. Depending on the time of year, the mirrors surrounding the multilevel bar near the entrance reflect thousands of hydrangeas, chrysanthemums, or poinsettias. Even the table linen matches whichever colors the resident botanist has chosen as the seasonal motif. Each person involved in food preparation spends a prolonged apprenticeship at restaurants in France before returning home to try his or her freshly sharpened talents on the taste buds of aristocratic Madrileños.

Representative specialties include crab bisque, fresh oysters, a petite marmite of fish and shellfish, imaginative preparations of salmon, fresh asparagus with mushrooms in puff pastry with parsley-butter sauce, a three-fish platter with fines herbes, brochette of filet of beef in pecadillo, and a light version of blanquette of monkfish so tender it melts in your mouth. The "festival of desserts" includes specials the chef has concocted that day, a selection of which is placed temptingly on your table.

⭐ **Jockey,** Amador de los Ríos 6. ☎ **319-24-25.**
   Cuisine: INTERNATIONAL. **Reservations:** Required. **Metro:** Cuzco.
   Prices: Appetizers 1,100–6,500 ptas. ($7.80–$46.20); main courses 2,500–6,800 ptas. ($17.80–$48.30). AE, DC, MC, V.
   Open: Lunch Mon–Sat 1–4pm; dinner Mon–Sat 9–11:30pm. **Closed:** Aug.

For decades this was considered Spain's premier restaurant, although competition for that title is now severe. At any rate, it's the favorite of international celebrities, diplomats, and heads of state, and some of the more faithful patrons look on it as their own private club. It was, in fact, once known as the "Jockey Club," although the *Club* was eventually dropped because it suggested exclusivity. The restaurant, with tables on two levels, isn't overly large. Wood-paneled walls and colored linen provide warmth. Against the paneling are a dozen prints of horses mounted by jockeys—hence the name.

Since Jockey's establishment shortly after World War II, the chef has prided himself on coming up with new and creative dishes. Sheiks from oil kingdoms can still order beluga caviar from Iran, but others might settle happily for Jockey's goose-liver terrine or slices of Jabugo ham. Cold melon soup with shrimp is soothing on a hot day, followed by such dishes as grill-roasted young pigeon from Talavera cooked in its own juice or sole filets with figs in chardonnay. Stuffed small chicken Jockey style is a specialty, as is tripe madrileña, a local specialty. Desserts are sumptuous, although people may end their meal with the Colombian coffee alone.

Inexpensive

Foster's Hollywood, calle Magallanes 1. ☎ **448-91-65.**
   Cuisine: AMERICAN. **Reservations:** Not required. **Metro:** Quevedo.
   Prices: Appetizers 450–600 ptas. ($3.20–$4.30); main courses 600–1,000 ptas. ($4.30–$7.10). AE, DC, MC, V.
   Open: Sun–Thurs 1pm–midnight, Fri–Sat 1pm–2am.

When Foster's opened in 1971, it was not only the first American restaurant in Spain but also one of the first in Europe. Since those days it has grown into a chain with more than 20 restaurants in Madrid and even several in Florida. A popular hangout for both locals and visiting Yanks, it offers a choice of dining venues—ranging from "classical club American" to studios, the latter evoking working movie studios with props. Its varied menu includes Tex-Mex selections; butterfly shrimp; steaks; sandwiches; freshly made salads; and, as its signature product, hamburgers grilled over natural charcoal in many variations. *The New York Times* once reported that it has "probably the best onion rings in the world."

Other locations where you can have a direct hook-up to the United States in Madrid are paseo de la Habana 1 (☎ **564-63-08**); Padre Damián 38 (☎ **457-36-42**), next to the Eurobuilding hotel; Apolonio Morales 3 (☎ **345-10-36**), in the Castellana area; avenida de Brasil 14 (☎ **597-16-74**), near the Meliá Castilla hotel; Princesa 13 (☎ **559-19-14**), near Plaza de España; Velázquez 80 (☎ **435-61-28**), in the Serrano shopping area; Tamayo y Baus 1 (☎ **531-51-15**), close to Plaza de Cibeles and the Prado; Plaza Sagrado Corazón de Jesús 2 (☎ **564-66-50**), next to the National Music Auditorium; Centro Comercial Arturo Soría (☎ **759-73-42**); and Centro Comercial La Vaguada (☎ **738-12-67**).

7 Chamartín

Very Expensive

★ **Zalacaín**, Alvarez de Baena 4. ☎ **561-48-40**.
   Cuisine: BASQUE. **Reservations:** Required. **Metro:** Rubén Darío.
   Prices: Appetizers 1,500–5,000 ptas. ($10.70–$35.50); main courses 3,500–4,200 ptas. ($24.90–$29.80). AE, DC, MC, V.
   Open: Lunch Mon–Fri 1:30–3:30pm; dinner Mon–Sat 9–11:30pm.
   Closed: Week before Easter and Aug.

Outstanding in both food and decor, Zalacaín, which opened in 1973, is reached by an illuminated walk from the paseo de la Castellana and housed at the garden end of a modern apartment complex. In fact, it's within an easy walk of such deluxe hotels as the Castellana and Miguel Angel. The name of the restaurant comes from the intrepid hero of Basque author Pío Baroja's 1909 novel, *Zalacaín el Aventurero*. Zalacaín is small, exclusive, and expensive. In an atmosphere of an elegant old mansion you can peruse the menu, perhaps at the rust-toned bar. The walls are covered with textiles, and some are decorated with Audubon-type paintings. Men should wear jackets and ties.

The menu is interesting and varied, often with nouvelle-cuisine touches along with many Basque and French specialties. It might offer a superb sole in green sauce, but it also knows the glory of grilled pigs' feet. Among the most recommendable main dishes are a stew of scampi in cider sauce; crêpes stuffed with smoked fish; ravioli stuffed with mushrooms, foie gras, and truffles; Spanish bouillabaisse; and veal escalopes in orange sauce. For dessert, I'd suggest baked apples stuffed with cinnamon-flavored custard.

Expensive

Asador Errota-Zar, Corazón de María 32. ☎ **413-52-24**.
   Cuisine: BASQUE. **Reservations:** Required. **Metro:** Alfonso XIII.
   Bus: 43.
   Prices: Appetizers 850–1,800 ptas. ($6–$12.80); main courses 2,500–3,000 ptas. ($17.80–$21.30). AE, DC, MC, V.
   Open: Lunch Mon–Sat 1–4pm; dinner Mon–Sat 9pm–midnight.
   Closed: Aug.

Asador Errota-Zar is one of Madrid's best *asadors*, restaurants that roast meat on racks or spits over an open fire (the technique is said to have been brought to the Basque country by repatriated emigrés who learned it in Argentina and Uruguay a century ago; since then the Basques have claimed it as their own and presumably do it better than anyone else). It's behind the stucco-and-stone walls of an antique mill and managed by Basque-born Segundo Olano and his wife, Eugenia.

You might begin your meal with slices of pork loin, grilled spicy sausage, scrambled eggs with boletus mushrooms, a savory soup made from Basque kidney beans, or perhaps red peppers stuffed with codfish. Other dishes include stewed hake with clams in a marina sauce, but the real specialties of the house are the succulent cuts of beef, fish, and pork that are first gently warmed, then seared, then cooked by the expert hand of Señor Olano himself. The restaurant is at its most interesting when groups of friends arrive, sharing portions of several appetizers among themselves before concentrating on a main course. The offerings of meat tend to be very fresh but rather limited. The culinary variety here lies in the appetizers.

El Bodegón, calle Pinar 15. ☎ 562-31-37.

Cuisine: INTERNATIONAL/BASQUE. **Reservations:** Required. **Metro:** Rubén Darío.
Prices: Appetizers 800–1,750 ptas. ($5.70–$12.40); main courses 2,200–2,950 ptas. ($15.60–$20.90). AE, DC, MC, V.
Open: Lunch Mon–Fri 1:30–4pm; dinner Mon–Sat 9pm–midnight.
Closed: Holidays, most of August.

El Bodegón is imbued with the atmosphere of a gentleman's club for hunting enthusiasts—in the country-inn style. International globe-trotters are attracted here, especially in the evening, because the restaurant is near such deluxe hotels as the Castellana and Miguel Angel. King Juan Carlos and Queen Sofia have dined here.

Waiters in black and white, with gold braid and buttons, bring dignity to the food service. Even bottled water is served champagne style, chilled in a silver floor stand. There are two main dining rooms—conservative and oak-beamed.

I recommend cream of crayfish bisque or velvety vichyssoise to launch your meal. Main-course selections include grilled filet mignon with classic béarnaise sauce or venison à la bourguignonne. Other main-course selections include shellfish au gratin Escoffier, quails Fernand Point, a tartare of raw fish marinated in parsley-enriched vinaigrette, and smoked salmon. For dessert, try homemade apple pie.

★ **El Cabo Mayor,** Juan Ramón Jiménez 37. ☎ 250-87-76.

Cuisine: SEAFOOD. **Reservations:** Recommended. **Metro:** Cuzco.
Prices: Appetizers 1,600–3,800 ptas. ($11.40–$27); main courses 2,500–3,900 ptas. ($17.80–$27.70). AE, DC, MC, V.
Open: Lunch Mon–Sat 1:30–4pm; dinner Mon–Sat 9pm–midnight.
Closed: One week in Aug.

In the prosperous northern edges of Madrid, this restaurant is not far from the city-within-a-city of Chamartín station. This is one of the best, most popular, and most stylish restaurants in Spain. The open-air staircase leading to the entranceway descends from a manicured garden on a quiet side street. You'll know you're here by the battalion of uniformed doormen who greet arriving taxis. The restaurant's decor is a nautically inspired mass of hardwood panels, brass trim, old-fashioned pulleys and ropes, a tile floor custom-painted into sea-green and blue replicas of waves, and hand-carved models of fishing boats. In brass replicas of portholes, some dozen bronze statues honoring fishers and their craft are displayed in illuminated positions of honor.

Menu choices include a superb version of paprika-laden peppers stuffed with fish, a salad composed of Jabugo ham and foie gras of duckling, fish soup from Cantabria (a province between the Basque country and Asturias), asparagus mousse, salmon in sherry sauce, and loin of veal in cassis sauce. Desserts include such selections as rice mousse with pine-nut sauce.

 El Olivo Restaurant, General Gallegos 1. ☎ **359-15-35.**
Cuisine: MEDITERRANEAN. **Reservations:** Recommended. **Metro:** Plaza de Castilla.
Prices: Appetizers 975–3,650 ptas. ($6.90–$25.90); main courses 2,500–3,500 ptas. ($17.80–$24.90); fixed-price meals 3,850–5,800 ptas. ($27.30–$41.20). AE, DC, MC, V.
Open: Lunch Tues–Sat 1–4pm; dinner Tues–Sat 9pm–midnight. **Closed:** Aug and four days around Easter.

Local wits praise the success of a non-Spaniard (in this case, French-born Jean-Pierre Vandelle) in recognizing the international appeal of two of Spain's most valuable culinary resources: olive oil and sherry. His likable restaurant, located in northern Madrid near the Chamartín station, pays homage to the glories of the Spanish olive. Designed in tones of green and amber that reflect the leaves and oil of the olive tree, it's probably the only restaurant in Spain with a trolley stocked with 40 regional olive oils that is wheeled from table to table. From the trolley, diners select one or another variety, a golden puddle of which is offered for taste testing; it is to be soaked up with chunks of rough-textured bread that is—according to your taste—seasoned with a dash of salt.

Menu specialties include grilled filet of monkfish marinated in herbs and olive oil, served with black-olive sauce over a compote of fresh tomatoes; and four preparations of codfish arranged on a single platter, served with a pil-pil sauce (named after the sizzling noise it makes as it bubbles on a stove, pil-pil sauce is composed of codfish gelatin and herbs whipped into a mayonnaiselike consistency with olive oil). Also popular are thinly sliced roulades of beef stuffed with foie gras of duckling, dredged in flour, and fried in top-quality olive oil. Desserts might be one of several chocolate pastries or *leche frite* served with orange sauce. A wide array of reasonably priced Bordeaux and Spanish wines can accompany your meal.

A final note: Many clients deliberately arrive early as an excuse to linger in El Olivo's one-of-a-kind sherry bar. Although other drinks are offered, the bar features more than 100 brands of vino de Jerez, more than practically any other establishment in Madrid. Priced at 300 to 800 ptas. ($2.10 to $5.70) per glass, they make the perfect apéritif.

Moderate

O'Pazo, calle Reina Mercedes 20. ☎ **553-23-33.**

> **Cuisine:** GALICIAN/SEAFOOD. **Reservations:** Required.
> **Metro:** Nuevos Ministerios or Alvarado. **Bus:** 3 or 5.
> **Prices:** Appetizers 900–2,400 ptas. ($6.40–$17); main courses 2,100–3,900 ptas. ($14.90–$27.70). MC, V.
> **Open:** Lunch Mon–Sat 1–4pm; dinner Mon–Sat 8:30pm–midnight.
> **Closed:** Aug.

O'Pazo is a deluxe Galician restaurant, considered by the local cognoscenti to be one of the top seafood places in the country. The fish is flown in daily from Galicia, and much of it is priced by the weight, depending on market quotations. In front is a cocktail lounge/bar, all in polished brass, with low sofas and paintings. The restaurant has carpeted floors, cushioned Castilian furniture, soft lighting, and colored-glass windows. Most diners begin with assorted smoked fish or fresh oysters.

The house specialty is hake Galician style, but you may prefer the sea bass, baked in the oven and served with a mustard sauce. O'Pazo sole is also recommended.

Inexpensive

 Alfredo's Barbacoa, Juan Hurtado de Mendoza 11. ☎ **345-16-39.**

> **Cuisine:** AMERICAN. **Reservations:** Recommended. **Metro:** Cuzco.
> **Prices:** Appetizers 375–675 ptas. ($2.70–$4.80); main courses 600–1,600 ptas. ($4.30–$11.40). AE, DC, MC, V.
> **Open:** Lunch Mon–Fri 1–4:30pm, Sat 2–5pm; dinner Mon–Thurs 8:30pm–midnight, Fri–Sat 8:30pm–1am.

Alfredo's is a popular rendezvous for Americans longing for homestyle food other than hamburgers. Al, the owner, directs his bar/restaurant wearing boots, blue jeans, and a 10-gallon hat; his friendly welcome has made the place a center for both his friends and newcomers to Madrid. You *can* have hamburgers here, but they're of the barbecued variety, and you might instead prefer the barbecue spareribs or chicken. The salad bar is an attraction. And it's a rare treat to be able to have corn on the cob. The original Alfred's Barbacoa, at Lagasca 5 (☎ **576-62-71;** Metro: Retiro). is still in business, also under Al's auspices.

8 Chueca

Inexpensive

Taberna Carmencita, Liberated 16. ☎ **531-66-12.**

> **Cuisine:** SPANISH. **Reservations:** Recommended. **Metro:** Chueca.
> **Prices:** Appetizers 600–1,000 ptas. ($4.30–$7.10); main courses 1,000–3,500 ptas. ($7.10–$24.90); fixed-price lunch menu 1,000 ptas. ($7.10). AE, DC, MC, V.
> **Open:** Lunch Mon–Fri noon–5pm; dinner Mon–Sat 8pm–midnight.

Carmencita, founded in 1840 and exquisitely restored, is a street-corner enclave of old Spanish charm, filled with 19th-century detailing and tilework that witnessed the conversations of a former patron, the poet Federico García Lorca. Meals might include entrecôte with green-pepper sauce, escalope of veal, braised mollusks with port, filet of pork, codfish with garlic, and Bilbao-style hake. Every Thursday the special dish is a complicated version of the famous cocido (stew) of Madrid.

Budget

El Inca, Gravina 23. ☎ **532-77-45.**

> **Cuisine:** PERUVIAN. **Reservations:** Required on weekends. **Metro:** Chueca.
> **Prices:** Appetizers 550–900 ptas. ($3.90–$6.40); main courses 1,000–1,600 ptas. ($7.10–$11.40); fixed-price lunch menu 2,500 ptas. ($17.80). AE, DC, MC, V.
> **Open:** Lunch Tues–Sat 1:30pm–4pm; dinner Tues–Sat 9pm–midnight.
> **Closed:** Aug.

Frommer's Cool for Kids: Restaurants

Casa de Campo (see "Cool for Kids" in Chapter 6) Children visiting Spain will delight in patronizing any of the restaurants at the Parque de Atracciones in the Casa de Campo.

A Picnic (see "Picnic Fare and Where to Eat It" under "Specialty Dining" in this chapter) Another good idea is to go on a picnic.

Fast-Food Chains For a taste of home, there are always the fast-food chains like McDonald's, Burger King, and Kentucky Fried Chicken. Remember, though, that because Spain is a foreign country, everything may have a slightly different taste.

Foster's Hollywood (see p. 137) This restaurant has some of the best hamburgers in Madrid, plus lots of fare familiar to American kids.

V.I.P. (see p. 152) This is the most centrally located member of a Madrid chain, serving fast food, hamburgers, and other foodstuffs that kids go for in a big way, especially the ice-cream concoctions.

For a taste of South America, try El Inca, decorated with Inca motifs and artifacts. Since it opened in the early 1970s, it has hosted its share of diplomats and celebrities, although on the average night you're more likely to see families and groups of local officeworkers. The house cocktail is a deceptively potent pisco sour—the recipe comes straight from the Andes. Many of the dishes contain potatoes, the national staple of Peru. The salad of potatoes and black olives is given an unusual zest with white-cheese sauce. Other specialties are *cebiche de merluza* (raw hake marinated with onions) and *aji de gallina* (a chicken-and-rice dish made with peanut sauce), a Peruvian favorite.

$ **La Argentina,** Gravina 18. ☎ **531-91-17.**

> **Cuisine:** INTERNATIONAL. **Reservations:** Not required. **Metro:** Chueca.
>
> **Prices:** Appetizers 375–850 ptas. ($2.70–$6); main courses 800–1,250 ptas. ($5.70–$8.90); fixed-price menu 1,200 ptas. ($8.50). No credit cards.
>
> **Open:** Lunch Tues–Sun noon–4pm; dinner Tues–Sat 9pm–midnight. **Closed:** July 25–Aug 31.

La Argentina, set within a building erected in 1941, is run under the watchful eye of owner Andrés Rodríguez. The restaurant has only 16 tables, but the food is well prepared, sort of Spanish family-style. The best bets are cannelloni Rossini, noodle soup, creamed spinach, and meat dishes, including entrecôte and roast veal. Chicken Villaroy is another special. All dishes are served with mashed or french-fried potatoes. For dessert, have a baked apple or rice pudding. The decor is simple and clean, and you're usually served by one of the two waitresses who have been here for years.

Nabucco, calle Hortaleza 108. ☎ **310-06-11.**

> **Cuisine:** ITALIAN. **Reservations:** Recommended. **Metro:** Alonso Martínez. **Bus:** 7 or 36.
>
> **Prices:** Pizzas 585–725 ptas. ($4.20–$5.10); appetizers 450–700 ptas. ($3.20–$5); main courses 725–1,300 ptas. ($5.10–$9.20). AE, DC, MC, V.
>
> **Open:** Lunch Mon–Sat 1:30–4pm; dinner Mon–Thurs 8:45pm–midnight, Fri–Sat 9pm–1am.

In a neighborhood of Spanish restaurants, the Italian format comes as a welcome change. The decor resembles a postmodern update of an Italian ruin, complete with faux-marble walls. Roman portrait busts and a prominent bar lend a dignified air. Menu choices include cannelloni, a good selection of veal dishes, and osso buco. You might begin with a selection of antipasti, then for dessert try the chocolate mousse.

Tienda de Vinos, Augusto Figueroa 35. ☎ **521-70-12.**

> **Cuisine:** SPANISH. **Reservations:** Not accepted. **Metro:** Chueca.
>
> **Prices:** Appetizers 200–600 ptas. ($1.40–$4.30); main courses 400–800 ptas. ($2.80–$5.70). No credit cards.
>
> **Open:** Breakfast and lunch, Mon–Sat 9am–4:30pm; dinner Mon–Sat 8:30pm–midnight.

Officially this restaurant is known as the Wine Store, but ever since the 1930s Madrileños have called it El Comunista. Its now-deceased owner was a fervent Communist, and many locals in sympathy with his political beliefs patronized the establishment. This rather rickety old wine shop, with a few tables in the back, is quite fashionable with actors and journalists looking for Spanish fare without frills. There is a menu, but no one ever thinks of asking for it—just ask what's available. Nor do you get a bill—you're just told how much. You sit at wooden tables and on wooden chairs and benches placed around the walls, which are decorated with old posters, calendars, pennants, and clocks. Start with garlic or vegetable soup or lentils, followed by lamb chops, tripe in spicy sauce, or meatballs and soft-set eggs with asparagus.

9   South of the Plaza Mayor

Expensive

Casa Lucio, Cava Baja 35. ☎ **365-32-52.**

> **Cuisine:** CASTILIAN. **Reservations:** Recommended. **Metro:** Sol or La Latina.
> **Prices:** Appetizers 1,000–2,000 ptas. ($7.10–$14.20); main courses 2,000–3,300 ptas. ($14.20–$23.40). AE, DC, MC, V.
> **Open:** Lunch Sun–Fri 1–4pm; dinner daily 9pm–midnight. **Closed:** Aug.

Set on a historic street whose edges once marked the perimeter of old Madrid, this is a time-honored tasca with all the requisite antique accessories. You'll pass a well-oiled bar accented with dozens of cured hams hanging from hand-hewn beams and mix with a loyal clientele of sometimes surprisingly well placed public figures. (Among them has been included even the present king of Spain and many prominent business moguls.) You'll be directed to one of two dining rooms on one of two floors, each with whitewashed walls, tile floors, and exposed brick. A well-trained staff offers classic Castilian food that might include *jamón de Jabugo* with broad beans; shrimp in garlic sauce; hake with green sauce; several types of roasted lamb; and *churrasco de la casa*, a thick steak served sizzling hot on a heated platter.

Las Cuevas de Luís Candelas, calle de Cuchilleros 1.
    ☎ **366-54-28.**

> **Cuisine:** SPANISH/INTERNATIONAL. **Reservations:** Required. **Metro:** Puerta del Sol.
> **Prices:** Appetizers 550–2,200 ptas. ($3.90–$15.60); main courses 1,200–2,800 ptas. ($8.50–$19.90). AE, DC, MC, V.
> **Open:** Lunch daily 1–4pm; dinner daily 7:30pm–2:30am.

Right down the steps from the Mesón del Corregidor is the even-better-known Las Cuevas de Luís Candelas, housed in a building from 1616. The restaurant itself opened its doors in 1900. It's entered through a doorway under an arcade on the steps leading to calle de Cuchilleros, the nighttime street of Madrid, teeming with restaurants, flamenco clubs, and rustic taverns. The restaurant is named after the legendary Luís Candelas, an 18th-century bandit sometimes known as "the Spanish Robin Hood." He is said to have hidden out in this maze of *cuevas* (caves). Although the menu is in English, the cuisine is authentically Spanish. Specialties include hake in the chef's own style. To begin your meal, another house dish is *sopa de ajo Candelas* (garlic soup). Roast suckling pig and roast lamb, as in the other restaurants on the Plaza Mayor, are the featured specialties.

El Schotis, Cava Baja 11. ☎ **365-32-30.**

> **Cuisine:** SPANISH. **Reservations:** Recommended. **Metro:** Sol or La Latina.
>
> **Prices:** Appetizers 400–750 ptas. ($2.80–$5.30); main courses 1,750–2,400 ptas. ($12.40–$17). Fixed-price menu 3,850 ptas. ($27.30). AE, DC, MC, V.
>
> **Open:** Lunch Tues–Sun 1–4pm; dinner Tues–Sat 9pm–midnight. **Closed:** Two weeks in Aug.

Set beside one of Madrid's oldest and most historic streets, El Schotis was established in 1962 in a solid-stone building with lots of nostalgic garnish. A series of large and pleasingly old-fashioned dining rooms is the setting for an animated crowd of Madrileños and foreign visitors. They are served ample portions of conservative, well-prepared vegetables, salads, soups, fish, and, above all, meat. Specialties of the house include roasted baby lamb, grilled steaks and veal chops, shrimp with garlic, fried hake in green sauce, and traditional desserts. There's a bar near the entrance for tapas and before- or after-dinner drinks.

Moderate

Los Galayos, calle Botoneras 5. ☎ **366-30-28.**

> **Cuisine:** SPANISH. **Reservations:** Recommended. **Metro:** Puerta del Sol.
>
> **Prices:** Appetizers 450–1,100 ptas. ($3.20–$7.80); main courses 1,100–3,700 ptas. ($7.80–$26.30). AE, MC, V.
>
> **Open:** Daily 12:30pm–12:45am.

This restaurant's position is among the most desirable in all of Spain, on a narrow side street about three steps from the arcades of the Plaza Mayor. In summer, cascades of vines accent a series of tables and chairs, perfect for tapa-sampling and people-watching, set on the cobblestones outside. Some visitors consider an evening here among the highlights of their trip to Spain.

The interior ambience, reflecting the accessories and accoutrements of Old Castile, is featured in several dining rooms with vaulted or beamed ceilings and lots of Iberian charm. The Grande family are your multilingual hosts. Among the dishes served you'll find traditional versions of fish, shellfish, pork, veal, and beef, as well as suckling pig, baby goat, and roasted lamb. Naturally, a carafe or bottle of wine goes well with virtually anything you select. Set within two separate houses, the restaurant and its tapas bar have flourished on this site since 1884.

Gure-Etxea (Restaurant Vasco), Plaza de la Paja 12.
☎ **365-61-49.**

Cuisine: BASQUE. **Reservations:** Recommended. **Metro:** La Latina.
Prices: Appetizers 1,200–1,800 ptas. ($8.50–$12.80); main courses
1,500–3,500 ptas. ($10.70–$24.90); fixed-price menu 3,500 ptas.
($24.90). AE, DC, MC, V.
Open: Lunch Mon–Sat 1:30–4pm; dinner Mon–Sat 9pm–midnight.
Closed: Aug.

This restaurant is in a stone-walled building that was the convent
for the nearby Church of San Andrés before the Renaissance.
Today—amid a decor enhanced by Romanesque arches, vaulted
tunnels, and dark-grained paneling—you can enjoy selections from
a small yet choice menu. Specialties include vichyssoise, rape (a
whitefish) in green sauce, Gure-Etxea's special filet of sole, and
bacalau al pil-pil (codfish in fiery sauce).

Inexpensive

La Chata, Cava Baja 24. ☎ **366-14-58.**

Cuisine: CASTILIAN/GALICIAN/NORTHERN SPANISH. **Reservations:**
Recommended. **Metro:** La Latina.
Prices: Appetizers 1,000–3,000 ptas. ($7.10–$21.30); main dishes
1,500–2,200 ptas. ($10.70–$15.60). V.
Open: Lunch daily 12:30–5pm; dinner Mon–Sat 8pm–midnight
or 2am.

Set behind a heavily ornamented tile facade, this place has a stand-
up tapas bar at the entrance and a formal restaurant in a side room.
Many locals linger at the darkly paneled bar, which is framed by
hanging Serrano hams, cloves of garlic, and photographs of
bullfighters. Full meals might include roast suckling pig, roast lamb,
calamares en su tinta (squid in its own ink), grilled filet of steak with
peppercorns, and omelets flavored with eel strips.

El Cuchi, calle de Cuchilleros 3. ☎ **366-44-24.**

Cuisine: MEXICAN/SPANISH. **Reservations:** Required. **Metro:** Puerta
del Sol.
Prices: Appetizers 450–1,350 ptas. ($3.20–$9.60); main dishes 900–
2,900 ptas. ($6.40–$20.60). AE, DC, MC, V.
Open: Lunch daily 1–4pm; dinner daily 8pm–midnight.

A few doors down from Hemingway's favorite restaurant (Sobrino
de Botín—see "Specialty Dining," below), El Cuchi defiantly claims
that "Hemingway never ate here." But about everybody else has,
attracted both to its low prices and to its labyrinth of dining rooms.
    A European link in Mexico's famous Carlos 'n' Charlie's restau-
rant chain, it stands off a corner of the Plaza Mayor. Ceiling beams
and artifacts suggest rusticity. Menu specialties here include black-
bean soup, ceviche, guacamole, quail Mozambique, "pregnant" trout,
and roast suckling pig (much cheaper than that served at Botín).

10 | Specialty Dining

Tasca Hopping

If you think you'll starve waiting for Madrid's fashionable 9:30 or 10pm dinner hour, you've been misinformed. Throughout the city you'll find tascas (bars) that serve wine, beer, and platters of tempting hot and cold hors d'oeuvres known as tapas, which may include mushrooms, salads, baby eels, shrimp, lobster, mussels, sausage, ham—and, in one establishment at least, bull testicles. Keep in mind that you can often save pesetas by ordering at the bar.

El Anciano Rey de los Vinos, Bailén 19. ☎ **548-50-52.**

Cuisine: TAPAS. **Metro:** Ópera.
Prices: Tapas 95–450 ptas. (70¢–$3.20). No credit cards.
Open: Thurs–Tues 10am–3pm and 5:30–11pm.

Lying near the Royal Palace, the bar here is jammed during most of the day with crowds of Madrileños out for a glass (or a carafe) of one of the four house wines, which range from dry to sweet and start at 100 ptas. (70¢) per glass. Beer is also served.

Antonio Sánchez, calle Mesón de Parades 13. ☎ **539-78-26.**

Cuisine: SPANISH. **Metro:** Tirso de Molina.
Prices: Bar, tapas 200–600 ptas. ($1.40–$4.30). Restaurant, appetizers 200–500 ptas. ($1.40–$3.60); main courses 1,000–1,600 ptas. ($7.10–$11.40); fixed-price lunch menu Mon–Fri 1,500 ptas. ($10.70). MC, V.
Open: Mon–Sat noon–4pm and 8pm–midnight, Sun noon–4pm.

Named in 1850 after the founder's son, who was killed in the bullring, Antonio Sánchez is full of bullfighting memorabilia, including the stuffed head of the animal that gored young Sánchez. Also featured on the dark-paneled walls are three works by the Spanish landscape painter and portraitist Ignacio Zuloaga (1870–1945), who held his last public exhibition in this restaurant. A limited array of tapas, including garlic soup, are served with Valdepeñas wine drawn from a barrel. Many guests ignore the edibles, though, in favor of smoking cigarettes and arguing the merits of this or that bullfighter. A restaurant in the back serves Spanish food with a vaguely French influence. The establishment lies close to the Plaza Tirso de Molina.

Cervecería Alemania, Plaza de Santa Ana 6. ☎ **429-70-33.**

Cuisine: TAPAS. **Metro:** Alonzo Martín or Sevilla.
Prices: Beer 95 ptas. (70¢); tapas 100–900 ptas. (70¢–$6.40). No credit cards.
Open: Sun–Mon and Wed–Thurs 10am–12:30pm. Fri–Sat 10am–1:30am.

Hemingway used to frequent this casual spot with the celebrated bullfighter Luís Miguel Dominguín—ask the waiter to point out "Hemingway's table." However, it earned its name because of its long-ago German clients. Opening directly onto one of the liveliest little plazas of Madrid, it clings to its turn-of-the-century traditions. Young

Madrileños are fond of stopping in for a mug of draft beer. You can sit at one of the tables, leisurely sipping beer or wine, since the wait staff make no attempt to hurry you along. To accompany your beverage, try the fried sardines or a Spanish omelet.

Cervecería Santa Barbara, Plaza de Santa Barbara 8.
☎ **419-04-49.**

Cuisine: TAPAS. **Metro:** Además. **Bus:** 3, 7, or 21.
Prices: Beer 150–290 ptas. ($1.10–$2.10); tapas 1,000–3,750 ptas. ($7.10–$26.60). No credit cards.
Open: Daily 11am–11pm.

Unique in Madrid, the Cervecería Santa Barbara is an outlet for a beer factory, and the management has spent a lot to make it modern and inviting. Hanging globe lights and spinning ceiling fans create an attractive ambience, as does the black-and-white checkerboard marble floor. You go here for beer, of course: *cerveza negra* (black beer) or *cerveza dorada* (golden beer). The local brew is best accompanied by homemade potato chips or by fresh shrimp, lobster, crabmeat, or barnacles. You can either stand at the counter or go directly to one of the wooden tables for waiter service.

Taberna Toscana, Ventura de la Vega 22. ☎ **429-60-31.**

Cuisine: TAPAS. **Metro:** Puerta del Sol or Sevilla.
Prices: Glass of wine 100 ptas (70¢); tapas 500–1,300 ptas. ($3.60–$9.20). No credit cards.
Open: Lunch Tues–Sat noon–4pm; dinner Mon and Wed–Sat 8pm–midnight. **Closed:** Aug.

Many Madrileños begin their nightly tasca crawl here. The aura is that of a village inn, far removed from 20th-century Madrid. You sit on crude country stools under time-darkened beams from which hang sausages, pimientos, and sheaves of golden wheat. The long tile tapas bar is loaded with tasty tidbits, including the house specialties: *lacón y cecina* (boiled ham), *babas* (broad beans) with Spanish ham, and *chorizo* (a sausage of pork and red peppers)—almost meals in themselves. Especially delectable are the kidneys in sherry sauce and snails in hot sauce.

Dining with a View

Cafe de Oriente, Plaza de Oriente 2. ☎ **541-39-74.**

Cuisine: FRENCH/SPANISH. **Reservations:** Recommended for the restaurant. **Metro:** Ópera.
Prices: Cafe, tapas 850 ptas. ($6); coffee 650 ptas. ($4.60). Restaurant, appetizers 950–2,700 ptas. ($6.70–$19.20); main courses 1,900–2,950 ptas. ($13.50–$20.90). AE, DC, MC, V.
Open: Lunch daily 1–4pm; dinner daily 9pm–midnight.

The Oriente is a café/restaurant complex, the former being one of the most popular in Madrid. From the cafe tables on its terrace, there's a spectacular view of the Palacio Real (Royal Palace) and the Teatro Real. The dining rooms—Castilian upstairs, French Basque downstairs—are frequented by royalty and diplomats. Typical of the refined cuisine are vichyssoise, fresh vegetable flan, and many savory meat and fresh-fish offerings; the service is excellent. Most visitors, however, patronize the cafe, trying if possible to get an outdoor table for a "ringside" view of the Royal Palace. The cafe is decorated in turn-of-the-century style, with banquettes and regal paneling, as befits its location. Pizza, tapas, and drinks (including Irish, Viennese, Russian, and Jamaican coffees) are served.

Hemingway's Roast Suckling Pig

 Sobrino de Botín, calle de Cuchilleros 17. ☎ 366-42-17.

Cuisine: SPANISH. **Reservations:** Required. **Metro:** La Latina or Ópera. **Prices:** Appetizers 430–2,400 ptas. ($3.10–$17); main courses 620–3,850 ptas. ($4.40–$27.30); fixed price menu 3,500 ptas. ($24.90). AE, DC, MC, V.
Open: Lunch daily 1–4pm; dinner daily 8pm–midnight.

Ernest Hemingway made Sobrino de Botín famous. In the final two pages of his novel *The Sun Also Rises* he had Jake invite Lady Brett there for the Segovian specialty, washed down with Rioja Alta.

By merely entering its portals, you step back to 1725, the year the restaurant was founded. You'll see an open kitchen with a charcoal hearth, hanging copper pots, and an 18th-century tile oven for roasting suckling pig. The aroma from a big pot of regional soup wafts across the tables, which sit under time-aged beams. Your host, Don Antonio, never loses his cool—even when he has 18 guests standing in line waiting for tables.

The two house specialties are roast suckling pig and roast Segovian lamb. From the à la carte menu you might try the "quarter-of-an-hour" soup, made with fish. Good main dishes include the baked Cantabrian hake and filet mignon with potatoes. The dessert list features strawberries (in season) with whipped cream. You can wash down your meal with Valdepeñas or Aragón wine, although most guests order sangría.

Hotel Dining

 Restaurant Belagua, in the Hotel Palacio Santo Mauro, calle Zurbano 36. ☎ 319-69-00.

Cuisine: INTERNATIONAL. **Reservations:** Recommended. **Metro:** Rubén Darío or Alonso Martínez.
Prices: Appetizers 900–2,400 ptas. ($6.40–$17); main courses 1,800–3,800 ptas. ($12.80–$27); fixed-price menu Mon–Thurs 1,800–2,380 ptas. ($12.80–$16.90); fixed-price menu Fri–Sun 2,500 ptas. ($17.80). AE, DC, MC, V.
Open: Lunch Mon–Sat 1–4pm; dinner Mon–Sat 8:30–11:30pm.
Closed: National holidays.

The building that contains this glamorous restaurant was created in 1894 as a small French neoclassical palace. In 1991, Catalán designer Josep Joanpere helped transform it into a carefully detailed hotel

(Palacio Santo Mauro—see entry under "Chamberí" in Chapter 4). Part of what emerged from the building's incarnation included this highly appealing postmodern restaurant, which today is considered one of the capital's finest.

Assisted by a well-mannered staff, you'll select from a menu whose inspiration and ingredients change with the seasons. Examples include watermelon-and-prawn salad, light cream of cold ginger soup, haddock baked in a crust of potatoes tinted with squid ink, duck with honey and black cherries, and a dessert specialty a waiter will define as a palette of seasonal flavors—depending on the efforts of the chef, it might include miniature portions of flan with strawberry sauce plus an array of the day's pastries. The restaurant's name, incidentally, derives from a village in Navarre known for its natural beauty.

Vegetarian

La Galette, Conde de Aranda 11. ☎ **576-06-41.**

> **Cuisine:** VEGETARIAN. **Reservations:** Recommended. **Metro:** Retiro.
> **Prices:** Appetizers 350–400 ptas. ($2.50–$2.80); main courses 550–750 ptas. ($3.90–$5.30); fixed-price menu 2,200 ptas. ($15.60). AE, DC, MC, V.
> **Open:** Lunch Mon–Sat 2–4pm; dinner Mon–Sat 9pm–midnight.

La Galette was one of Madrid's first vegetarian restaurants, and it remains one of the best. Small and charming, it lies in a residential/shopping area in the exclusive Salamanca district, near the Plaza de la Independencía and the northern edge of Retiro Park. There's a limited selection of meat dishes, but the true allure lies in this establishment's imaginative use of vegetarian fare. Examples include baked stuffed peppers, omelets, eggplant croquettes, and even vegetarian "hamburgers." Some of the dishes are macrobiotic. The place is also noted for its mouth-watering pastries. La Galette's owners also operate La Galette II in the same building complex.

Afternoon Tea

The most delightful spot in Madrid for enjoying afternoon tea is a sidewalk table at the **Café de Oriente** (see "Dining with a View," above), overlooking the Royal Palace.

Light, Casual & Fast Food

Chez Lou Crêperie, Pedro Munguruza 6. ☎ **350-34-16.**

> **Cuisine:** FRENCH. **Reservations:** Required on weekends. **Metro:** Plaza de Castilla. **Bus:** 27 or 147.
> **Prices:** Appetizers 500–775 ptas. ($3.60–$5.50); crêpes 600–1,000 ptas. ($4.30–$7.10). No credit cards.
> **Open:** Lunch Mon–Fri 1:30–4pm; dinner Mon–Fri 8:30pm–1am.

Near the Eurobuilding hotel in Madrid's northern sector, this restaurant stands near the huge Joan Miró mural, which is worth the trek up here even if you don't try Chez Lou. In this intimate setting you get well-prepared and reasonably priced French food. The restaurant serves pâté as an appetizer, then a large range of crêpes with many fillings. Folded envelope style, the crêpes are not tearoom size, and they're perfectly adequate as a main course. I've sampled several variations, finding the ingredients nicely blended yet distinct enough to retain their identity. A favorite is the large crêpe stuffed with minced onions, cream, and smoked salmon. The ham-and-cheese crêpe is also tasty. The price of your dessert and drink is extra. Come here if you're seeking a light supper when it's too hot for one of those table-groaning Spanish meals.

$ La Plaza, in the Galería del Prado, Plaza de las Cortés 7. ☎ 429-65-67.

Cuisine: SPANISH. **Reservations:** Not required. **Metro:** Sevilla. **Prices:** Appetizers 335–660 ptas. ($2.40–$4.70); main courses 1,100–1,800 ptas. ($7.80–$12.80); fixed-price menus 1,100–1,400 ptas. ($7.80–$9.90). AE, MC, V.
Open: Mon–Fri 9am–10pm, Sat 11am–10:30pm.

This restaurant serves as the underground centerpiece of one of Madrid's shopping complexes, La Galería del Prado. Surrounded by thick marble-sheathed walls, it has a bunker-style position that means no natural sunlight can stream through windows. Nevertheless, it offers an attractive option: refreshing meals within an expensive neighborhood near the Prado. Some of its tables overflow into the rotunda of the shopping mall; most diners, however, sit in a glossy series of lattices whose rooms form a garden-inspired enclave near a well-stocked salad bar (visits here are priced according to the portions you take). You might begin with Serrano ham, mountain-fermented goat cheese, or a homemade pâté. Daily specials include such dishes as ragoût of veal. Platters of pasta also provide a zesty way to fill up.

Ríofrío, in the Centrol Colón, Plaza de Colón 1. ☎ 319-29-77.

Cuisine: INTERNATIONAL. **Reservations:** Not required. **Metro:** Colón. **Bus:** 5, 6, 14, 27, or 45.
Prices: Appetizers 400–1,700 ptas. ($2.80–$12.10); main courses 950–3,200 ptas. ($6.70–$22.70); sandwiches 460–850 ptas. ($3.30–$6). AE, DC, MC, V.
Open: Daily noon–1:30am.

Overlooking the Columbus Circle of Madrid, this is a sort of all-purpose place for drinking, eating, dining, and/or nightclubbing. The least expensive way to eat here is to patronize one of the two self-service cafeterias, where average meals run from 1,000 to 1,500 ptas. ($7.10 to $10.70). There's also a large restaurant serving international cuisine, with meals averaging 3,500 ptas. ($24.90), plus yet another dining room for informal lunches, dinners, snacks, or apéritifs. The spacious glassed-in terrace, open year round, is known for serving some of the city's best paella. Finally, there's even a nightclub, should you desire to make an evening of it: El Descubrimiento serves dinner costing from 4,500 ptas. ($32) that includes not only the meal but also a show to follow. Sandwiches are available throughout the day if you'd like just a light bite in the hot Madrid sun.

V.I.P. Gran Vía 43. ☎ **411-60-44.**

> **Cuisine:** FAST FOOD. **Reservations:** Not required. **Metro:** Callao.
> **Prices:** Appetizers 450–725 ptas. ($3.20–$5.10); main courses 650–
> 1,200 ptas. ($4.60–$8.50). AE, DC, MC, V.
> **Open:** Daily 9am–3am.

This place looks like a bookstore from the outside, but in back it is
a cafeteria serving fast food. You might begin with a cup of soothing
gazpacho. Hamburgers are the rage here. There are more than a dozen
V.I.P.s scattered throughout Madrid, but this is the most central one.

Local Favorites

La Bola, calle la Bola 7. ☎ **547-69-60.**

> **Cuisine:** MADRILEÑA. **Reservations:** Required **Metro:** Plaza de España
> or Ópera. **Bus:** 1 or 2.
> **Prices:** Appetizers 700–2,000 ptas. ($5–$14.20); main courses 1,200–
> 1,900 ptas. ($8.50–$13.50); fixed-price menu 2,125 ptas. ($15.10). No
> credit cards.
> **Open:** Lunch Mon–Sat 1–4pm; dinner Mon–Sat 9pm–midnight.

If you'd like to savor 19th-century Madrid, this *taberna*, just north
of the Teatro Real, is an inspired choice. It's one of the few restaurants
(if not the only one) left in Madrid that's painted with a blood-red
facade; once, nearly all fashionable restaurants were so coated. La Bola
hangs on to tradition like a tenacious bull. Time has galloped forward,
but not inside this restaurant, where the soft traditional atmosphere,
the gentle and polite waiters, the Venetian crystal, the Carmen-red
draperies, and the aging velvet preserve the 1870 ambience, Ava
Gardner, with her entourage of bullfighters, used to patronize this
establishment, but that was long ago, before La Bola became so well
known to tourists. Grilled sole is regularly featured, as is filet of veal
or roast veal. Basque-style hake and grilled salmon are also well
recommended. A host of refreshing dishes to begin a meal includes
grilled shrimp, red-pepper salad, or lobster cocktail.

Casa Ciriaco, calle Mayor 84. ☎ **548-50-66.**

> **Cuisine:** SPANISH. **Reservations:** Recommended. **Metro:** Ópera.
> **Prices:** Appetizers 450–1,500 ptas. ($3.20–$10.70); main courses
> 1,800–3,500 ptas. ($12.80–$24.90); *menu del día* 1,725 ptas. ($12.20).
> No credit cards.
> **Open:** Lunch Thurs–Tues 1–4pm; dinner Thurs–Tues 8:30pm–midnight.
> **Closed:** Aug.

Since 1906 this has been a special restaurant in one of the most
romantic parts of Old Madrid. It enjoys associations with the Spanish
painter Ignacio Zuloaga. The chef features dishes from Navarre and
Andalusia, but Castilian specialties predominate. Gazpacho makes a
fine opener, then you can order Navarre-style trout or tender slices
of veal.

Casa Mingo, paseo de la Florida 2. ☎ **57-79-18.**

> **Cuisine:** SPANISH. **Reservations:** Not accepted. **Metro:** Norte, then
> a 15-minute walk.

Prices: Main courses 450–1,050 ptas. ($3.20–$7.50). No credit cards.
Open: Daily 10am–midnight.

Casa Mingo has been known for decades for its Asturian cider, both still and bubbly. The perfect accompanying tidbit is a piece of the local Asturian *cabrales* (goat cheese), but the roast chicken is the specialty of the house, with an unbelievable number of helpings served daily. There's no formality here—customers share big tables under the vaulted dining room ceiling. In summer the staff places some tables and wooden chairs out on the sidewalk. In the strictest sense, Casa Mingo is not a restaurant but a bodega/taverna that serves food.

$ Hylogui, Ventura de la Vega 3. ☎ 429-73-57.
  Cuisine: CASTILIAN. **Reservations:** Recommended. **Metro:** Sevilla.
  Prices: Appetizers 425–900 ptas. ($3–$6.40); main courses 850–1,850 ptas. ($6–$13.10). AE, MC, V.
  Open: Lunch daily 1–4:30pm; dinner Mon–Sat 9pm–midnight.

Hylogui, a local legend, is one of the largest dining rooms along Ventura de la Vega, but there are many arches and nooks for privacy. One globe-trotting American wrote enthusiastically that he took all his meals here in Madrid, finding the soup pleasant and rich, the flan soothing, and the regional wine dry. The food is old-fashioned Spanish homestyle cooking.

Taberna del Alabardero, calle Felipe V 6. ☎ 547-25-77.
  Cuisine: BASQUE/SPANISH. **Reservations:** Required for restaurant only. **Metro:** Ópera.
  Prices: Bar, tapas 450–1,200 ptas. ($3.20–$8.50); glass of house wine 95 ptas. (70¢). Restaurant, appetizers 950–1,600 ptas. ($6.70–$11.40); main courses 1,900–3,100 ptas. ($13.50–$22). AE, DC, V.
  Open: Lunch daily 1–4pm; dinner daily 9pm–midnight.

Because of its proximity to the Royal Palace, most patrons visit this little Spanish classic for its selection of tasty tapas, ranging from squid cooked in wine to fried potatoes dipped in hot sauce. Photographs of former patrons, including Nelson Rockefeller and race-car driver Jackie Stewart, line the walls. The restaurant in the rear is said to be one of the city's "best-kept secrets." Decorated in typical tavern style, it serves savory Spanish Basque cuisine using market-fresh ingredients.

Picnic Fare & Where to Eat It

On a hot day, do as the Madrileños do. Secure the makings of a picnic lunch and head for the **Casa de Campo** (Metro: El Batán), those once-royal hunting grounds in the west of Madrid across the Manzanares River. Children delight in this adventure, for they can also visit a boating lake, the Parque de Atracciones, and the Madrid Zoo.

Your best choice for picnic fare is **Mallorca,** Velázquez 59 (☎ 431-99-09; Metro: Velázquez). This place has all the makings for a deluxe picnic and is open daily from 9am to 9pm.

Another good bet is **Rodilla,** Precíados 25 (☎ **522-57-01;** Metro: Callao), where you can find sandwiches, pastries, and takeaway tapas. Sandwiches, including vegetarian, meat, and fish, begin at 75 ptas. (50¢). It's open Monday through Saturday from 8:30am to 10:30pm and Sunday from 2:30 to 10:30pm.

6

What to See & Do in Madrid

Tourist officials in Madrid often confide, "We spend so much fuss trying to get people to visit Madrid. But when we get them here and they've seen the Prado and a bullfight, we send them off to El Escorial or Toledo." Too true—and regrettably so. As European capitals go, Madrid is hard to get to know. The city's mainstream attractions— tree-shaded parks, wide paseos, bubbling fountains, the Prado's art treasures—are obvious. And, of course, it's this Madrid the routine visitor sees quickly before striking out for the next adventure, usually to one of the satellites, such as Segovia. However, for the more determined traveler, willing to invest the time and stamina, the Spanish capital tucks away many hidden treasures.

Suggested Itineraries

If You Have 1 Day

If you have just arrived in Spain after a long flight, don't tackle too much on your first day. Spend the morning at the Prado, one of the world's great art museums, arriving when it opens at 9am (closed Monday). Have lunch and then visit the Palacio Real (Royal Palace). Enjoy an early dinner near the Plaza Mayor.

If You Have 2 Days

Spend Day 1 as described above. On your second day take a trip to Toledo, where you can visit El Greco's House and Museum, the Santa Cruz Museum, the Church of Santo Tomé, and the Alcázar. Return to Madrid in the evening.

If You Have 3 Days

Follow the suggestions above for Days 1 and 2. On Day 3 take the train (one hour) to the Monastery of San Lorenzo del Escorial, in the foothills of the Sierra de Guadarrama. Return to Madrid in the evening.

If You Have 5 Days

Follow the suggestions for Days 1 to 3. Day 4 would be very busy indeed if you visited the Thyssen-Bornemisza Museum in the morning (it opens at 10am), took a walking tour of medieval Madrid (see Chapter 7), and visited the Museo Nacional Centro de Arte Reina Sofía in the late afternoon or early evening (it closes at 9pm on most nights). There you can see Picasso's *Guernica*, plus other great 20th-century art. Have dinner once again at one of the many restaurants off the Plaza Mayor.

On Day 5 take a trip to Segovia in Old Castile. Be sure to see its Alcázar, Roman aqueduct, and cathedral. Sample the region's specialties at lunch and return to Madrid for dinner in the old town.

1 The Top Attractions

★ **Museo del Prado,** paseo del Prado. ☎ **420-28-36.**

Many Madrileños go once or twice a month all their lives just to gaze upon their particular favorites (the reproductions at home are never adequate). But first-time visitors, with less than a lifetime to spend, will have to limit their viewing—see the two-hour walking tour of the Prado in Chapter 7. That task is difficult, as the Prado owns more than 7,000 paintings and is ranked among the top three art museums of the world.

In an 18th-century neoclassic palace designed by Juan de Villanueva, the Prado has been considerably improved in the past few years, especially its lighting. The most hurried trekker may want to focus attention on the output of three major artists: the court painters Velázquez and Goya, plus El Greco, who was in fact a Greek (born in Crete in 1541). But don't overlook the exceptional visions of Hieronymus Bosch, the 15th-century Flemish artist who peopled his canvases with fiends and ghouls and conjured up tortures that far surpassed Dante's *Inferno*. In particular, seek out his triptychs, *The Hay Wagon* and *The Garden of Earthly Delights*.

Most of the works of these artists are on the second floor. However, on the ground floor you'll find Goya's "black paintings" and his remarkable drawings. The Prado's single most famous work is *Las Meninas*—the maids in waiting—the masterpiece of Velázquez. In the Goya room is displayed his *Naked Maja*, certainly one of the most recognizable paintings in the West—said to have been posed for by the woman the artist loved, the Duchess of Alba. As a court painter to Charles IV and his adulterous queen, María Luisa, Goya portrayed all their vulgarity of person and mind—and got them to pay for the results.

Other paintings—by Raphael, Botticelli, Correggio, Titian, (Titzano), Pieter Breughel the Elder, Murillo, Ribera, and Fra Angelico—will make the morning fade quickly into dusk.

Admission: 450 ptas. ($3.20).

Open: Tues–Sat 9am–7pm, Sun and holidays 9am–2pm. **Closed:** Jan 1, Good Friday, May 1, Dec 25. **Metro:** Banco de España or Atocha. **Bus:** 10, 14, 27, 34, 37, 45, or M6.

★ **Thyssen-Bornemisza Museum,** Palacio de Villahermosa, paseo del Prado 8. ☎ **420-39-44.**

Until around 1985, this museum's contents of virtually overflowed the premises of a legendary villa near Lugano, Switzerland. Considered one of the most frequently visited sites of Switzerland, the collection had been laboriously amassed over about 60 years by the Thyssen-Bornemisza family, scions of a shipping/banking/mining/chemical fortune whose roots began around 1905 in Holland, Germany, and Hungary. Experts had proclaimed it one of the world's most extensive and valuable privately owned collections, rivaled only by Elizabeth II's legendary holdings.

For tax and insurance reasons and because the collection had outgrown the boundaries of the lakeside villa that contained it, the collection was discreetly marketed in the early 1980s to the world's major museums. Amid endless intrigue, a litany of glamorous supplicants from eight nations came calling. Among them were Prime Minister Margaret Thatcher and Prince Charles of the United Kingdom; trustees of the Getty Museum in Malibu, California; the president of West Germany; the Duke of Badajoz, brother-in-law of Juan Carlos II; and even emissaries from Disney World in Orlando, Florida—all hoping to acquire the collection for their respective countries or entities.

Eventually, thanks partly to the lobbying by Baron Hans Heinrich Thyssen-Bornemisza's fifth wife, a Spanish-born beauty (and former Miss Spain) named Tita, the collection was awarded to Spain. An agreement born as a nine-year lend-lease arrangement eventually evolved, pending final negotiations, into an outright $350-million purchase by the Spanish government. Although this amount was far less than the market value of the collection if each painting had been sold individually, controversies over the public cost of the acquisition raged for months throughout every level of Spanish society. Despite the brouhaha, various estimates have placed the value of this collection at anywhere between $1 and $3 billion.

To house the collection, an 18th-century building adjacent to the Prado, the Villahermosa Palace, was retrofitted with the appropriate lighting and security devices and renovated at a cost of $45 million. Since the rooms are arranged numerically(numbered 1 through 48, spread out over three floors), visitors can follow a logical sequence of European painting from the 13th through the 20th century. The nucleus of the collection consists of 700 world-class paintings by, among others, El Greco, Velázquez, Dürer, Rembrandt, Watteau, Canaletto, Caravaggio, Frans Hals, Hans Memling, and Goya.

Unusual among the world's great art collections because of its eclecticism, the Thyssen group also contains an abundance of 19th- and 20th-century paintings by many of the notable French impressionists, as well as works by Picasso, Sargent, Kirchner, Nolde, and Kandinsky—artists whose absence within Spanish museums had become increasingly obvious until the Thyssen acquisition. This museum has attracted millions of visitors since its long-awaited opening, so be prepared for magnificent art and long lines.

Admission: 650 ptas. ($4.60).

Open: Tues–Sun 10am–7pm. **Metro:** Banco de España. **Bus:** 1, 2, 5, 9, 10, 14, 15, 20, 27, 34, 45, 51, 52, 53, 74, 146, or 150.

★ **Museo Nacional Centro de Arte Reina Sofía,** Santa Isabel 52. ☎ **467-50-62.**

Filling for the world of modern art the role the Prado has filled for traditional art, the MoMA of Madrid (its nickname) reigns without challenge as Spain's greatest repository of 20th-century art. Set within the echoing, futuristically renovated walls of the former General Hospital (built between 1776 and 1781), the museum is a high-ceilinged, sprawling showplace named after the Greek-born wife of Spain's present king. Once designated "the ugliest building in Spain" by Catalán architect Oriol Bohigas, the building is said to be one of the largest museums—and probably the most security conscious—in Europe. The design hangs in limbo somewhere between the 18th and the 21st century and incorporates a 50,000-volume art library and database; a cafe; a theater; a bookstore; Plexiglas-sided elevators; and systems that carefully calibrate the security, temperature, humidity, and quality of light surrounding the exhibits.

Special emphasis is paid to the great artists of contemporary Spain: Juan Gris, Dalí, Miró, and Picasso (the museum has been able to acquire a handful of his works). What many critics claim to be Picasso's masterpiece, *Guernica* (1937), now rests at this museum after a long and troubling history of traveling. Banned in Spain during Franco's era (Picasso refused to have it displayed there anyway), it hung for years on world view at New York's Museum of Modern Art until it was returned after Franco's death. The antiwar piece of art immortalizes the shameful blanket bombing of Guernica (Gernika) by the German Luftwaffe, fighting for Franco during the Spanish Civil War. The town was the cradle of the Basque nation, and Picasso's canvas made it a household name around the world.

An important showplace of 20th-century Spanish art, the museum has also acted as a huge magnet for the relocation within its neighborhood of several new art galleries and cultural institutions that collectively promise to upgrade both the neighborhood and Spain's cultural quality of life.

Admission: 450 ptas. ($3.20).

Open: Wed–Mon 10am–9pm. **Metro:** Atocha. **Bus:** 6, 14, 26, 27, 32, 45, 57, or C.

⭐ **Palacio Real (Royal Palace)**, Plaza de Oriente, Bailén 2. ☎ 248-74-04.

Alfonso XIII, grandfather of Juan Carlos I, and his queen, Victoria Eugénie, were the last to use the Palacio Real as a royal abode, in 1931 before they fled into exile. Franco used the Royal Palace (also known as the Palacio de Oriente) for state functions and elaborate banquets for foreign dignitaries, but guides like to point out that he never sat on the king's chair in the Throne Room.

King Juan Carlos and Queen Sofia are more modest in their requirements. They have turned the Royal Palace over to history, choosing to live in their much smaller suburban palace, the Zarzuela, named after the Spanish operetta, or musical comedy.

On the landmark site of the former Alcázar of Madrid (destroyed by fire on Christmas 1734), the Royal Palace was launched in 1738. Its first tenant was Charles III, the "enlightened despot" of the House of Bourbon. The rooms—many added at a later date—total around 1,800. Not all are open to the public, of course—nor need they be, for the tour would then take a week.

Visitors are conducted on a guided tour of the State Apartments, the Reception Salons, the Royal Armory, and the Royal Pharmacy.

Madrid Attractions

If you're rushed and want just a quick glimpse of the grandeur of the palace, then you should confine your sightseeing to the State Apartments and the Reception Rooms.

After your tour, you can skip across the courtyard to the **Royal Armory,** considered one of the most impressive in Europe. Recalling the days of jousting and equestrian warfare, many of the exhibits

300 m
330 y
0

N

Calle de Genova

Calle de la Palma

Calle de Fuencarral

27

Calle Fernando VI

Plaza de
la Villa

Plaza
de Colón
COLÓN

26

SERRANO
Calle de Goya

Jardines
del
Descubrimiento

25

Calle de Serrano

El Escorial

Calle de San Pablo

Hortaleza

Calle de
Gravina del Almirante

CHUECA

Calle Bárbara
de Braganza

el Pez

Corredera Baja de San Pablo

Calle de Valverde

Calle de Fuencarral

Calle de Augusto Figueroa

Calle de Prim

Paseo Recoletos

GRAN VÍA
Red. de
San Luis

Avenida de Gran Vía

Calle de Barquillo

Plaza de
la Cibeles

Calle de Alcalá

24

Plaza de la
Independencia

Calle Montera

Calle de Alcalá

BANCO
DE ESPAÑA

23

Calle de Montalbán

SEVILLA

22

Paseo del Prado

SOL

Carrera de San Jerónimo

Plaza de
la Lealtad

Calle A. Maura

Calle de Alfonso XII

aza Jacinto
Benavente

Calle de la Cruz

Plaza
de las
Cortes

Calle del Prado

Calle de
Cervantes

Plaza C.
del Castillo

21

Parque
del
Retiro

20

19

Calle Atocha

Calle de las Huertas

15

T. DE MOLINA
Calle de la Magdalena

ANTON
MARTIN

Calle de Gobernador

Calle de Espalter

Calle de Alfonso XII

18

Calle de la Cabeza

14

Calle Jesús y María

Calle Atocha

17

Calle del Amparo

Calle de Santa Isabel

Real
Jardín
Botánico

Calle Mesón de Paredes

Plaza
Lavaples

16

LAVAPIES

ATOCHA

Calle Miguel Servet

Estación
de Atocha

Ronda de Atocha

Sta. María de la Cabeza

Paseo de la Infanta Isabel

ⓘ Information

✉ Post Office

✝ Church

date from the reign of Charles V (Charles I of Spain) of the Hapsburg Empire. The collection spans about 200 years of the Spanish Empire.

The **Royal Pharmacy** also merits a visit. It was, in its heyday, the "cure-all" source for any ailment that plagued the royal family.

Worth a detour, the **Museo de Carruajes Reales** (Carriage Museum) is also on the palace grounds. Here you can view the horse-drawn vehicles Spanish aristocrats used in the days when a person was judged solely on appearance.

After your whirlwind tour, you can wind down by strolling through the Campo del Moro, the gardens of the palace.

Admission: Palace, 500 ptas. ($3.60); Carriage Museum 200 ptas. ($1.40).

Open: Mon–Sat 9am–6pm, Sun 9am–3pm. **Metro:** Ópera or Plaza de España.

Real Fábrica de Tapices (Royal Factory of Tapestries), calle Fuenterrabia 2. ☎ 551-34-00.

The making of tapestries—based on original designs (called cartoons) by Goya, Francisco Bayeu (Goya's brother-in-law), and others—is still a flourishing art in Madrid. You can actually visit the factory where the *tapices* are turned out and chat with the workers. Some of the hand-looms on which they work date back to the days of Goya. The great Spanish artist sketched numerous cartoons that were converted into tapestries to adorn the walls of the Royal Palace not only in Madrid but also in Aranjuez and La Granja. One of the most famous, reproduced hundreds of times, is *El Cacharrero* (The Pottery Salesman).

Some craftspeople have copied the same design all their lives, so now they can work on it without thinking. Others, less cavalier, prefer to watch the design carefully through a mirror.

Admission: 450 ptas. ($3.20).

Open: Mon–Fri 9am–12:30pm. **Closed:** Aug. **Metro:** Menéndez Pelayo. **Bus:** 10, 14, 26, 32, 37, C, or M9.

Museo Lázaro Galdiano, Serrano 122. ☎ 561-60-84.

Deserving of far more visitors than it receives, this remarkable, compact, and art-stuffed museum spans the centuries of artistic development with seeming ease. An elevator takes you to the top floor of what was once one of Madrid's great mansions. It belonged to José Lázaro Galdiano, a famous 20th-century patron of the arts. You weave your way from room to room (37 in all), descending the stairs as you go.

The collection begins with vestments, some dating from the 15th century. Along the way you can stop and stare at an assemblage of weapons, daggers, and swords, some with elaborate handles dating from the 15th century. Seals, such as one belonging to Napoleon, are displayed; and there's a rare exhibition of Spanish fans, one a possession of Isabella II.

In Room XX are two Flemish paintings by the incomparable Bosch—rats crawling through the eyes of humans and so on. In the following room (XXI) is a portrait of Saskia signed by her husband, Rembrandt, dating from 1634. In other salons, several of the major artists of Spain are represented: Velázquez, Zurbarán, El Greco, Valdés Leal, Murillo, and Ribera. Room XXV is the salon of English-speaking portraitists: Gainsborough, Sir Joshua Reynolds, Gilbert Stuart, and Constable. Many well-known works by Goya are in his salon (XXX), including some of the "black paintings" and portraits of Charles IV and his voluble spouse.

Other intriguing showcases are filled with 16th-century Limoges crystal, French and Italian ivory carving from the 14th and 15th centuries, and a 15th-century Maltese cross. In Room VI hangs a small portrait of the Savior as an adolescent, encased in green velvet. Although some critics attribute this painting to Leonardo da Vinci, other art historians dispute this claim.

Admission: 450 ptas. ($3.20).

Open: Tues–Sun 10am–2pm. **Closed:** Holidays, Aug. **Metro:** Avenida de América. **Bus:** 9, 16, 19, 51, or 89.

⭐ **Convento de las Descalzas Reales,** Plaza de las Descalzas Reales. ☎ **248-74-04.**

What would you do if you were a starving nun surrounded by a vast treasure house of paintings, gold, jewelry, and tapestries? Sell them? Not possible. The order of the Franciscan Clarissas convinced the government to let them open the doors of the convent to the general public—with the pope's permission, of course. The museum is still an operational convent housing approximately 30 sisters.

The collection includes tapestries based on Rubens's cartoons, 16th- and 17th-century vestments, a silver forearm said to contain bones of St. Sebastian, and a statue of the Virgin wearing earrings, as is the custom in Andalusia. The most interesting chapel is dedicated to Our Lady of Guadalupe (the statue of the Virgin is made of lead).

The most valuable oil is Titian's *Caesar's Money,* worth millions of pesetas. The Flemish Hall contains other superb canvases—for example, one of a processional by Hans der Berken. You must wait for a guided tour.

Did You Know . . . ?

- Casa Botín, a Hemingway favorite, claims to be the world's oldest restaurant. It was founded in 1725.

- The only public statue anywhere dedicated to the Devil stands in Madrid's Retiro Park.

- A Mexican composer wrote the unofficial anthem "Madrid, Madrid, Madrid," and he had never been to Madrid.

- Napoleon once established his brother Joseph on the throne in Madrid.

- The ghost of the mistress of Philip II, who mysteriously disappeared, is said to haunt the Plaza del Rey at night.

- The Prado owns Pieter Breughel the Elder's *Triumph of Death*, considered the most frightening canvas ever painted.

- A tablet at the Puerta del Sol proclaims it to be *kilométrico zero*, the point from which all the roads radiating from Madrid are measured.

- The harmonious Plaza Mayor was the site of executions and *autos-de-fé*, inventive acts of death by torture conceived by the Inquisition.

Admission: 475 ptas. ($3.40) adults; 250 ptas. ($1.80) children.
Open: Tues–Thurs 10:30am–12:30pm and 4–5:30pm, Fri 10:30am–12:30pm, Sun 11am–1:30pm. **Metro:** Puerta del Sol, Callao, or Ópera. **Bus:** 1, 2, 5, 20, 46, 52, 53, 74, M1, M2, M3, or M5. **Directions:** From Plaza del Callao, off Gran Vía, walk down Postigo de San Martín to Plaza de las Descalzas Reales; the convent is on the left.

Panteon de Goya, Glorieta de San Antonio de la Florida.
☎ 542-07-22.

Emulating Tiepolo, Goya frescoed the Church of San Antonio de la Florida in 1798. Although he depicted in part the miracles of St. Anthony of Padua, his work was nearly secular in its execution. This has been called Goya's Sistine Chapel. Already deaf when he began the painting, Goya labored dawn to dusk for 16 weeks, painting with sponges rather than brushes. By depicting common street life—stone masons, prostitutes, and beggars—Goya raised the ire of the nobility, who held judgment until the patron, Carlos IV, viewed it. When the monarch approved, the formerly outrageous painting was deemed acceptable. Mirrors are placed to better allow you to see the beauty of the ceiling. The figure of a woman draped in a cape is one of the most celebrated subjects in Goya's work.

The hermitage is located at the northwestern edge of the city, near the western edge of the Parque Oeste, beyond the Príncipe Pío (north) station. Goya died in exile in Bordeaux, France, in 1828, but his bones were later removed from there and interred here in the memorial he unknowingly created for himself. In transit his skull disappeared, presumably stolen by a souvenir hunter.

Some church officials once considered Goya's frescoes irreverent—hence the hermitage was not a fit place of worship. A twin of the 18th-century church was erected alongside it, and services are conducted there now. Facing both of them, go into the one on the right to pay your respects to Goya.

Admission: 225 ptas. ($1.60).
Open: Apr–Oct, Thurs–Tues 10am–1pm and 4–7pm; Nov–Mar, Thurs–Tues 10am–2pm and 4–8pm. **Metro:** Norte. **Bus:** 41, 46, 75, or C.

2 More Attractions

Museums

Museo de la Real Academia de Bellas Artes de San Fernando (Fine Arts Museum), calle de Alcalá 13.
☎ 522-14-91.

Right on Madrid's busy boulevard, an easy stroll from the Puerta del Sol, the Fine Arts Museum is housed in the restored and remodeled

---

Frommer's Favorite Madrid Experiences

Tasca **Hopping**   The quintessential Madrid experience and the fastest way for a visitor to tap into the local scene. *Tascas* are Spanish pubs that serve tantalizing *tapas* (appetizers). You can go from one to the next, sampling the special dishes and wines in each tavern.

Eating "Around Spain"   The variety of gastronomic experiences is staggering. You can literally restaurant hop from province to province—without ever leaving Madrid.

Viewing the Works of Your Favorite Artist   Spend an afternoon at the Prado, savoring the works of your favorite Spanish artist, such as Goya or Velázquez, devoting all your attention to one painter.

Bargain Hunting at El Rastro   Madrid has one of the greatest flea markets in Europe, if not the world. Wander through its many offerings, discovering that hidden treasure you've been searching for.

A Night of Flamenco   Flamenco folk songs (*cante*) and dances (*baile*) are an integral part of the Spanish experience. Spend at least one night in a flamenco tavern listening to the heartrending laments of gypsy sorrows, tribulations, hopes, and dreams.

Outdoor Cafe Sitting   This is a famous Madrid experience for the summer, when Madrileños come alive again on their *terrazas*. The drinking and good times can go on until dawn. From glamorous hangouts to lowly street corners, the cafe scene takes place mainly along an axis shaped by paseo de la Castellana, paseo del Prado, and paseo de Recoletos.

---

baroque palace of Juan de Goyeneche, a banker who constructed it in 1710. It houses more than 1,500 paintings and 570 sculptures by such masters as Goya, Murillo, and El Greco, plus drawings by Rubens, Ribera, and Velázquez. The collection ranges from the 16th century to the present and was started in 1752 when the academy was founded during the reign of Fernando VI (1746–59). The emphasis is on works of Spanish, Flemish, and Italian artists, and you can see masterpieces by the artists mentioned above, plus Zurbarán, Sorolla, Cano, and Coello.

   Admission: 225 ptas. ($1.60) adults; children free.

   Open: Tues–Fri 9am–7pm, Sat–Mon 9am–2:30pm. **Metro:** Puerta del Sol or Sevilla.

Museo Taurino (Museum of Bullfighting), calle de Alcalá 237, in the Plaza de Teros de las Ventas (the Patio de Caballos).
   ☎ **255-18-57.**
   Ideally, you should visit this museum before you see your first Spanish bullfight, as it serves as a good introduction to "the tragedy" in the arena. It's located beneath the Moorish arcade of the largest bullfight stadium in Madrid. The complete history of the *torero*, as well

as a lot of bullfighting trivia, is traced in pictures, historic bullfight posters, and scale models. Works of art include a Goya painting of a matador, plus an exquisite bust, sculpted in bronze, of Manolete.

Admission: Free.

Open: May–Sept, Tues–Fri 9:30am–1:30pm, Sun 10am–1pm; Oct–Apr, Mon–Fri 10am–1pm. **Bus:** 12, 21, 38, 53, 146, M1, or M8.

Museo Municipal, Fuencarral 78. ☎ 522-57-32.

Perhaps more than any other museum in Madrid, the Municipal Museum documents the explosion of Madrid from a sleepy and dusty backwater into a world-class city. It contains exhibits on local history, archaeology, art, porcelain, plans, engravings, and photographs, all depicting the history of Madrid. In a churrigueresque baroque structure, the museum displays deal especially with 18th-century Bourbon Madrid, whose paseos with strolling couples are shown on huge tapestry cartoons. Paintings from the royal collections are here, plus period models of the best-known city squares and a Goya that was painted for the Town Hall.

Admission: 450 ptas. ($3.20).

Open: Tues–Fri 9:30am–8pm, Sat–Sun 10am–2pm. **Metro:** Tribunal. **Bus:** 3, 7, 40, or M10.

Museo Arqueológico Nacional (Archeological Museum), calle Serrano 13. ☎ 577-79-12.

For some reason, Iberian archaeological museums tend to be dull—surprising, since so many civilizations (prehistoric, Roman, Visigothic, Muslim) have conquered the peninsula. An exception, however, is this stately mansion in Madrid, a storehouse of artifacts from prehistoric times to the heyday of the baroque; it also houses the National Library. One of the prime exhibits here is the Iberian statue *La Dama de Elche*, a piece of primitive carving—probably from the 4th century B.C.—discovered on the southeastern coast of Spain, as well as the splendidly polychromed *Dama de Baza* discovered in Granada province, from the same period.

Treasures from the discovery of some of the finest Punic relics in Europe on the Balearic island of Ibiza—many found in a Carthaginian and Roman necropolis—are on display. Excavations from Paestum, Italy, are shown: The statuary of Imperial Rome includes a statue of Tiberius enthroned and one of the controversial Livia, mother of Tiberius and wife of Augustus. The Islamic collection from Spain is outstanding. The collection of Spanish Renaissance lusterware, as well as Talavera pottery and Retiro porcelain, is shown to good advantage, along with some rare 16th- and 17th-century Andalusian glassware.

The "classic" artifacts are impressive, and the contributions from medieval days up through the 16th century are highly laudable. Many of the exhibits were ecclesiastical treasures removed from churches and monasteries. A much-photographed choir stall from Palancia—hand-painted and crude but remarkable nevertheless—dates from the 14th century.

Worthy of a look are the reproductions of the prehistoric Altamira cave paintings discovered near Santander in northern Spain in 1868. Joseph Dechelette called them "the Sistine Chapel of Quaternary art." The original caves have been closed except to a carefully arranged handful of monthly visitors, so this is your chance to see an excellent copy.

Admission: 450 ptas. ($3.20).

Open: Museum, Tues–Sun 9:30am–8:30pm; caves, Tues–Sun 9:30am–1:30pm. **Metro:** Serrano or Retiro. **Bus:** 1, 9, 19, 51, 74, or M2.

Museo Nacional de Artes Decorativas (Decorative Arts Museum), calle de Montalbán 12, near the Plaza de la Cibeles. ☎ 521-34-40.

In 62 rooms spread over several floors, this museum displays a rich collection of furniture, ceramics, and decorative pieces from all regions of Spain. It's especially rich in works of the 16th and 17th centuries, though the collection is eclectic, with many surprises— including bronzes from the Ming Dynasty in China. You're greeted by an 18th-century Venetian sedan chair in the vestibule. This bit of whimsy is only a preview of what awaits you: Gothic carvings, tapestries, alabaster figurines, vestments, festival crosses, elaborate dollhouses, Andalusian antique glass, elegant baroque four-poster beds, a chapel covered with leather tapestries, even kitchens from the 17th century. Just keep climbing one flight of steps after another; the surprises continue until you reach the top floor of what must have been one of the grandest mansions in Madrid.

Admission: 450 ptas. ($3.20).

Open: Tues–Fri 9am–3pm, Sat–Sun 10am–2pm. **Metro:** Banco de España. **Bus:** 14, 27, 34, 37, 45, or M6.

Museo del Ejército (Army Museum), calle Mendez Núñez 1. ☎ 522-89-77.

Behind the Prado, this museum has some outstanding exhibits from military history, including the original sword of El Cid. Isabella carried this same sword when she took Granada from the Moors. In addition, you can see the tent used by Charles V in Tunisia, along with relics from explorers Pizarro and Cortés. The collection of armor is also exceptional. The museum contains a piece of the cross that Columbus carried with him when he landed in the New World and weapons and memorabilia from the grisly Spanish Civil War. The museum is housed in the Buen Retiro Palace, which dates from 1631 and was destroyed (and subsequently rebuilt in a smaller form) during the Napoleonic Wars.

The museum has a notorious founder: Manuel Godoy, who rose from relative poverty to become the lover of María Luisa of Parma, wife of Carlos IV.

Admission: 125 ptas. (90¢).

Open: Tues–Sat 10am–2pm, Sun 10am–1:30pm. **Metro:** Banco de España.

Museo Naval (Naval Museum), paseo del Prado 5. ☎ **379-52-99.**
The history of nautical science and the Spanish navy comes alive at this museum. For me, the most fascinating exhibit is the map of the new discoveries of land that the mate of the *Santa Maria* made to show the Spanish monarchs. There are also souvenirs of the Battle of Trafalgar.

Admission: Free.

Open: Tues–Sun 10:30am–1:30pm. **Closed:** Aug. **Metro:** Banco de España. **Bus:** 10, 14, 27, 34, 37, 45, or M6.

Museo Sorolla, General Martínez Campos 37. ☎ **410-15-84.**
Appreciation of the work of painter Joaquin Sorolla (1863–1923) is an acquired taste. In his day he was celebrated, as autographed portraits from Alfonso XIII and U.S. President Taft reveal. From 1912 he and his family occupied this elegant Madrileño town house off paseo de la Castellana. Two years after his death his widow turned it over to the government—and it is now maintained as a memorial to the artist, inaugurated in 1932. Much of the house remains as Sorolla left it, right down to his stained paintbrushes and pipes. In the museum wing, however, a representative collection of the artist's paintings is displayed. All the works owned by the museum can't be exhibited, however, because of the lack of space.

Although Sorolla painted portraits of Spanish aristocrats, he was essentially interested in "the people," often in their native costumes, such as those once worn in Avila and Salamanca. He was especially fond of painting beach scenes on what is now the Costa Blanca. His favorite subjects are depicted either "before" or "after" their bath, and he was interested in the subtle variations of the Spanish sunlight. One critic wrote that Sorolla "may fail to please certain individuals, contaminated by an unhealthy leaning toward things decadent, pessimistic, and tragic."

Seek out not only the artist's self-portrait but also the paintings of Madame Sorolla and their handsome son. The house and garden alone are worth the trip. The museum is entered through an Andalusian-style patio.

Admission: 450 ptas. ($3.20).

Open: Tues–Sun 10am–3pm. **Closed:** Holidays. **Metro:** Iglesia or Rubén Darío. **Bus:** 5, 16, 61, 40, or M3.

Museo Romantico (Romantic Museum), San Mateo 13.
☎ **448-10-71.**
Of special interest and limited appeal, this museum attracts those seeking the romanticism of the 19th century. Decorative arts festoon the mansion in which the museum is housed: crystal chandeliers, faded portraits, oils from Goya to Sorolla, opulent furnishings, porcelain, jewelry, ceramics, even *la grande toilette.* Many of the exhibitions date from the days of Isabella II, the high-living, fun-loving queen who was forced into exile and eventual abdication of the throne (she lived in Paris until her death in 1904).

Admission: 450 ptas. ($3.20).

Open: Tues–Sat 9am–3pm, Sun 10am–2pm. **Closed:** Aug.
Metro: Alonso Martínez.

Religious Sites

Real Basílica de San Francisco El Grande, on the Plaza de San
Francisco El Grande, at San Buenaventura 1. ☎ **365-38-00.**

In lieu of a great cathedral, Madrid possesses this church, which has
a dome larger than that of St. Paul's in London. Constructed on the
site of a much earlier church, San Francisco dates from the late 18th
century and owes much of its appearance to Sabatini, a celebrated
architect of his day.

Its interior of Doric columns and Corinthian capitals is cold and
foreboding, although 19th-century artists labored hard to adorn its
series of chapels flanking the nave. The best painting—that of St.
Bernardinus of Siena preaching—is by Goya.

You are conducted through the church by a guide, who notes the
most outstanding artwork, especially the choir stalls dating from the
16th century.

Admission: 125 ptas. (90¢).

Open: Tues–Sat 11am–1pm and 4–7pm. **Metro:** La Latina or
Puerta del Toledo. **Bus:** 3, 60, C, or M4.

Templo de Debod, on calle Ferraz, at paseo de Rosales.

This Egyptian temple once stood in the Valley of the Nile, 19 miles
from Aswan. When the new dam built there threatened to overrun
its site with water, the Egyptian government agreed to have the temple
dismantled and presented to the Spanish people. It was taken down
stone by stone in 1969 and 1970, then shipped to Valencia. From
that Mediterranean port, it was sent by rail to Madrid, where it was
reconstructed and opened to the public in 1971. Photos upstairs in
the temple depict its long history. The temple stands right off the
Plaza de España.

Admission: Free.

Open: Tues–Fri 10am–1pm and 4–7pm, Sat–Sun 10am–1pm.
Closed: National and Catholic holidays. **Metro:** Plaza de España or
Ventura Rodríguez. **Bus:** 1, 2, 44, or 74.

Parks & Gardens

PARQUE DE RETIRO The most prominent and famous park
in Madrid sprawls over 350 acres. A reminder of the large forests that
once stood proudly in Castile, the Retiro was originally a royal playground for the exclusive use of the Spanish monarchs and their guests.
The huge palaces that stood here were destroyed in the early 19th
century. Only the palace's former dance hall, the Casón del Buen
Retiro (housing some of the Prado's modern works), and the building containing the army museum remain. The park is filled with
numerous fountains (one dedicated to an artichoke) and statues (one
honors Lucifer, strangely heretical in Catholic Spain), and there's a
large lake where soldiers meet their girlfriends during the hotter

months. There is also a pair of exposition centers, the Velázquez and Crystal Palaces (built to honor the Philippines in 1887), plus a lakeside monument, erected in 1922, to Alfonso XII. In summer the rose gardens are worth the visit, and you'll find several places where you can have inexpensive snacks and drinks.

The park is technically open all day and night, but it's at its most popular (and safest) between 7am and 8:30pm. Entrance is free, and hundreds of Madrileños, especially on hot midsummer days, are likely to be here, too.

Across calle de Alfonso XII, abutting the southwest corner of the Retiro, are the famous **Royal Botanical Gardens** (Real Jardín Botánico), Plaza de Murillo 2 (☎ **585-47-00**). Founded by Carlos III and in its present location since the 18th century, these gardens contain more than 104 species of trees and 3,000 types of plants. They surround a library specializing in botany and an exhibition hall. The gardens are open daily from 10am to 8pm, charging 200 ptas. ($1.40) per person. Metro: Atocha. Bus: 10, 14, 19, 32, or 45.

CASA DE CAMPO   Many visitors to Madrid never make it to the former royal hunting grounds, the Casa de Campo—miles and miles of parkland lying south of the Royal Palace, across the Manzanares. You can see the gate through which the kings and queens rode out of the palace grounds—either on horses or in carriages—and headed for the retiro. Presently, of course, you will have to take less elegant transportation: the Metro to El Lago or El Batán.

The park has a variety of trees and a lake usually filled with rowers. You can have drinks and light refreshments around the lake, or you can go swimming in an excellent municipally operated pool.

Madrileños like to keep the place to themselves; on a hot night or a Sunday morning, the park is thronged with people trying to escape the heat. If you have an automobile you can go for a drive, as the grounds are extensive. The park is open daily from 8am to 9pm. It's cool, pleasant, and refreshing—a cheap way to spend an evening.

3 Cool for Kids

The Spanish have always loved children and have created diversions for kids that many Spanish adults remember with great fondness in later years. Here's a sampling:

Museo de las Figuras de Cera (Wax Museum), paseo de Recoletos 41. ☎ **319-26-49**.

In this wax museum famous personalities seem to come to life, sometimes in eerily disconcerting ways. Some parents consider it a good way to imbue children with a sense of history. There are scenes depicting Columbus calling on Ferdinand and Isabella, Romans battling with Celts, Arabs fighting with Spaniards, and characters from *Don Quixote de La Mancha*. Twentieth-century international figures aren't neglected either; we see Jacqueline Kennedy Onassis drinking champagne and Garbo all alone. The heroes and villains of World War II—everyone from Eisenhower to Hitler—are highlighted by the presence of Marlene Dietrich singing "Lili Marlene." The 400 figures that inhabit the 38 tableaux were created by out-of-work film-makers, who succeeded best with backdrops, falling shortest in their depictions of contemporary celebrities. A film gives a 30-minute re-cap of Spanish history from the days of the Phoenicians to today.

Admission: 750 ptas. ($5.30) adults; 500 ptas. ($3.60) children.

Open: Daily 10:30am–1:30pm and 4-8pm. **Metro:** Colón. **Bus:** 27, 45, or 53.

Aquapolis, Villanueva de la Canada, carretera de El Escorial.

☎ **815-69-11.**

Just 16 miles northwest of Madrid lies a watery attraction where your kids might happily intermingle with hundreds of other children. Scattered amid shops, a picnic area, and a barbecue restaurant are water slides, wave-making machines, and tall slides that spiral chil-dren (and an occasional adult) into the swimming pool below. These water sports are available in summer only.

Admission: 2,000 ptas. ($14.20) adults; 1,250 ptas. ($8.90) children.

Open: Daily 10am–8pm. **Closed:** Oct–Apr. **Transportation:** Free bus runs several times a day during park's open hours, leaving Madrid from calle de los Reyes, next to Coliseum Cinema, on east-ern edge of the Plaza de España.

Parque de Atracciones, Casa de Campo. ☎ **463-29-00.**

At its most popular in July and August, this park was created in 1969 to amuse the young at heart with an array of rides and concessions. The numerous attractions include a tobaggan slide, a carousel, pony rides, an adventure into "outer space," a walk through a transparent maze, a visit to "jungleland," a motor-propelled series of cars disguised as a tail-wagging dachshund puppy, and a gyrating whirligig clutched in the tentacles of an octopus named El Pulpo. The most popular rides are a pair of roller coasters named 7 Picos and Jet Star.

Admission: 225 ptas. ($1.60) adults; 75 ptas. (50¢) children under 9. An all-inclusive ticket—good for all rides—is 1,400 ptas. ($9.90).

Open: Apr–June, Tues–Fri noon–9pm, Sat–Sun noon–1am; July–Aug, Tues–Fri 6pm–1am, Sat 6pm–2am, Sun noon–1am; Sept, Tues–Sun (variable hours—call to check before going); Oct–Mar, Sat noon–8pm (sometimes 9pm), Sun 11am–8pm (sometimes 9pm). **Directions:** Take the *teleférico* cable car (see below). At the end of the ride, "microbuses" will take you the rest of the way. Alternatively, take the suburban train from Plaza de España and stop near the en-trance to the park (Entrada de Batán).

Zoo de la Casa de Campo, in the Casa de Campo, at the edge of the Parque de Atracciones. ☎ **711-99-50.**

Children are invariably delighted by the zoo, which in Madrid lies in the Parque de Atracciones (see above). The zoo was developed in the 1970s using up-to-date theories about layout and planning. Most of the animals are in a simulated natural habitat, with moats sepa-rating them from the public. There's an area where small animals may be petted by children. Sprawling over 50 carefully landscaped acres, it contains animals from Spain and throughout the world. It allows you to see, through its division by continents, the wildlife of Africa, Asia, the Americas, and Europe, with about 2,500 animals on display.

Admission: 1,240 ptas. ($8.80) adults; 895 ptas. ($6.40) children 3–8; children 2 and under free.

Open: Daily 10am–sunset. **Metro:** Batán. **Bus:** 33. **Directions:** Exit on the right side for the park, turn left, and walk up to Plaza de España, which takes you directly to the zoo.

Teleférico, paseo del Pintor Rosales, at the corner of calle Marqués de Urquijo. ☎ **541-19-97.**

Strung high above several of Madrid's verdant parks, this cable car was built in 1969 as part of a public fairgrounds (the Parque de Atracciones) modeled vaguely along the lines of Disneyland. Today, even for visitors not interested in visiting the park, the *teleférico* retains an allure of its own as a high-altitude method of admiring the cityscape. The cable car departs from the paseo Pintor Rosales at the eastern edge of the Parque del Oeste (at the corner of the calle Marqués de Urquijo) and carries you high above two parks and railway tracks and over the Manzanares River to a spot near a picnic ground/restaurant in the Casa de Campo. Weather permitting, there are good views of the Royal Palace along the way. The ride takes 11 minutes.

Prices: 300 ptas. ($2.10) one way; 500 ptas. ($3.60) round trip.

Service: Mar–Oct, daily noon–9pm; Nov–Feb, Mon and Thurs–Fri noon–2pm and 4–7pm, Sat–Sun noon–7pm. **Metro:** Plaza de España or Argüelles. **Bus:** 74.

Planetarium, Tierno Galván Park, Méndez Alvaro. ☎ **467-34-61.**

This planetarium has a projection room with optical and electronic equipment—including a multivision system—designed to reproduce outer space.

Admission: 375 ptas. ($2.70) adults; 200 ptas. ($1.40) children.

Open: Tues–Sun shows at 11:30am and 12:45, 5:30, 6:45 and 8pm. **Closed:** 2 weeks in Jan. **Metro:** Méndez Alvaro. **Bus:** 148.

4   Special-Interest Sightseeing

For the Literary Enthusiast

Casa de Lope de Vega, Cervantes 11. ☎ **429-92-16.**

Ironically, the House of Lope de Vega stands on a street named after Cervantes, his competitor for the title of the greatest writer of the Golden Age of Spain. The house is considered a *perfecta* reconstruction of the casa in which Lope de Vega lived, and it's furnished with pieces indigenous to his time (1562–1635). The Spanish writer, the major dramatist of Hapsburg Spain, wrote more than 1,000 plays, many of which have been lost to history. You'll be shown through the house, with its volumes upon volumes of manuscript reproductions, and then allowed to roam at random in the garden in back.

Admission: 200 ptas. ($1.40).

Open: Tues and Thurs 9:30am–3pm, Sat 10am–4pm. **Metro:** Anton Martín.

Hemingway Haunts

Chicote, Gran Vía 12. ☎ **532-67-37.**

Hemingway used Chicote as a setting for his only play, *The Fifth Column*. He would sit here night after night, gazing at the *putas* (it was a famed hooker bar back then) as he entertained friends with such remarks as "Spain is a country for living and not for dying." The bar still draws a lively crowd. A whisky and soda costs 850 ptas. ($6).

Open: Mon–Sat 1:30pm–3am. **Metro:** Gran Vía.

Museo del Prado, paseo del Prado. ☎ **420-28-36.**

Of the Prado, A. E. Hotchner wrote in his *Papa Hemingway:* "Ernest loved the Prado. He entered it as he entered cathedrals." More than any other, one picture held him transfixed, Andrea del Sarto's *Portrait of a Woman.* (For details on the museum, see "The Top Attractions," earlier in this chapter.)

Sobrino de Botín, Cuchilleros 17. ☎ **366-42-17.**

In the final two pages of Hemingway's novel *The Sun Also Rises,* Jake invites Lady Brett here for the Segovian specialty, roast suckling pig, washed down with Rioja Alta. In another book, *Death in the Afternoon,* Hemingway told his mythical "Old Lady": "I would rather dine on suckling pig at Botín's than sit and think of casualties my friends have suffered." Since that time, thousands upon thousands of Americans have visited Botín (see Chapter 5 for details). It's a perennial favorite of all visiting Yankees.

For the Architecture Enthusiast

⭐ **PLAZA MAYOR** In the heart of Madrid, this famous square was known as the Plaza de Arrabal in medieval times, when it stood outside the city wall.

The original architect of the Plaza Mayor itself was Juan Gómez de Mora, who worked during the reign of Philip III. Under the Hapsburgs the square rose in importance as the site of public spectacles, including the gruesome *autos-da-fé,* in which "heretics" were burned. Bullfights, knightly tournaments, and festivals were also staged here.

Three times the buildings on the square burned—in 1631, 1672, and 1790—but each time the Plaza Mayor bounced back. After the last big fire, it was completely redesigned by Juan de Villanueva.

Nowadays a Christmas fair is held around the equestrian statue of Philip III (dating from 1616) in the center of the square. On summer nights the Plaza Mayor becomes the virtual living room of Madrid, as tourists sip sangría at the numerous cafes and listen to music, which is often spontaneous.

PUERTA DE TOLEDO   The Puerta de Toledo is one of the two surviving town gates (the other is the Puerta de Alcalá). Constructed during the brief and unpopular rule of Joseph Bonaparte, this one marks the spot where citizens used to set out for the former imperial capital of Toledo. On an irregularly shaped square, it stands at the intersection of ronda de Toledo and calle de Toledo. Its original purpose was as a triumphal arch to honor Napoleon Bonaparte. In 1813 it became a symbol of Madrid's fierce independence and the loyalty of its citizens to their Bourbon rulers, who had been restored to the throne in the wake of the Napoleonic invasion. Metro: Puerta de Toledo.

5   Organized Tours

A large number of agencies in Madrid book organized tours and excursions to sights and attractions both within and outside the city limits. Although your mobility and freedom might be somewhat hampered, some visitors appreciate the ease, convenience, and efficiency of being able to visit so many sights in a single well-organized day. Also, the hassles of navigating from one sight to the next are almost eliminated as you entrust your itinerary to the bus driver and bilingual guide.

Many of the city's hotel concierges and travel agents can book you for a guided tour of Madrid or its environs with one of Spain's largest tour operators, **Pullmantours,** Plaza de Oriente 8 (☎ 541-18-07). Regardless of destination and duration, virtually every tour departs from the Pullmantour terminal at that address. Half-day Madrid tours include an "artistic tour" priced at 4,300 ptas. ($30.50) per person, which includes entrance to a selection of the city's museums, and a panoramic tour for 2,600 ptas. ($18.50).

Southward treks to Toledo are the most popular full-day excursions outside the city limits. These tours—costing 6,900 ptas. ($49) and including lunch—depart daily at 8:30am from the above-mentioned departure point, last all day, and include ample opportunities for wandering at will through the city's narrow streets. You can, if you wish, take an abbreviated morning tour, without stopping for lunch, for 4,470 ptas. ($31.70).

Another popular tour stops briefly in Toledo and continues on to visit both the monastery at El Escorial and the Valley of the Fallen (Valle de los Caídos) before returning the same day to Madrid. With lunch included, this all-day excursion costs 9,410 ptas. ($66.80).

Other worthwhile full-day tours include visits to Segovia and the Bourbon dynasty's 18th-century La Granja palace costing 5,515 ptas. ($39.20) without lunch and 8,520 ptas. ($60.50) with lunch. A half-day tour of Aranjuez and Chinchón, without lunch, costs 5,200 ptas. ($36.90).

The hop-off, hop-on **Madrid Vision Bus** lets you set your own pace and itinerary. A scheduled panoramic tour lasts half an hour, providing you don't get off the bus. Otherwise, you can opt for an unlimited number of stops, exploring at your leisure. The Madrid Vision makes four complete tours daily, two in the morning and two in the afternoon; on Sunday and Monday buses depart only in the morning. Check with the Madrid tourist office for times of your departure, which are variable. The panoramic tour (without your getting off the bus) costs 560 ptas. ($4); the full-day tour with unlimited stops is 1,050 ptas. ($7.50).

6   Sports & Recreation

Spectator Sports

⭐ **THE BULLFIGHT**   Madrid draws the finest matadors in Spain: If a matador hasn't proved his worth in Madrid's major ring, he just hasn't been recognized as a top-flight artist. The major season begins during the Fiestas de San Isidro, patron saint of Madrid, on May 15. This is the occasion for a series of fights during which talent scouts are part of the audience. Matadors who distinguish themselves in the ring are signed up for Majorca, Málaga, and other places.

For tickets to the biggest bullfight stadium in Madrid, go to the box office of the **Plaza Monumental de Toros de las Ventas,** calle de Alcalá 237 (☎ **356-22-00;** Metro: Ventas). Many hotels have good seats you can buy. Front-row seats are known as *barreras.* Third-row seats (*delanteras*) are available in both the *alta* (high) and *baja* (low) sections. The cheapest seats, *filas,* afford the worst view and are in the sun (*sol*) during the entire performance. The best seats are in the shade (*sombra*). Bullfights are held on Sunday and holidays at 7pm from Easter through October; in late September and October they often begin at 5pm. Fights by neophyte matadors are sometimes staged on Saturday at 11pm. On the day of the fight, arrive early to avoid the crowds. You'll want to leave the fight before the very end again to avoid the crowds. Admission to the bullring ranges from 600 to 15,000 ptas. ($4.30 to $106.50). The box office is open Friday through Sunday from 10am to 2pm and 5 to 8pm.

HORSE RACING   At the **Hipódromo de la Zarzuela,** carretera de la Coruña, Km 7.8 (☎ **207-01-40**), there are two racing seasons: spring (February through June) and fall (mid-September through early December). Races, often six or seven, are generally held on Sunday and holidays at 11am, with a series of night races held at 11pm on weekends in July and August. A restaurant and bar are at the hippodrome, which is 11 miles (18 km) from the center of Madrid on the N-VI. Admission is 500 ptas. ($3.60). To get there, take the tree bus that leaves from Moncloa, across the Air Ministry.

SOCCER   *Futból* is played with a passion year round in Madrid. Saturday and Sunday league matches run from September through May, culminating in the annual summer tournaments. Madrid has two teams in the top division. **Real Madrid** plays at the Estadio Santiago Bernabéu, Concha Espina 1 (☎ **344-00-52;** Metro: Lima).

Club Atlético de Madrid plays at the Estadio Vicente Calderón, paseo de la Virgen del Puerto 67 (☎ **366-47-07;** Metro: Pirámides). Tickets for each team, starting at 1,500 ptas. ($10.70), can be obtained from their respective stadium.

Recreation

FITNESS CENTERS   Although Madrid has scores of gyms, body-building studios, and aerobic-exercise centers, many are private. For one open to the public, try **Atenas,** Victor de la Serna 37 (☎ **345-16-75;** Metro: Colombia). This facility for men and women has an indoor pool, workout equipment, a sauna, and such personal services as massage. It's open Monday through Saturday from 8am to 9:30pm.

JOGGING   The **Parque del Retiro** and the **Casa de Campo** both have jogging tracks. For details on how to get there, see "Parks and Gardens" under "More Attractions," earlier in this chapter.

SWIMMING & TENNIS   The best swimming and tennis facilities are found at the **Casa de Campo,** avenida del Angel (☎ **463-00-50;** Metro: Batán or Lago), a 4,300-acre former royal hunting preserve that lies on the right bank of the Manzanares River. Today it's a public park, serving as a playground for Madrileños.

7

Strolling Around Madrid

You will need public transportation to get around New Madrid, since it sprawls for miles in all directions; however, walking is the best way to savor the unique charms of Old Madrid.

This chapter is organized into a series of walking tours for those who want to use their own shoe leather to discover the major attractions and districts of the Spanish capital.

Unless you're in Madrid for a long time, it's virtually impossible to see all that's of interest in the city. Much of the dusty environs of Madrid—filled with ugly modern apartment houses and industry—is of little interest to visitors. However, some districts of Madrid are of such architectural interest that every street you wander down holds some fascination.

Chief of these is Medieval Madrid (Walking Tour 1). After visiting the highlights of the oldest part of the city, you can then explore a section built later: Hapsburg Madrid (Walking Tour 2), whose chief attraction is the Royal Palace (see Chapter 6).

Walking Tour 3 explores Bourbon Madrid, built at a time when the city was already an established world-class center. This section is the site of the Prado and the Puerta del Sol. For those who still haven't exhausted their feet, Walking Tour 4 explores some of the major districts and arteries of Madrid, including the Plaza de España and the Gran Vía.

Finally you could wander for weeks in the Prado and still not see everything—but surveys have shown that many visitors have only two hours to devote to this repository of world art. For those rushed individuals, I've recommended only some of the major masterpieces or schools of paintings in Walking Tour 5.

Warning: As you walk around Madrid with your head buried in a map or a guidebook, maintain your usual vigilance against potential muggers, as tourists are frequently victims of robberies.

Walking Tour 1
Medieval Madrid

Start   Plaza de la Villa.
Finish   Plaza de la Puerta Cerrada.
Time   2½ hours.
Best Times   Any sunny day.
Worst Times   Monday through Saturday from 7:30 to 9:30am and 5 to 7:30pm—because of heavy traffic.

The oldest part of the city was a flourishing Muslim area before Madrid became the capital.

Begin your tour at the:

1. **Plaza de la Villa,** which stands beside calle Mayor, between the Palacio Real (Royal Palace) and the Puerta del Sol. In the center, note the bronze statue of Don Alvaro de Bazán, an admiral under Philip II, best remembered for defeating

the Turks at Lepanto. With your back to calle Mayor, you'll see the red-brick 17th-century facade of the:

2. **Ayuntamiento de Madrid (Town Hall)** on your right. It was built as a prison and today houses the Museo Municipal (see Chapter 6). On the square's south side rises the depressingly somber stone-and-brick facade of the 15th-century:

3. **Torre de los Lujanes,** a tower whose simple granite entrance is one of Madrid's few remaining examples of Gothic architecture. Beside the tower, behind a Gothic-Mudéjar archway, lies the tomb of Beatriz Galindo, nicknamed "La Latina" because she taught Latin to the adolescent Isabella I.

   With your back to calle Mayor, you'll see two narrow streets stretching parallel to each other to the south. Take the one on the left (calle del Cordón) and walk for about one short block to the:

4. **Plaza del Cordón** (you won't see any street signs here). You'll find yourself amid a complex of unmarked 16th- and 17th-century municipal buildings, protected and patrolled by uniformed guards. Turn left at the entrance to the Plaza del Cordón, walk about 50 feet, and notice the semicircular convex entrance to the baroque:

5. **Church of San Miguel,** San Justo 4, built by Giacomo Bonavia in the 18th century. A few steps farther, flanking the right side of the church, is a narrow alley, the Pasadizo del Panecillo, where 17th-century priests distributed bread to hungry paupers. Facing the front of the church is one of the oldest houses in Madrid, a grim, rather dingy-looking stone building. Look for the heraldic shields carved into its fortresslike facade. Historical sources report that the legendary Isidro, patron saint of Madrid, worked as a servant in this baronial, now much-faded residence, which today contains private apartments. Its address, although you probably won't see a street sign until you reach the bottom of the hill, is calle del Doctor Letamendi.

   Walk down this cobblestone street (you'll have to walk back about 10 feet and enter it from an edge of the Plaza del Cordón). Follow it one block and cross busy calle de Segovia. Then turn right and walk about three blocks (the street will now rise sharply). Look down the Costanilla San Pedro, to your left, and notice the Mudéjar tower of the:

6. **Church of San Pedro el Viejo (Old St. Peter's),** which marks the border of Madrid's Muslim quarter. The church's mid-14th-century tower is one of the few remnants of medieval architecture in Madrid. The church itself, however, dates from the 17th century; it was severely looted during the Civil War in 1936. Although the houses

in this neighborhood look small, they're considered among the most chic and expensive in Madrid.

Walk one more uphill block along calle de Segovia until you reach the Costanilla San Andrés. Before you turn left onto this narrow street, note to the north of calle de Segovia the:

7. **Plaza de la Cruz Verde,** whose centerpiece is a 19th-century baroque fountain commemorating the end of the Spanish Inquisition. In the background you'll see the back side and the massive brick tower of the:

8. **Iglesia del Sacramento,** where memorial services for soldiers killed in war or by terrorists are performed. Now, ascend the steep cobblestones of Costanilla San Andrés. Around you is the:

9. **Arab Quarter.** Many buildings that were erected during the past two centuries were built upon foundations of Muslim structures. Very shortly you'll reach the triangular and steeply sloping grounds of the:

10. **Plaza de la Paja,** whose lovely trees and calm give no hint that this was once the most important produce market in the region. Today the neighborhood waits sleepily in the intense sunlight for night to bring business to the several famous restaurants that ring its perimeter. To your left as you climb the square is the:

11. **Capilla del Obispo (Bishop's Chapel),** entered from the Plaza de la Paja. The mortal remains of San Isidro were interred here from 1518 to 1657. Notice its Renaissance doors. The high altar is considered a masterpiece of Plateresque (the late Gothic style of Castile). At the top of the square, follow the continuation of Costanilla San Andrés to the right side of the chapel. You'll discover that it abuts the back of the more imposing:

12. **Church of San Andrés,** Plaza de San Andrés. In one of the most colorful parts of the old town, the church dates from medieval times but was rebuilt in the 17th century. A 1936 fire destroyed its greatest treasures. Keep walking and you'll come to the fountains of the:

13. **Plaza de los Carros,** the first of four interconnected squares, each with its own name and allure. Descend the steps at the far edge of the Plaza de los Carros and turn left onto the Plaza de Puerta de Moros. Diagonally across the street, you'll soon notice the modern brick-and-concrete dome of the:

14. **Mercado de la Cebada.** In its echoing interior are open-air markets, open Monday through Saturday from 8am to 2pm and 5 to 8pm. The square has by this time changed its name to the:

15. **Plaza del Humilladero.** Directly in your path are two streets. The one that forks to the left is:

Walking Tour — Medieval Madrid

Map legend:

1. Plaza de la Villa
2. Ayuntamiento de Madrid (Town Hall)
3. Torre de los Lujanes
4. Plaza del Cordón
5. Church of San Miguel
6. Church of San Pedro el Viejo (Old St. Peter's)
7. Plaza de la Cruz Verde
8. Iglesia del Sacramento
9. Arab Quarter
10. Plaza de la Paja
11. Capilla del Obispo (Bishop's Chapel)
12. Church of San Andrés
13. Plaza de los Carros
14. Mercado de la Cebada
15. Plaza del Humilladero
16. Calle de la Cava Baja
17. La Chata
18. Plaza de la Puerta Cerrada

16. **Calle de Cava Baja** (the other is calle la Cava Alta). Some 600 years ago these streets defined the city limits of Madrid. Take calle de Cava Baja, which is filled with some of the most typical cafes, bars, and restaurants in Madrid.

Refueling Stop

There's a restaurant in back at **17. La Chata,** calle de Cava Baja 24 (% 366-14-58), but its stand-up bar up front is more popular. Here, locals chatter amid hanging Serrano hams and photographs of famous bullfighters. On a hot day, order a glass of beer or some tapas. The bar is open Monday and Wednesday through Saturday from noon to 5pm and Wednesday through Monday from 8pm to midnight.

The tour ends at the end of calle de Cava Baja, at the:

18. Plaza de la Puerta Cerrada, with its simple white-stone cross.

Walking Tour 2
Hapsburg Madrid

Start   Southeastern corner of the Palacio Real.

Finish   Calle del Arenal.

Time   Three hours.

Best Times   Saturday or Sunday, when you can also visit the flea market of El Rastro.

Worst Times   Monday through Saturday from 7:30 to 9:30am and 5 to 7:30pm—because of heavy traffic.

This tour encompasses 16th- and 17th-century Madrid, including the grand plazas and traffic arteries that the Hapsburg families built to transform a quiet town into a world-class capital.

Begin your tour at the:

1. **Palacio Real (Royal Palace),** at the corner of calle de Bailén and calle Mayor. The latter was built by Philip II in the 1560s to provide easy access from the palace to his preferred church, San Jerónimo el Real. Walk east on:

2. **Calle Mayor,** on the south side of the street. Within a block you'll reach a black bronze statue of a kneeling angel, erected in 1906 to commemorate the aborted assassination of Alfonso XIII (grandfather of the present king, Juan Carlos). Across the street from the kneeling angel is the:

3. **Palacio de Abrantes,** calle Mayor 86, today occupied by the Italian Institute of Culture. On the same side of the street as the kneeling angel, to the statue's left, is the:

4. **Palacio de Uceda,** calle Mayor 79, today the headquarters of Spain's military. Both these palaces are considered among the best examples of 17th-century civil architecture in Madrid.

Walk half a block east, crossing to the north side of calle Mayor and detouring about 20 yards to the left, down narrow calle de San Nicolás, and you'll come to the somber facade of the oldest church in Madrid, the 12th-century:

Walking Tour — Hapsburg Madrid

MADRID

Río Manzanares

☐ Hapsburg Madrid

1 Palacio Real
2 Calle Mayor
3 Palacio de Abrantes
4 Palacio de Uceda
5 Church of St. Nicolás
6 Plaza de San Miguel
7 Plaza Mayor
8 Café Bar Los Galayos
9 Calle de Toledo
10 Iglesia de San Isidro
11 Colegio Imperial
12 El Rastro
13 Calle de Segovia
14 Calle de Cuchilleros
15 Calle Bordadores
16 Church of San Ginés

✝️■ Church   ◆ Metro

5. **Church of St. Nicolás,** Plaza de San Nicolás. Only a brick tower remains from the original building, one of the few examples of the Mudéjar style in the capital. The reredos at the high altar is the work of Juan de Herrera, also the architect of El Escorial.

Retrace your steps to calle Mayor. Turn left and continue to walk east. You'll pass the Plaza de la Villa on your right, and, one block later, the:

6. **Plaza de San Miguel,** an iron-canopied meat-and-vegetable market. You might stock up on ingredients for a picnic here. (The market is open Monday through Friday from 9am to 2pm and 5 to 8pm and Saturday from 9am to 2pm.)

Leave the Plaza de San Miguel by Ciudad Rodrigo (there might not be a sign), which leads under a soaring granite archway and up a sloping street to the northwestern corner of the:

7. **Plaza Mayor,** the landmark square that's at the heart of Old Madrid.

Refueling Stop

At Plaza Mayor 1, **8. Café Bar Los Galayos** (☎ **366-30-28**) has long been one of the best places for *tapas* along this square. If you're taking the walking tour during the day, you may want to return to this cafe/bar at night, since it's most lively then (see Chapter 5). In summer you can select one of the outdoor tables for your drinks and *tapas*.

Stroll through the Plaza Mayor, crossing it diagonally, and exit at the closer of its two southern exits. A dingy, steep flight of stone stairs leads down to the beginning of:

9. **Calle de Toledo.** Note in the distance the twin domes of the yellow-stucco–and–granite:

10. **Iglesia de San Isidro,** legendary burial place of Madrid's patron saint and his wife, Santa María de La Cadeza. The church lost its status as a cathedral in 1992, when the honor went to the larger Church of La Almudena. Adjacent to San Isidro is the baroque facade of the:

11. **Colegio Imperial,** which was also run by the Jesuits. Lope de Vega, Calderón, and many other famous men studied at this institute. If your tour takes place on a Saturday or Sunday before 3 pm, visit:

12. **El Rastro,** Madrid's world-famous flea market. Continue along calle de Toledo, then fork left onto calle Estudios and proceed to the Plaza de Cascorro, named after a hero of the Cuban wars. El Rastro begins here. If your tour takes place Monday through Friday, skip the Rastro neighborhood. Instead, turn right onto:

13. **Calle de Segovia,** which intersects calle de Toledo just before it passes in front of the Iglesia de San Isidro. Walk one block and turn right onto the first street:

14. **Calle de Cuchilleros.** Follow it north past 16th- and 17th-century stone-fronted houses. Within a block a flight of

granite steps forks to the right. Climb the steps (a sign identifies the new street as calle Arco de Cuchilleros) and you'll pass one of the most famous *mesones* (typical Castilian restaurants) of Madrid, the Cueva de Luís Candelas.

Once again you will have entered the Plaza Mayor, this time on the southwestern corner. Walk beneath the southernmost arcade and promenade counterclockwise beneath the arcades, walking north underneath the square's eastern arcade. Then walk west beneath its northern arcade. At the northwest corner, exit through the archway onto calle 7 de Julio. Fifty feet later, cross calle Mayor and take the right-hand narrow street before you. This is:

15. Calle Bordadores, which during the 17th century housed Madrid's embroidery workshops, staffed exclusively by men. As you proceed, notice the 17th-century brick walls and towers of the:

16. Church of San Ginés, Arenal 15. The church of one of Madrid's oldest parishes owes its present look to the architects who reconstructed it after a devastating 1872 fire. At the end of this tour, you'll find yourself on the traffic-congested calle del Arenal, at the doorstep of many interesting old streets.

Walking Tour 3
Bourbon Madrid

Start   Puerta de Alcalá.
Finish   Plaza de Oriente.
Time   Three hours.
Best Times   Early morning or late afternoon in summer (or any sunny day in winter).
Worst Times   Monday through Saturday from 7:30 to 9:30am and 5 to 7:30pm—because of heavy traffic.

By the time the Bourbons came to power in Spain, Madrid was firmly ensconced as a political and cultural center, proud of its role as head of a centralized government. This tour shows off the broad boulevards, spectacular fountains, and interconnected plazas that put Madrid on a par architecturally with other European capitals. Much of this tour goes through neighborhoods planned by Charles III in the 18th century.

Begin your tour at the:

1. Puerta de Alcalá (Alcalá Gate), Plaza de la Independencia. One of the grand landmarks of Madrid, the Alcalá Gate was designed by Francesco Sabatini and built from 1769 to 1778. In neoclassical style, it replaced a baroque arch that used to mark the entry into the city; with its five arched passages, it soon became a symbol of the new Bourbon "enlightenment" that swept over Madrid. Today it guards the approach to the major artery leading to northeastern Spain and on to France. Walk west, slightly downhill, along calle de Alcalá to the:

2. **Plaza de la Cibeles,** the most beautiful square in Madrid. In the center of the square is the Fuente de Cibeles, showing the Roman goddess Cybele driving an elaborate chariot pulled by two docile lions, which symbolize elegance and harmony. José Hermosilla and Ventura Rodríguez, architects of paseo del Prado (see below), designed the fountain. To your left, on the corner of calle de Alcalá and Plaza de la Cibeles, is the most magnificent post office in Europe, the Palacio de Comunicaciones. Its lavish embellishments give it the air of an ecclesiastical palace. It dates from 1904.

   From the Plaza de la Cibeles you'll see two monuments—the pink-sided Palacio de Buenavista, the army headquarters of Spain, on the right side of the square; and immediately opposite you on the far side of the square, the Banco de España. You're now at the beginning of the most monumental part of Bourbon Madrid. Promenade beneath the leafy canopy of:

3. **Paseo del Prado,** which incorporates two busy one-way streets separated by a wide pedestrian promenade. Walk south down the world-famous promenade, passing shrubbery, trees, and benches. Paseo del Prado links the Plaza de la Cibeles with the Plaza del Emperador Carlos V, site of the Atocha train station, the paseo's southern terminus. It's part of the busy north-south axis of the city. This whole section, called the Salón del Prado, incorporates more world-class art masterpieces than any other area of similar size in the world. On your left, as you head south toward the Plaza del la Lealtad, you'll pass the:

4. **Museo Naval,** paseo del Prado 5. Adjacent to it, behind a gracefully angled row of neoclassical columns, stands the Madrid stock exchange (La Bolsa), dating from the 19th century. Continue down paseo del Prado to the:

5. **Monument to the Heroes of the Second of May.** This 19th-century obelisk, on your left behind a barrier of trees, honors the "unknown soldiers" who fell in the Napoleonic wars of independence. To your right, a few paces later, is the:

6. **Palacio de Villahermosa,** paseo del Prado 8. This neoclassical palace holds one of the world's greatest artistic bequests, the Thyssen-Bornemisza Museum. In the center of the Plaza Canovas del Castillo (also called the Plaza de Neptuno) is a fountain dedicated to the Roman god Neptune. Continue walking south and you'll reach the:

7. **Museo del Prado,** paseo del Prado, one of the world's great art museums. The original core of its paintings, which came

Walking Tour —Bourbon Madrid

Calle de Alfonso XI

① start here
Plaza de la Independencia

RECOLETOS

Paseo Recoletos

② Plaza de la Cibeles

BANCO

Calle de Prim

Calle de Augusto Figueroa

③ ④ ⑤
PASEO DEL PRADO

Calle Juan de Mena

Plaza de la Lealtad

Calle de Felipe IV

Real Jardín Botánico

⑦ ⑧
PASEO DEL PRADO
Plaza de Murillo
Plaza C. del Castillo
DEL PRADO

⑥ Plaza de las Cortes
SAN JERÓNIMO

Calle de Zorrilla

Calle del Prado

Calle de Cervantes

Calle de Moratín

Calle de Atocha

AVENIDA DE GRAN VÍA
CALLE DE ALCALÁ

SEVILLA

Calle Sevilla

Plaza Canalejas
⑪ ⑩ CARRERA
⑫ Puerta del Sol

Calle de las Huertas

A. MARTIN

GRAN VÍA
Calle Montera

Calle de la Cruz
Calle de Carretas

Calle de la Magdalena

CALLAO

Calle del Carmen
Calle del Preciados
Calle de la Salud
Calle de Tetuán

⑬ SOL

T. DE MOLINA

Calle de la Colegiata

PL. ESPAÑA
AVENIDA DE GRAN VÍA

STO. DOMINGO

Plaza Descalzas
Plaza de Isabel II

OPERA
CALLE DEL ARENAL

Calle Marqués Viudo de Pontejos

CALLE MAYOR

Calle Duque de Alba

LA LATINA

finish here

Jardines del Cabo Noval
⑮ CALLE CARLOS III
Plaza de Oriente

Calle de Bailén

300 m
330 y
0

N

⊠ Post Office   ◈ Metro

MADRID
Bourbon Madrid
Río Manzanares

- ① Puerta de Alcalá (Alcalá Gate)
- ② Plaza de la Cibeles
- ③ Paseo del Prado
- ④ Museo Naval
- ⑤ Monument to the Heroes of the Second of May
- ⑥ Palacio de Villahermosa
- ⑦ Museo del Prado
- ⑧ Real Jardín Botánico
- ⑨ Carrera de San Jerónimo
- ⑩ Plaza Canalejas
- ⑪ Lhardy
- ⑫ Puerta del Sol
- ⑬ La Mallorquina
- ⑭ Plaza de Isabel II
- ⑮ Plaza de Oriente

from royal palaces throughout Spain, was hugely increased in the 19th century by private bequests. Much of the museum's layout results from the efforts of Charles III in the late 1700s. He commissioned the construction of a neoclassical brick-and-stone palace to house a Natural History Museum, named El Prado de San Jerónimo

(St. Jerome's Meadow). It had barely been completed before Napoleon's troops sacked and burned it. Under Ferdinand VII the museum was restored and finally opened to the public in 1819. Continue south along paseo del Prado to the:

8. **Real Jardín Botánico,** a fine oasis on a hot day. Head back up paseo del Prado, crossing the street. When you reach the Plaza Cánovas del Castillo, turn left toward the ancient heart of Madrid along calle de las Cortés, which leads into:

9. **Carrera de San Jerónimo** (its name will briefly be the Plaza de las Cortés). Walk along the right side. On your left you'll pass the facade of the deluxe Palace Hotel. Turn around and look behind you for a distant view of the Gothic spire of the Iglesia de San Jerónimo.

Keep walking uphill. On your right you'll pass the Corinthian columns and twin bronze lions flanking the entrance to the Spanish Parliament, built around 1850. Facing it in a small three-sided park is a statue of Cervantes. At this point, the street will narrow considerably, funneling itself into the:

10. **Plaza Canalejas,** around which sit several late-19th- and early-20th-century buildings. On the left side of the square, notice the twin spires of one of the neighborhood's most whimsically appealing structures. Built around 1920, it was designed as an eclectic combination of 17th-century styles, including shells, neoclassical obelisks, and heraldic lions holding shields.

Pass along this square back onto carrera de San Jerónimo, by now a busy, congested, and commercial street lined with stores.

Refueling Stop

At carrera de San Jerónimo 8, **11. Lhardy** (☎ **521-33-85**) opened its doors in 1839. It soon became the gathering place of Madrid's literati, political leaders, and executives. Today this place has a decor called "Isabella Segundo" and gives off an aura of another era. Upstairs is a restaurant, but for refueling you can stop downstairs, as have thousands of visitors before you, and enjoy a cup of consommé from a large silver samovar; or in summer, a soothing gazpacho. Each cup costs 119 ptas. (80¢). It's open Monday through Saturday from 1 to 3:30pm and 9 to 11:30pm and closed from late July to early September.

Continue along carrera de San Jerónimo to the geographical heart of Spain, the:

12. **Puerta del Sol.** Two-thirds of the way along its half-moon–shaped expanse you'll come upon a small brass plaque from which all the distances in Spain are measured,

placed immediately in front of a red-brick municipal building called Communidad de Madrid, on the southern edge of the square.

Refueling Stop

The most famous pastry shop in Madrid, **13.** La Mallorquina, Puerta del Sol 8 (☎ **521-12-01**), occupies a position at the southwest corner of the Puerta del Sol. It was founded before the turn of the century and became known for one specialty, a Napoletana, filled with cream and studded with almond slices. You can order sandwiches, coffee, and pastries on the ground floor, or head upstairs, where there's sit-down service. It's open daily from 9am to 9:15pm.

At the far end of the Puerta del Sol are two main streets, calle Mayor and calle del Arenal, forking off to the right. Take Arenal, passing the red-brick neoclassical facade of the Iglesia de San Ginés on your left. Within a short distance, you'll come upon the:

14. Plaza de Isabel II, graced with a bronze statue of the 19th-century music-loving queen whose efforts helped construct an opera house for Madrid, the Teatro Real. Follow calle del Arenal, now called calle Carlos III, around the southern edge of the opera house to the:

15. Plaza de Oriente, with its view of the Palacio Real (Royal Palace).

Walking Tour 4
Grandeur: Past & Present

Start   Gran Vía at Plaza del Callao.
Finish   Plaza de la Encarnación.
Time   Three hours.
Best Times   Any day except Monday, when the collections are closed.
Worst Times   Monday.

Begin your tour at the:

1. Gran Vía, the major street of central Madrid, at the Plaza del Callao. The shop-flanked Gran Vía was opened at the end of World War I, and long before deluxe hotels started to sprout up north on paseo de la Castellana, the hotels of Gran Vía were the most expensive and elegant in the Spanish capital. The street runs from calle de Alcalá to the Plaza de España and is at the heart of the modern city, with banks, department stores, and office blocks, plus an array of cinemas.

Begin your promenade at the Plaza del Callao, dominated by the Palacio de la Prensa (press), dating from 1924, and the Capitol, the most fashionable looking building, dating from 1931.

From Gran Vía, head west toward the Plaza de España. This section of the Gran Vía is considered the most American in inspiration. The architects of the Gran Vía at that time were much influenced by the 1930s style sweeping New York, especially as reflected by the Roxy and Paramount buildings. The Gran Vía comes to an end at the:

2. **Plaza de España,** with its two tower blocks from the 1950s, the Edificio de España and the Torre de Madrid. This vast square, overshadowed by these skyscrapers, is at a hub separating Old Madrid from the modern city. Once a military barracks, it's now one of the busiest traffic intersections in Madrid. In the center of the square stands a monument to Cervantes (erected in 1928), with figures of Don Quixote and his faithful Sancho Panza.

From the square, walk up calle de la Princesa, turning to your left (south) as you approach calle de Ventura Rodríguez, where you'll come upon one of the esoteric treasure houses of Madrid, the:

3. **Museo Cerralbo,** Ventura Rodríguez 17 (☎ **547-36-46;** Metro: Plaza de España or Ventura Rodríguez). This town house, dripping with the gilt and red-velvet romanticism of the 19th century, was once inhabited by the family of the Marquis of Cerralbo, who filled its every nook and cranny with decorative bric-a-brac and art treasures. Note the crystal chandeliers and the fashionable, opulently colored glass imported from Venice. The Cerralbo clan were art collectors as well, purchasing well-known works by Zurbarán, Ribera, and El Greco. Especially intriguing is the library/study of the late marquis, preserved just as he left it. Admission costs 250 ptas. ($1.80). It's open Tuesday through Saturday from 9:30am to 2:30pm and Sunday from 10am to 2pm; closed in August.

Returning to the Plaza de España, go to the southeastern corner of the square and head down calle de Bailén to the semicircular:

4. **Plaza de Oriente,** created in 1840, one of the most famous squares in Spain and the site of the Palacio Real. The square was designed to provide a harmonious panoramic vista between the Royal Palace and the Puerta del Sol. At the overthrow of the Napoleonic dynasty, work ended and the square was not completed until the reign of Isabella II. An equestrian statue of Philip IV stands in the center of the square, the work, based on drawings by Velázquez, of Italian sculptor Pietro Tacca.

1. Gran Vía
2. Plaza de España
3. Museo Cerralbo
4. Plaza de Oriente
5. Café de l'Oriente
6. Convento de la Encarnación

Refueling Stop

At Plaza de Oriente 2, **5. Café de Oriente** (☎ **541-39-74**) gives you a chance to have a drink and *tapas* with a view of the Royal Palace. The cafe's entrance is a well-marked doorway set behind shaded sidewalk tables and a turn-of-the-century decor.

From the Plaza de Oriente, take a tiny side street to the northeast of the square, calle de Pavia, which will lead to the:

6. **Convento de la Encarnación** (☎ **247-05-10;** Metro: Ópera), on one of the most charming squares in Madrid, the Plaza de la Encarnación. The convent and adjoining church were completed in 1616. A Spanish-speaking guide will show you around, pointing out the most important ecclesiastical paintings and Ribera's *St. John the Baptist.* Other works include a gory Christ with serpentine hair by Gregorio Fernández. The cloisters are filled with richly decorated chapels, one in the Pompeiian style. Admission is 450 ptas. ($3.20). The convent is open Wednesday and Saturday from 10:30am to 12:30pm and 4 to 5:30pm and Sunday from 11am to 1:30pm.

Walking Tour 5
The Prado in Two Hours

Start   Velázquez door (western entrance).
Finish   Room 57A.
Time   Two hours.
Best Times   At the 9am opening.
Worst Times   12:30 to 3pm (too crowded) or Monday (when it's closed).

Considered the most precious cultural institution in all of Spain and the seat of a deep-seated pride in the country's artistic heritage, the Prado places Madrid firmly on the artistic map of Europe. It's also one of the capital's most consistently reliable tourist attractions, as witnessed by the more than 2 million visitors who enter its corridors every year.

But because of the Prado's *embarras de richesses* (only a third of the collection can be displayed at any given time), you may need some guidance to see at least some of the world-acclaimed masterpieces. You could devote weeks to the Prado, but regrettably many visitors have only two hours. Here's how to make the most of that limited time.

Because the lines there tend to be shorter, I usually prefer to enter via the:

1. **Velázquez door,** the Prado's western (central) entrance, near the larger-than-life bronze statue of the seated artist, Spain's most famous painter. Resolutely ignoring (for the time being) the riches on the museum's street level, climb to the upper floor, using the building's central (western) staircase, which lies a short distance to the right of the entrance turnstile. At the top of the stairs, a short hall will deposit you into the museum's famous:

Walking Tour—The Prado In Two Hours

MADRID

The Prado Museum ■

1 Velázquez door
2 Long Gallery
3 Oil paintings by Goya
4 Paintings by Murillo, Ribera, and Zurbarán
5 Paintings by Velázquez
6 Paintings by El Greco
7 Italian Renaissance paintings
8 Old Master Flemish and Dutch paintings
9 The Black Paintings of Goya
10 Paintings by Bosch, Breughel the Elder, and Dürer

MAIN FLOOR

GROUND FLOOR

VELÁZQUEZ ENTRANCE

start here

finish here

LECTURE HALL

Temporary Exhibitions

Temporary Exhibitions

2. **Long Gallery.** Though referred to as a gallery, it's more technically the interconnected series of Rooms 24 through 32. Echoing, marble-sheathed, and often very crowded, these rooms are the main traffic artery of the Prado's second showcase floor. Walk south through Rooms 28 and 29,

admiring large-scale works by mainly Italian Renaissance painters as you go. Specific artworks will include representations by Raphael, Titian, Tintoretto, and Fra Angelico. The gallery will eventually funnel into an octagonal room (no. 32) containing:

3. **Oil paintings by Goya,** including his most famous portraits—the cruel depictions of the family of Charles IV. You're standing amid the museum's densest concentration of oils by Goya. The best of these lie a few steps to the east. With your back to the Long Gallery, turn left into the long and narrow Room 31. At the end of no. 31, turn left into Room 22. This and four of its neighbors (specifically Rooms 19 through 23, which lie in a straight uninterrupted line) contain many of Goya's cartoons (sketches for tapestries) that the artist designed for eventual execution by teams of weavers. Walk southward into Room 18 to see:

4. **Paintings by Murillo, Ribera, and Zurbarán.** Along with its immediate neighbors (Rooms 18A and 17A), you'll find clustered together works by Murillo (1617–82), Ribera (1588–1652), and Zurbarán (1598–1664). Each of these artists is considered a superlative contemporary of the most acclaimed artwork ever to emerge from Spain, the:

5. **Paintings by Velázquez.** These lie ahead of you, in about half a dozen rooms whose contents are considered the centerpiece of the Prado. Wander through Rooms 16A, 15A, 14, 16, and 13, in any order that appeals to your roving eye. You'll probably intuitively gravitate to the Prado's architectural and artistic centerpiece, Room 12. Though masterpieces await you on all sides, note in particular *Las Meninas* (Ladies of the Court), whose enigmatic grouping has intrigued observers for centuries.

   Now, exit from Room 12's northern door into Room 11, turn left into Room 11A, then turn immediately right into Room 10B and 9B. This series of rooms contains one of Europe's most important collections of:

6. **Paintings by El Greco.** Famous for his nervous depictions of mystical ecstasy, his dramatically lurid colors, and the elongated limbs of his characters (who seem to be physically rising upward to heaven), El Greco was the premier exponent of the late-baroque school of Mannerism.

   Time will by now be rushing by. If you choose to prolong your visit, you might want to gaze briefly at the contents of Rooms 8B, 9, 8, 7, 7A, 8A, and 9A, an array of:

7. **Italian Renaissance paintings.** These interconnected rooms lie within a few steps of one another, and each contains more world-class examples of works by such Italian masters as Tintoretto, Titian, and Paolo Veronese. Know at this point that you have by now seen—albeit

briefly—many of the grandest artworks of the Prado's upper floor.

Now, head quickly for the nearest staircase. (You might prefer to ask a guard at this point, but in any event, the museum's most important staircases lie off the Long Gallery, which—as stated earlier, is comprised of Rooms 24 through 32.) Midway along its length, look for the staircase and descend to the museum's ground floor. When you reach it, head south through the very long Room 75. Midway down its length, turn left into Room 61B, the beginning of the Prado's superb collection of:

8. **Old Master Flemish and Dutch paintings.** These are in Room 61B (famous for Rubens's *Martyrdom of St. Andrew*) and continue in a cluster of rooms that includes Rooms 62B, 63B, 63, 62, and 61. Room 61 contains some of the most famous paintings in history: Rubens's *The Three Graces* and the somewhat less well known *Judgment of Paris.*

Your tour is nearing an end, but if time remains, a final excursion back into the artistic vision of Goya would not be amiss. For views of some of the most depressing paintings in the history of Spain, brilliant for their evocation of neurotic emotional pain and anguish, leave the Flemish section by walking to the ground floor's southeastern corner. There, in Rooms 65, 66, and 67, you'll find:

9. **The Black Paintings of Goya.** Refresh yourself, if time remains, at the cafeteria, which lies close nearby (signs are prominently posted). Before concluding your tour, however, you might be tempted to view the weird and hallucinogenic paintings of Dutch artist Hieronymus Bosch ("El Bosco," 1450–1516). To reach them, walk briskly to the northeastern corner of the museum's ground floor, where the artist's works lie scattered amid Rooms 55 through 57A. In these rooms you can also gaze upon:

10. **Paintings by Bosch, Breughel the Elder, and Dürer.** The most important of these works includes *The Garden of Earthly Delights,* whose convoluted and bizarre images have provided fodder for the nightmares of generations of children.

8

Madrid Shopping

Practically everything you'd want to buy is available in Madrid, which 17th-century playwright Tirso de Molina called "a shop stocked with every kind of merchandise." Madrid has been one of the major shopping centers of Spain ever since the court moved here. Today its merchandise has expanded and is so diverse in its offerings that it has become a city for people "born to shop." So whatever your travel schedule, try to budget time for exploring some of the more than 50,000 stores in Madrid, selling everything from high-fashion clothing (for both men and women) to flamenco guitars to art and ceramics.

If your time is limited and you want a quick overview of Madrid offerings, go to one of the big department stores (see below). Each carries a "bit of everything."

1 The Shopping Scene

BEST BUYS   Spain has always been revered for the dedication of its craftspeople, many of whom still work in the time-honored, labor-intensive traditions of their grandparents. It's hard to go wrong if you limit your purchases to the handcrafted objects the Spanish have always executed so beautifully. These include hand-painted tiles, sturdy ceramics, and fine porcelain. Shipping can be arranged by any reputable dealer, who will send the object to its destination swathed in protective padding.

Hand-woven rugs, handmade sweaters, and intricate embroideries are also good buys. And you'll find some of the best leather in the world. Jewelry—especially gold set with Majorca pearls, which have been produced in Spain for centuries—represents good value and unquestioned luxury.

Antiques, although no longer the giveaway bargains they were before World War II, are still available in Spain and are sold in many retail outlets. Better suited to the budgets of many travelers, however, are the flea markets whose weekly bartering and haggling have become an elaborate ritual in modern Madrid.

Spain, although hardly the center for haute couture that Milan and Paris are, is still making inroads into fashion. Its young designers are regularly featured in the fashion magazines of Europe. You'll also find some well-made shoes. *Warning:* Shoes and quality clothing are generally more expensive in Madrid than in the United States.

SHOPPING DISTRICTS   Drawing on its historical origins as the most interesting part of Madrid, the **center of Madrid** has a dense concentration of all kinds of shops. Their sheer diversity is staggering, interspersing the most old-fashioned mom-and-pop outlets for salt, meat, fish, and staples with high-tech, high-fashion boutiques. The neighborhood's densest concentration of shops lies immediately north of the Puerta del Sol, radiating out from calle del Carmen, calle Montera, and calle de Preciados.

The **calle Mayor and calle del Arenal district,** although technically in the center (not far from the Puerta del Sol), still seems to exist as a separate shopping entity. Unlike their more stylish neighbors to the north, shops in this district tend toward the small, slightly dusty enclaves of coin and stamp collectors, family-owned souvenir shops, clockmakers, sellers of military paraphernalia, and (thanks to the nearness of the Teatro Real and the Music Conservatory) an abundance of stores selling musical scores for obscure orchestral works.

The **Gran Vía** was conceived, designed, and built in the 1910s and 1920s as a showcase for the city's best shops, hotels, and restaurants. Since those days its allure has been battered by the emergence of other shopping districts, yet the art-nouveau/art-deco glamour of the Gran Vía still survives in the hearts of most Madrileños. The bookshops here are among the best in the city, as are outlets for fashion, shoes, jewelry, furs, and handcrafted accessories from all regions of Spain.

Most visitors are so immediately enamored by the architectural symmetry of the **Plaza Mayor** that they overlook its neighborhood as a shopping opportunity. Within three or four blocks in each direction from the square you'll find more than the predictable concentration of souvenir shops. Under the arcades of the square itself are exhibitions of lithographs and oil paintings, and every Saturday and Sunday there's a loosely organized market of collectible stamps and coins. One of the city's headquarters for the sale of bolts of cloth, threads, and buttons lies amid the stores on calle Marqués Viudo de Pontejos, which runs east from the Plaza Mayor. Also running east of the square, on calle de Zaragoza, are collections of silversmiths and small jewelry shops. On the more practical end of the spectrum, calle Posetas contains shops selling housewares, underwear, soap powders, and almost everything a person would need to create a happy (and clean) home.

Near **carrera de San Jerónimo,** several blocks east of the Puerta del Sol, is Madrid's densest concentration of gift shops, craft shops, and antiques dealers—a decorator's delight. Its most interesting streets include calle del Prado, calle de las Huertas, and the Plaza de las Cortés. Because of the nearness of some of Madrid's most expensive and posh hotels and the upscale nature of the neighborhood, don't expect any bargains.

A few blocks east of the Parque del Oeste, the verdant and well-heeled neighborhood of **northwest Madrid** is well stocked with luxury goods and staples for middle-class and upscale homes. Identified by its Metro stop, Argüelles, its main thoroughfare is calle de la Princesa, which contains a bevy of shops selling shoes, handbags, fashions, gifts, and children's clothing. Thanks to the influence and presence of the nearby university, there's also a dense concentration of bookstores, especially on calle Isaac Peral and calle Fernando el Católico (which lie several blocks north and northwest, respectively, from the Argüelles subway stop).

The **Salamanca** district is known throughout Spain as the quintessential upper-bourgeois neighborhood, as uniformly prosperous as anything you're likely to find in Iberia. Its shops are correspondingly exclusive. They include outlets run by interior decorators; furniture shops; fur and jewelry shops; Spanish couture; several department stores; and design headquarters whose output ranges from the solidly conservative to the high-tech *outré* of Europe. The main streets of this district are calle Serrano and calle Velázquez. The district lies northeast of the center of Madrid, a few blocks north of Retiro Park. Its most central Metro stops are Serrano and Velázquez.

HOURS & SHIPPING   Major stores are open (in most cases) Monday through Saturday from 9:30am to 8pm; many small stores take a siesta between 1:30 and 4:30pm. Of course, there is never any set formula, and hours can vary greatly from store to store depending on the owner's idiosyncracies and schedules.

Many art and antiques dealers will crate and ship bulky objects for an additional fee. Any especially large or heavy item, such as a piece of furniture, should probably be sent by ship. Every antiques dealer in Spain maintains lists of reputable maritime shippers. One reliable option is **Emery Ocean Freight** (☎ toll free **800/488-9451** in the U.S.), which maintains branch offices in Barcelona, Alicante, Madrid, Málaga, Bilbao, and Valencia. The main Spanish office of their representative is S.J. Rubert, S.L. (I.T.E. Ltd, c/o Emery) International Freight Forwarding and Customs Agents, Explanada de España 2, Aptdo 8, 03002 Alicante (☎ **96/521-4011**).

For most small and medium-size shipments, air freight isn't much more expensive than shipping by sea. **Iberia's Air Cargo Division** (☎ toll free **800/221-6002** in the U.S.) offers air-freight service from Spain to New York, Miami, or Los Angeles. For shipments from either Barcelona or Madrid to New York, a shipment under 100 kg (220 pounds) costs 760 ptas. ($5.40) per kilo. The per-kilo price goes down as the weight increases, reaching 427 ptas. ($3) per kilo for shipments weighing more than 100 kilos. Regardless of what you ship, there's a minimum 8,500 ptas. ($60.40) charge.

For an additional fee, Iberia or one of its representatives will pick up your package. For truly precious cargo, ask the seller to build a

---

Frommer's Smart Traveler: Shopping

1. Read "Tax and How to Recover It" on page 200. There's red tape, but refunds can mean substantial savings.

2. Fine-tune your haggling skills in Madrid's open-air flea market (El Rastro). You can come up with some good buys with strong, steady, firm bargaining.

3. If you pay cash, some smaller stores will lower the price.

4. Shop the July and August sales.

5. Don't assume that because a certain product is "made in Spain" it's cheaper in Spain. It pays to know what something costs at home before you make a substantial purchase.

crate for it. Within Spain, information about air-cargo shipments is available by calling Iberia's cargo division at Madrid's Barajas Airport (☎ **91/587-8890**) or its division at Barcelona's airport (☎ **93/401-3426**).

Remember that your air-cargo shipment will need to clear customs after it's brought into the United States. This involves some additional paperwork; costly delays; and, in some cases, a trip to the airport where the shipment first entered the United States. It's usually easier (and, in some cases much easier) to hire a commercial customs broker to do the work for you. **Emery Worldwide,** a division of CF Freightways, can clear your goods for around $125 for most shipments, which you'll pay in addition to any applicable duty you owe your home government. For information, call toll free **800/323-4685** within the United States.

TAX & HOW TO RECOVER IT   If you're a nonresident and make purchases in Spain worth more than 82,400 ptas. ($585), you can get a tax refund. The internal tax, known as value-added tax (VAT) in most of Europe, is called IVA—pronounced *ee*-bah—in Spain. Depending on the goods, the rate usually ranges from 6% to 12% of the total worth of your merchandise. Luxury items are taxed at 33%.

To get this refund, you must complete three copies of a form the store will give you detailing the nature of your purchase and its value. Citizens of non-EU countries show the purchase and the form to the Spanish Customs Office. The shop is supposed to refund the amount due you. Inquire at the time of purchase how they will do so and discuss in what currency your refund will arrive.

TRADITIONAL SALES   The best sales are usually in summer. Called *rebajas*, they start in July and go through August. As a general rule, merchandise is marked down even more in August to make way for the new fall wares.

DUTY FREE—WORTH IT OR NOT?   Before you leave home, check the regular retail price of items you're most likely to buy. Duty-free prices vary from one country to another and from item to item. Sometimes you're better off purchasing an item in a discount store at home. If you don't remember back-home prices, you can't tell when you're getting a good deal.

BARGAINING   The days of bargaining are, for the most part, long gone. Most stores have what is called *precio de venta al público* (PVP), a firm retail price not subject to negotiation.

With street vendors and in flea markets it's a different story. Here, haggling *à la española* is expected. However, you'll have to be very skilled to get the price reduced a lot, as most of these street-smart vendors know exactly what their merchandise is worth—and they are old hands at getting it.

2   Shopping A to Z

Antiques

In the 19th century, Spain's imperial traditions and status-conscious bourgeoisie created a market for enormous amounts of furniture. Much of these highly desirable antiques are available today.

Centre de Arte y Antiguedades, calle Serrano 5. ☎ **576-96-82.**

Other than at the flea market or in the new Mercado de la Puerta de Toledo shopping mall (see below), one of the densest concentration of antiques stores is in the Centre de Arte y Antiguedades. Set in a mid-19th-century building, it has several unusual antiques dealers (plus) a large carpet emporium. Each establishment maintains its own hours, but they tend to be open Monday through Saturday from 10am to 2pm and 4:30 to 8pm. Metro: Retiro. Bus: 1, 2, 9, or 15.

Centro de Anticuarios Lagasca, calle Lagasca 36. No phone.

Another possibility, this center contains about a dozen shops specializing in antique furniture. Open Monday through Saturday from 10am to 1:30pm and 5 to 8pm. Metro: Serrano or Velázquez.

Art Gallery

Galería Kreisler, Hermosilla 8. ☎ **431-42-64.**

One successful entrepreneur on Madrid's art scene is the Kreisler family, whose gallery specializes in relatively conservative paintings, sculptures, and graphics. The gallery prides itself on occasionally displaying and selling the works of artists who are critically acclaimed in Spain and displayed in its museums. Open Monday through Saturday from 10:30am to 2pm and 5 to 9pm; closed Saturday afternoon from July 15 to September 15 and all of August. Metro: Serrano. Bus: 27, 45, or 150.

Capes

Capas Seseña, calle Cruz 23. ☎ **531-68-40.**

Memories of Zorro have prompted some visitors to Madrid to search out similar attire. If you're looking for the perfect cape, head for Capas Seseña. Founded shortly after the turn of the century, it has been manufacturing and selling the finest wool capes for both men and women for many years. The wool comes from the mountain town of Béjar, near Salamanca. Open Monday through Friday from 9:30am to 1:30pm and 5 to 8pm and Saturday from 9:30am to 1:30pm. Metro: Sevilla or Tirso de Molina.

Carpets

Ispahan, Serrano 5. ☎ **575-20-12.**

In this 19th-century building, behind handmade bronze doors, are three floors devoted to carpets from around the world, notably Afghanistan, India, Nepal, Iran, Turkey, and the Caucasus. One section is devoted to silk carpets. In addition, the Art Gallery of the

Louvre, Ispahan II, displays both old masters and contemporary art. Open Monday through Saturday from 10am to 2pm and 4:30 to 8:30pm. Metro: Retiro. Bus: 1, 2, 9, or 15.

Ceramics

Antigua Casa Talavera, Isabel la Católica 2. ☎ **547-34-17.**

Called "the first house of Spanish ceramics," this shop has a sampling of ceramic styles from every major region of Spain. Sangría pitchers, dinnerware, tea sets, plates, vases—all are handmade, and the buyers work hard to find pieces with character. One of the showrooms has an interesting selection of tiles, painted with reproductions of everything from scenes from *Don Quixote* to bullfights, dances, and folklore. There's also a series of tiles depicting famous paintings at the Prado. At its present location since 1904, the shop is only a short walk from the Plaza de Santo Domingo. Open Monday through Friday from 10am to 1:30pm and 5 to 8pm and Saturday from 10am to 1:30pm. Metro: Santo Domingo. Bus: 1, 2, 46, 70, 75, or 148.

Crafts

El Arco de los Cuchilleros Artesania de Hoy, Plaza Mayor 9 (basement level). ☎ **365-26-80.**

Set within one of the 17th-century vaulted cellars of the Plaza Mayor, this shop is entirely devoted to unusual craft items from throughout Spain. The merchandise—one-of-a-kind and, in most cases, contemporary—includes a changing array of pottery, leather, textiles, wood carvings, glassware, wickerwork, papier mâché, and silver jewelry. They deal directly with the artisans who produce each item, ensuring a wide inventory of handcrafts that can sometimes contribute profoundly to the aesthetics of any traveler's private home. The staff is familiar with the rituals of applying for tax-free status of purchases here and speak several different languages. Open daily from 11am to 8pm in off-season, till 9pm in summer. Metro: Puerta del Sol.

Department Stores

Despite the presence of innumerable boutiques scattered throughout the city, many Madrileños appreciate the congregation of thousands of items under one roof. Department-store shopping is definitely a Spanish *institución.* Many visitors also prefer the convenience of making all their purchases in one store, rather than running from boutique to boutique.

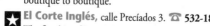

⭐ **El Corte Inglés,** calle Precíados 3. ☎ **532-18-00.**

The flagship of Spain's largest department-store chain, El Corte Inglés is considered by some shopping devotees to be one of Europe's best department stores. Despite the throngs of shoppers jamming the corridors and escalators, it manages to retain the upper-crust image of a store loaded with practical goods. Salespeople rarely speak English but are so tuned in to the merchandise and to the needs of shoppers they can often be of great help anyway.

El Corte Inglés sells all kinds of souvenirs and Spanish handcrafts, such as damascene steelwork from Toledo, flamenco dolls, and embroidered shawls. Some astute buyers report it also sells glamorous fashion articles such as Pierre Balmain for about a third less than elsewhere in Europe.

The chain has a multitude of services that foreign visitors appreciate, including interpreters, currency-exchange facilities, and parcel delivery either to a local hotel or overseas. It will also arrange for all the necessary formalities regarding the IVA refund. (For more information on this, see "Tax and How to Recover It" under "The Shopping Scene," above.)

Madrid boasts several branches of this chain. This store is open Monday through Saturday from 10am to 9pm (without interruption). Metro: Puerta del Sol.

Galerías Preciados, Plaza de Callao 1. ☎ 522-47-71.

Fiercely competitive with El Corte Inglés is the Galerías Preciados, really two stores connected by an underground passageway. It's slightly more downscale than its famous competitor but with quite presentable ready-made clothing for men, women, and children. There's a top-floor snack bar/restaurant. Some good buys I've noted in the past include guitars, men's suede jackets and Spanish capes, and women's full-length suede coats. There's a tailoring department on the store's second floor where men can have a suit made to order. The selection of fabrics—solids, herringbones, or stripes—can be made into whatever style you prefer. Open Monday through Saturday from 10am to 8pm. Metro: Callao.

Embroideries

Casa Bonet, calle Núñez de Balboa 76. ☎ 575-09-12.

Throughout the 19th and 20th centuries, the intricately detailed embroideries produced in Spain's Balearic Islands (especially Majorca) have been avidly sought out for bridal chests and elegant dinner settings. One outlet that stocks and sells them is Casa Bonet. A few examples are displayed on the walls, but a true concept of the store's inventory comes when tablecloths, sheets, napkins, and pillowcases are unrolled on velvet-covered Spanish tables. You'll find a full range of cottons, linens, and polyesters here, many embroidered into patterns fit for a bride. Open Monday through Friday from 9:45am to 2pm and 5 to 8pm and Saturday from 10:15am to 2pm. Metro: Núñez de Balboa.

Espadrilles

Espadrilles are those lighthearted shoes no self-respecting Iberian fisher would do without. Although many styles exist, the tops are usually crafted from canvas and the soles from tightly woven hemp. (The hemp is first woven into ropes, then stitched in oval patterns into what is eventually used as a sole.) Despite these shoes' humble origins, some consumers consider espadrilles perfect for beachwear and occasionally as a kind of casually chic shoe to wear to summer parties.

Casa Hernanz, calle de Toledo 18. ☎ **366-54-50.**

If you want to stock up on this kind of Iberian accessory, head for Casa Hernanz. Located on a busily trafficked street a brisk walk south of the Plaza Mayor, it has been in business since the 1840s. In addition to espadrilles, the shop sells shoes in other styles and hats. The staff are cordial but don't speak English. Open Monday through Friday from 9am to 1:30pm and 4:30 to 8pm and Saturday from 10am to 2pm. Metro: Puerta del Sol, Ópera, or La Latina.

Fans & Umbrellas

A true mistress of the fan-bearing art can convey a multitude of messages through the way she manipulates her fan, and part of the fun of a trip to Spain is the attempt to figure out the various signals. Fans and umbrellas have traditionally been sold from the same shops in Spain.

Casa de Diego, Puerta del Sol 12. ☎ **522-66-43.**

One well-known shop that can supply you with all the ingredients you'll need for your own Spain-inspired flirtation is Casa de Diego. Fans sold here range from plain to fancy, from plastic to exotic hardwood, from cost-conscious to lavish, in an assortment that will probably tempt you to become (at least during a candlelit evening or two) a bit more *espagnole*. In summer the shop is open Monday through Saturday from 9:30am to 8pm; off-season hours are Monday through Saturday from 9:30am to 1:30pm and 5 to 8pm. Metro: Puerta del Sol.

Fashions

The dowdiness of Franco-era Spain has long disappeared as designers, typified by Paloma Picasso, have transformed the fashion landscape. The array of desirable boutiques is endless, but a representative list might include the following:

FOR WOMEN

Don Carlos, calle Serrano 92. ☎ **575-75-07.**

Don Carlos strictly maintains its status as a boutique, with a limited but tasteful array of carefully chosen clothing for women and a somewhat smaller selection for men. Open Monday through Saturday from 10am to 2pm and 5 to 8:30pm. Metro: Núñez de Balboa.

Herrero, calle Preciados 16. ☎ **521-29-90.**

The sheer size and buying power of this popular retail outlet make it a reasonably priced emporium for all kinds of feminine garb. An additional outlet lies on the same street at no. 7 (same phone). Open Monday through Saturday from 10:45am to 2pm and 4:30 to 7pm. Metro: Puerta del Sol or Callao.

Jesús de Poso, calle Almirante 28. ☎ **531-66-76.**

This shop markets the collections of one of Spain's most fashionable designers for women. The fabrics are beautiful and the garments expensive. Open Monday through Saturday from 10am to 1:30pm and 5 to 8pm. Metro: Banco de España.

Modas Gonzalo, Gran Vía 43. ☎ **547-12-39.**

This boutique's gilded baroque atmosphere evokes the 1940s, but its fashions are strictly up-to-date, well made, and intended for stylish adult women. No children's garments are sold. Open Monday through Saturday from 10am to 1:30pm and 4:30 to 8pm. Metro: Callao or Puerta del Sol.

FOR MEN

For the man on a budget who wants to dress reasonably well, the best outlet for off-the-rack clothing is **El Corte Inglés** department store (see above). Most men's boutiques in Madrid are very expensive and may not be worth the investment.

Flea Markets

In addition to the thousands of conventional shops, the Spanish capital has a strong tradition of open-air markets whose haggling and informality have become part of Madrileño lore. Foremost among these is **El Rastro** (which is translated as either "flea market" or "thieves' market"). Located on a meandering network of streets and plazas a few minutes' walk south of the Plaza Mayor, it will warm the heart of anyone attracted to fascinating junk interspersed with bric-a-brac and paintings. (Don't expect to find a Goya.) The neighborhood is also lined with permanent stores that are open, with exceptions, Tuesday through Sunday from 9:30am to 1:30pm and 5 to 8pm. These sell a mixture of dusty junk and antiques and should be visited during the week if you're seriously interested in buying (or just looking for) antiques. On Sunday between 9am and 2pm, it seems half of Madrid and many people from the surrounding countryside jostle one another through the narrow streets, searching for real and imagined bargains.

The flea market occupies a roughly triangular district of streets whose center is the Plaza Cascarro and Ribera de Curtidores. As its name implies, thieves are rampant here, so proceed carefully. It's open Tuesday through Sunday from 9:30am to 1:30pm and 5 to 8pm. Metro: La Latina. Bus: 3 or 27.

Food & Wine

⭐ **Mallorca,** calle Velázquez 59. ☎ **431-99-09.**

Each of the European capitals has its own legendary gourmet shop where you can eat, drink, and carry away succulent tidbits for consumption at home or on your picnic. Madrid's Mallorca was originally established in 1931 as an outlet for a pastry called an *ensaimada.* Consumed as part of the coffee-drinking ritual, it's still the store's most famous product. (They emerge ultrafresh every hour from the ovens.) There are also a tempting array of cheeses; canapés; roasted and marinated meats; sausages; about a dozen kinds of pâté; and a mind-blowing array of tiny pastries, tarts, and chocolates.

Don't overlook the displays of wine and brandies. There's also a *tapas* bar, where clients stand—three deep sometimes—sampling the wares before buying. Hostesses of chic cocktail parties—and marauding families organizing picnics—sometimes make take-out from Mallorca the gastronomic focal point of their events. *Tapas* cost 250 to 500 ptas. ($1.80 to $3.60) per *racion* (portion). Open daily from 9am to 9pm. Metro: Velázquez.

Hats & Headgear

Casa Yustas, Plaza Mayor 30. ☎ 366-50-84.

If your sessions with the analyst have revealed a fetish for unusual hats, you can satisfy your inclinations at this extraordinary emporium established in 1894. Picture yourself as a Congo explorer, a Spanish sailor, an officer in the Kaiser's army, a Rough Rider, a priest, or even Napoleon. You'll also find sombreros and berets for both men and women. Open Monday through Friday from 9:45am to 1:30pm and 4:30 to 8pm and Saturday from 9:45am to 1:30pm. Metro: Puerta del Sol.

Leather

Loewe, Gran Vía 8. ☎ 522-68-15.

Loewe has been the most elegant leather store in Spain since 1846. Its gold medal–winning designers have always kept abreast of changing tastes and styles, but there remains a timeless chic to much of their goods. The store sells luggage, handbags, and jackets (leather or suede) for men and women. Much of the inventory is in the supple and soft shade of medium brown for which the store is known. Open Monday through Saturday from 9:30am to 8pm. Metro: Banco de España.

Musical Instruments

Real Musical, Carlos III no. 1. ☎ 541-30-07.

If you're looking to buy a Spanish guitar, a piano, a string or wind instrument, or simply a record, CD, or pieces of sheet music, head for Real Musical. Open Monday through Friday from 9:30am to 2pm and 5 to 8pm and Saturday from 10am to 2pm. Metro: Ópera.

Perfume

Perfumería Padilla, calle Precíados 17. ☎ 522-66-83.

This store sells a competitively priced large assortment of Spanish and international scents for women. It also maintains a branch at calle del Carmen 78 (same phone). Both branches are open Monday through Saturday from 9:45am to 8:30pm. Metro: Puerta del Sol.

Urgulola, calle Mayor 1. ☎ 521-59-05.

Located at the western edge of the Puerta del Sol, this time-tested shop carries one of the most complete stocks of perfume in Madrid—both national and international brands. It also sells gifts, souvenirs, and costume jewelry. Open Monday through Saturday from 10am to 8pm. Metro: Puerta del Sol.

Porcelain

Some visitors prefer the thick and rustic pottery and stoneware that Spanish artisans churn out by the thousands at potters' wheels throughout the country. Others search out only the delicately realistic porcelain sculptures whose elongated limbs and whimsically yearning expressions were probably inspired by El Greco's Mannerist paintings. Foremost among the manufacturers of this style of porcelain sculpture is Lladró. Many shops have concessions to sell Lladró porcelain.

Lasarte, Gran Vía 44. ☎ **521-49-22.**

An imposing outlet for Lladró porcelain, this store is devoted almost exclusively to its distribution. The staff can usually tell you about new designs and releases the Lladró company is planning for the near future. Open Monday through Friday from 9:30am to 8pm and Saturday from 9:30am to 2pm. Metro: Callao.

Shopping Malls

Galería del Prado, Plaza de las Cortés 7.

Spain's top designers are represented in this marble-sheathed concourse below the Palace Hotel. It opened in 1989 with 47 shops, many featuring *moda joven* (fashions for the young). Merchandise changes with the season, but you'll always find a good assortment of fashion, Spanish leather goods, cosmetics, perfumes, and jewelry. You can also eat and drink here. The entrance is in front of the hotel, facing the broad tree-lined paseo del Prado across from the Prado itself. Open Monday through Saturday from 10am to 9pm. Metro: Banco de España or Atocha.

⭐ **Mercado Puerta de Toledo,** Puerta de Toledo. No phone.

This is one of Spain's most upscale, ambitious, and architecturally unusual malls. More than 150 of the most glamorous names in Spanish retail are collected into the slightly run-down neighborhood just southwest of the historic center. Fashion and antiques are featured—an unusual contrast for a building that once served as Madrid's central fish market. Today, thanks to many pesetas invested by the municipal government, the complex is perceived as a showcase, and some observers have compared it to London's revitalized Covent Garden marketplace. Interspersed among the stores are museum-quality temporary expositions devoted to such subjects as the pottery of Talaverde or the Toledo-based art of metalworking.

Highly stylized and futuristic, the market rises five floors above a sun-flooded courtyard that contains an artistic rendering of a lunar clock and sun dial. You won't go hungry between shopping binges because of the many restaurants, *tapas* bars, and cafes on the premises. Each individual shop maintains hours of its own choosing, but most do business Monday through Saturday from 10am to 8:30pm. Metro: Puerta de Toledo.

9

Madrid Nights

Madrileños are called *gatos* (cats) because of their excessive fondness for prowling around at night. If you're going to a club, it's best to go as late as possible. If you arrive too early, you'll probably have the place to yourself.

In recent years nightlife in Madrid has changed more dramatically than that in any other European capital. There's something going on at night to interest virtually everyone. The young people of Madrid rarely seem to stay home watching television. They're out exploring the many nocturnal facets of their city.

Nightlife is so plentiful in Madrid that the city can be roughly divided into "night zones." These areas can also be dangerous (muggings, for example), so explore them with caution, especially late at night. The most popular nightlife area—both traditionally and from the standpoint of tourist interest—is the **Plaza Mayor/Puerta del Sol** district. It is filled with *tapas* bars and *cuevas* (drinking "caves"). Here it's customary to begin a *tasca* crawl, going from tavern to tavern, sampling the wine in each, along with a selection of tapas. The major streets for such a crawl are Cava de San Miguel, Cava Alta, and Cava Baja. You can order *pinchos y raciones* (tasty snacks and tidbits).

Nightlife along the **Gran Vía** is confined mainly to cinemas and theaters. Most of the after-dark action takes place on little streets branching off the Gran Vía.

Another area much frequented by tourists is the section around **Plaza de Isabel II** and **Plaza de Oriente,** site of the Royal Palace. Both are in the center of Madrid. Many restaurants and cafes flourish in this area, including the famous Café de Orient.

Chueca—embracing such streets as Hortaleza, Infantas, Barquillo, and San Lucas—is the gay nightlife district, with many clubs. Cheap restaurants, along with a few striptease joints, are also found here. Again, this area can be dangerous at night, so be alert for pickpockets and muggers. As of late, there has been greater police presence at night.

For university students, the area of **Argüelles/Moncloa** sees most of the action. However, if it's a weeknight and there are classes the next day, most students head home by 11pm. Many discos are found in the area, along with ale houses and fast-food joints. The area is bounded by Pintor Rosales, Cea Bermúdez, Bravo Murillo, San Bernardo, and Conde Duque.

FREE EVENTS & DISCOUNTS In summer Madrid becomes a virtual free festival, as the city sponsors a series of plays, concerts, and films. Pick up a copy of the *Guía del Ocio* (available at most newsstands) for listings of these events. This guide also provides information about occasional discounts for commercial events, such as concerts staged in Madrid's parks. Also check the program of the **Fundación Juan March,** calle Castelló 77 (☎ **435-42-40;** Metro: Núñez de Balboa), which frequently gives free concerts.

FLAMENCO & DISCOS Flamenco in Madrid is geared mainly to tourists with fat wallets, and nightclubs are expensive. But since

Madrid is preeminently a city of song and dance, you can often be entertained at very little cost—in fact, for the price of a glass of wine or beer, if you sit at a bar with live entertainment.

Discos also tend to be expensive, but they often open for what is called "afternoon" sessions (from 7 to 10pm). Although discos charge entry fees, at an "afternoon" session the cost might be as low as 300 ptas. ($2.10), rising to 2,000 ptas. ($14.20) and beyond for a "night" session—that is, one beginning at 11:30pm and lasting until the early-morning hours. Therefore, get there early, dance till 10pm, then go on to dinner (you'll be eating at the fashionable hour).

1   The Performing Arts

Madrid is home to a wide variety of large-scale theaters, opera companies, and ballet groups. To discover the specific cultural events occurring during your visit, pick up a copy of the *Guía del Ocio* for 85 ptas. (60¢) at a city newsstand.

TICKETS   Admission to dramatic and musical events usually ranges from 700 to 2,000 ptas. ($5 to $14.20), with discounts of up to 50% on certain days (usually Wednesday and early performances on Sunday). The concierges at most major hotels can usually get you tickets to specific concerts; however, he or she will charge a considerable markup. You'll save money if you go directly to the box office. If the event you choose is sold out, you may be able to get tickets (with a considerable markup attached) at the **Localidades Galicia** at the Plaza del Carmen (☎ 531-27-32; Metro: Puerta del Sol). This agency also markets tickets to bullfights and sports events. It's open Tuesday through Sunday (except holidays) from 10am to 1pm and 4:30 to 7:30pm.

Major Performing Arts Companies ——————————

Madrid offers many theater performances that may be enjoyable only if your Spanish is fluent. If it isn't, check out *Guía del Ocio* for performances by English-speaking companies on tour from Britain or select a concert or subtitled movie instead.

Major Concert & Performance Halls

Auditorio Nacional de Música, calle Príncipe de Vergara 136.
☎ 337-01-00.

Auditorio del Real Conservatorio de Música, Plaza Isabel II.
☎ 337-01-00.

Centro Cultural de la Villa, Plaza de Colón. ☎ 532-57-62.

Teatro Calderón, calle Atocha 18. ☎ 369-14-34.

Teatro de la Comedia, calle Príncipe 14. ☎ 521-49-31.

Teatro Español, calle Príncipe 25. ☎ 429-62-97.

Teatro María Guerrero, Tamayo y Baus 4. ☎ 319-47-69.

For those who speak Spanish, the **Companía Nacional de Nuevas Tendencias Escénicas** is an avant-garde troupe that performs new—often controversial—works by undiscovered writers. On the other hand, the **Companía Nacional de Teatro Clásico,** as its name suggests, is devoted to the Spanish classics, including works by the ever-popular Lope de Vega or Tirso de Molina.

Among dance companies, the national ballet of Spain—devoted exclusively to Spanish dance—is the **Ballet Nacional de España.** Their performances are always well attended. The national lyrical ballet company of the country is the **Ballet Lírico Nacional.** Check *Guía del Ocio* to see if the **Compagñía Nacionale de Danza** is appearing in Madrid at the time of your visit. This outstanding company, which has appeared around the world in such major cities as New York, is directed by Nacho Duato, considered the finest choreographer in Spain.

Madrid's opera company is **Teatro de La Ópera,** and its symphony orchestra is the outstanding **Orquesta Sinfónica de Madrid.** The national orchestra of Spain—widely acclaimed on the continent—is the **Orquesta Nacional de España,** which pays homage to Spanish composers in particular.

Major Concert Halls & Auditoriums

In addition to those listed below, there are another 30 formally designated concert halls in Madrid. Dozens of impromptu concerts—sometimes in churches—are given throughout the capital. And as part of their regular program, bars often feature music.

Auditorio Nacional de Música, calle Príncipe de Vergara 136. ☎ 337-01-00.

The ultramodern home (1988) of both the National Orchestra and the National Chorus is considered a major addition to the competitive circles of classical music in Europe; it's sheathed in slabs of Spanish granite, marble, and limestone and capped with Iberian tiles. Standing just north of Madrid's Salamanca district, it's devoted exclusively to the performance of symphonic, choral, and chamber music. In addition to the *auditorio principal* (Hall A), whose capacity is almost 2,300, there's a hall for chamber music (Hall B) and a small auditorium for intimate concerts seating 250 spectators or fewer. The lofty space of the main hall is noteworthy for having absolutely no sound-absorbing materials of any kind (such as carpeting or curtains). This and a smooth-finished wooden ceiling give it a sound experts say is distinctive. Metro: Cruz del Rayo.

Admission: Tickets, 1,500–4,000 ptas. ($10.70–$28.40).

Auditorio del Real Conservatorio de Música, Plaza Isabel II. ☎ 337-01-00.

This is one of the home bases of the Spanish Philharmonic Orchestra, which presents its concerts between September and May. The space is sometimes lent to relatively unknown musical newcomers, who perform at admission-free concerts. Also presented are concerts by chamber-music ensembles visiting from abroad. Containing only about 400 seats, the hall is sometimes sold out long in advance, especially for such famous names as tenor Plácido Domingo. Metro: Ópera.

Admission: Tickets, 1,500–7,500 ptas. ($10.70–$53.30).

Fundación Juan March, calle Castelló 77. ☎ **435-42-40.**

There are free weekly concerts at lunchtime here, although the schedule is notoriously difficult to predict. Metro: Núñez de Balboa.

Admission: Free.

Auditorio del Parque de Atracciones, Casa de Campo.

This theater's schedule might include everything from rock to the more highbrow warm-weather performances of visiting symphonic orchestras. It can hold 3,500 spectators and is in the most complete amusement park in Spain. Check with Localidades Galicia to see what's on at the time of your visit (see "Tickets," above). Metro: Lago or Batán.

Admission: Ticket prices depend on the event.

Ballet

Centro Cultural de la Villa, Plaza de Colón. ☎ **573-57-62.**

Ballet, Spanish style, is presented at this cultural center. Tickets go on sale five days before each event, and performances are usually presented at 8 and 10:30pm. Metro: Serrano or Colón.

Admission: Tickets, 1,200–4,000 ptas. ($8.50–$28.40), depending on the event.

Theater

In addition to those listed below, there are at least 30 other theaters in Madrid—including one devoted almost entirely to performances of children's plays, the **Sala La Bicicleta,** in the Ciudad de los Niños in the Casa de Campo. Dozens of other plays are staged by nonprofessional groups in such places as churches. All that are open to the public will be listed in *Guía del Ocio.*

Teatro Calderón, calle Atocha 18. ☎ **369-14-34.**

The largest theater in Madrid, the Calderón has a seating capacity for 1,700. It's known for its popular reviews, performances of popular Spanish plays, and flamenco. Metro: Tirso de Molina.

Admission: Tickets, 900–3,000 ptas. ($6.40–$21.30).

Teatro de la Comedia, calle Príncipe 14. ☎ **521-49-31.**

More prestigious is the home of the Compañía Nacional de Teatro Clásico. Here, more than anywhere else in Madrid, you're likely to see performances from the classic repertoire of great Spanish drama. Metro: Seville. Bus: 15, 20, or 150. Closed: Thurs and July to Aug.

Admission: Tickets, 1,000–1,500 ptas. ($7.10–$10.70).

Teatro Español, calle Príncipe 25. ☎ **429-62-97.**

This theater is funded by Madrid's municipal government. Its repertoire is a time-tested assortment of great and/or favorite Spanish plays. Metro: Sevilla.

Admission: Tickets, from 1,300 ptas. ($9.20).

Teatro María Guerrero, Tamayo y Baus 4. ☎ 319-47-69.

Also funded by the government, this theater works in cooperation with the Teatro Español (see above) to stage performances of works by such classic Spanish playwrights as García Lorca and Lope de Vega. The theater was named after a much-loved Spanish actress. Metro: Banco de España or Colón.

Admission: Tickets, 900–2,000 ptas. ($6.40–$14.20).

Local Cultural Entertainment

FLAMENCO

The strum of a guitar and the sound of hands clapping rhythmically signal that flamenco is about to start. Soon, colorfully dressed women, and occasionally men, will flounce onto the stage to swirl in time with the music. The staccato beat of castanets and the tapping of heels make the rafters ring. Flamenco is the incomparable Spanish performing art.

Flamenco personifies the blood and guts of Andalusia, where it originated. Nowadays, gypsies have virtually taken over the art form, making flamenco part of their own folklore. Their fire and flair add another dimension to an already passionate dance.

The songs are chanted in a passionate, tense tone, almost Arabic in origin. Age doesn't keep an artist off the center stage. Flamenco singers (*cantores*) seem to perform forever.

Many of the major flamenco clubs in Madrid are patronized almost exclusively by foreigners searching for a glimpse of an earlier era. For that privilege you'll pay dearly, but some visitors still consider it worth the expense.

★ **Café de Chinitas,** calle Torija 7. ☎ 559-5135.

Known throughout Madrid as one of the best flamenco clubs in town, the Café de Chinitas is set one floor above street level in a 19th-century building midway between the Ópera and the Gran Vía. It features an array of (usually) gypsy-born flamenco artists from Madrid, Barcelona, and Andalusia whose acts and performers change about once a month. You can arrange for dinner before the show, although many Madrileños opt for dinner somewhere else, then arrive here just for drinks and the flamenco. It's open Monday through Saturday, with dinner served from 9 to 11pm; the show lasts from 10:30pm to 2am. Reservations are recommended. Metro: Santo Domingo. Bus: 1 or 2.

Admission: Dinner and show 8,000 ptas. ($56.80); cover charge for show without dinner (but with one drink included) 3,900 ptas. ($27.70).

Corral de la Morería, calle de la Morería 17. ☎ 365-84-46.

This club is in the old town, the Morería—meaning a quarter where Moors reside. It sizzles more in its flamenco than in its skillet. Strolling performers, colorfully costumed, get the proceedings under way around 11pm, but they're there only to warm up the audience. A flamenco showcase follows, with at least 10 dancers who initiate the stage for the star, who always appears late and with an almost hyperbolic drama.

The management has devised ways of putting tables in the most unlikely places; reserve near the front and go early if you really want a ringside table. The show and an à la carte dinner, served any time after 9:30pm, costs 9,000 ptas. ($63.90). It's open daily from 9pm to at least 3am. Metro: La Latina or Puerta del Sol.

Admission (including first drink): 3,800 ptas. ($27).

Zambra, in the Hotel Wellington, Velázquez 8. ☎ 435-49-28.

Zambra is a subterranean supper club in the Hotel Wellington's premises. Some of Spain's best flamenco singers and dancers appear here before enthusiastic audiences. The doors open Monday through Saturday at 9:30pm for dinner. The show is scheduled to begin at 10:15pm, although it's occasionally delayed, perhaps for dramatic effect. It ends around 3am. With dinner included, the show costs 9,500 ptas. ($67.50) per person. Reservations are suggested. Metro: Velázquez.

Admission (including first drink): 3,750 ptas. ($26.60).

ZARZUELA

For an authentic Spanish experience, you can attend a *zarzuela*, a Spanish operetta with turn-of-the-century music, lots of Iberian panache, bright costumes, and what usually turns out to be a predictably sentimental plot with plenty of schmaltz. Sometimes the theaters sandwich flamenco numbers and musical revues between excerpts from the time-tested librettos.

Teatro Lirico Nacional de la Zarzuela, calle Jovellanos 4. ☎ 429-82-25.

Near the Plaza de la Cibeles, this theater of potent nostalgia produces ballet and an occasional opera in addition to *zarzuela.* Show times vary. Metro: Sevilla.

Admission: Tickets, 1,100–4,500 ptas. ($7.80–$32).

Teatro Nuevo Apolo, Plaza Tirso de Molina 1. ☎ 369-14-67.

The Nuevo Apolo is the permanent home of the renowned Antología de la Zarzuela company. It is on the restored site of the old Teatro Apolo, where these musical variety shows were performed since the 1930s. Prices and times depend on the show. The box office is open daily from 11:30am to 1:30pm and 5 to 8pm; show times vary. Metro: Tirso de Molina.

Admission: Tickets, usually 2,500 ptas. ($17.80).

2 The Club & Music Scene

Cabaret & Spectacles

Madrid's nightlife is no longer steeped in prudishness, as it was (at least officially) during the Franco era. You can now see glossy cabarets and shows with lots of nudity.

Las Noches de Cuple, calle de la Palma 51. ☎ **532-71-15.**

More subtle and sometimes vastly more poignant than the show at Scala Melía Castilla (see below) is this nostalgic cabaret of a type that's fading fast. Its entrance is on a crowded street barely wide enough for the pedestrians and cars that compete for space. Like everything else in Madrid, the show begins very late and ends when dawn begins to trickle through the alleyways. Inside, a long room with a vaulted ceiling and a tiny stage are the forum for the still-charming former beauty Señora Olga Ramos, who conducts an evening of Iberian song. The charm of her all-Spanish act is increased by the discreet humor of an octogenarian accompanist with an ostrich-feather tiara and a fuchsia-colored boa. If you want dinner, it will cost from 7,500 ptas. ($53.30). After your first drink (see below), each additional drink will cost 1,100 ptas. ($7.80). Dinner is served between 9:30pm and midnight (don't go too early), and the show usually begins around midnight. Even if you don't speak Spanish, the evening's kitsch, unabashed camp, and sometimes lavish sentimentality will give you something to remember. It's open Monday through Saturday from 9:30pm until 2:30am. Metro: Noviciado.

Admission: One-drink minimum at 3,000 ptas. ($21.30).

Scala Melía Castilla, calle Capitán Haya 43 (entrance at Rosario Pino 7). ☎ **571-44-11.**

Madrid's most famous dinner show is a major Las Vegas–style spectacle, with music, water, light, and color. The program is varied—you might see international or Spanish ballet, magic acts, ice skaters, whatever. Most definitely you'll be entertained by a live orchestra. It is open Monday through Saturday from 8:30pm to 3am. Dinner is served beginning at 9pm; the show is presented at 10:30pm. The show with dinner costs 8,500 ptas. ($60.40), and if you partake you don't have to pay the admission charge, because it's included in the show/dinner price. Reservations are required. Metro: Cuzco.

Admission (including first drink): 4,700 ptas. ($33.40)

Jazz Clubs

Café Berlin/Oba-Oba, calle Jacometrezo 4. ☎ **531-08-10** (for Café Berlin) or **531-06-40** (for Oba-Oba).

This establishment carries a double whammy thanks to its dual nature. In its basement lies Oba-Oba, whose specialty is Caribbean- and Brazilian-inspired jazz, to which an animated clientele dances the lambada, the salsa, and an occasional paso doble. If you haven't yet mastered these steps, don't be shy—there will almost certainly be someone there to teach you. Upstairs, the Café Berlin has live jazz concerts that pack spectators tightly inside whenever the music is playing. You'll pay from 750 ptas. ($5.30) for each drink. They're both open nightly from 6pm until 4 or 5am, sometimes even later. Here, like everywhere else, it's most crowded after 11pm. Metro: Callao.

Admission: Free.

Café Central, Plaza del Angel 10. ☎ **468-08-44.**

Off the Plaza de Santa Ana, beside the famed Gran Hotel Victoria, the Café Central has a vaguely art deco interior with an unusual series of stained-glass windows. Many customers read newspapers and talk at the marble-top tables during the day, but the ambience is far more animated during the nightly jazz sessions. Open Monday through Thursday from 1pm to 1:30am and Friday through Sunday from 1pm to 2:30am; live jazz is presented daily from 10pm to 2am. Drinks begin at 400 ptas. ($2.80). Metro: Antón Martín.

Admission: Mon–Thurs 500 ptas. ($3.60), Fri–Sun 600 ptas. ($4.30)—but prices vary depending on show.

Café Populart, calle Huertas 22. ☎ **429-84-07.**

This cafe is known in town for hiring talented jazz groups that encourage the audience to dance. Run by an engaging entrepreneur named Arturo, it specializes in Brazilian, Afro-bass, reggae, and "new African-wave" music. Patrons are charged 350 ptas. ($2.50) for a beer and 650 ptas. ($4.60) for whisky and soda when live music isn't playing (when the music starts, prices of drinks nearly double). Open daily from 6pm to 4 or 5am. Metro: Antón Martín or Sevilla. Bus: 6 or 60.

Admission: Free.

⭐ **Calalú,** in the Park Hyatt Villa Magna, paseo de la Castellana 22. ☎ **576-75-00.**

Calalú, run by what many view as the city's most elegant deluxe hotel, is the only terrace in Madrid where you can enjoy live jazz performed on Tuesday through Saturday. The relaxed atmosphere comes alive with melodic rhythms ranging in sound from New Orleans to Brazil. It's a warm and vibrant place to enjoy an evening with friends, tropical drinks, and tasty food. Calalú offers a variety of Cajun-style apéritifs and appetizers to go with your drinks. Waiters are outfitted in black trousers, white shirts, bow ties, and bowler hats. Potted palms, subdued lighting, and intimate table lamps create the illusion of a tropical island in the center of Madrid. Drinks begin at 900 ptas. ($6.40). Open daily from 10pm to 2am. Metro: Rubén Darío.

Admission: Free.

Clamores, calle Alburquerque 14. ☎ **445-79-38.**

Clamores is the largest jazz club in Madrid, accommodating some 450 people. With dozens of small tables and a huge bar in its somewhat dark interior, the club serves beer, whisky, wine, and the best Catalán champagne to go with the music of bands from Spain and the rest of Europe. Established in the early 1980s, it has thrived because of its changing programs of American and Spanish-jazz bands. Jazz is presented only Tuesday through Saturday; on those nights, performances begin at 11:30pm, with an additional show every Saturday night at 1:30am. There are no live performances on Sunday or Monday nights, when the format is recorded disco music and there's no cover charge. Regardless of the night of the week you consume them, drinks begin at around 700 ptas. ($5) each. Open daily from 6pm to around 3am. Metro: Bilbao.

Admission: Tues–Sat 500–800 ptas. ($3.60–$5.70), depending on the act; Sun–Mon free.

Whisky Jazz, Diego de León 7. ☎ **561-11-65.**

Whisky Jazz is a hideaway for jazz enthusiasts just a block from the U.S. Embassy. If you arrive at the right time, you'll be presented with one of Spain's best showcases of jazz. In the interior of the two-story brick building is a stairway leading to an open mezzanine that projects over a downstairs bar. The walls and a glass case contain intriguing jazz memorabilia, including autographs and photos from its heyday in Chicago and New Orleans. Open Monday through Saturday from 9pm to 3:30am. Metro: Núñez de Balboa.

Admission: From 1,000 ptas. ($7.10), depending on the act.

Dance Clubs & Discos

Some discos and dance clubs are spectacular, complete with the latest sound systems and lasers. Others are little cellar dives where the owner plays records to special but fickle late-night cliques who desert him the next day for a newer club. Be assured of one thing: It's a matter of *gato* pride that no club worth its entrance charge will be crowded and hot until at least 11pm.

Archy, calle Marqués de Riscal 11. ☎ **308-31-62.**

In the cellar of an old apartment building, this art deco–style dance club is fashionable as of this minute. If you're a woman, it's best to show up looking like a young Cher if you'd like to join what Madrileños call the *Gente guapa* (beautiful people). Leave your T-shirts and jeans back in the hotel or the security guards may not let you in. There's also an elegant restaurant and pub here. Drinks range from 790 to 1,200 ptas. ($5.60 to $8.50). Hours are daily from 9pm to 5am. Metro: Colón.

Admission: No cover.

Joy Eslava, calle de Arenal 11. ☎ **366-37-33.**

Joy Eslava is housed in an old theater whose walls have been painted almost entirely black. It's filled with up-to-date lighting and sound equipment and a prominent array of bars, with imitation lasers that shoot bursts of light into almost every corner. If you don't feel like dancing, comfortable chaises longues are scattered throughout. Libations begin at 1,200 ptas. ($8.50) each. Open daily from 11:30pm to 7am (unless it's closed for a private party). Metro: Puerta del Sol or Ópera.

Admission: 2,000 ptas. ($14.20).

Vog, Padre Damian 23. ☎ **350-6444.**

Set in an upscale neighborhood north of city center, on the street level of the hotel-and-office grouping known as the Eurobuilding, this is one of Madrid's leading nightspots. It prides itself on maintaining its allure for a well-heeled clientele, many of whom show up in expensively chic dresses and jackets and ties. Suitably dressed newcomers apply for membership in what is considered almost a semiprivate club, especially on those evenings when it's reserved for private parties. Drinks cost 1,800 ptas. to 2,300 ptas. ($12.80 to $16.30). Open Monday through Saturday from midnight to 5am. Metro: Colombia or Cuzco.

Admission: Fri–Sat nights 2,000 ptas. ($14.20); otherwise free.

3   The Bar Scene

Pubs & Bars

Balmoral, calle Hermosilla 10. ☎ **431-41-33.**

Balmoral is unashamedly Anglo-Saxon. Its exposed wood and comfortable chairs evoke something you'd expect to find in London. Its clientele tends toward journalists, politicians, army brass, owners of large estates, bankers, diplomats, and an occasional literary star. *Newsweek* once dubbed it "one of the best bars in the world." Beer costs around 400 ptas. ($2.80), whiskey with soda from 800 ptas. ($5.70). No food, other than *tapas,* is served. Open daily from 7:30pm to 2am. Metro: Serrano.

Balneario, Juan Ramón Jiménez 37. ☎ **458-24-20.**

Balneario serves gratifyingly potent drinks in an enclave of fresh flowers, white marble, and the kind of stone bathtub that might have been used by Josephine Bonaparte. Near the Chamartín station in one of the capital's northern edges, it's one of the most stylish and upmarket bars in Madrid. Many guests precede a meal at the restaurant El Cabo Mayor (see Chapter 5) with a drink here; the two establishments share a well-tended garden a few steps away. *Tapas* such as endive with smoked salmon, asparagus mousse, and anchovies with avocadoes cost 550 to 1,750 ptas. ($3.90 to $12.40). Drinks run 550 to 950 ptas. ($3.90 to $6.70). Open Monday through Saturday from noon to 2:30am. Metro: Cuzco.

Bar Cock, calle de la Reina 16. ☎ **532-28-26.**

The name comes from the word *cocktail,* or so they say. Cock attracts some of Madrid's most visible artists, actors, models, and filmmakers, including award-winning Spanish director Pedro Almodóvar, who is rumored to be here frequently, although he owns his own bar in Madrid. The decoration is elaborately antique, perhaps in delicate contrast to its clientele. Drinks start at 700 ptas. ($5). Open Monday through Saturday from 9pm to 3am; closed December 24 to 31. Metro: Gran Vía.

Los Gabrieles, calle Echegaray 17. ☎ **429-62-61.**

Located in the heart of one of Madrid's most visible warrens of narrow streets, in a district that pulsates with after-dark nightlife options, this historic bar served throughout most of the 19th century as a sales outlet for a Spanish wine merchant. In the 1980s its two rooms were transformed into a bar and cafe, where you can admire lavishly tiled walls with detailed scenes of courtiers, dancers, and Andalusian maidens peering from behind mantillas and fans. Beer costs 350 ptas. ($2.50). Open daily from 1pm to 2:30am. Metro: Tirso de Molina.

★ **Hanoi,** calle Hortaleza 81. ☎ **319-66-72.**

Hanoi is a stylish and minimalist assemblage of stainless steel, curving lines, and space-age angles. Its clientele is fun, young, attractive, and articulate. The mood is amusedly permissive, and the crowd blends comfortably with both heterosexual and homosexual expressions. There's a small restaurant in the rear, a bevy of male and female models who seem to be in constant attendance, eight video screens showing adventure shows from some long-defunct TV series, and up-to-date music. No matter who you are, you'll probably have fun in Hanoi. Drinks begin at 850 ptas. ($6). Open daily from 9:30pm to 3:30am. Metro: Alonso Martínez.

Hispano Bar/Buffet, paseo de la Castellana 78. ☎ **411-48-76.**

This establishment does a respectable daily lunch trade for members of the local business community, who crowd in to enjoy the amply portioned *platos del día.* These might include roast duck with figs or orange sauce or suprême of hake. After around 5pm, however, the ambience becomes that of a busy after-office bar, with dozens of stylishly dressed women and local entrepreneurs. The hubbub continues into the night. Full meals at lunchtime cost from around 3,500 ptas. ($24.90), while beer, depending on the time of day, ranges from 250 ptas. to 350 ptas. ($1.80 to $2.50). Open daily from 1:30pm to 1:30am. Metro: Nuevos Ministerios.

Mr. Pickwick's, Marqués de Urquijo 48, at the corner of paseo del Pintor Rosales. ☎ **559-51-85.**

For homesick English expatriates, no other establishment in Madrid better captures the pub atmosphere than Mr. Pickwick's, a 10-minute walk from the Plaza de España. Although only a few of the staff speak fluent English, the decor includes everything you might expect in London: framed prints of Dickens characters, brass hunting horns, and pewter and ceramic beer mugs. Loners can drink at the bar, or you can sit at one of the small tables, sinking into the soft sofas and armchairs. Beer begins at 340 ptas. ($2.40), whisky at 700 ptas. ($5). Open daily from 6pm to 1am. Metro: Argüelles.

Oliver Piano Bar, calle Almirante 12, off the paseo de la Castellana. ☎ **521-73-79.**

This popular bar is a pub-style hangout for show-biz people, with a good sprinkling of foreign personalities. The street-floor room evokes a stage setting by one of London's designers. There's a pastoral mural on the ceiling, a formal fireplace, and recessed alcoves containing shelves of books. On the walls hang old paintings and engravings. The color scheme is aged Mediterranean: faded red, sienna, bronze, and gold.

At the bottom of a winding staircase is a lower level ringed with couches. Often someone plays the piano softly. You pay 450 ptas. ($3.20) for a beer at a table; it's slightly less at the stand-up bar. Music begins most evenings about 30 minutes after midnight. Open daily from 4pm to 6am. Metro: Chueca. Bus: 70.

★ **Palacio Gaviria,** calle del Arenal 9. ☎ **526-6069.**

Its 1847 construction was heralded as the architectural triumph of one of the era's most flamboyant aristocrats, the Marqués de Gaviria. Famous as one of the paramours of then-queen Isabella II, he outfitted his palace with the heavily ornate jumble of neoclassical and baroque styles that later became known as *Isabelino.* In 1993, after extensive renovations, the building was opened to the public as a concert hall for the occasional presentation of classical music and as a late-night cocktail bar. Ten high-ceilinged rooms now function as richly decorated multipurpose areas for clients to wander in, drinks in hand, reacting to whatever or whomever happens to be there at the time. (One room is discreetly referred to as the bedroom-away-from-home of the queen herself.) No food is served, but the list of libations includes many stylish cocktails and wines. At press time, talks were underway for the presentation of either disco music or a cabaret. Open Sunday through Wednesday from 9:30pm to 3am, Thursday from 9:30pm to 4am, and Friday and Saturday from 9:30pm to 5:30am. Metro: Puerta del Sol or Ópera.

Admission (including first drink): 1,500 ptas. ($10.70). Second drink from 1,000 ptas. ($7.10) to 1,750 ptas. ($12.40).

Viva Madrid, calle Manuel Fernández y González 7. ☎ **410-55-35.**

With its lushly ornate tiled facade and the animated crowd that sometimes spills out onto the sidewalk during peak hours, Viva Madrid is hard to resist. It sits near the Plaza Santa Ana in a neighborhood of narrow streets loaded with marauding *gatos* searching for friendship, love, and fulfillment (sometimes successfully). A congenial mixture of students, artists, foreign tourists, and visiting Yanks crams into its turn-of-the-century interior, where tilework murals and carved animals contribute an undeniable charm. Beer begins at 450 ptas. ($3.20), drinks start at 800 ptas. ($5.70). Open Sunday through Friday from noon to 1am and Saturday from noon to 2am. Metro: Antón Martín.

Gay & Lesbian Bars

Spain has witnessed an explosion of gay life since the 1970s, perhaps as a reaction against the omnipresent pressures of machismo and traditional models of femininity. Many gay Spaniards agree, however, that the segregation of gay men from lesbians simply doesn't apply with the rigid boundaries you might have expected. In the most sophisticated clubs, people of all sexual orientations mix comfortably.

Black & White, calle Gravina, at the corner of Libertad. ☎ **531-11-41.**

This is Madrid's major gay bar, in the center of the Chueca district. A guard will open the door to a large room—painted, as you might expect, black and white. There's a disco in the basement, but the street-level bar is the premier gathering spot, featuring drag shows, male striptease, and videos. Old movies are shown against one wall. Drinks are 450 ptas. ($3.20). Open daily from 8pm to 5am. Metro: Chueca.

Café Figueroa, Augusto Figueroa 17, at the corner of Hortaleza.
☎ **521-16-73.**

This turn-of-the-century cafe attracts a diverse clientele, including a large number of gay men and lesbians. It's one of the city's most popular gathering spots for drinks and conversation. Drinks are 400 ptas. ($2.80); beer is 350 ptas. ($2.50). Open daily from 1pm to 2am. Metro: Chueca.

Cruising, Perez Galdos 5. ☎ **521-51-43.**

Considered one of Madrid's predominant gay bars, a center for consciousness-raising and cruising (as its name suggests), this place has probably been visited at least once by virtually every gay male in Castile. It doesn't get crowded or lively until late at night. Beer costs from 450 ptas. ($3.20). Open daily from 10:30pm to 3am. Metro: Chueca.

Duplex, calle Hortaleza 64. ☎ **531-37-92.**

Attracting a young crowd of disco-loving gays, lesbians, and straights, this bar contains a modern decor, a disco with recent and very danceable music, and an amply stocked bar. Drinks are 800 ptas. ($5.70); beer is 450 ptas. ($3.20). Open Friday and Saturday from 10pm to 5am. Metro: Chueca.

No Sé los Digas a Nadie, calle Ventura de la Vega 7. ☎ **420-29-80.**

"Don't Tell Mama" defines itself as a politically correct women's entertainment center, although it seems to attract an almost equal number of men to its two floors, hidden behind a black garage door on this street of budget restaurants. Inside, there is an art gallery, a bar/cafe, a mostly lesbian staff with information on women's activities in Madrid, and live or recorded music every evening after 11pm. Drinks range from 350 to 800 ptas. ($2.50 to $5.70). Open Tuesday through Saturday from 9:30am to 3 or 4am. Metro: Puerta del Sol, Sevilla, or Antón Martín.

Summer *Terrazas*

At the first hint of spring, Madrileños rush outdoors to drink, talk, and sit at a string of open-air cafes *terrazas* throughout the city. The best ones—and also the most expensive—are along the paseo de la Castellana between Plaza de la Cibeles and Plaza Emilio Castelar, but there are dozens more.

You can wander up and down the boulevard, selecting one that appeals to you; if you get bored, you can go on later to another. Sometimes these *terrazas* are called *chiringuitos.* You'll also find them along other paseos, the Recoletos and the Prado, both fashionable areas though not as hip as the Castellana. For old, traditional atmosphere, the terrazas at the Plaza Mayor win out. The terrazas of Plaza Santa Ana also have several atmospheric choices within the old city. Friday and Saturday are the most popular nights for drinking; many locals sit here all night.

Cave Crawling

To capture a peculiar Madrid *joie de vivre* of the 18th century, visit some *mesones* and *cuevas*, many found in the so-called *barrios bajos*. From the Plaza Mayor, walk down calle Arco de Cuchilleros until you find a gypsylike cafe that fits your fancy. Young people love to meet in the taverns and caves of Old Madrid for communal drinking and songfests. The sangría flows freely, the atmosphere is charged, the room usually packed; the sound of guitars wafts into the night air. Sometimes you'll see a strolling band of singing students (*tuna*) go from bar to bar, colorfully attired, with ribbons fluttering from their outfits.

Mesón Austrias, Cava de San Miguel 11. No phone.

One of several tapas bars just behind the Plaza Mayor, Mesón Austrias has a number of sit-down cells stretching toward a second bar in the rear. Most customers prefer to stand near the front entrance. In winter the favorite spot is by the open fireplace in the front room, when a pitcher of sangría is the thing to order. There's often accordion music at night. Beer costs 300 ptas. ($2.10); a pitcher of sangría is 1,200 ptas. ($8.50); tapas are from 550 ptas. ($3.90). Open daily from 6:30pm to 1:30am. Metro: Puerta del Sol or Ópera.

Mesón del Champiñon, Cava de San Miguel 17. No phone.

The barmen keep a brimming bucket of sangría behind the long stand-up bar as a thirst-quencher for the many people who crowd in. The name of the establishment translates as "mushroom," and that's what you see delineated in various sizes along sections of the vaulted ceilings. A more appetizing way to experience a *champiñon* is to order a *ración* of grilled, stuffed, and salted mushrooms, served with toothpicks. A portion costs 500 ptas. ($3.60) at the bar or 550 ptas. ($3.90) at a table. The pair of slightly dank tiny rooms in back is where Spanish families jam in for the organ music played by a stalwart musician performing in one corner. Sangría runs 1,200 ptas. ($8.50). Open daily from 6pm to 2am. Metro: Puerta del Sol, Ópera, or La Latina.

Mesón de la Guitarra, Cava de San Miguel 13. ☎ 559-95-31.

My favorite *cueva* in the area, Mesón de la Guitarra is loud and exciting any night of the week and as warmly earthy as anything you'll find in Madrid. The decor combines terra-cotta floors, antique brick walls, hundreds of sangría pitchers clustered above the bar, murals of gluttons, old rifles, and faded bullfighting posters. Like most things in Madrid, the place doesn't get rolling until around 10:30pm, although you can stop in for a drink and tapas earlier. Don't be afraid to start singing an American song if it has a fast rhythm—60 people will join in, even if they don't know the words. Beer goes for 175 ptas. ($1.20); wine costs 100 ptas. (70¢); tapas are 500 to 700 ptas. ($3.60 to $5). Open daily from 6:30pm to 1:30am. Metro: Puerta del Sol or Ópera.

Sesamo, calle Príncipe 7. ☎ **429-65-24.**

Despite its rustic bohemian appearance (or perhaps because of it), "Sesame" has hosted Truman Capote and many other celebrities. Styles and cultural heroes rise and fall, but Sesamo seems to go on forever. Its two cellar rooms are reached via a long flight of steps. Downstairs, you'll find seats gathered around tiny tables. Guests have been known to bring their guitars or banjos, spontaneously singing folk songs, laments of love, or political protests. When no one in the audience is particularly musical, management provides a piano player. Like virtually everything else in Madrid, the action here doesn't get going until around 11pm. If you're with a group, it's customary to order a pitcher of sangría for 1,200 ptas. ($8.50). Beer costs 300 ptas. ($2.10). Open daily from 6pm to 2am. Metro: Sevilla or Puerta del Sol.

---

4 More Entertainment

FILMS Spanish film director José Luís Garci has written that no other city in the world treats films and the pronouncements of publicity agents with greater respect than Madrid. Recent cinematic releases from Paris, New York, Rome, and Hollywood come quickly to Madrid, where an avid audience often waits in long lines for tickets. Most foreign films are dubbed into Spanish, unless they're indicated as *V.O.* (original version).

The city's premier theaters are the slightly faded enormous movie palaces of the Gran Vía, whose huge marquees announce in lurid colors whichever romantic or adventure *espectáculo* happens to be playing at the moment.

Madrid boasts at least 90 legitimate movie houses (many have several theaters under one roof), and many others running pictures for adults only. All listings are in the *Guía del Ocio*, in the *Guía de Diario 16* (also available at newsstands), or in the film listings of Madrileño newspapers.

If you want to see a film while in Madrid, one of the best places is the quadriplex **Alphaville,** calle Martín de los Héros 14 (☎ **559-38-36;** Metro: Plaza de España), showing English-language films with Spanish subtitles. If the film is not too long, there are four daily showings at 4:30, 6:30, 8:30, and 10:30pm; on Saturday and Sunday, there's a show at 12:30am. The complex also includes a bookstore and an art deco cafe.

For classic revivals and foreign films, check the listings at Filmoteca in the **Cine Doré,** calle Santa Isabel 3 (☎ **369-11-25;** Metro: Antón Martín). Movies here tend to be shown in their original language, with tickets costing around 300 ptas. ($2.10). There are a bar and a simple restaurant on the premises.

A CASINO   The **Casino Gran Madrid** is at Km 28,300 de la Ctra. Nacional VI–Madrid–La Coruña, Apdo 62, Torrelodones 28250 (☎ **856-11-00**). Even nongamblers sometimes make the trek here from the capital, for the casino's many entertainment facilities are considered by some to be the most exciting around. Its scattered attractions include two restaurants, four bars, and a nightclub. The casino is open Sunday through Thursday from 2pm to 4am and Friday, Saturday, and holiday evenings from 2pm to 5am. For an entrance fee of 500 ptas. ($3.60), you can sample the action in the gaming rooms, including French and American roulette, blackjack, punto y banco, baccarat, and chemin de fer.

An à la carte restaurant in the French Gaming Room offers international cuisine, with dinners costing from 8,000 ptas. ($56.80). The American Gaming Room's buffet will cost around 3,000 ptas. ($21.30). The restaurants are open from 9:30pm to 2am. The casino is about 17 miles (27 km) northwest of Madrid, along the Madrid–La Coruña N-BI highway. If you don't feel like driving, the casino has buses that depart from Plaza de España 6, every afternoon and evening at 4:30, 6, 7:30, 9, and 11:30pm. Note that between October and June, men must wear jackets and ties; jeans and tennis shoes are forbidden in any season. To enter, a European visitor must present an identity card and a non-European visitor must present a passport.

10

Easy Excursions from Madrid

Sᴏᴍᴇ ᴏꜰ Eᴜʀᴏᴘᴇ'ꜱ ᴍᴏꜱᴛ ɪɴᴛᴇʀᴇꜱᴛɪɴɢ ᴀɴᴅ ᴠᴀʀɪᴇᴅ ꜱᴄᴇɴᴇʀʏ ᴀɴᴅ ᴀᴛᴛʀᴀᴄᴛɪᴏɴꜱ lie in the satellite cities and towns ringing Madrid. These include Toledo with its El Greco masterpieces, Aranjuez with its autumn/ spring Bourbon palace, San Lorenzo with its monastery that's considered the eighth wonder of the world (El Escorial), Segovia with its castles that "float" in the clouds, and La Granja with its summer palaces of the Bourbon dynasty.

If your time is short, go at least to Toledo, which captures the ages of Spain in miniature. Many tourists combine a tour of Toledo with a stopover at the royal palace of Aranjuez.

1 **Toledo**

42 miles (68 km) SW of Madrid, 85 miles (137 km) SE of Ávila

GETTING THERE • By Train RENFE trains run frequently every day. Those departing Madrid's Atocha railway station for Toledo run from 8:15am to 8:55pm; those leaving Toledo for Madrid run daily from 6:25am to 9:50pm. Travel time is approximately 90 minutes. For train information in Madrid, call **527-31-60;** in Toledo, call **22-12-71.**

• **By Bus** Buses are faster and more direct than trains. Galiano Continental (☎ **22-29-61**) runs about 12 different buses daily, departing every half an hour from 6:30am to 10pm from the lower level of Estación Sur de Autobuses, Canarías 17 (Metro: Palos de la Frontera). Buses take about 1¹/₄ hours to complete the trip between Madrid and Toledo and are usually marked "ꜱᴀɴᴛᴀ Bᴀʀʙᴀʀᴀ" or "ᴘᴏʟɪɢᴀɴᴏ." In Toledo, you'll be deposited at the Estación Sur de Autobuses on the outskirts of central Toledo, where you can either walk into town or take a city bus.

• **By Car** Exit Madrid via Cibeles (Paseo del Prado) and take the N-401 south.

ESSENTIALS Toledo's **telephone area code** is 925. The **Tourist Information Office** is at Puerta Nueva de Bisagra (☎ **925/22-08-43**).

The ancient capital of Spain looms on the horizon like an El Greco painting, seemingly undisturbed by the ages. The See of the Primate of Spain, the ecclesiastical center of the country, Toledo is medieval but well preserved. The Tagus River loops around the granite promontory on which Toledo rests, surrounding the Imperial City on three sides like a snake.

Toledan steel, known as early as the 1st century B.C., has sliced its name down through the ages. Many a Mexican or Peruvian—if he had lived—could attest to the deadly accuracy of a Toledan sword. But except for its steel and damascene work, the lack of major industrial activity has kept Toledo a virtual museum. Many of its buildings are intact, having survived countless battles, the most recent being the bloody fighting the city witnessed in the Spanish Civil War. It's not uncommon for mansions to preserve their original coats-of-arms in their facades.

The natural fortress that is Toledo is a labyrinth of narrow and precipitous streets, decaying palaces, towers, and squares—all tourist-trodden. The Spanish government has seen fit to preserve all of Toledo as a "national monument." One critic labeled the entire city "a gallery of art," with every style represented from Romanesque to Moorish to Gothic (best exemplified by the cathedral) to Renaissance.

Essentially, Toledo is a blending of the widely diverse cultures that made Spain what it is today: Roman, Visigothic, Moorish, Jewish, and Christian. Perhaps for that reason, Tirso de Molina, the 17th-century dramatist, called Toledo "the heart of Spain." He named three of his dramas *Los cigarrales de Toledo* (The Grasshopper Fields of Toledo), which brings us to a most important suggestion: Before you leave the Imperial City, you should—preferably in the late afternoon—traverse the **carretera de Circunvalación**, that most scenic of roads across the left bank of the Tagus. Along the slopes of the hills, you'll find the *cigarrales*, the rustic houses. From this side of the river, you can obtain the best panorama and see the city in perspective as El Greco did. With luck, you'll be perched on some belvedere as the sun goes down. Then you'll know why Toledo's sunsets are called violet.

What to See & Do

You can see all the major attractions in one day, provided you arrive early and stay late.

⭐ **Cathedral of Toledo,** Arco de Palacio. ☎ **22-22-41.**

Built at the flowering peak of the Gothic era of architecture, the cathedral, which stands directly east of the Plaza del Ayuntamiento in the heart of Toledo, is one of the greatest in Europe. It was erected principally between 1226 and 1493, although there have been later additions. The monument is a bastion of Christian architecture, but a great deal of the actual construction work was carried out by the Moors, master builders themselves.

The cathedral witnessed many prime moments in Spanish history—such as a proclamation naming "Juana la Loca" (the insane daughter of Isabella I) and her husband, Philip the Handsome, heirs to the throne of Spain.

Inside, the Transparente—the altar completed in 1732 by Narciso Tome—is a landmark in European architecture. Lit by a "hole" cut through the ceiling, this production includes angels on fluffy clouds, a polychrome *Last Supper*, and a Madonna winging her way to heaven.

Dating from the 16th century, the cathedral's iron gate is in the plateresque style. Works of art include *The Twelve Apostles* by El Greco and paintings by Velázquez, Goya, Morales, and van Dyck. El Greco's first painting in Toledo was commissioned by the cathedral. Called *El Expolio*, it created a furor when the devout saw the vivid coloring of Christ's garments. The artist was even hauled into the courts. Many elaborately sculpted tombs of both the nobility and the ecclesiastical hierarchy are sheltered inside.

Don't fail to visit the Gothic cloister, the Capilla Mayor, and the Renaissance-style Choir Room (elaborate wood carvings), and you should see the rose windows, preferably near sunset. In the Treasure Room is a 500-pound monstrance, dating from the 16th century and said to have been made, in part, from gold Columbus brought back from the New World. To celebrate Corpus festivities, the monstrance is carried through the streets of Toledo. The Mozarabic Chapel dates from the 16th century and contains paintings by Juan de Borgoña (a mass using Mozarabic liturgy is still conducted here).

Admission: Cathedral, free; Treasure Room, 350 ptas. ($2.50).

Open: July–Aug, Mon–Sat 10:30am–1pm and 3:30–7pm, Sun 10:30am–1:30pm and 4–7pm; Sept–June, Mon–Sat 10:30am–1pm and 3:30–7:30pm, Sun 10:30am–1:30pm and 4–6pm. **Bus:** 5 or 6.

Museo de Santa Cruz, calle de Miguel Cervantes 3. ☎ 22-10-36.

Built in the form of a Greek cross, this 16th-century plateresque hospice has been turned into a museum of fine arts and archeology. As a hospital, it was founded by Cardinal Mendoza. It's of such beautiful construction—especially its paneled ceilings—that it's a question of the "frame" competing with the pictures inside.

In the Fine Arts Museum are 18 paintings by El Greco (*The Burial of Conde de Orgaz* is a copy of his masterpiece). *The Assumption of the Virgin* is his most important canvas here. Other works are by Ribera and Goya. Flemish tapestries, antique furnishings, and jewelry round out the exhibit.

In the Archeological Museum the past ages of Toledo are peeled away: prehistoric, Iberian, Roman (note the mosaics), Moorish, Visigothic, and Gothic. The museum is an easy walk from the Plaza de Zocodover in the very heart of Toledo.

Admission: 225 ptas. ($1.60).

Open: Tues–Sat 10am–6:30pm, Sun–Mon 10am–2pm. **Bus:** 5 or 6. **Directions:** Pass beneath the granite archways piercing the eastern edge of the Plaza de Zocodover and walk about one block.

Casa y Museo del Greco, calle de Samuel Leví. ☎ 22-40-46.

The famous painter Doménikos Theotokópoulos, called El Greco because he was born in Crete, arrived in Toledo in 1577 and lived here with Doña Jerónima, a noted beauty (either his wife or his mistress) until his death in 1614. His living quarters stood in the *antiguo barrio judío*, or the old Jewish quarter, on calle de Samuel Leví in the heart of Toledo. It is believed the painter moved to this site in 1585.

Samuel Ha-Leví, chancellor of the exchequer to Pedro the Cruel, is said to have built a series of houses here, forming a complex in the 14th century. These little interconnected houses were often called "apartments." Ha-Leví had subterranean passages dug to hide his treasury; and a Don Enrique de Villena, it is said, practiced alchemy in these underground cellars.

The apartments or houses were torn down in the late 19th

Easy Excursions From Madrid

1 Toledo   **3** Aranjuez
2 Segovia   **4** San Lorenzo de
       El Escorial

century, but many people in Toledo say El Greco's house or apartment was rescued. Perhaps it was, but critics aren't sure. What emerged, nevertheless, was identified for visitors as "Casa del Greco." Eventually a neighboring house was incorporated to shelter a museum with 19 pictures by El Greco.

Visitors are admitted into the so-called studio of El Greco, which contains a painting by the artist. Especially interesting are the garden and kitchen.

Admission: 225 ptas. ($1.60); children under 20 free.

Open: July–Sept, Tues–Sat 10am–1:45pm and 3:30–6:45pm, Sun 10am–1:45pm; Oct–June, Tues–Sat 10am–2pm and 3:30–6pm, Sun 10am–1:45pm. Check with the tourist office to see if it's reopened after a restoration. **Bus:** 5 or 6.

San Juan de los Reyes, calle de los Reyes Católicos 17.
☎ 22-38-02.

This church was founded by Ferdinand and Isabella to commemorate their 1476 triumph over the Portuguese at Toro. Its construction was started in 1477, according to the plans of architect Juan Guas. It was finished, together with the splendid cloisters, in 1504, dedicated to St. John the Evangelist and used, from the very beginning, by the Franciscan Friars. It's a perfect example of Gothic-Spanish-Flemish style.

San Juan de los Reyes was restored after being damaged in the invasion of Napoleon and abandoned in 1835. Actually, the national monument has been entrusted again to the Franciscans since 1954.

Admission: 125 ptas. (90¢); children under 9 free.

Open: Daily 10am–1:45pm and 3:30–6pm. **Bus:** 5 or 6.

Iglesía de Santo Tomé, Plaza del Conde 2, calle de Santo Tomé.
☎ 21-02-09.

Except for its mudéjar tower, this little 14th-century chapel is rather unprepossessing. But by some strange twist it was given the honor of exhibiting El Greco's masterpiece, *The Burial of the Conde de Orgaz*. Long acclaimed for its composition, the painting is a curious work in its blending of realism with mysticism.

Admission: 125 ptas. (90¢).

Open: Daily 10am–1:45pm and 3:30–6:45pm (until 5:45pm in winter). **Closed:** Jan 1 and Dec 25.

Alcazar, calle General Moscardó 4. ☎ 22-30-38.

The characteristic landmark dominating the skyline of Toledo is the Alcázar, in the very center of the city. It attracted worldwide attention during the 1936 siege of the city, when Nationalists held the fortress for 70 days until relief troops could respond to their plea for help, arriving on September 27, 1936.

The most famous event surrounding that battle was a telephone call the Republicans placed to the Nationalist leader inside. He was informed his son was being held captive and would be executed if the Alcázar were not surrendered. He refused to comply with their demands, and his son was sacrificed.

The Alcázar was destroyed. The one standing in its place today is a reconstruction that houses an Army Museum. A monument out front is dedicated to the heroes of that 1936 siege.

Admission: 150 ptas. ($1.10); children under 9 free.

Open: Oct–June, Tues–Sun 10am–1:30pm and 4–5:30pm (until 6:30pm July–Sept). **Bus:** 5 or 6.

Sínagoga del Tránsito, calle de Samuel Leví. ☎ 22-36-65.

Down the street from El Greco's museum is the once-important place of worship for the large Jewish population that used to inhabit the

Toledo

City Wall

Hospital de Santa Cruz

Plaza de Zocodover

Cuesta del Alcázar

Plaza Magdalena

Plaza de Alfonso VI

Paseo de Madrid

Plaza Tendillas

Palacio de Fuensalida

Río Tajo

Puente de la Peña Nueva

⊕ N

Church †   Post Office ⊠   Information ⓘ

Alcázar ❼
Casa y Museo del Greco ❹
Cathedral of Toledo ❽
Museo de Santa Cruz ❶
San Juan de los Reyes ❺
Santo Tomé ❷
Sinagoga del Tránsito ❸
Sinagoga de Santa María La Blanca

Madrid ☆
Toledo ○
SPAIN

9144

city, living peacefully with both Christians and Arabs. This 14th-century building is noted for its superb stucco and its Hebrew inscriptions. There are some psalms along the top of the walls and on the east wall a poetic description of the temple. The construction of the synagogue was ordered by Don Samuel Ha-Leví, the chancellor of the exchequer to Pedro el Cruel (Peter the Cruel). The name of the king appears clearly in a frame in the Hebrew inscription.

The synagogue is the most important part of the **Museo Sefardi,** which was inaugurated in 1971 and contains tombstones with Hebrew epigraphy dating from before 1492 and other art works.

Admission: 200 ptas. ($1.40).

Open: Tues–Sat 10am–2pm and 4–6pm, Sun 10am–2pm. **Bus:** 5 or 6.

Sínagoga de Santa María la Blanca, calle de los Reyes Católicos 2. ☎ 22-72-57.

In the late 12th century, the Jews of Toledo erected an important synagogue in the *almohade* style, which employs graceful horseshoe arches and ornamental horizontal moldings. Although by the early 15th century it had been converted into a Christian church, much of the orginal remains, including the five naves and elaborate Mudéjar decorations—mosquelike in their effect. The synagogue lies on the western edge of the city, midway between the El Greco museum and San Juan de los Reyes.

Admission: 125 ptas. (90¢)

Open: Apr–Sept, daily 10am–2pm and 3:30–7pm; Oct–Mar, daily 10am–2pm and 3:30–6pm. **Bus:** 2

Hospital de Tavera, paseo de Madrid. ☎ 22-04-51.

This 16th-century Greco-Roman palace north of Toledo's medieval ramparts was built by Cardinal Tavera; it now houses a private art collection. Titian's portrait of Charles V hangs in the banqueting hall, and the museum owns five paintings by El Greco: *The Holy Family; The Baptism of Christ;* and portraits of St. Francis, St. Peter, and Cardinal Tavera. Ribera's *The Bearded Woman* also attracts many. The libarary's collection of books is priceless. In the nearby church is the mausoleum of Cardinal Tavera, designed by Alonso Berruguete.

Admission: 500 ptas. ($3.60)

Open: Daily 10:30am–1:30pm and 3:30–6pm.

Where to Stay ─────────────────────────────

EXPENSIVE

 Parador Nacional de Conde Orgaz, Cerro del Emperador, 45002 Toledo. ☎ **925/22-18-50.** Fax 925/22-51-66. 76 rms. MINIBAR TV TEL **Directions:** Drive across Puente San Martín and head south for 2¹/₂ miles (4 km).

Rates: 10,300 ptas. ($73.10) single; 15,000 ptas. ($106.50) double. Breakfast 1,200 ptas. ($8.50) extra. AE, DC, MC, V. **Parking:** Free.

Make reservations well in advance for this parador, built on the ridge of a rugged hill where El Greco is said to have painted the *View of Toledo.* The main living room/lounge has fine furniture—old chests, brown-leather chairs, heavy tables—and leads to a sunny terrace overlooking the city. On chilly nights you can sit by the fireplace. A stairway and balcony lead to dark oak-paneled doors opening onto the guest rooms, the most luxurious in all Toledo. Spacious and beautifully furnished, they contain reproductions of regional antique pieces.

Dining/Entertainment: See the restaurant recommendation under "Where to Dine," below.

Services: Room service, laundry/valet.

Facilities: Outdoor pool.

MODERATE

★ **Hostal del Cardenal,** Paseo de Recardo 24, 45005 Toledo.
☎ **925/22-49-00.** Fax 925/22-29-91. 27 rms, 2 suites.
$ A/C TV TEL **Bus:** 2 from rail station.

Rates: 5,900 ptas. ($41.90) single; 9,500 ptas. ($67.50) double; 13,300 ptas. ($94.40) suite. Breakfast 650 ptas. ($4.60) extra. AE, DC, MC, V.

The entrance to this unusual hotel is set into the stone fortifications of the ancient city walls, a few steps from the Bisagra Gate. Inside you'll find flagstone walkways, Moorish fountains, rose gardens, and cascading vines. To reach the hotel you must climb a series of terraces to the top of the crenellated walls of the ancient fortress. There, grandly symmetrical and very imposing, is the former residence of the 18th-century cardinal of Toledo, Señor Lorenzana. The establishment has tiled walls; long, narrow salons; dignified Spanish furniture; and a smattering of antiques.

Hotel Carlos V, calle Trastamara 1, 45001 Toledo. ☎ **925/22-21-00.**
Fax 925/22-21-05. 69 rms. A/C TEL **Bus:** 5 or 6.

Rates: 7,195 ptas. ($51.10) single; 10,500 ptas. ($74.60) double. Breakfast 645 ptas. ($4.60) extra. AE, DC, MC, V.

This old favorite midway between the Alcázar and the cathedral has a handsome, albeit somber, exterior. It looks more expensive than it is. The guest rooms are well appointed, and the service is fine. Dining is available at the Carlos V, with lunch or dinner costing 2,500 ptas. ($17.80).

Hotel María Cristina, Marqués de Mendigorría 1, 45003 Toledo.
☎ **925/21-32-02.** Fax 925/21-26-50. 60 rms, 3 suites.
A/C TV TEL

Rates: 6,995 ptas. ($49.70) single; 10,615 ptas. ($75.40) double; 13,800 ptas. ($98) suite. Breakfast 600 ptas. ($4.30) extra. AE, DC, MC, V. **Parking:** 650 ptas. ($4.60).

Located adjacent to the historic Hospital de Tavera, near the northern perimeter of the old town, this stone-sided, awning-fronted hotel resembles a palatial country home. Originally built as a convent and later used as a hospital, it was transformed into this comfortably stable hotel in the early 1980s. Sprawling, historic, and generously proportioned, it contains clean and amply sized guest rooms, each attractively but simply furnished.

Dining/Entertainment: On site is the very large and well-recommended restaurant El Abside, where fixed-price lunches and dinners begin at 3,000 ptas. ($21.30). There's also a bar.

Services: 24-hour room service, laundry, concierge, babysitting.

Facilities: Tennis courts.

Hotel Pintor El Greco, Alamillos del Tránsito 13, 45002 Toledo.
☎ **925/21-42-50.** Fax 925/21-58-19. 33 rms. A/C TV TEL

Rates: 7,440 ptas. ($52.80) single; 9,300 ptas. ($66) double. Breakfast 650 ptas. ($4.60) extra. AE, DC, MC, V.

In the old Jewish quarter, one of the most tradition laden and historic districts of Toledo, this hotel was converted from a typical *casa Toledana* that had once been used as a bakery. With careful restoration, especially of its antique facade, it was converted into one of Toledo's best and most atmospheric small hotels. The old patio with a fountain was restored, and decoration in both the public rooms and the guest rooms is in a traditional Castilian style. Automatic phones, piped-in music, satellite TV, and individual security boxes were added to the immaculately kept guest rooms. At the hotel's doorstep are such landmarks as the Iglesia de San Juan de los Reyes, Sínagoga de Santa María la Blanca, Sínagoga del Tránsito, Casa y Museo de El Greco, and Iglesia de Santo Tomé.

Hotel Residencia Alfonso Vi, calle General Moscardó 2, 45001 Toledo. ☎ **925/22-26-00.** Fax 925/21-44-58. 88 rms. A/C TV TEL **Bus:** 5 or 6.

Rates: 7,595 ptas. ($53.90); 10,900 ptas. ($77.40) double. Breakfast 645 ptas. ($4.60) extra. AE, DC, MC, V.

Although built in the early 1970s, this hotel has been kept up-to-date. It sits near a great concentration of souvenir shops in the center of the old city, at the Alcázar's southern perimeter. Inside you'll discover a high-ceilinged, marble-trimmed decor with a scattering of Iberian artifacts, copies of Spanish provincial furniture, and dozens of leather armchairs. You can dine in the stone-floored dining room, where fixed-price meals are 2,500 ptas. ($17.80).

INEXPENSIVE

$ **Hotel Imperio,** Cadenea 5, 45001 Toledo. ☎ **925/22-76-50.** Fax 925/25-31-83. 21 rms. A/C TV TEL **Bus:** 5 or 6.

Rates: 3,700 ptas. ($26.30) single; 5,500 ptas. ($39.10) double. Breakfast 400 ptas. ($2.80) extra. MC, V.

Just off calle de la Plata, one block west of the Plaza de Zocodover, the Imperio is the best bet for those on a tight budget. The rooms are clean and comfortable but small. Most overlook a little church with a wall overgrown with wisteria.

Hotel Maravilla, Plaza de Barrio Rey 7, 45001 Toledo.
☎ **925/22-33-00.** Fax 925/25-05-58. 18 rms. A/C TEL **Bus:** 5 or 6.

Rates: 3,800 ptas. ($27) single; 6,600 ptas. ($46.90) double. Breakfast 500 ptas. ($3.60) extra. AE, MC, V.

If you enjoy hotels with lots of local color, then this little place will please you. It's only one block south of the Plaza de Zocodover and opens directly onto its own cobblestone plaza. Semimodernized in 1971, the building has many bay windows; the guest rooms are modest but adequate, the furnishings so-so. You can hang your laundry on the roof and use an iron in the downstairs laundry room.

NEARBY PLACES TO STAY

For readers who have a car or don't mind one or two taxi rides a day, there are a couple of excellent accommodations across the Tagus.

La Almazara, carretera Toledo-Argés-Cuerva, Km 3400, 45080 Toledo. ☎ **925/22-38-66.** 21 rms. TEL **Directions:** Follow the road to the Parador of Cuidad Real, then take the C-781 to Cuerva.

Rates: 3,500 ptas. ($24.90) single; 6,000 ptas. ($42.60) double. Breakfast 450 ptas. ($3.20) extra. AE, MC, V. **Closed:** Nov 1–Mar 15. **Parking**: Free.

Taking its name from an olive-oil mill that used to stand here, La Almazara offers some of the most offbeat accommodations around. Hidden away in the hills, this old-fashioned country villa, with its own courtyards and vineyards, offers a rare opportunity to soak up the atmosphere of Old Spain, far removed from the pace of city life. It has an exceptional view of Toledo. You may be assigned either a spacious chamber in the main house or a room in the annex.

Hotel los Cigarrales, carretera Circunvalación 32, 45000 Toledo. ☎ **925/22-00-53.** Fax 925/21-55-46. 36 rms. A/C TEL **Bus:** Chamartín from rail station.

Rates: 3,800 ptas. ($27) single; 5,900 ptas. ($41.90) double. Breakfast 450 ptas. ($3.20) extra. MC, V. **Parking:** Free.

About a mile south of the city center, this hotel offers quiet seclusion. Built in the 1960s in traditional red brick, it looks like a private villa with a garden; the friendliness of the family owners adds to this feeling. Most of the interior is covered with blue and green tiles. The rooms are clean and sunny, decorated with heavy Spanish furniture. The dining room offers meals for 1,675 ptas. ($11.90). From the cozy bar's flower-filled terrace you can see the towers of medieval Toledo.

Where to Dine

MODERATE

 Asador Adolfo, calle La Granada 6. ☎ **22-73-31.**

Cuisine: SPANISH. **Reservations:** Recommended. **Bus:** 5 or 6.

Prices: Appetizers 650–1,200 ptas. ($4.60–$8.50); main courses 1,850–2,500 ptas. ($13.10–$17.80); fixed-price menus 4,500 ptas. ($32). AE, DC, V.

Open: Lunch daily 1–4pm; dinner Mon–Sat 8pm–midnight.

Located less than a minute's walk north of the cathedral, in a warren of narrow medieval streets, this is considered by many residents the finest and most renowned restaurant in Toledo. Sections of the building were constructed during the 1400s, although recent renovations in the kitchens have enabled its chefs to prepare many modern variations of traditional Toledo-derived dishes. The ceilings of the several dining rooms are supported by massive beams and occasionally contain faded frescoes dating from the year of the building's original construction.

The house specialties include different preparations of game dishes, which are said to be among the best anywhere. These might include partridge with white beans, venison, or any of the wild game birds the region produces in such abundance. Nongame dishes include hake flavored with local saffron and any of a wide array of beef, veal, or lamb dishes. To begin, try the *pimientos rellenos* (red peppers stuffed with pulverized shellfish). The house dessert is marzipan; it's prepared in a wood-fired oven and is noted for its lightness.

The restaurant lies at the corner of calle Hombre de Palo, behind a discreet sign.

Casa Aurelio, calle de la Sínagoga 6 and calle de Sinagoga 1.
☎ **22-20-97.**

Cuisine: CASTILIAN. **Reservations:** Recommended. **Bus:** 5 or 6.
Prices: Appetizers 600–1,100 ptas. ($4.30–$7.80); maincourses 1,900–2,500 ptas. ($13.50–$17.80); fixed-price menu 3,250 ptas. ($23.10). AE, DC, MC, V.
Open: Lunch daily 1–4pm; dinner daily 8–11:30pm.

Established in the late 1940s near the northern edge of the cathedral, Casa Aurelia occupies two separate dining rooms, with two separate entrances a few feet apart. It's considered one of Toledo's restaurant staples, offering plentiful food, Castilian ambience, and efficient service. Menu items usually include traditional versions of *sopa castellana;* grilled hake; *lubina a la sal* (whitefish cooked in salt); fresh salmon; roast lamb; and, at certain times of year, Toledo partridge or roast suckling pig. Note that the main outlet of this restaurant (at calle de la Sinagoga 6) is usually closed every Wednesday, although the smaller of the restaurant's two dining rooms (at calle de la Sínagoga 1) remains open.

⭐ **Hostal del Cardenal,** paseo de Recaredo 24. ☎ **22-49-00.**

Cuisine: SPANISH. **Reservations:** Required. **Bus:** 2 from the station.
Prices: Appetizers 425–2,200 ptas. ($3–$15.60); main courses 800–2,350 ptas. ($5.70–$16.70); fixed-price menu 2,500 ptas. ($17.80). AE, DC, MC, V.
Open: Lunch daily 1–4pm; dinner daily 8:30–11:30pm.

You may want to treat yourself to Toledo's best-known restaurant, owned by the same people who run Madrid's Casa Botín, so beloved by Hemingway. The menu is very similar. You might begin with "quarter of an hour" (fish) soup or white asparagus, then move on to curried prawns, baked hake, filet mignon, or smoked salmon. Roast suckling pig is a specialty, as is partridge in casserole. Arrive early and enjoy a sherry in the bar or in the courtyard.

Parador Nacional de Conde Orgaz, Cerro del Emperador.
☎ **22-18-50.**

Cuisine: CASTILIAN. **Reservations:** Not accepted. **Directions:** Drive across Puente San Martín and head south for 2¹/₂ miles (4 km).
Prices: Appetizers 1,200–1,500 ptas. ($8.50–$10.70); main courses 2,000–2,600 ptas. ($14.20–$18.50); fixed-price menu 3,600 ptas. ($25.60). AE, DC, MC, V.

Some of the best Castilian regional cuisine is combined here with one of the most panoramic views from any European restaurant. Located in a fine parador (see "Where to Stay," above), the restaurant is on the crest of a hill—said to be the spot that El Greco selected for his *View of Toledo*. The fixed-price meal might include tasty Spanish hors d'oeuvres, hake, then perhaps either veal or beef grilled on an open fire, plus dessert. If you're dining lightly, try a local specialty, *tortilla española con magra* (potato omelet with ham or bacon). There's a bar on the upper level.

Venta de Aires, Circo Romano 35. ☎ **22-05-45.**

> **Cuisine:** SPANISH. **Reservations:** Recommended.
> **Prices:** Appetizers 850–1,500 ptas. ($6–$10.70); main courses 1,900–2,500 ptas. ($13.50–$17.80); fixed-price menu 4,500 ptas. ($32). AE, DC, MC, V.
> **Open:** Lunch daily 1–4pm; dinner Mon–Sat 8–11pm.

Just outside the city gates, directly southwest of the Circo Romano (Roman Circus), this restaurant has served Toledo's pièce de résistance—*perdiz* (partridge)—since 1891, when the place was only a little roadside inn. On the à la carte menu, this dish is best eaten with the red wine of Méntrida, but if you want to keep your tab low, you'd better stick to the fixed-price menu. For dessert, try the marzipan, an institution in Toledo. On your way out, take note of former President Nixon's entry in the guest book (he dined here in 1963).

INEXPENSIVE

$ **El Emperador,** carretera del Valle 1. ☎ **22-46-91.**

> **Cuisine:** SPANISH. **Reservations:** Recommended. **Bus:** Carretera del Valle.
> **Prices:** Appetizers 600–900 ptas. ($4.30–$6.40); main courses 800–1,800 ptas. ($5.70–$12.80); fixed-price menu 1,400 ptas. ($9.90). MC, V.
> **Open:** Lunch Tues–Sun 1–4pm; dinner Tues–Sun 8–11pm.

A modern restaurant on the outskirts of Toledo, southwest of the historic core, El Emperador is reached via an arched bridge. Its terraces overlook the river and the towers of Toledo, while the tavern-style interior has leather-and-wooden chairs, heavy beams, and wrought-iron chandeliers. It was established in 1974 by a proud family who still owns and manages it today. Service is attentive. The fixed-price menu might include a choice of soup (beef, vegetable, or noodle), followed by a small steak with french fries, then fresh fruit, plus wine.

$ **Maravilla,** Plaza de Barrio Rey 5. ☎ **22-33-00.**

> **Cuisine:** SPANISH. **Reservations:** Not accepted. **Bus:** 5 or 6.
> **Prices:** Appetizers 650–1,380 ptas. ($4.60–$9.80); main courses 1,300–2,100 ptas. ($9.20–$14.90); fixed-price menus 1,075–1,800 ptas. ($7.60–$12.80). AE, MC, V.
> **Open:** Lunch Tues–Sun 1–4pm; dinner Tues–Sun 8–11pm.

238

Located in the Barrio Rey, a small square off the historic Plaza de Zocodover that's filled with budget restaurants and cafes that change their names so often it's virtually impossible to keep track, Maravilla offers the best all-around dining bargain. Its kitchen serves a typically Castilian menu, specializing in the famous *perdiz* (partridge) but also preparing *cordero asado* (roast lamb).

La Parilla, Horno de los Bizcochos 8. ☎ **21-22-45.**

Cuisine: SPANISH. **Reservations:** Not accepted. **Bus:** 5 or 6.
Prices: Appetizers 650–950 ptas. ($4.60–$6.70); main courses 1,500–2,200 ptas. ($10.70–$15.60); fixed-price menu 2,300 ptas. ($16.30). AE, DC, MC, V.
Open: Lunch daily 1–4pm; dinner daily 8–11pm.

This classic Spanish restaurant, lying within a thick-walled medieval building, stands on a cobbled street near the Hotel Alfonso VI, just east of the cathedral. The menu offers no surprises, but it's reliable. Likely inclusions on the bill of fare are roast suckling pig, spider crabs, Castilian baked trout, stewed quail, baked kidneys, and La Mancha rabbit.

A TAPAS BAR

Bar Ludeña, Plaza de la Horn Madelena 13, Corral de Don Diego 10. ☎ **22-33-84.**

Cuisine: TAPAS. **Reservations:** Not accepted.
Prices: Tapas 250–750 ptas. ($1.80–$5.30). No credit cards.
Open: Thurs–Tues 10am–midnight.

Delectable combinations of tapas are served here to a loyal clientele. Sometimes glasses of wine are passed through a small window to clients who are standing outside enjoying the view of the square. The bar is little more than a narrow corridor, serving *raciones* of tapas that are so generous they make little meals, especially when served with bread. The roasted red peppers in olive oil are especially tasty, along with the stuffed crabs. Huge dishes of pickled cucumbers, onions, and olives are available. A tiny dining room behind a curtain at the end of the bar serves inexpensive fare.

2 Aranjuez

29 miles (47 km) S of Madrid, 30 miles (48 km) NE of Toledo

GETTING THERE • By Train   Trains run about every 20 minutes to and from Madrid's Atocha station (50 minutes). Trains run less often along the east-west route to and from Toledo (40 minutes). The Aranjuez station lies about a mile outside town. You can walk it in about 15 minutes, but taxis and buses line up on calle Stuart (two blocks from the tourist office). The bus that makes the run from the center of Aranjuez to the railway station is marked "N-Z."

• By Bus   Buses bound for Aranjuez depart from Madrid's Estación Sur de Autobuses, Canarias 17 (call **468-45-11** in Madrid for information). Buses run about seven times a day between Aranjuez and Madrid. They arrive at and depart from the City Bus Terminal, calle Infantas 8 (☎ **891-01-83**), in Aranjuez.

• **By Car**   Driving is easy and takes about 30 minutes once you reach the southern city limits of Madrid. To reach Aranjuez, follow the signs to Aranjuez and Granada, taking the N-IV highway.

ESSENTIALS   The **telephone area code** of Aranjuez is 91. The **Tourist Information Office** is at Plaza Puente de Barcas (☎ **91/ 891-04-27**).

On the Tagus River, Aranjuez strikes visitors as a virtual garden. It was mapped out in the 18th century by the royal architects and landscapers of Ferdinand VI. The natural setting has been blended with wide boulevards and fountain- and statuary-filled gardens.

Surrounded in late spring by beds of asparagus and heavily laden strawberry vines, Aranjuez exudes the spirit of May. But for some visitors, autumn best reveals the royal town. It's then that the golden cypress trees cast lingering shadows in countless ponds, evoking a painting by Santiago Rusiñol Prats.

What to See & Do

⭐ **Palacio Real**, Plaza del Palacio. ☎ **891-13-44**.

Since the beginning of a united Spain, the climate and natural beauty of Aranjuez have attracted Spanish monarchs, notably Ferdinand and Isabella and Philip II, who managed to tear himself away from El Escorial. But the Palacio Real, lying immediately west of the center, in its present form dates primarily from the days of the Bourbons, who used to come here mainly in the autumn and spring, reserving La Granja, near Segovia, for their summer romps. The palace was also favored by Philip V and Charles III.

Fires have swept over the structure numerous times, but most of the present building dates from 1778. William Lyon, writing in the Madrid weekly, the *Guidepost*, called its dominant note one of "deception: in almost each of its widely varying rooms there is at least one thing that isn't what it first appears." Mr. Lyon cites assemblages of mosaics that look like oil paintings, a trompe-l'oeil ceiling that seems three-dimensional although it's flat, and a copy of a salon at Granada's Alhambra Palace.

In spite of these eye-fooling tricks, the palace is lavishly and elegantly decorated. Especially notable are the dancing salon, the throne room, the ceremonial dining hall, the bedrooms of the king and queen, and a remarkable Salon de Porcelana (Porcelain Room). Paintings include works by Lucas Jordan and José Ribera.

Admission: 600 ptas. ($4.30).

Open: Apr–Sept, Tues–Sun 10am–6:30pm; Oct–Mar, Tues–Sun 10am–5:30pm. **Bus:** Routes from the rail station converge at the square and gardens at the westernmost edge of the palace.

Jardín de la Isla, Palacio Real. ☎ **891-07-40**.

These gardens appear somehow forgotten, their mood melancholic. They lie to the east of the Palacio Real, adjoining a royal ornamental garden called the Parterre. From the Parterre, two bridges lead to the "garden of the island." The "Non Plus Ultra" fountain is dazzling.

Under linden trees, the fountain of Apollo is romantic, and others honor the king of the sea and Cybele, goddess of agriculture. The most delightful stroll is along an avenue of trees, called Salón de los Reyes Católicos, which lies along the river.

Admission: Free.

Open: Apr–Sept, daily 8am–8:30pm; Oct–Mar, daily 8am–6:30pm. **Bus:** See Palacio Real entry, above.

Casita del Labrador, calle de la Reina. ☎ 891-13-44.

"The little house of the worker" is a classic example of understatement. Actually, it was modeled after the Petit Trianon at Versailles. If you visit the Royal Palace in the morning, you can spend the afternoon here in the northeastern part of town. Those with a car can motor to it through the tranquil **Jardín del Príncipe,** with its black poplars.

The little palace was built in 1803 by Charles IV, who later abdicated in Aranjuez. The queen came here with her youthful lover, Godoy (whom she had elevated to the position of prime minister), and the feebleminded Charles didn't seem to mind a bit. Surrounded by beautiful gardens, the "bedless" palace is lavishly furnished in the grand 18th- and 19th-century style. The marble floors represent some of the finest workmanship of that day. The brocaded walls emphasize luxurious living—and the royal bathroom is a sight to behold (in those days, royalty preferred an audience). The clock here is one of the treasures of the house.

Admission: 400 ptas. ($2.80).

Open: Apr–Sept, Tues–Sun 10am–6:30pm; Oct–Mar, Tues–Sun 10am–5:30pm. **Bus:** See Palacio Real entry, above.

Where to Stay

Hostal Castilla, carretera Andalucía 98, 28300 Aranjuez.
☎ 91/891-26-27. 17 rms. MINIBAR TV TEL

Rates: 3,900 ptas. ($27.70) single; 5,100 ptas. ($36.20) double. Breakfast 400 ptas. ($2.80) extra. AE, DC, V.

On one of the town's main streets north of the Royal Palace and gardens, the Castilla consists of the ground floor and part of the first floor of a well-preserved early-18th-century house. Most accommodations overlook a courtyard with a fountain and flowers. The owner, Joaquin Suárez, speaks English fluently. There are excellent restaurants nearby, and the hostal has an arrangement with a neighboring bar that provides guests here with an inexpensive lunch. The Castilla is a good location from which to explore either Madrid or Toledo on a day trip.

Where to Dine

Casa Pablo, Almibar 42. ☎ 891-14-51.

Cuisine: SPANISH. **Reservations:** Recommended.
Prices: Appetizers 700–900 ptas. ($5–$6.40); main courses 1,900–2,500 ptas. ($13.50–$17.80); four-course fixed-price menu 2,700 ptas. ($19.20). MC, V.

Open: Lunch daily 1–4:30pm; dinner daily 8pm–midnight. **Closed:** Aug.

An unpretentious and well-managed restaurant near the bus station in the town center, Casa Pablo was established in 1941. At tables set outside under a canopy, you can dine while enjoying the tree-lined street and the red and pink geraniums; in cooler weather you can eat either upstairs or in the cozy rear dining room. The fixed-price menu includes four courses, a carafe of wine, bread, and service. If it's hot and you don't want a heavy dinner, try a shrimp omelet or half a roast chicken; once I ordered just a plate of asparagus in season, accompanied by white wine. If you want a superb dish, try a fish called mero (Mediterranean pollack of delicate flavor), grilled over an open fire.

La Rana Verde, calle de la Reina 1. ☎ **891-32-38.**

Cuisine: SPANISH. **Reservations:** Recommended.

Prices: Appetizers 650–850 ptas. ($4.60–$6); main courses 1,050–2,200 ptas. ($7.50–$15.60); fixed-price menu 2,200 ptas. ($15.60). MC, V.

Open: Daily noon–midnight.

The Green Frog, just east of the Royal Palace and next to a small bridge spanning the Tagus, is still the traditional choice for many. The restaurant looks like a summer house with its high-beamed ceiling and soft ferns drooping from hanging baskets. The preferred tables are in the nooks overlooking the river. As in all the restaurants of Aranjuez, asparagus is a special feature. Game, particularly partridge, quail, and pigeon, can be recommended in season; fish, too, including fried hake and fried sole, makes a good choice. Strawberries are served with sugar, orange juice, or ice cream.

3 San Lorenzo de El Escorial

30 miles (48 km) W of Madrid, 32 miles (52 km) SE of Segovia

GETTING THERE • By Train More than two dozen trains depart daily from Madrid's Atocha, Nuevos Ministerios, and Chamartín railway stations. During the summer extra coaches are added. The railway station for San Lorenzo de El Escorial is located about a mile outside town. The Herranz bus company meets all arriving trains with a shuttle bus that ferries passengers to and from the Plaza Virgen de Gracia, about a block east of the entrance to the monastery.

• **By Bus** Madrid's Empresa Herranz, calle Isaac Peral 8 (☎ **543-36-45**), runs about 15 buses daily to El Escorial from the capital. It leaves passengers at the Plaza Virgen de Gracia, about a block east of the entrance to the monastery. This same company also sells tickets for the single trip per day it makes between El Escorial's Plaza Virgen de Gracia and the Valley of the Fallen (see below). A round-trip ticket from El Escorial to this sight costs 565 ptas. ($4). Departure is at 3:15pm; return to El Escorial is at 6:15pm (5:30pm in winter). Travel time is 20 minutes each way.

• **By Car** Follow the N-VI highway (on some maps marked as the A-6) from the northwestern perimeter of Madrid, in the direction of Lugo, La Coruña, and San Lorenzo de El Escorial. After about half an hour, fork left onto the C-505 toward San Lorenzo de El Escorial. Driving time is about an hour.

ESSENTIALS   San Lorenzo de El Escorial's **telephone area code** is **91.** The **Tourist Information Office** is at Floridablanca 10 (☎ **91/890-15-54**).

Next to Toledo, the most important excursion from Madrid is the austere Royal Monastery of San Lorenzo de El Escorial. Philip II ordered the construction of this granite-and-slate rectangular monastery in 1563, two years after he moved his capital to Madrid. Once the haunt of aristocratic Spaniards, El Escorial is now a summer resort where hotels and restaurants flourish in summer, as hundreds flock here to escape the capital's heat. Despite the appeal of its climate, the town of San Lorenzo itself is not very noteworthy. But because of the monastery's size, you might decide to spend a night or two at San Lorenzo—or more if you have the time.

San Lorenzo makes an ideal base for visiting the cities and towns of nearby Segovia and Ávila, the royal palace of La Granja, the Valley of the Fallen, and even the more distant university city of Salamanca.

What to See & Do

 Real Monasterio de San Lorenzo de El Escorial, calle San Lorenzo de El Escorial 1. ☎ **890-59-02.**

In the Guadarrama mountain resort of El Escorial stands this imposing monastery, which many refer to as the eighth wonder of the world. Both a palace and a monastery, it was ordered built south of the town by Philip II to commemorate the 1557 triumph of his forces at the Battle of San Quentin. Escorial was dedicated to St. Lawrence, the martyred saint burned to death.

The original architect of El Escorial in 1563 was Juan Bautista de Toledo. After his death the monumental task was assumed by the greatest architect of Renaissance Spain, Juan de Herrera, who completed it in the shape of a gridiron in 1584.

The severe lines of the great pile of granite strike many as being as austere as the pious Philip himself. Architectural critic Nikolaus Pevsner called it "overwhelming, moving no doubt, but frightening."

In the **Charter Hall** is one of the greatest art collections in Spain outside the Prado, the canvases dating primarily from the 15th to the 17th century. Among the most outstanding are El Greco's *The Martyrdom of St. Maurice,* Titian's *Last Supper,* Velázquez's *The Tunic of Joseph,* van der Weyden's *Crucifixion,* and another version of Bosch's *The Hay Wagon* (see also a remarkable tapestry based on a painting by "El Bosco" as the Spanish call this artist); there are also works by Ribera, Tintoretto, and Veronese.

The **Biblioteca**—one of the most important libraries in the world—has an estimated number of volumes in excess of 50,000. The collection, started by Philip II, ranges far and wide: Muslim codices; a Gothic 13th-century "Cántigas" from the reign of Alfonso X (known as "The Wise King"); and signatures from the Carmelite nun St. Teresa de Jesús, who conjured up visions of the devil and of angels sticking burning-hot lances into her heart.

For many sightseers, the tour's highlight is a visit to the **Apartments of Philip II,** which contain many of the original furnishings. He died in 1598, in the "cell for my humble self" that he ordered built. He desired quarters that were spartan, and so they remain today—graced by a painting by Bosch, a copy he made of his *The Seven Capital Sins,* now at the Prado.

The **Apartments of the Bourbons** reflect a different style—a complete break from the asceticism imposed by the Hapsburg king. They are richly decorated, with a special emphasis on tapestries (many resembling paintings) based on Goya and Bayeu cartoons at the Royal Factory in Madrid.

From a window in his bedroom, a weak and dying Philip II could look down at the services being conducted in the **basilica.** As the dome clearly indicates, the church was modeled after Michelangelo's drawings of St. Peter's in Rome. Works of art include a crucifix by Benvenuto Cellini, choir stalls by Herrera, and sculpted groups of father and son (Charles V and Philip II), along with their wives, flanking the altar.

The **Royal Pantheon,** burial place of Spanish kings from Charles V to Alfonso XII, is under the altar. (The Bourbon king Philip V is interred at La Granja, and the body of Ferdinand VI was placed in a tomb in a Madrid church.) In the octagonal mausoleum you'll see the tombs of queens who were mothers of kings. In 1993, Don Juan de Borbón, the count of Barcelona and the father of Juan Carlos II (Franco "passed over" the count and never allowed him to ascend to the throne), was interred here.

On the lower level rests one of the curiosities of El Escorial: a "wedding cake" tomb for royal children. The Whispering Hall, with its odd sound effects, is also intriguing.

Allow about three hours for a visit.

Admission: Comprehensive ticket 800 ptas. ($5.70) adults, 300 ptas. ($2.10) children.

Open: Apr–Sept, daily 10am–7pm; Oct–Mar, daily 10pm–6pm.

Casa de Príncipe (Prince's Cottage), calle de la Reina.
☎ 891-03-05.

This small but elaborately decorated 18th-century palace near the railway station was originally a hunting lodge built for Charles III by Juan de Villanueva. Most visitors stay in El Escorial for lunch, visiting the cottage when it reopens in the afternoon.

Admission: Included in the comprehensive ticket, above.

Open: Tues–Sat 10am–1pm and 3:30–6:30pm.

El Valle de los Caídos (Valley of the Fallen). ☎ 890-56-11.

This architectural marvel took two decades to complete and is dedicated to those who died in the Spanish Civil War. Its detractors say it represents the worst of Neo-Fascist design; its admirers say they have found renewed inspiration by coming here.

A gargantuan cross, nearly 500 feet high, dominates the Rock of Nava, a peak of the Guadarrama Mountains. Directly under the cross is a basilica in mosaic, completed in 1959. Here José Antonio Primo de Rivera, the founder of the Falange party, is buried. When this Nationalist hero was buried at El Escorial, many, especially influential monarchists, protested that he was not a royal. Infuriated, Franco decided to erect another monument. Originally it was slated to honor the dead on the Nationalist side only, but the intervention of several parties led to a decision to include all the *caídos* (fallen). In time the mausoleum claimed Franco as well; his body was interred behind the high altar.

On the other side of the mountain is a Benedictine monastery that has sometimes been dubbed "the Hilton of monasteries" because of its seeming luxury.

Admission: 400 ptas. ($2.80).

Open: Tues–Sun 10am–7pm (until 6pm in winter).

Directions: Drive to the valley entrance, about 5 miles (8 km) north of El Escorial in the heart of the Guadarrama Mountains. Once there, drive 3¹/2 miles (6 km) along a dusty road west to the underground basilica. **Bus:** Autocares. Empresa Herranz in El Escorial runs a bus here at 3:15pm, returning at 5:30pm (at 6:15pm in winter); the trip takes 15 minutes. Tour buses from Madrid usually include an excursion to the Valley of the Fallen on their one-day trips to El Escorial. **Funicular:** It extends from near the entrance to the basilica to the base of the gigantic cross erected on the mountaintop above (where there's a superb view). The fare is 250 ptas. ($1.80), and the funicular runs daily from 10:30am to 1:15pm and 4 to 6pm.

Where to Stay

$ Hostal Cristina, Juan de Toledo 6, 28200 San Lorenzo de El Escorial. ☎ **91/890-19-61.** 16 rms.

Rates: 4,000 ptas. ($28.40) single; 5,400 ptas. ($38.30) double. Breakfast 350 ptas. ($2.50) extra. MC, V.

One of the best choices for those on a budget, this hotel is run by the Delgado family, who opened it in the mid-1980s. About 50 yards from the monastery, it stands in the town center, offering clean and comfortable rooms. The helpful staff will direct you to their small garden. Since the food is both good and plentiful, many Spanish visitors prefer to book here for a summer holiday. Meals begin at 1,600 ptas. ($11.40).

Hotel Victoria Palace, calle Juan de Toledo 4, 28200 San Lorenzo de El Escorial. ☎ **91/890-15-11.** Fax 91/890-12-48. 87 rms, 4 suites. TV TEL

Rates: 9,900 ptas. ($70.30) single; 13,750 ptas. ($97.60) double; 25,000 ptas. ($177.50) suite. Breakfast 950 ptas. ($6.70) extra. AE, DC, MC, V. **Parking:** Free.

Victoria Palace, with its view of El Escorial, is the finest hotel in town—a traditional establishment that has been modernized without losing its special aura of style and comfort. It's surrounded by beautiful gardens and has an outdoor pool. The rooms, some with private terrace, are well furnished and maintained. The rate—reasonable enough, and a bargain for a four-star hotel—also includes admission to El Escorial. The dining room serves some of the best food in town, with a meal averaging 3,500 ptas. ($24.90). Laundry and room service are provided.

Miranda & Suizo, calle Floridablanca 18, 28200 San Lorenzo de El Escorial. ☎ **91/890-47-11.** Fax 91/890-43-58. 48 rms. TV

Rates: 6,000 ptas. ($42.60) single; 8,500 ptas. ($60.40) double. Breakfast 500 ptas. ($3.60) extra. AE, DC, MC, V.

On a tree-lined street in the heart of town, within easy walking distance of the monastery, this excellent middle-class establishment ranks as a leading two-star hotel. The Victorian-style building has good guest rooms, some with terraces. The furnishings are comfortable, the beds often have brass frames, and sometimes you'll find fresh flowers on the table. In summer there's outside dining.

Where to Dine

Charolés, calle Floridablanca 24. ☎ **890-59-75.**
   Cuisine: SPANISH/INTERNATIONAL. **Reservations:** Required.
   Prices: Appetizers 1,075–1,950 ptas. ($7.60–$13.80); main courses 1,450–3,700 ptas. ($10.30–$26.30); fixed-price menu 4,800 ptas. ($34.10). AE, DC, MC, V.
   Open: Lunch daily 1–4pm; dinner daily 9pm–midnight.

The thick and solid walls of this establishment date, according to its managers, "from the monastic age" and probably predate the town's larger and better-known monastery of El Escorial. The restaurant contained within was established around 1980 and has been known ever since as the best dining room in town. It has a flower-ringed outdoor terrace, for use during clement weather, and a wide choice of menu items based entirely on fresh fish and meats. These include such dishes as grilled hake with green or hollandaise sauce, shellfish soup, monkfish in butter-and-herb sauce, succulent charolais of beef with fresh vegetables and herbs, pepper steak, *pastel* of fresh vegetables with crayfish, and herb-flavored baby lamb chops. Strawberry or kiwi tart is a good dessert choice.

Mesón la Cueva (The Cave), San Antón 4. ☎ **890-15-16.**
   Cuisine: CASTILIAN. **Reservations:** Recommended.
   Prices: Appetizers 850–950 ptas. ($6–$6.70); main courses 1,200–2,200 ptas. ($8.50–$15.60); menu del día 3,000 ptas. ($21.30). No credit cards.
   Open: Lunch Tues–Sun 1–4pm; dinner Tues–Sun 8:30–11:30pm.

Founded in 1768, this restaurant captures the world of Old Castile, and it lies only a short walk from the monastery. A *mesón típico*, built around an enclosed courtyard, it boasts such nostalgic accents as stained-glass windows, antique chests, faded engravings, paneled doors, and iron balconies. The cooking is on target, the portions generous. Regional specialties include Valencian paella and *fabada asturiana* (pork sausage and beans), but fresh trout broiled in butter may be best of all. The menu's most expensive items are Segovian roast suckling pig and roast lamb (tender inside, crisp outside). Off the courtyard through a separate doorway is La Cueva's *tasca*, filled with Castilians quaffing their favorite before-dinner drinks.

NEAR THE VALLEY OF THE FALLEN

Hostelbrie Valle de los Caídos, Valle de los Caídos.
☎ **890-55-11.**
Cuisine: SPANISH. **Reservations:** Not accepted.
Prices: Appetizers 575–650 ptas. ($4.10–$4.60); main courses 900–1,500 ptas. ($6.40–$10.70); fixed-price menu 1,200 ptas. ($8.50). No credit cards.
Open: Lunch only, daily 2–4pm.

This restaurant is probably the most likely bet for clients heading up into the Valley of the Fallen. Set amid an arid but dramatic landscape halfway along the inclined access road leading to Franco's monuments and reachable only by car or bus, it's a mammoth modern structure with wide terraces, floor-to-ceiling windows, and a well-established pattern of feeding busloads of foreign tourists. The *menu del día* usually includes such dishes as cannelloni Rossini, pork chops with potatoes, a dessert choice of flan or fruit, and wine.

4 Segovia

54–63 miles (87–101 km) NW of Madrid, 42 miles (68 km) NE of Ávila

GETTING THERE • By Train About a dozen trains leave Madrid's Chamartín station every day and arrive two hours later in Segovia, where you can board bus no. 3, which departs every quarter of an hour for the Plaza Mayor. The station lies on the paseo Obispo Quesada s/n (☎ **42-07-74**), a 20-minute walk southeast of the town center.

• By Bus Buses arrive and depart from the Estacionamiento Municipal de Autobuses, paseo de Ezequile González 10 (☎ **42-77-25**), near the corner of the avenida Fernández Ladreda and the steeply sloping paseo Conde de Sepúlveda. There are 10 to 15 buses a day to and from Madrid (which depart from the paseo de la Florida 11; Metro: Norte), and about four a day traveling between Ávila, Segovia, and Valladolid. One-way tickets from Madrid cost around 690 ptas. ($4.90).

• By Car Take the N-VI (on some maps it's known as the A-6) or the Autopista del Nordeste northwest from Madrid, toward León and Lugo. At the junction with Route 110 (signposted Segovia), turn northeast.

ESSENTIALS   Segovia's **telephone area code** is 921. The **Tourist Information Office** is at Plaza Mayor 10 (☎ **921/43-03-28**).

In Old Castile, Segovia is one of the most romantic of Spanish cities, its glory of another day. Isabella I was proclaimed Queen of Castile here in 1474. Segovians live with the memory of the time when their star was in the ascendancy.

The capital of a province of the same name, it lies on a slope of the snow-capped Sierra de Guadarrama mountains, between two ravine-studded valleys and the Eresma and Clamores Rivers (actually streams). As it appears on the horizon, dominated by its Alcázar and its Gothic cathedral, Segovia is decidedly of the Middle Ages.

The city was of strategic importance to the Roman troops, and one of its greatest monuments, the Aqueduct, dates from those times. The skyline is characterized by the Romanesque belfries of the churches and the towers of its old and decaying palaces.

The Upper Town is mainly encased by its old walls; but the part outside the walls is of interest, too, especially for views of the Alcázar.

What to See & Do

★ **El Alcazar,** Plaza de la Reina Victoria Eugenia. ☎ **43-01-76.**

If you've ever dreamed of castles in the air, then all the fairy-tale romance of childhood will return when you view the Alcázar. Many have waxed poetic about it, comparing it to a giant boat sailing through the clouds. See it first from down below, at the junction of the Clamores and Eresma Rivers. It's on the west side of Segovia, and you may not spot it when you first enter the city, but that's part of the surprise.

The castle dates back many hundreds of years—perhaps to the 12th century. But a large segment of it—notably its Moorish ceilings—was destroyed by fire in 1862. Over the years, under an ambitious plan, the Alcázar has been restored.

Inside you'll discover a facsimile of Isabella's dank bedroom. It was at the Alcázar that she first met Ferdinand, preferring him to the more "fatherly" King of Portugal. But she wasn't foolish enough to surrender her "equal rights" after marriage. In the Throne Room, with its replica chairs, you'll note that the seats are equally proportioned. Royal romance continued to flower at the Alcázar. Philip II married his fourth wife, Anne of Austria, here.

After you inspect the polish on some medieval armor inside, you may want to walk the battlements of this once-impregnable castle, whose former occupants poured boiling oil over the ramparts onto their uninvited guests below. Or you can climb the tower, originally built by Isabella's father as a prison, for a supreme view of Segovia. (In particular, note the so-called pregnant-woman mountain.)

Admission: 350 ptas. ($2.50) adults, 150 ptas. ($1.10) children 8–14; children 7 and under free.

Open: Apr–Sept, daily 10am–7pm. Oct–Mar, daily 10am–6pm. **Directions:** Take either calle Vallejo, calle de Velarde, calle de Daoiz, or Paseo de Ronda. **Bus:** 3.

⭐ **Roman Aqueduct**, Plaza del Azoguejo.

The aqueduct, an architectural marvel, is still used to carry water, even though it was constructed by the Romans almost 2,000 years ago. It's not only the most colossal reminder of Roman glory in Spain, but also one of the best-preserved Roman architectural achievements in the world. It consists of 118 arches, and in one two-tiered section—its highest point—it soars 95 feet. You'll find no mortar in these granite blocks brought from the Guadarrama Mountains. The Spanish call it El Puente, and it spans the Plaza del Azoguejo, the old market square, stretching out to a distance of nearly 800 yards. When the Moors took Segovia in 1072, they destroyed 36 arches. However, Ferdinand and Isabella ordered that they be rebuilt in 1484. You can see it anytime night or day since it's an integral landmark of Segovia.

Cabildo Catedral de Segovia, Plaza Mayor, calle Marqués del Arco. ☎ **43-53-25.**

Constructed between 1515 and 1558, this structure lays claim to being the last Gothic cathedral built in Spain. Fronting the historic Plaza Mayor, the Cathedral of Segovia stands on the spot where Isabella I was proclaimed Queen of Castile. It's affectionately called "la dama de las catedrales." Inside, it contains numerous treasures, such as the Blessed Sacrament Chapel (created by the flamboyant Churriguera), stained-glass windows, elaborately carved choir stalls, and 16th- and 17th-century paintings, including a reredos portraying the deposition of Christ from the cross by Juan de Juni. Older than the cathedral are the cloisters, which belong to a former church destroyed in the War of the Communeros. The cathedral's museum exhibits jewelry, paintings, and a rare collection of antique manuscripts, along with the inevitable vestments.

Admission: Cathedral free; cloisters, museum, and chapel room 200 ptas. ($1.40).

Open: Spring and summer, daily 9am–7pm; off-season, daily 9:30am–noon and 3–6pm. **Bus:** 3.

Iglesia de la Vera Cruz, carretera de Zamarramala. ☎ **43-14-75.**

Built in either the 11th or 12th century by the Knights Templar, this is the most fascinating Romanesque church in Segovia. It stands in isolation outside the old town's walls, overlooking the Alcázar. Its unusual 12-sided design is believed to have been copied from the Church of the Holy Sepulchre in Jerusalem. Inside you'll find an inner temple, rising two floors, where the knights conducted nightlong vigils as part of their initiation rites.

Admission: 125 ptas. (90¢).

Open: Apr–Sept, Tues–Sun 10:30am–1:30pm and 3:30–7pm; Oct–Mar, Tues–Sun 10:30am–1:30pm and 3:30–6pm.

Monasterio del Parral, calle del Marqués de Villena (across the Ersema River). ☎ **43-23-98.**

The restored Monastery of the Grape was established for the Hironymites by Henry IV, a Castilian king (1425–74) known as "The

Segovia

Legend (right side): Church ✝■ Post Office ⊠ Information ⓘ

❷ Catedral de Segovia
❶ El Alcázar
❸ Roman Aqueduct

Inset map: Madrid ⊛ — SPAIN

Impotent." The monastery's major art treasure is a large retable (1528) by Juan Rodríguez. A robed monk guides you through.

Admission: Free.

Open: Mon–Fri 10am–1:30pm and 4–7pm. **Directions:** Take Ronda de Sant Lucía, cross the Ersema River, and head down calle del Marqués de Villena.

Iglesia de St. Martín, Plaza de la Sirenas. No phone.

Located in the center of Segovia, this church was once the most out-standing in Old Castile. The porticoes of the 12th-century Romanesque structure are especially striking, but except for the rare altar, the interior is less interesting. The square on which the church stands, the Plaza de las Sirenas, was modeled after the Piazza di Spagna in Rome. A fountain commemorates the legend of Juan Bravo, the hero of the War of the Communeros against Charles V. Nearby is the 15th-century **Mansion of Arias Davila,** one of the old houses of the Segovian aristocracy.

Admission: Free.

Open: Apr–Sept, daily 10:30am–1:30pm and 3:30–7pm; Oct–Mar, daily 10:30am–1:30pm and 3:30–6pm.

Where to Stay

Gran Hotel las Sirenas, Juan Bravo 30, 40001 Segovia.
☎ **921/43-40-11.** Fax 921/43-06-33. 39 rms. A/C TV TEL
Rates: 4,000 ptas. ($28.40) single; 6,000 ptas. ($42.60) double. Breakfast 500 ptas. ($3.60) extra. AE, DC, MC, V.

Standing on Segovia's most charming old plaza, opposite the Church of St. Martín, this hotel was built around 1950 and has been renovated several times since. Modest but clean and decorated in a conservative, traditional style, it ranks as one of the town's most visible hotels. Each well-maintained guest room is filled with functional, uncomplicated furniture. No meals other than breakfast are served, but the staff at the reception desk can direct clients to any of the several cafes and tascas nearby.

Hotel Los Linajes, Dr. Velasco 9, 40003 Segovia. ☎ **921/46-04-75.** Fax 921/46-04-79. 55 rms, 10 suites. TV TEL **Bus:** 1.
Rates: 6,900 ptas. ($49) single; 10,500 ptas. ($74.60) double; 13,200 ptas. ($93.70) suite. Breakfast 750 ptas. ($5.30) extra. AE, DC, MC, V. **Parking:** 725 ptas. ($5.10).

In the historic district of St. Stephen, at the northern edge of the old town, stands this hotel, the former home of a Segovian noble family. While the outside facade dates from the 11th century, the interior is modern except for some Castilian decorations. One of the best hotels in town, Los Linajes offers gardens and patios where guests can enjoy a panoramic view over the city. The hotel also has a bar/lounge, coffee shop, disco, and garage.

Parador de Segovia, carretera Valladolid s/n (N-601), 40003 Segovia. ☎ **921/44-37-37.** Fax 921/43-73-62. 113 rms, 7 suites. A/C MINIBAR TV TEL
Rates: 12,000 ptas. ($85.20) single; 15,000 ptas. ($106.50) double; from 22,000 ptas. ($156.20) suite. Breakfast 1,200 ptas. ($8.50) extra. AE, DC, MC, V. **Parking:** 1,000 ptas. ($7.10).

This 20th-century tile-roofed parador sits on a hill 2 miles northeast of Segovia (take the N-601). It stands on an estate called El

Terminillo, which used to be famous for its vines and almond trees, a few of which still survive. The guest rooms are deluxe. The vast lawns and gardens contain two lakelike pools, and there is also an indoor pool. Other facilities include saunas and tennis courts. You can eat in the dining room for 3,600 ptas. ($25.60) and up.

Where to Dine

El Bernardino, calle Cervantes 2. ☎ 43-32-25.

Cuisine: CASTILIAN. **Reservations:** Recommended.

Prices: Appetizers 400–2,000 ptas. ($2.80–$14.20); main courses 1,100–2,000 ptas. ($7.80–$14.20); fixed-price menu 2,500 ptas. ($17.80). AE, DC, MC, V.

Open: Lunch daily 1–4:15pm; dinner daily 8–11:15pm.

El Bernardino, a three-minute walk west of the Roman aqueduct, is built like an old tavern. Lanterns hang from beamed ceilings, and the view over the red-tile rooftops of the city is delightful. The *menu del día* might include a huge paella, roast veal with potatoes, flan or ice cream, plus bread and wine. You might begin your meal with *sopa castellana* (made with ham, sausage, bread, egg, and garlic). The roast dishes are exceptional here, including roast suckling pig from a special oven and roast baby lamb. You can also order grilled rib steak or stewed partridge.

Casa Duque, calle Cervantes 12. ☎ 43-05-37.

Cuisine: CASTILIAN. **Reservations:** Recommended.

Prices: Appetizers 575–1,750 ptas. ($4.10–$12.40); main courses 975–1,800 ptas. ($6.90–$12.80); fixed-price menus 1,500–3,800 ptas. ($10.70–$27). AE, DC, MC, V.

Open: Lunch daily 12:30–5pm; dinner daily 8–11:30pm.

Duque—the *maestro asador,* as he calls himself—supervises the roasting of the pig, the house specialty, in this *mesón típico* founded in 1985. Waitresses wearing the traditional garb of the mayoress of Zamarramala will serve you other Segovian gastronomic specialties, such as *sopa castellana* or a cake known as *ponche alcázar.* There is a tavern below so you may enjoy a predinner drink.

José María, Cronista Lecea 11. ☎ 46-11-11.

Cuisine: SEGOVIAN. **Reservations:** Recommended.

Prices: Appetizers 400–1,800 ptas. ($2.80–$12.80); main dishes 1,200–2,800 ptas. ($8.50–$19.90); fixed-price menu 3,800 ptas. ($27). AE, DC, MC, V.

Open: Lunch daily 1–4pm; dinner daily 8–11:30pm.

This centrally located bar/restaurant, a block east of the Plaza Mayor, serves quality regional cuisine in a rustic stucco-and-brick dining room. Before dinner, locals crowd in for tapas at the bar, then move into the dining room for such Castilian specialties as roast suckling pig, rural-style conger eel, and freshly caught sea bream. Try the cream of crabmeat soup, roasted peppers, salmon with scrambled eggs, grilled veal steak, or house-style hake. For dessert, try the ice-cream tart with whiskey sauce.

La Oficina, Cronista Lecea 10. ☎ **43-16-43.**

Cuisine: CASTILIAN. **Reservations:** Not required.

Prices: Appetizers 650–1,000 ptas. ($4.60–$7.10); main courses 1,600–2,800 ptas. ($11.40–$19.90); fixed-price menus 1,300–2,000 ptas. ($9.20–$14.20). AE, DC, MC, V.

Open: Lunch Wed–Mon 1–4:30pm; dinner Wed–Mon 7–11:30pm.

Closed: Three weeks in Nov.

A meal here provides many insights into the traditions and aesthetics of Old Spain. Established in 1893, Oficina has been maintained ever since by three subsequent generations of the original owner. As such, it has probably welcomed virtually every resident of Segovia into the thick brick-and-stone walls that give it a distinctive Castilian flavor. Few changes, other than repairs, seem to have been made to the decor since its founding, a fact that contributes significantly to its charm. Set adjacent to the Plaza Mayor, a short walk east of the cathedral, it offers a stand-up bar accessible through a separate entrance, where locals usually opt for a wine or sherry apéritif. The owners have won various awards for the quality of their roast suckling pig, prepared and served with suitable pomp and ceremony by the well-trained staff.

★ **Mesón de Candido,** Plaza del Azoguejo 5. ☎ **42-59-11.**

Cuisine: CASTILIAN. **Reservations:** Recommended.

Prices: Appetizers 700–1,600 ptas. ($5–$11.40); main courses 1,800–2,600 ptas. ($12.80–$18.50); fixed-price menu 2,500 ptas. ($17.80). AE, DC, MC, V.

Open: Lunch daily 12:30–4:30pm; dinner daily 8–11:30pm or midnight.

For years this beautiful old Spanish inn, standing on the old town's eastern edge, has maintained a monopoly on the tourist trade. The oldest part of the building housing the restaurant dates from 1822, and the restaurant has gradually been enlarged since then. The proprietor of the House of Candido is known as *mesonero mayor de Castilla* (the major innkeeper of Castile). He has been decorated with more medals and honors than paella has grains of rice and has entertained everyone from King Hussein to Hemingway. The restaurant's popularity can be judged by the flocks of hungry diners who fill every seat in the six dining rooms. It offers an à la carte menu that includes *cordero asado* (roast baby lamb) or *cochinillo asado* (roast suckling pig).

Mesón el Cordero, calle de Carmen 4. ☎ **43-51-96.**

Cuisine: CASTILIAN/IBERIAN. **Reservations:** Recommended.

Prices: Appetizers 400–1,500 ptas. ($2.80–$10.70); main courses 1,400–2,500 ptas. ($9.90–$17.80). AE, DC, MC, V.

Open: Lunch daily 12:30–4:30pm; dinner daily 8–11:30pm.

This restaurant is known throughout the town for the flavorful roasted meats it serves. It was built in the 1800s as a Carmelite convent, near the base of the town's Roman aqueduct; in the 1970s a pair of hardworking partners added dozens of rustic artifacts and enlarged its premises to create the charming restaurant you see to-day. One noteworthy specialty is roast suckling lamb (*cordero lechal*), served on the bone and seasoned with fresh herbs that include ample amounts of rosemary and thyme. The wine list includes an array of suitably robust reds from Rioja, Rivera, and southern France.

A Side Trip to La Granja

To reach La Granja, 7 miles (11 km) southeast of Segovia, you can take a 20-minute bus ride from the city center. About 12 buses a day leave from paseo Conde de Sepulveda at avenida Fernández Ladreda.

$ Palacio Real de la Granja, Plaza de España 17, San Ildefonso (Segovia). ☎ **911/47-00-19.**

San Ildefonso de la Granja was the summer palace of the Bourbon kings of Spain, who imitated the grandeur of Versailles here in this Segovia province. Set against the snow-capped Sierra de Guadarrama, the slate-roofed palace dominates the village (nowadays a summer resort) that grew up around it.

The founder of La Granja was Philip V, grandson of Louis XIV and the first Bourbon king of Spain (his body, along with that of his second queen, Isabel de Fernesio, is interred in a mausoleoum in the Collegiate Church). Philip V was born at Versailles in 1683, which partially explains why he wanted to re-create that atmosphere at Segovia.

Before the palace was built in the early 18th century, a farm stood here—hence the totally inappropriate name *granja*, meaning "farm" in Spanish. Inside you'll find valuable antiques (many in the Empire style), paintings, and a remarkable collection of tapestries of Flemish design and others based on Goya cartoons from the Royal Factory in Madrid.

Most visitors, however, seem to find a stroll through the gardens more to their liking, so allow adequate time for it. The fountain statuary is a riot of gods and nymphs cavorting with abandon, hiding indiscretions behind jets of water. The gardens are studded with chestnuts and elms.

Admission: 600 ptas. ($4.30) adults; 150 ptas. ($1.10) children 5–14; children 4 and under free.

Open: Apr–May, Mon–Fri 10am–1:30pm and 3–5pm, Sat–Sun 10am–6pm; June–Sept, daily 10am–6pm; Oct–Mar, Mon–Sat 10am–1:30pm and 3–5pm, Sun 10am–2pm.

11

The Costa del Sol

Sᴘᴀɪɴ's ᴍᴏsᴛ ᴘᴏᴘᴜʟᴀʀ ʙᴇᴀᴄʜ sᴛʀɪᴘ—ᴀɴᴅ Eᴜʀᴏᴘᴇ's ᴍᴏsᴛ sᴘᴇᴄᴛᴀᴄᴜʟᴀʀ real-estate boom—begins at the port of Algeciras and stretches eastward all the way to Almería. Against the backdrop of once-pagan Andalusia, the Sun Coast curves gently along the Mediterranean, studded with beaches, sandy coves, lime-washed houses, high-rise apartments, tennis courts, golf courses, swimming pools, and hotels of every type and description.

Sun-seekers from all over Europe and North America are drawn to the mild climate and virtually guaranteed sunshine. You can bathe in the sun year round, but in January and February only northern Europeans dare the sea. The less hardy splash in sheltered, heated pools. The mean temperature in January, the coldest month, is 56° Fahrenheit. In August, the hottest month, the mean temperature is about 75°F, as prevailing sea breezes mercifully keep the heat down.

Once the Sun Coast was only a spring-to-autumn affair. Now, so many shivering refugees have descended from the cold cities of northern Europe that the strip is alive year round. From June through October, however, "alive" isn't the half of it. Bullfights, flamenco,

---

What's Special About the Costa del Sol

Beaches
- Marbella, 17 miles of sandy beaches.
- Torremolinos, sandy but crowded beaches—try Bajondillo or El Lido.
- Fuengirola, 3¹/₂ miles of beaches. Best bets: Las Gaviotas, Carrajal, Santa Amalja.

Great Resorts
- Marbella, where glitter and hype reach their pinnacle—visit the "Golden Mile" strip of the super-wealthy.
- Torremolinos, the "eye" of the Costa del Sol hurricane.

Great Villages
- Mijas, an Andalusian pueblo.
- Nerja, fishing village transformed into a resort.

Historic City
- Málaga, former harbor for the Moorish kingdom of Granada.

Architectural Highligths
- Marbella's old quarter, around the Plaza de los Naranjos.
- Alcazaba at Málaga, an 11th-century fortress with a Hispano-Muslim garden.

Pocket of Posh
- Puerto Banús, a yacht-clogged harbor for the rich.

Festivals
- Málaga's major festivals on religious occasions: a big annual *feria* (fair) in August.
- Marbella's flamenco festival in the second half of June.

and fiestas crowd its calendar all year. Holy Week in Málaga, for example, is among the most stunning celebrations in Spain—it rivals that of Seville. And then there's Málaga's winter festival, packed with cultural and sporting events ranging from horse racing to folk songs and dances. On August fiesta days, Málaga's bullfights are second to none. There are hundreds of good restaurants along the Sun Coast for those desiring to escape from their hotel dining rooms. I'll review only a sampling of the many possibilities.

First, a word about the food specialties of the area. In this part of the Mediterranean, fish (such as whitebait), chopitos, and anchovies are the major part of the banquet. Particular specialties include fish soup (*sopa de pescado*), a fisher's rice dish of crayfish and clams (*arroz a la marinera*), and grilled sardines (*espetones de sardinas*). In all of Andalusia, soothing gazpacho is a refreshing opener to many a meal. Of course, everything's better when washed down with the renowned wines of Málaga, including Pedor Ximénez and Muscatel.

Seeing the Costa del Sol

GETTING THERE • By Plane   None of the airlines that fly into Spain from North America touches down in Málaga. Transfers are required in either Madrid or Barcelona, although some airlines (such as the well-recommended British Airways) offer flights to Málaga nonstop from such other European cities as London.

For passengers who opt for a transfer through Madrid, the largest operator, with the greatest number of connections, is **Iberia** (☎ toll free **800/772-4642**), the national airline of Spain. Iberia offers daily nonstop service to Madrid from New York, Miami, Los Angeles, Montréal, and Toronto. Iberia offers an even greater selection of itineraries into Málaga through its affiliate airlines, which include Binter, Viva, and Aviaco. Flights on any of these airlines can be booked via Iberia's toll-free reservations line.

• By Train & Bus   Málaga maintains good rail connections with Madrid: at least five trains a day, and the trip takes 8 to 10 hours. Many visitors arrive by train after having explored the Andalusian city of Seville. There are at least three trains a day connecting Seville with Málaga, a four-hour run. It's also possible to go from Madrid to Málaga by bus. Three major coaches make the nine-hour run from Madrid to Málaga daily. For rail information in Málaga, call RENFE (☎ **95/221-31-22**), and for bus information call Málaga's new central bus station (☎ **95/235-00-61**).

GETTING AROUND THE COAST   Once at Málaga, you can go by train along the coast as far west as the resort of Fuengirola. There is rail service every 50 minutes between Málaga and Fuengirola. The run to Torremolinos takes only 30 minutes by train. For train information, there's a RENFE office in Málaga at calle Strachan 2 (☎ **95/221-31-22**). Here you can not only get information but also purchase tickets. It's open Monday through Friday from 9am to 1:30pm and 4:30 to 7:30pm.

If you're in Málaga and plan to go to Marbella, you'll need to take a bus. Buses leave about every 30 minutes in either direction and the ride takes about 1¹/₂ hours. It's also possible to get to Nerja by bus from Málaga in about 1¹/₂ hours. The Málaga bus depot lies just behind the RENFE offices, opening onto paseo de los Tilos (☎ 95/235-00-61).

If you're planning to rent a car and drive along the coast, exercise extreme caution. The impossibly overcrowded highway running along the Costa del Sol is considered one of the most dangerous in the world in terms of accidents: Many of the drivers (some, such as the British, unfamiliar with driving on the right-hand side) are drunk on Spanish wine. However, the road isn't quite as notorious as it once was, as it has been turned into a major highway, with only one-way (two-lane) traffic going each way. A series of traffic circles allows for directional changes. However, if you want to chance it, you may want to arrange your car rental in advance with one of the major companies with toll-free numbers in the United States. For more details about rentals, and the financial advantages of reserving a car in advance, see "Getting Around" in Chapter 3.

1   Málaga

340 miles (547 km) S of Madrid, 82 miles (132 km) E of Algeciras

GETTING THERE   See "Getting There," earlier in this chapter.

By Car   From the resorts in the west (such as Torremolinos and Marbella), head east along the N-340 to Málaga. If you're in the east at the end of the Costa del Sol (Almería), take the N-340 west to Málaga, with a recommended stopover at Nerja.

ESSENTIALS   The **telephone area code** for Málaga is 95. The **Tourist Information Office** is at pasaje de Chinitas 4 (☎ 95/221-34-45).

Warning: Málaga has one of the highest crime rates in Spain. The most common complaint is purse-snatching, with an estimated 75% of the crimes committed by juveniles. Stolen passports are also a problem—if it happens to you, contact the U.S. Consulate, Edificio El Ancla, calle Ramón y Cajal, Apt. 502, in nearby Fuengirola (☎ 95/247-98-91).

One of the most important seaports on the Mediterranean, Málaga is the major city of the Costa del Sol and the second-largest city of Andalusia, after Seville. At the foot of Mt. Gibralfaro, it's marked by orange trees, flower markets, and fishing boats. The best way to see the city in true 19th-century style is in a horse-drawn carriage. If possible, visit the vegetable and fish markets.

Málaga's winter climate ranks as one of Europe's most idyllic—perhaps sufficient explanation for the luxuriant vegetation in the city's parks and gardens. Truly, El Parque, which dates from the 19th century and is filled with many botanic species, ranks among the most handsome parks in Spain.

The most festive time in Málaga is the first week in August, when the city celebrates its reconquest by Ferdinand and Isabella in 1487. The big *feria* (fair) is the occasion for parades and bullfights. A major tree-shaded boulevard of the city, paseo del Parque, is transformed into a fairground featuring amusements and restaurants.

Málaga's most famous citizen is Pablo Picasso, born here in 1881 at the Plaza de la Merced, in the center of the city. The co-founder of cubism, who would one day paint his *Guernica* to express his horror of war, unfortunately left little of his spirit in his birthplace and only a small selection of his work.

What to See & Do

After sightseeing, head back to town and do some shopping on calle Larios and its satellite alleys, all of which contain stores brimming with Spanish handcrafts.

Museo de Bellas Artas (Fine Arts Museum), San Agustín 6. ☎ 221-83-82.

Málaga is not especially known for its art treasures, even though Pablo Picasso, as mentioned above, was born here. This museum owns two of his works, an oil and a watercolor, both done when he was a teenager. The museum is located behind the cathedral.

Admission: 250 ptas. ($1.80).

Open: Mon–Fri 10:30am–1:30pm and 5–7pm, Sat–Sun 10:30am–1:30pm. **Bus:** 4, 18, 19, or 24.

The Alcazaba and Archeological Museum, Plaza de la Aduana, Alcazabilla. ☎ 221-60-05.

The Alcazaba forms the remains of the ancient palace of Málaga's former Moorish rulers. Towers encircle two walled precincts. In ruins, it's considered an outstanding example of Moorish-Spanish architecture. Troops loyal to Isabella and Ferdinand fought a savage battle with the Arabs to take it. When the Catholic monarchs conquered Málaga, they lodged at the castle. Right in the center of town, it offers panoramic views. Wander at your leisure through the open patios, tile-lined pools, and flower gardens.

Inside is an archeological museum that contains artifacts found in prehistoric caves in Málaga province. Other exhibits document cultures ranging from Greek to Phoenician to Carthaginian.

Admission: Museum, 30 ptas. (20¢).

Open: Museum, Apr–Sept, Tues–Sat 9:30am–1:30pm and 5–8pm, Sun 10am–2pm; winter, Tues–Fri 10am–1pm and 5–7pm, Sat 10am–1pm and 5–8pm, Sun 10am–2pm. **Bus:** 4, 18, 19, or 24.

Cathedral of Málaga, Plaza Obispo. ☎ 221-59-17.

The Cathedral of Málaga was begun in 1528. Its 300-foot tower stands as a lone sentinel, without a mate. Although never finished, the cathedral took so long to build it's a mélange of styles, roughly classified as Spanish Renaissance. Inside, seek out in particular its ornate choir stalls.

Admission: 100 ptas. (70¢).

The Costa Del Sol

30 km
20 mi

Open: Mon–Sat 10am–12:30pm and 4–5:30pm. **Bus:** 14, 18, 19, or 24.

Castillo de Gibralfaro, Cerro de Gibralfaro.

On a hill overlooking Málaga and the Mediterranean are the ruins of an ancient Moorish castle-fortress of unknown origin. It's near the government-run parador and might easily be tied in with a luncheon visit.

Warning: Don't walk to Gibralfaro Castle from town. Readers have reported muggings along the way, and the area around the castle is dangerous. Take the bus (see below).

Admission: Free.

Open: Daily dawn–dusk. **Microbus:** H, leaving hourly from the cathedral.

Where to Stay

For such a large city in a resort area, Málaga has a surprising lack of hotels. The best ones in all price ranges are documented below. **Note:** Reserve well in advance for all paradores.

EXPENSIVE

Hotel Guadalmar, Urbanización Guadalmar, carretera de Cádiz, Km 238, 29080 Málaga. ☎ **95/231-17-03.** 190 rms. A/C MINIBAR TV TEL

Rates: 9,950 ptas. ($70.60) single; 12,950 ptas. ($91.90) double. Children under 12 stay free in parents' room. MC, V. **Parking:** Free.

The Guadalmar is a nine-story resort hotel located 2 miles (3 km) from the city center and about 1 mile (2 km) from the airport. The hotel has its own private beach, and all the guest rooms open onto the pool and garden. Each well-furnished accommodation is spacious, with a private sea-view balcony. For those traveling with children, there are cribs, babysitters, and special menus available, as well as a playground. Take your meals in the dining room, La Bodega, which opens onto the sea and is decorated in a rustic theme. For a live combo to listen and dance to, go straight to La Corrida, the hotel bar.

Málaga Palacio, Cortina del Muelle 1, 29015 Málaga. ☎ **95/221-51-85.** Fax 95/221-51-85. 207 rms, 16 suites. A/C MINIBAR TV TEL **Bus:** 4, 18, 19, or 24.

Rates: 11,600 ptas. ($82.40) single; 17,500 ptas. ($124.30) double; 23,650 ptas. ($167.90) suite. Breakfast 950 ptas. ($6.70) extra. AE, DC, MC, V. **Parking:** 1,000 ptas. ($7.10) nearby.

One of the leading hotels in the town center, the Palacio opens directly onto a tree-lined esplanade near the cathedral and the harbor. The 1960s building was constructed flat-iron style, rising 15 stories and crowned by an open-air pool and refreshment bar. Most of the balconies open onto views of the port, and down below you can see turn-of-the-century horse-drawn carriages. The guest rooms are traditionally furnished. The street-floor lounges mix antiques with more modern furnishings. Other facilities include hairdressers for both men and women, a cafeteria, and boutiques.

Parador Nacional del Golf, carretera de Málaga, Apdo. 324, 29080 Torremolinos, Málaga. ☎ **95/238-12-55.** Fax 95/238-21-41. 60 rms. A/C MINIBAR TV TEL

Rates: 10,000–11,200 ptas. ($71–$79.50) single; 12,500–14,000 ptas. ($88.80–$99.40) double. Breakfast 1,100 ptas. ($7.80) extra. AE, DC, MC, V. **Parking:** Free.

This is a tasteful resort hotel created by the Spanish government. Surrounded by an 18-hole golf course on one side, the Mediterranean on another, it is arranged hacienda-style, with several low tile buildings. You're greeted by chirping birds and grounds planted with flowers. Each guest room has a private balcony with a view of the green, the circular pool, or the water. The furnishings are attractive. There are no single rooms. Long tile corridors lead to the public rooms, graciously furnished lounges, and a bar and restaurants. The parador is less than 2 miles from the airport, 6¹/₂ miles west of Málaga, and 2¹/₂ miles east of Torremolinos.

MODERATE

Hotel Los Naranjos, paseo de Sancha 35, 29016 Málaga.
☎ **95/222-43-19.** Fax 95/222-59-75. 40 rms, 1 suite.
A/C MINIBAR TV TEL **Bus:** 11.
Rates: 10,100 ptas. ($71.70) single; 13,500 ptas. ($95.90) double; 19,500 ptas. ($138.50) suite. Breakfast 800 ptas. ($5.70) extra. AE, DC, MC, V. **Parking:** 920 ptas. ($6.50).

Hotel Los Naranjos is one of the more reasonably priced (and safer) choices in the city. This is a well-run and well-maintained hotel lying just outside the heart of town on the eastern side of Málaga past the Plaza de Toros (bullring). It's in the vicinity of the best beach in Málaga, Baños del Carmen. The rooms are contemporary with private baths or showers. The public rooms are decorated in the typical Andalusian style, with colorful tiles and ornate wood carving. Breakfast is the only meal served.

Parador de Málaga-Gibralfaro, Monte Gibralfaro, 29016 Málaga.
☎ **95/222-43-16.** Fax 95/222-19-04. 40 rms. A/C MINIBAR TV TEL **Directions:** Take the coast road, paseo de Reding, which becomes avenida Casa de Pries and finally paseo de Sancha: turn left onto Camino Nuevo and follow the small signs the rest of the way.
Rates: 10,000 ptas. ($71) single; 12,000 ptas. ($85.20) double. Breakfast 1,200 ptas. ($8.50) extra. AE, DC, MC, V. **Parking:** Free.

Restored in 1994 and slated for reopening in early 1995, this is one of Spain's oldest, tradition-laden paradors. It enjoys a scenic location high on a plateau near an old fortified castle, overlooking the city and the Mediterranean, with views of the bullring, mountains, and beaches. Imagine a building of rugged stone with long arched open corridors and guest rooms furnished with hand-loomed fabrics. Each room comes with a sitting area and a terrace bedecked with garden furniture. However, don't attempt to walk down to the heart of Málaga—it's not safe: Many readers have been mugged. The location is 1¹/₂ miles north of the center.

INEXPENSIVE

 El Cenachero, Barroso 5, 29001 Málaga. ☎ **95/222-40-88.**
14 rms (all with bath or shower). **Bus:** 15.
Rates: 2,700 ptas. ($19.20) single with shower; 4,000–4,600 ptas. ($28.40–$32.70) double with shower; 5,000 ptas. ($35.50) double with bath. No credit cards.

Opened in 1969, this modest little hotel is five blocks from the park (near the harbor). All the nicely carpeted guest rooms are unique; half have showers, the rest baths. Everything is kept clean. No meals are served here.

Hostal Residencia Carlos V, Cister 6, 29015 Málaga.
☎ **95/221-51-20.** 50 rms. TEL **Bus:** 15 from the rail station.
Rates: 2,682–2,925 ptas. ($19–$20.80) single; 5,300–6,095 ptas. ($37.60–$43.30) double. Breakfast 500 ptas. ($3.60) extra. AE, DC, MC, V. **Parking:** 1,090 ptas. ($7.70)

This hotel has a good central location near the cathedral as well as an interesting facade decorated with wrought-iron balconies and *miradores.* The lobby is fairly dark, but this remains an old, safe haven. An elevator will take you to your room, furnished in a no-frills style.

$ **Hotel Residencia Derby,** San Juan de Dios 1, 29015 Málaga.
☎ **95/222-13-01.** 16 rms (8 with bath or shower). TEL **Bus:** 15.
Rates: 2,500 ptas. ($17.80) single without bath or shower; 3,000 ptas. ($21.30) single with shower; 3,000 ptas. ($21.30) double without bath or shower; 3,500 ptas. ($24.90) double with shower; 4,000 ptas. ($28.40) double with bath. No credit cards.

The Derby is a real find. This fourth-floor boarding house right in the heart of Málaga, on a main square directly north of the train station, has some rooms with excellent views of the Mediterranean and the port of Málaga. The hostal is quite clean, and all rooms have hot and cold running water. No breakfast is served.

A NEARBY RETREAT

★ **La Bobadilla,** Finca La Bobadilla (Apdo. 53), 18300 Loja (Granada). ☎ **958/32-18-61.** Fax 958/32-18-10. 60 rms, 8 suites. A/C MINIBAR TV TEL **Directions:** From the airport at Málaga, follow the signs toward Granada, but at km 178 continue through the village of Salinas. Take the road marked Salinas/Rute but after 2 miles (3 km) follow the signposts for the hotel to the entrance.
Rates (including breakfast): 18,600–22,800 ptas. ($132.10–$161.90) single; 25,600–35,800 ptas. ($181.80–$254.20) double; from 49,800 ptas. ($353.60) suite. AE, DC, MC, V. **Parking:** Free.

An hour's drive northeast of Málaga, La Bobadilla is the most luxurious retreat in the south of Spain. A secluded oasis, it lies in the foothills of the Sierra Nevada near the town of Loja, 44 miles north of Málaga. La Bobadilla is a 13-mile drive from Loja.

The hotel complex is built like an Andalusian village, a cluster of whitewashed *casas* (cottages) constructed around a tower and a white church. Every casa in this re-created village is complete with a roof terrace and balcony overlooking the olive grove–studded district. Each accommodation is individually designed, from the least expensive doubles to the most expensive King's Suite, the latter with plenty of room for bodyguards. The hotel service is perhaps the finest in all of Spain.

Superb craftsmanship is reflected at every turn, from the wrought-iron gates to the Andalusian fountains. The hotel breeds its own domestic animals and grows much of its own food, including fruit and vegetables.

If you get bored in this lap of luxury, you can always drive to Granada in only an hour. Should you decide to marry your companion at this resort, you'll find a chapel with an organ 30 feet high with 1,595 pipes.

Dining/Entertainment: Even the King of Spain has dined at La Finca, which serves both a Spanish national and an international cuisine; meals begin at 4,500 ptas. ($32). El Cortijo, on the other hand, specializes in a regional cuisine. Concerts, featuring flamenco, are presented on Friday and Saturday nights.

Services: Room service, laundry/valet, massage, babysitting.

Facilities: Two tennis courts, horseback riding, archery, outdoor swimming pool, heated indoor pool, Jacuzzis, Finnish sauna, Turkish steam bath, fitness club.

Where to Dine

VERY EXPENSIVE

Café de Paris, Vélez Málaga 8. ☎ 222-50-43.

> **Cuisine:** FRENCH. **Reservations:** Required. **Bus:** 13.
>
> **Prices:** Appetizers 600–1,800 ptas. ($4.30–$12.80); main courses 1,800–2,500 ptas. ($12.80–$17.80); *menu del día* 3,050 ptas. ($21.70). AE, DC, MC, V.
>
> **Open:** Lunch Mon–Sat 12:30–4pm; dinner Mon–Sat 8:30pm–midnight. **Closed:** Aug 30–Sept 10.

The Café de Paris brings elegance and a refined French cuisine to Málaga. The location is La Malagueta, the district surrounding the Plaza de Toros (bullring). This is the domain of the proprietor and chef de cuisine, José García Cortés, who has worked in many important dining rooms before carving out his own niche. Some critics have suggested that the chef's cuisine is pitched too high for the taste of the average Malagueño patronizing this establishment—at least too high for the pocketbook. By that, reference is made to such costly items as caviar, game (including partridge), and foie gras often featured on the menu.

Much of his cuisine has been adapted from classic French dishes to please the Andalusian palate. Menus are changed frequently, reflecting both the chef's imagination and the availability of produce in the Málaga markets. You might on any given night be served *crêpes gratinées* (filled with baby eels) or local white fish baked in salt (it doesn't sound good but is excellent). Meat Stroganoff is made here not with the usual cuts of beef but with ox meat. Save room for the creative desserts. Try, for example, a citrus-flavored sorbet made with champagne. One pleased diner pronounced the custard apple mousse "divine."

MODERATE

Antonio Martín, paseo Marítimo 4. ☎ 222-21-13.

> **Cuisine:** SPANISH. **Reservations:** Required. **Bus:** 13.

Prices: Appetizers 900–1,500 ptas. ($6.40–$10.70); main courses 1,750–2,300 ptas. ($12.40–$16.30). AE, DC, MC, V.
Open: Lunch daily 1–4pm; dinner Mon–Sat 8pm–midnight.

Although this brick building is close to a busy intersection near the Plaza de Toros, you'll hardly be aware of the traffic outside. Three dining rooms with natural brick walls are clustered under a peaked wooden ceiling. The most rustic of them, the Rincón de Ordóñez, honors one of Spain's top matadors. On the wall is the head of the last bull Ordóñez killed before retiring as well as the suit he wore. Before your meal, you can stop for an apéritif and tapas at the entrance bar, which is crowded with local residents and taurine memorabilia. In summer the shaded harborfront terrace makes an ideal place to dine. Menu items include grilled sirloin, leg of baby lamb, grilled salmon, mixed fried fish, fresh fried anchovies, shrimp cocktail, and shellfish soup. Service is both fast and attentive.

Parador de Málaga-Gibralfaro, Monte Gibralfaro.
☎ **222-19-02.**

Cuisine: SPANISH. **Reservations:** Not required. **Microbus:** H. leaving hourly from the cathedral.
Prices: Appetizers 650–950 ptas. ($4.60–$6.70); main courses 1,800–2,200 ptas. ($12.80–$15.60). AE, DC, MC, V.
Open: Lunch daily 1–4pm; dinner daily 8:30–11pm.

Government-owned, this restaurant sits on a mountainside high above the city and is preferred for its view. You can look down into the heart of the Málaga bullring, among other things. Meals are served in the attractive dining room or under the arches of two wide terraces that provide coastal views. Featured are hors d'oeuvres parador—your entire table literally covered with tiny dishes of tasty tidbits. Another specialty is an omelet of chanquetes—tiny whitefish popular in this part of the country—or chicken Villaroi.

Parador Nacional del Golf, carretta de Málaga. ☎ **238-12-55.**

Cuisine: SPANISH. **Reservations:** Not required.
Prices: Appetizers 850–1,700 ptas. ($6–$12.10); main courses 1,600–2,000 ptas. ($11.40–$14.20); fixed-price menu 1,800–2,200 ptas. ($12.80–$15.60). AE, DC, MC, V.
Open: Lunch daily 1:30–4pm; dinner daily 8:30–11pm.

Another government-owned restaurant, this has an indoor/outdoor dining room that opens onto a circular pool, golf course, and private beach. The interior dining room, furnished with reproductions of antiques, has a country-club atmosphere. Before-lunch drinks at the modern bar tempt golfers, among others, who then proceed to the covered terrace for their Spanish meals.

Refectorium, calle Cervantes 8. ☎ **221-89-90.**

Cuisine: SPANISH. **Reservations:** Recommended on weekends and at all bullfights.
Prices: Appetizers 650–1,100 ptas. ($4.60–$7.80); main courses 1,400–1,800 ptas. ($9.90–$12.80). AE, V.
Open: Lunch daily 1–4pm; dinner daily 9pm–2am.

Behind Málaga's bullring, this place becomes hectic during any bullfight, filling up with aficionados and, after the fight, often with the matadors themselves. But it can be visited at any time, especially when the pace here is less frantic. The cuisine has a certain old-fashioned flair, and the servings are more than generous, so take that into consideration when ordering.

You might begin with a typical soup of the Málaga district, called *ajo blanco con uvas* (cold almond soup flavored with garlic and garnished with big muscatel grapes). A classic opener—also popular in the north of Spain—is garlic-flavored mushrooms seasoned with bits of sweet-tasting ham. The fresh seafood is generally a delight, including rape or angler fish. Lamb might be served with a savory saffron-flavored tomato sauce, and you might finish with a homemade dessert, such as rice pudding.

INEXPENSIVE

$ La Manchega, Marín García 4. ☎ 222-21-80.

Cuisine: SPANISH. **Reservations:** Not required. **Bus:** 7 or 9.
$ Prices: Appetizers 300–500 ptas. ($2.10–$3.60); main courses 550–1,300 ptas. ($3.90–$9.20). No credit cards.
Open: Lunch daily 11:30am–4:30pm; dinner daily 7:30–11:30pm.

This restaurant has thrived as a tavern since its establishment in 1954. Set within a 1920s building on a popular pedestrian-only street in Málaga's downtown commercial zone, it offers sidewalk tables, a ground-floor bar with tile walls, and a decorator's attempt to create an indoor Andalusian courtyard. A *salón comedor* offers additional space for dining on an upper floor. Menu items include a peppery version of fish soup; shrimp omelets; Málaga-style soup; beans with Serrano ham; snails; eels; and a full array of fish, including grilled shrimp, hake, monkfish, clams, and mussels.

$ Mesón Danes (Faarup), Barroso 7. ☎ 222-74-42.

Cuisine: DANISH/SPANISH. **Reservations:** Not accepted. **Bus:** 15.
Prices: Appetizers 200–600 ptas. ($1.40–$4.30); main courses 1,095–1,850 ptas. ($7.80–$13.10); *menu del día* 1,350 ptas. ($9.60). V.
Open: Lunch Mon–Sat noon–4pm; dinner Mon–Sat 8–11:30pm.
Closed: Aug.

Here you can enjoy Danish and Spanish snacks at low prices, with choices including Danish or Spanish soup, fish, and meat. Also available is a special Faarup plate with assorted food. The cheaper *menu del día* represents one of the best food values in Málaga. Mesón Danes is located near the harbor and city center.

Las Trevedes, in the El Corte Inglés Department Store, Andalucía 4. ☎ 230-00-00.

Cuisine: SPANISH. **Reservations:** Not required. **Bus:** 15.
Prices: Appetizers 575–580 ptas. ($4.10–$6); main courses 1,200–1,900 ptas. ($8.50–$13.50). Buffet 1,950 ptas. ($13.80) per person. AE, DC, MC, V.
Open: Lunch only, Mon–Sat 1–4:30pm.

Although it originated as a sales incentive to lure shoppers into Málaga's best-accessorized department store, this restaurant quickly adopted a clientele of its own. Set on the sixth floor of El Corte Inglés, the local branch of the nationwide chain, it offers a buffet table of salads and hot and cold meats and fish, as well as à la carte service. The setting is dignified and comfortable, with a well-trained staff who serve such dishes as green peppers stuffed with shellfish, filet of pork in pepper-cream sauce, several kinds of brochettes, and a long list of wines.

Evening Entertainment

Bar Loqüeno, calle de Marín García 12. ☎ **222-30-48.**

This place offers basically the same tapas as its neighbor, La Tasca (see below). The entrance is behind a wrought-iron–and–glass door that leads into a stucco-lined room decorated in a "local tavern style" with a vengeance. There are enough hams, bouquets of garlic, beer kegs, fish nets, and sausages to feed an entire village for a week. There's hardly enough room to stand, and you'll invariably be jostled by a busy waiter shouting "Calamari" to the cooks in the back kitchens. Tapas cost from 125 ptas. (90¢) for a potato croquette to 1,600 ptas. ($11.40) for Serrano ham. Hours are daily from 12:30 to 4:30pm and 7:30pm to 1:30am. Bus: 15.

La Tasca, calle de Marín García 1. ☎ **222-20-82.**

La Tasca is not the place to go if you're looking for a quiet and mellow tasca where no one ever raises his or her voice. The most famous bar in Málaga, this is really a hole in the wall, but it has style, conviviality, and a large staff crowded behind the bar to serve the sometimes-strident demands of practically everyone in Málaga—many of whom bring their children with them. You can have a choice of beer from the tap, wine, and an array of tapas. Try the croquettes (croquetas) and pungent shish kebabs laced with garlic and cumin. If you see an empty seat, try to commandeer it politely—otherwise you'll stand in what might be awestruck observation of the social scene around you. Tapas cost from 200 ptas. ($1.40), beer from 115 ptas. (80¢). Between calle Larios and calle Nueva, the bar's open daily from noon to 4pm and from 7pm to midnight. Just opposite La Tasca is La Tasca 2, an offshoot restaurant serving a reasonably priced cuisine. Bus: 15.

2 Nerja

33 miles (53 km) E of Málaga, 341 miles (549 km) S of Madrid, 104 miles (167 km) W of Almería

GETTING THERE • By Bus Nerja is well serviced by buses from Málaga, at least 10 per day (1½ hours). If you're coming from Almería in the east, there are four buses a day (3 hours).

• By Car Head along the N-340 east from Málaga or take the N-340 west from Almería.

ESSENTIALS   Nerja's **telephone area code** is 95. The **Tourist Information Office** is at calle Puerta del Mar 2 (☎ 95/252-15-31).

Nerja is known for its good beaches and small coves, its seclusion, its narrow streets and courtyards, and its whitewashed flat-roofed houses. Nearby is one of Spain's greatest attractions: the Cueva de Nerja (Cave of Nerja—see below).

At the mouth of the Chillar River, Nerja gets its name from an Arabic word, *narixa,* meaning "bountiful spring." Its most dramatic spot is the **Balcón de Europa,** a palm-shaded promenade that juts out into the Mediterranean. The sea-bordering walkway was built in honor of an 1885 visit from the Spanish king Alfonso XIII in the wake of an earthquake that had shattered part of nearby Málaga. The phrase *Balcón de Europa* is said to have been coined by the king during one of the speeches he made in Nerja praising the beauty of the panoramas around him. To reach the best beaches, head west from the Balcón and follow the shoreline.

The most popular outing from either Málaga or Nerja is to the ✪ **Cueva de Nerja,** carretera de Maro, C.D. 29787 (☎ 95/252-95-20), which scientists believe was inhabited from 100,000 to 40,000 B.C. This prehistoric stalactite and stalagmite cave lay undiscovered until 1959, when it was found by chance by a handful of boys. When fully opened, it revealed a wealth of treasures left from the days of the cave dwellers, including Paleolithic paintings depicting horses and deer; as of this writing, they are not open to public view. The archeological museum in the cave contains a number of prehistoric artifacts; don't miss walking through its stupendous galleries. The ceiling soars to a height of 200 feet.

The cave, located in the hills near Nerja where there is a panoramic view of the countryside and sea, is open daily from 10:30am to 2pm and from 3:30 to 6pm. Admission is 400 ptas. ($2.80) for adults and 200 ptas. ($1.40) for children 6 to 12. Children under 6 are admitted free.

Nerja Cave–bound buses leave hourly everyday from Muelle de Heredia in Málaga from 7am until 8:15pm. Return buses are also hourly until 8:15pm. The journey takes one hour.

Where to Stay

EXPENSIVE

Hotel Mónica, Playa de la Torrecilla s/n, 29780 Nerja.
   ☎ 95/252-11-00. Fax 95/252-11-62. 234 rms, 1 suite. A/C TV TEL
Rates: 7,000–8,600 ptas. ($49.70–$61.10) single; 10,000–13,500 ptas. ($71–$95.90) double; 15,800 ptas. ($112.20) suite. Breakfast 850 ptas. ($6) extra. AE, MC, V. **Parking:** 2,650 ptas. ($18.80).

Hotel Mónica looks something like a three-pronged propeller if you view it from the air. At ground level as you approach the entrance, you see that it has North African arches and green-and-white panels. This hotel opened in 1986, a four-star establishment in an isolated position about a 10-minute walk from the Balcón de Europa on a low-lying curve of beachfront.

The glistening white marble in its lobby is highlighted with such neobaroque touches as elaborately detailed cast-iron balustrades, curved marble staircases, bas-reliefs, paintings, and sculptures. Some of the stairwells even contain oversize copies, set in tiles, of the beach scenes of Claude Monet. A nautical theme is carried out in the bar with brass navigational instruments, models of clipper ships, and comfortable sofas. Both the hotel's restaurants have outdoor terraces or patios for indoor/outdoor dining. A *menu del día* costs 2,650 ptas. ($18.80). A curved pool was built into a terrace a few feet above the beach. The comfortable guest rooms offer private balconies.

★ **Parador Nacional de Nerja,** calle Almuñecar 8, Playa de Burriana-Tablazo, 29780 Nerja. ☎ **95/252-00-50.** Fax 95/252-19-97. 73 rms. A/C MINIBAR TV TEL

Rates: 9,600-11,200 ptas. ($68.20–$79.50) single; 12,000–14,000 ptas. ($85.20–$99.40) double; 13,500–15,100 ptas. ($95.90–$107.20) suite. Breakfast 1,100 ptas. ($7.80) extra. AE, DC, MC, V. **Parking:** Free.

On the outskirts of town, a five-minute walk from the center, this government-owned hotel takes the best of modern motel designs and blends them with a classic Spanish ambience of beamed ceilings, tile floors, and hand-loomed draperies. It's built on the edge of a cliff, around a flower-filled courtyard with a splashing fountain, and its social life centers around a large swimming pool. There is a sandy beach below, reached by an elevator, and lawns and gardens. The guest rooms are spacious and furnished in an understated but tasteful style. International and Spanish meals are served in the hotel restaurant, where a complete dinner costs 3,500 ptas. ($24.90).

MODERATE

Hotel Balcón de Europa, paseo Balcón de Europa 1, 29780 Nerja. ☎ **95/252-08-00.** Fax 95/252-44-90. 85 rms, 20 suites. A/C TV TEL

Rates: 5,200–8,400 ptas. ($36.90–$59.60) single; 7,450–11,200 ptas. ($52.90–$79.50) double; 14,200–18,500 ptas. ($100.80–$131.40) suite. Breakfast buffet 650 ptas. ($4.60) extra. AE, DC, MC, V. **Parking:** 750 ptas. ($5.30).

Occupying the best position in town at the edge of the Balcón de Europa, this 1970s hotel offers rooms with private balconies overlooking the water and the rocks. At a private beach nearby, parasol-shielded tables offer a place to gaze upon the peaceful vista. The comfortable bedrooms are decorated with modern furniture and terra-cotta floors. There's a private garage a few steps away.

Guests can dine at the fourth-floor Restaurant Azul, which offers a panoramic view, or at the beach restaurant, Nautico. An international menu is served. Azul offers a *menu del día* for 2,100 ptas. ($14.90). The Nautico is open only for lunch in winter but for both lunch and dinner in summer. Facilities include a sauna, health club, and solarium, and services include babysitting, laundry, and room service.

BUDGET

Cala-Bela, Puerta del Mar 8, 29780 Nerja. ☎ **95/252-07-00.** 10 rms. TEL

Rates: 2,500–3,500 ptas. ($17.80–$24.90) single; 3,750–5,000 ptas. ($26.60–$35.50) double. Breakfast 400 ptas. ($2.80) extra. AE, DC, MC, V.

Built as a private house in 1895 but much modernized since, this is a well-positioned hotel only a minute's walk from the Balcón de Europa. Cala-Bela offers guest rooms opening onto the sea. They may be small, but they're clean—and what a view! The lounge is charming. In the seafront dining room, seated in a bone-white Valencian chair, you are served a fixed-price meal for 1,500 ptas. ($10.70). The food is good, so even if you're not staying at the hotel, you may want to give the restaurant a try. Enjoy the filet of pork in sherry sauce, paella, grilled crayfish, or trout with cream.

 Hostal Mena, Alemania 15, 29780 Nerja. ☎ **95/252-05-41.** 14 rms (8 with bath). TV TEL

Rates: 1,700 ptas. ($12.10) single without bath; 3,000 ptas. ($21.30) double without bath; 3,700 ptas. ($26.30) double with bath. No credit cards.

This century-old little residencia near the Balcón de Europa has a lot of charm about the place, including the central hallway whose back walls are lined with hundreds of blue and white Andalusian tiles. The family running the hostal are very helpful. Bedrooms are plain and functional, but clean. No meals are served.

Hostal Miguel, calle Almirante Ferrándiz 31, 29780 Nerja. ☎ 95/252-15-23. Fax 95/252-34-85. 9 rms.

Rates: 2,500 ptas. ($17.80) single; 3,500 ptas ($24.90) double. Breakfast 250 ptas. ($1.80) extra. MC, V.

The Miguel is a pleasant, unpretentious inn with simply furnished rooms. Housed in a 19th-century building with iron-rimmed balconies, it's situated on a quiet back street about a three-minute walk from the Balcón de Europa. Breakfast is the only meal served.

Where to Dine

Casa Luque, Plaza Cavana 2. ☎ 252-10-04.

Cuisine: ANDALUSIAN. **Reservations:** Required.

Prices: Appetizers 475–1,100 ptas. ($3.40–$7.80); main courses 1,100–1,900 ptas. ($7.80–$13.50); *menu degustación* 2,450 ptas. ($17.40). AE, MC, V.

Open: Lunch Mon–Sat 1–4pm; dinner Mon–Sat 7:30pm–midnight.

With its impressive canopied and balconied facade, Casa Luque looks like a dignified private villa near the heart of town. The interior has an Andalusian courtyard, and in summer there is a seaview terrace. Meals might include *pâté maison* with raspberry sauce; shoulder of ham; osso buco; pork filet; hot-pepper chicken Casanova; grilled meats; or a limited selection of fish, including grilled Mediterranean grouper.

Casa Paco y Eva, El Barrio 50. ☎ 252-15-27.

    Cuisine: INTERNATIONAL. **Reservations:** Required.

    Prices: Appetizers 650–850 ptas. ($4.60–$6); main courses 1,600–2,200 ptas. ($11.40–$15.60). MC, V.

    Open: Lunch Thurs–Tues noon–4pm; dinner Thurs–Tues 7pm–midnight.

This air-conditioned Andalusian restaurant lies a five-minute walk from the Balcón de Europa. The decor is bright and typically Spanish. The food is excellent, and the owner/chef prepares a varied menu. His special dishes include *sopa de marisco* (shellfish soup); giant prawns cooked *a la plancha* (grilled) with garlic or in whiskey sauce; sole cooked in fresh orange sauce; and tender steaks, either grilled or served with pepper-and-cream sauce. You might also try his pheasant cooked with grapes or, in season, his partridge. Finish off with a homemade crème Catalán. The house Rioja wine goes well with most dishes.

El Colono, calle Granada 6. ☎ 252-18-26.

    Cuisine: ANDALUSIAN/FRENCH. **Reservations:** Required.

    Prices: Wed and Fri flamenco shows with fixed-price menus 1,995–2,795 ptas. ($14.20–$19.80); other nights, fixed-price dinner 1,250 ptas. ($8.90); fixed-price lunch 1,250 ptas. ($8.90). No credit cards.

    Open: Wed–Mon lunch noon–3:30pm; dinner Wed–Mon 8pm–midnight. **Closed:** Nov 15–Dec 20.

A family place for a night of Spanish fun—that's El Colono, near the Balcón de Europa, a three-minute walk from the main bus stop at Nerja. Guitar music and flamenco dancing account for the entertainment highlights, and you can also dine here in a tavern atmosphere, enjoying set menus featuring local specialties. If you just want a glass of wine, you can still enjoy the shows (three per evening, from 8pm until "the wee hours").

Pepe Rico Restaurant, Almirante Ferrándiz 28. ☎ 252-02-47.

    Cuisine: INTERNATIONAL. **Reservations:** Recommended.

    Prices: Appetizers 650–1,050 ptas. ($4.60–$7.50); main courses 1,300–2,100 ptas. ($9.20–$14.90); fixed-price menu 2,800 ptas. ($19.90). DC, MC, V.

    Open: Lunch Wed–Mon 12:30–3pm; dinner Wed–Mon 7–11pm. **Closed:** Nov 20–Dec 20.

Established in 1966, Pepe Rico is today one of the finest places for food in Nerja. It's housed in a white building with grill windows and little balconies. The rooms open onto a large rear balcony, which overlooks a flower-filled courtyard. Dining is in a tavern room, half wood paneled, with handmade wooden chairs, plaster walls, and ivy vines—the vines creep in from the patio, where you can also order meals al fresco.

    The specialty of the day, which might be a Spanish, German, Swedish, or French dish, ranges from almond-and-garlic soup to Andalusian gazpacho, available only in the summertime. The list of hors d'oeuvres is impressive—including Pepe Rico salad, smoked swordfish, salmon mousse, and prawns pil-pil (with hot chile peppers). Main dishes include filet of sole Don Pepe, roast leg of lamb, prawns Café de Paris, and steak dishes. Considering the quality of the food, the prices are reasonable.

Restaurante de Miguel, calle Pintada 2. ☎ **252-29-96.**

> **Cuisine:** INTERNATIONAL. **Reservations:** Recommended.
> **Prices:** Appetizers 450–850 ptas. ($3.20–$6); main courses 1,290–1,800 ptas. ($9.20–$12.80). MC, V.
> **Open:** Lunch Mon–Sat 1–3pm; dinner Mon–Sat 7–1pm. **Closed:** Feb.

This restaurant was established in 1986 by the son of a Nerja resident. At first it was patronized only by local families hoping for their friend to succeed. Since then, however, mostly because of the excellent food, the place has attracted a devoted coterie of foreign visitors and expatriate residents of the Costa del Sol. It sits in the center of town near the busiest traffic intersection, behind a plate-glass aquarium loaded with fresh lobsters, fish, and shellfish. Its not-very-large air-conditioned interior is one of the most decidedly upscale places in Nerja, with white-marble floors, elegant crystal and porcelain, and crisply ironed white napery. The menu lists a full array of international dishes, including cream of shrimp soup flavored with Cognac, tournedos with a sauce made from goat-milk cheese, sea bass with Pernod and fennel, a wide selection of beef and steak dishes, and concoctions composed from the cornucopia of fish from the aquarium.

$ Restaurant Rey Alfonso, paseo Balcón de Europa s/n. ☎ **252-09-58.**

> **Cuisine:** SPANISH/INTERNATIONAL. **Reservations:** Recommended.
> **Prices:** Appetizers 375–650 ptas. ($2.70–$4.60); main courses 850–2,100 ptas. ($6–$14.90); fixed-price menu 950 ptas. ($6.70). MC, V.
> **Open:** Lunch Thurs–Tues 11am–4pm; dinner Thurs–Tues 7–11pm. **Closed:** Nov.

Few visitors to the Balcón de Europa realize they're standing directly above one of the most unusual restaurants in town. You enter from the bottom of a flight of stairs skirting the rocky base of what was originally designed in the late 19th century as a *miradore* (viewing station), which juts seaward as an extension of the town's main square.

The restaurant's menu and interior decor don't hold many surprises, but the close-up view of the crashing waves makes dining here worthwhile. Have a drink at the bar if you don't want a full meal. Specialties include *paella valenciana*, Cuban-style rice, five different preparations of sole (from grilled to meunière), several versions of tournedos and entrecôte, beef Stroganoff, fondue bourguignonne, crayfish in whiskey sauce, and crêpes Suzette for dessert.

3 ## Torremolinos

9 miles (15 km) W of Málaga, 76 miles (122 km) E of Algeciras, 353 miles (568 km) S of Madrid

GETTING THERE • **By Plane**   Málaga airport is nearby.

• **By Train**   There are frequent departures from the terminal at Málaga.

• **By Bus**   Buses run frequently between Málaga and Torremolinos.

• **By Car**   Take the N-340 west from Málaga or the N-340 east from Marbella.

ESSENTIALS   The **telephone area code** for Torremolinos is 95. The **Tourist Information Office** at La Nogalera 517 (☎ **95/238-15-78**). In winter the weather can get chilly, so pack accordingly.

On a rocky promontory in the heart of the Costa del Sol, this resort dominates a magnificent bay at the foot of the Sierra Mijas. This international tourist center achieved prominence because of its 5-mile-long beach, one of the finest along the Mediterranean, although its level of pollution has long been under attack by the media.

If you get up at daybreak and go to the beach, you'll see the fishers bringing in their nets; but by 10am the sun worshipers have taken over. Many stay on the beach all day, depending on vendors who come around selling snacks and drinks. The once-sleepy fishing village pulsates with life in its high-rise apartments, hotels of every hue, discos, flamenco clubs, wine bodegas, boutiques, restaurants, and numerous bars—some with such unlikely names as Fat Black Pussycat.

The original village runs along **calle de San Miguel,** still distinctively Andalusian despite its boutiques and restaurants. Reached past a zigzag of buildings leading down to the beach, **La Carihuela** was the old fishers' village—it still is, if you ignore the hotels and apartments. Opposite is **Montemar,** a smart residential quarter of villas and gardens. For a slice of old Andalusia, see **El Calvario,** an area of whitewashed houses, donkeys, and street vendors.

In the evening, the sidewalk cafe life flourishes. You can spend an entire evening along the traffic-free **calle del Cauce,** with its open-air restaurants and bars (sample before-dinner *tapas* here).

If you want to do some shopping, you won't be disappointed: the best stores of Barcelona and Madrid operate branches in Torremolinos.

Where to Stay

At first, everything in town looks like a hotel, a restaurant, a bar, or a souvenir shop—and that's about it. Actually, considering the number of visitors, Torremolinos doesn't have as many hotels as you'd expect. That's because many European visitors rent apartments on short-term leases during their vacation stays. Hotels are clustered not only in Torremolinos but in nearby Benalmádena Costa (see below).

Many of the hotels in Torremolinos are filled with package-tour groups. The quality of accommodations is wide-ranging: everything from expensive choices (but nothing to equal the luxury of some of the Marbella hostelries) to cheap *hostales* (some of the latter seem popular with revelers who like to party until dawn on cheap wine). The best advice if you're planning to make Torremolinos your center in the Costa del Sol is to pick and choose carefully among the hotels, looking for one compatible with your interests and, most definitely, your budget.

EXPENSIVE

Aloha Puerto Sol, calle Salvador Allende 45, 29620 Torremolinos.
☎ **95/238-70-66,** or toll free **800/336-3542** in the U.S. Fax 95/238-57-01. 430 rms. A/C MINIBAR TV TEL

Rates (including buffet breakfast): 6,143–9,408 ptas. ($43.60–$66.80) single; 7,000–13,550 ptas. ($49.70–$96.20) double. AE, DC, MC, V.

Heralded as one of the most modern hotels along the Costa del Sol when it was built in 1972, this hotel stands on the seashore in the residential suburb of El Saltillo; it's on the southwestern edge of Torremolinos, beside the coastal road leading to Marbella. Away from the noise of the town center, it offers spacious rooms, defined by the hotel as minisuites. Each faces the sea, the Benalmádena marina, or the beach and contains a separate sitting area.

Amid all the accessories of a resort, guests are given a choice of two restaurants and four bars. The most popular lunchtime option is a poolside buffet, where each diner pays 1,500 ptas. ($10.70) for an all-you-can-eat medley of meats, salads, and seafood. Many guests spend their days beside one of the two pools, one of which is heated. Spanish evenings at El Comodoro, one of the several bars on the premises, last well into the early-morning hours.

Don Pablo, paseo Marítimo s/n, 29620 Torremolinos.
☎ **95/238-38-88.** Fax 95/238-37-83. 443 rms. A/C MINIBAR TV TEL

Rates (including buffet breakfast): 10,350–14,450 ptas. ($73.50–$102.60) single; 13,250–18,350 ptas. ($94.10–$130.30) double. AE, DC, MC, V.

One of the most desirable hotels in Torremolinos is housed in a modern building, located a minute from the beach, and surrounded by its own garden and playground areas. There are two unusually shaped open-air pools, with terraces for sunbathing and refreshments, and a large indoor pool as well. The surprise is the glamorous interior, which borrows heavily from Moorish palaces and medieval castle themes. Arched tile arcades have splashing fountains, and life-size stone statues of nude figures in niches line the grand staircase. The comfortably furnished guest rooms have sea-view terraces.

The hotel has a full day-and-night entertainment program, including fitness classes, dancing at night to a live band, and a disco. Piano music is also played in a wood-paneled English lounge, and the hotel has video movies shown on a giant screen every night. At lunch, a buffet is spread before you.

Hotel Cervantes, calle las Mercedes s/n, 29620 Torremolinos.
☎ **95/238-40-33.** Fax 95/238-48-57. 370 rms. A/C TV TEL

Rates (including breakfast): 7,844–9,540 ptas. ($55.70–$67.70) single; 11,256–14,000 ptas. ($79.90–$99.40) double. Half board 4,500 ptas. ($32) per person extra. AE, DC, MC, V.

The Cervantes is a four-star hotel that's about a seven-minute walk to the beach. It has its own garden and is adjacent to a maze of patios and narrow streets of boutiques and open-air cafes. The Cervantes is self-contained, with a sun terrace, a sauna, massage, two pools (one covered and heated), hairdressers, a gift shop, a TV and video lounge, and a game room. The guest rooms have streamlined modern furniture, music, safes, TVs, and spacious terraces; many have sea-view balconies.

A restaurant, a bar with an orchestra and entertainment programs, and a coffee shop are among the attractions. You can enjoy lunch or dinner for 2,438 ptas. ($17.30) and up. Los Molinos Grill on the top floor offers excellent grill meals. In midsummer, this hotel is likely to be booked with tour groups from northern Europe.

Melía Costa del Sol, paseo Marítimo 19, 29620 Torremolinos. ☎ **95/238-66-77**, or toll free **800/336-3542** in the U.S. Fax 95/238-64-17. 540 rms, 18 suites. A/C TV TEL

Rates: 6,550–9,550 ptas. ($46.50–$67.80) single; 8,350–11,900 ptas. ($59.30–$84.50) double; 22,500–31,500 ptas. ($159.80–$223.70) suite. Breakfast 700 ptas. ($5) extra. AE, DC, MC, V. **Parking:** Free.

There are two Melía hotels in Torremolinos, both operated by a popular hotel chain in Spain, but this one is preferred by many clients because of its more central location. It's practically twice the size of the smaller hotel and offers modern and well-maintained guest rooms. However, the hotel is popular with package-tour groups, and you may not feel a part of things if you're here alone. There's a garden, pool, Thalassotherapy center, disco, shopping arcade, and hair-dressing salon. Once a week a free flamenco show is presented to house guests, and on the other nights there is a pianist who plays for dancing couples.

Melía Torremolinos, avenida de Carlotta Alessandri 109, 29620 Torremolinos. ☎ **95/238-05-00**, or toll free **800/336-3542** in the U.S. Fax 95/238-05-38. 275 rms, 6 suites. A/C TV TEL

Rates: 9,440–12,000 ptas. ($67–$85.20) single; 11,800–15,000 ptas. ($83.80–$106.50) double; 22,000–27,000 ptas. ($156.20–$191.70) suite. Breakfast 950 ptas. ($6.70) extra. AE, DC, MC, V. **Parking:** Free. **Closed:** Nov–Mar.

This is the more luxurious of the two Melía hotels at the resort, but it's farther removed from the center. The hotel deliberately lowered its official rank from five stars to four, which means you can enjoy the amenities and service of a five-star hotel but at lower prices. Rising six floors from a position on the western outskirts of town, on the road to Cádiz, it stands in its own gardens. The guest rooms are generally spacious and always well furnished and maintained; many contain minibars. The public areas were renovated and upgraded in 1993. The hotel features a seemingly endless series of buffets, costing

2,300 ptas. ($16.30) per person. Other facilities include a pool and tennis courts, and flamenco shows are occasionally presented.

MODERATE

Hotel Los Arcos, avenida de Carlotta Alessandri 192, 29620 Torremolinos. ☎ **95/238-08-22.** Fax 95/238-02-20. 51 rms. A/C TV TEL

> **Rates** (including breakfast): 4,550 ptas. ($32.30) single; 7,900 ptas. ($56.10) double. AE, DC, MC, V.

Built in 1958 as a grand villa evocative of Beverly Hills in the 1920s, this Spanish-style house was remodeled and modernized in the 1990s. Eclectic furnishings are placed throughout. The guest rooms are pleasant, all with balconies and garden views and half with minibars. A complete lunch or dinner is available for 1,260 ptas. ($8.90). The hotel stands 225 yards from the beach and ³/₄ mile (1 km) from the town center.

Sidi Lago Rojo, Miami, 1, 29620 Torremolinos. ☎ **95/238-76-66.** Fax 95/238-08-91. 144 rms. A/C TV TEL

> **Rates:** 7,500 ptas. ($53.30) single occupancy of double room; 9,950 ptas. ($70.60) double. Breakfast 625 ptas. ($4.40) extra. AE, DC, MC, V.

In the heart of the still-preserved fishing village of La Carihuela, this hotel is only 150 feet from the beach and the waterside fish restaurants and bars. It's the finest place to stay in the fishing village, with its own surrounding gardens and pool, along with terraces for sunbathing and a refreshment bar. The modern hotel offers studio-style doubles, tastefully appointed with contemporary Spanish furnishings, tile baths, and terraces with views. The bar, with a sophisticated decor, is a popular gathering point. In the late evening there's disco dancing. The hotel also has a good restaurant, with meals costing 2,000 ptas. ($14.20).

Sol Palomas, Carmen Montes 1, 29620 Torremolinos. ☎ **95/238-50-00.** Fax 95/238-64-66. 345 rms. TEL

> **Rates** (including half board): 3,640–7,265 ptas. ($25.80–$51.60) per person. AE, DC, MC, V.

Built during the heyday of Torremolino's construction boom (1968), this well-managed hotel is one of the town's most attractive, surrounded as it is with carefully tended gardens. Located near the coastal road, a 1-minute walk from the beach and a 10-minute walk south of the center of town, it has an Andalusian decor that extends into the guest rooms, a formal entrance, and a devoted clientele of repeat visitors who hail mostly from France, Belgium, and Holland. Each room contains a private balcony, a tiled bath, and furniture inspired by southern Spain. None contains air conditioning, although many clients compensate by opening windows and balcony doors to let in the sea breezes. The hotel contains a sauna, three pools (one reserved for children), some form of entertainment going on throughout the day and early evening, a handful of shops, and an unending series of lunchtime and dinner buffets.

INEXPENSIVE

Hostal Los Jazmines, avenida del Lido s/n, 29620 Torremolinos.
☎ **95/238-50-33.** Fax 95/237-27-02. 85 rms. TEL

Rates: 3,000–4,700 ptas. ($21.30–$33.40) single; 4,000–5,900 ptas. ($28.40–$41.90) double. Breakfast 330 ptas. ($2.30) extra. AE, MC, V.

On one of the best beaches in Torremolinos, facing a plaza at the foot of the shady avenida del Lido, this choice for sunseekers is replete with terraces, lawns, and an irregularly shaped pool. Meals are served al fresco or in the appealing dining room, furnished with Spanish reproductions. A set menu costs 1,500 ptas. ($10.70). The guest rooms, all doubles, seem a bit impersonal, but they have their own little balconies, coordinated colors, and compact baths. From here it's a good hike up the hill to the town center.

Hotel El Pozo, Casablanca 4, 29620 Torremolinos. ☎ **95/238-06-22.** 28 rms. TV TEL

Rates: 4,000 ptas. ($28.40) single; 5,500 ptas. ($39.10) double. Breakfast 325 ptas. ($2.30) extra. DC, MC, V.

This hotel isn't for light sleepers, and it's usually filled with budget travelers, including many northern European students. It's in one of the liveliest sections of town, a short walk from the train station. The lobby-level bar has an open fireplace, heavy Spanish furniture, cool white tiles, and a view of a small courtyard. From your window or terrace you can view the promenades below. Rooms are furnished in a simple, functional style. The double rooms have TVs, and some are air-conditioned.

$ Miami, calle Aladino 14, 29620 Torremolinos. ☎ **95/238-52-55.** 27 rms. TEL

Rates: 3,340 ptas. ($23.70) single; 5,700 ptas. ($40.50) double. Breakfast 290 ptas. ($2.10) extra. No credit cards.

Near the Carihuela section, the Miami is like one of those Hollywood movie-star homes of the 1920s. It may even bring back silent-screen memories of Vilma Banky and Rod La Rocque. Its pool is isolated by high walls and private gardens. In the rear patio fuchsia bougainvillea climbs over arches. A tile terrace is used for sunbathing and refreshments. The country-style living room contains a walk-in fireplace, plus lots of brass and copper. The guest rooms are furnished with style, each traditional and comfortable with a balcony. Breakfast is the only meal served.

NEARBY PLACES TO STAY

Where Torremolinos ends and Benalmádena-Costa in the west begins is hard to say. Benalmádena-Costa has long since become a resort extension on the western frontier of Torremolinos, and it's packed with hotels, restaurants, and tourist facilities.

★ **Hotel Torrequebrada**, carretera de Cádiz, Km 220, 29630 Benalmádena. ☎ **95/244-60-00.** Fax 95/244-57-02. 317 rms, 33 suites. A/C MINIBAR TV TEL

Rates (including breakfast): 15,300–18,000 ptas. ($108.60–$127.80) single; 19,000–22,500 ptas. ($134.90–$159.80) double; 28,500–31,500 ptas. ($202.40–$223.70) suite. Discounts for stays of 5 or more days. AE, DC, MC, V. **Parking:** Free.

In the late 1980s this became one of the largest five-star luxury hotels to rise along the Costa del Sol. Lying 3 miles (5 km) west of Torremolinos, it opens onto its own beach and offers a wide range of facilities and attractions, including one of the largest casinos in Europe and a world-class golf course. In addition, it has an array of restaurants, bars, pools, gardens, a nightclub, a health club, a beach club, and tennis courts. You'll almost need a floor plan to navigate your way around the complex. Nine levels of underground parking accommodate motorists. The hotel is furnished in muted Mediterranean colors, and both antique and modern furniture is used.

The hotel offers handsomely furnished and coordinated guest rooms in two 11-story towers. All accommodations have large terraces with sea views and private safes.

A specialty restaurant, Café Royal, overlooks the gardens and the sea, enjoying a five-fork rating for its international cuisine. Meals begin at 5,000 ptas. ($35.50). At garden level, the Pavillion provides buffet and cafeteria service throughout the day. A flamenco show is presented at 11pm on Thursday, Friday, and Saturday, costing 3,500 ptas. ($24.90), including two drinks.

Tritón, avenida António Machado 29, 29491 Benalmádena-Costa. ☎ **95/244-32-40.** Fax 95/244-26-49. 196 rms, 10 suites. A/C MINIBAR TV TEL

Rates (including breakfast): 14,800–15,800 ptas. ($105.10–$112.20) single; 19,100–21,000 ptas. ($135.60–$149.10) double; from 39,600 ptas. ($281.20) suite. AE, DC, MC, V. **Parking:** Free.

Less than 2 miles north of Torremolinos, the Tritón is a Miami Beach–style beachfront resort colony in front of the marina of Benalmádena-Costa. It features a high-rise stack of guest rooms (with roomwide windows opening onto sun balconies) as well as an impressive pool and garden area. Surrounding the pool are subtropical trees and vegetation, plus thatched sun-shade umbrellas.

Among the public rooms are multilevel lounges and two bars with wood paneling and handmade rustic furniture (one has stained-glass windows). For food, there's the main dining room with its three-tiered, mouth-watering display of hors d'oeuvres, fruits, and desserts; a barbecue grill; plus a luncheon terrace where ferns and banana trees form the backdrop. The Tritón also offers tennis courts, a Swedish sauna, and a piano player in the bar.

Where to Dine

The cuisine in Torremolinos is more American and continental than Andalusian. The hotels often serve elaborate four-course meals. If you're on a budget you may want to seek out the food court called **La Nogalera,** the major gathering place in Torremolinos, located between the coast road and the beach. Head down calle del Cauce to this compound of modern whitewashed Andalusian buildings. Open to pedestrian traffic only, it features a maze of passageways, courtyards, and patios for eating and drinking. If you're seeking anything from sandwiches to Belgian waffles to scrambled eggs to pizzas, you'll find it here.

AT LA NOGALERA

$ El Gato Viudo, La Nogalera 8. ☎ 238-51-29.

Cuisine: SPANISH. **Reservations:** Not required. **Prices:** Appetizers 400–800 ptas. ($2.80–$5.70); main courses 700–1,850 ptas. ($5–$13.10). AE, DC, MC, V.

Open: Lunch Thurs–Tues 1–4pm; dinner Thurs–Tues 6–11:30pm.

Simple and amiable, this old-fashioned tavern occupies the street level and cellar of a building off the calle San Miguel. It offers sidewalk seating for those who prefer it and a tradition with local diners that dates back to its 1960 founding. The menu includes grilled fish; marinated hake; roast pork, steak, and veal; calamari with spicy tomato sauce; grilled shrimp; and shellfish or fish soup. The atmosphere is informal, and the staff has grown accustomed over the years to coping with clients from virtually everywhere.

Golden Curry, calle Guetaria s/n, La Nogalera, Bloque 6. ☎ 237-4855.

Cuisine: INDIAN. **Reservations:** Not required. **Prices:** Appetizers 400–550 ptas. ($2.80–$3.90); main courses 850–1,400 ptas. ($6–$9.90). AE, MC, V.

Open: Lunch daily 1–4pm; dinner daily 7pm–1am.

Set one floor above street level in the commercial heart of Torremolinos, this restaurant specializes in traditional Mogul dishes of India that have been adapted and altered to suit British tastes. The two chefs and the Calcutta-born owner all worked in Indian restaurants in London prior to emigrating to Spain, and today they receive much of their business from British holidaymakers. Menu items—served in a single dining room amid a scattering of Indian paintings—include chicken Madras; chicken in onion sauce; lamb slow-cooked in spices and served with lentils; and succulent versions of prawns. Vegetarian dishes are also served, the best of which arrive as an array of small dishes that, when several are combined, create satisfying meatless meals.

IN THE CENTER

Restaurante Cantón, Plaza de la Gamba Alegre 22. ☎ 238-21-17.

Cuisine: CHINESE. **Reservations:** Recommended. **Bus:** 4 to town center.

Prices: Appetizers 195–450 ptas. ($1.40–$3.20); main courses 500–925 ptas. ($3.60–$6.60); fixed-price menu 950 ptas. ($6.70). AE, MC, V.

Open: Lunch Wed–Mon 1–4pm; dinner Wed–Mon 7:30pm–midnight.

Near the main shopping center of Torremolinos is one of the resort's most reasonably priced restaurants. Its very popular set menu includes a spring roll, sweet-and-sour pork, beef with onions, steamed white rice, dessert, and a drink. Special combination platters start at 500 ptas. ($3.60). You can also order à la carte, partaking of such specialties as chicken with almonds and grilled king prawn Chinese style. The staff is efficient and cordial.

AT LA CARIHUELA

If you want to get away from the brash high-rises and honky-tonks, head to nearby Carihuela, the old fishing village on the western outskirts of Torremolinos, where some of the best bargain restaurants are found. You can walk down a hill toward the sea to reach it.

$ **Casa Prudencio,** Carmen 41. ☎ **238-14-52.**

Cuisine: SEAFOOD. **Reservations:** Recommended.

Prices: Appetizers 550–750 ptas. ($3.90–$5.30); main courses 850–1,800 ptas. ($6–$12.80); fixed-price menu 1,500 ptas. ($10.70). AE, MC, V.

Open: Lunch Tues–Sun 1–5pm; dinner Tues–Sun 7:30pm–midnight. **Closed:** Dec 25–Feb 15.

Tops with locals and visitors alike, this seaside restaurant 1 1/4 miles (2 km) west of the center is the oldest surviving restaurant in the fishing hamlet of Carihuela. The decor inside is rustic. In summer the favored place is a reed-canopy–covered open-air terrace where you dine elbow to elbow. The owner choreographs the waiters at a fast and nervous pace. Service is haphazard but friendly. For an appetizer, a soothing gazpacho is ideal. Most diners are fascinated by the specialty of the house, *lubina a la sal* (salted fish). Cooked in an oblong pan, the fish is completely covered with white salt, which is then scraped away in front of the diner to get to the well-flavored, tender white flesh inside. Other main courses are swordfish, shish kebab, and a special paella. For dessert, try the fresh strawberries.

El Roqueo, calle del Carmen 35. ☎ **238-49-46.**

Cuisine: SEAFOOD. **Reservations:** Recommended.

Prices: Appetizers 550–850 ptas. ($3.90–$6); main courses 1,400–2,200 ptas. ($9.90–$15.60); fixed-price menu 1,300 ptas. ($9.20). AE, DC, MC, V.

Open: Lunch Wed–Mon 1–4pm; dinner Wed–Mon 7pm–midnight. **Closed:** Nov.

Right in the heart of this fisherman's village, El Roqueo, which was established in 1975, makes the perfect place for a seafood dinner. Spanish families often fill up some of the tables and gorge themselves on an array of fresh fish. Diners may begin with a savory *sopa de mariscos* (fish soup). Some dishes are priced by the gram and can be expensive, so order carefully. A special is fish baked in rock salt. Grilled sea bass and grilled shrimp are favorites. For dessert, why not try that Spanish standard, carmelized flan (custard)?

AT PLAYAMAR

El Vietnam del Sur, Bloque 9. ☎ **238-67-37.**

Cuisine: VIETNAMESE. **Reservations:** Required.

Prices: Appetizers 475–600 ptas. ($3.40–$4.30); main courses 750–1,200 ptas. ($5.30–$8.50). AE, MC, V.
Open: Lunch Sun 1–4pm; dinner Thurs–Tues 7pm–midnight. **Closed:** Jan–Feb.

Vietnam del Sur will wake up your taste buds after you've had a lazy day on the beach. The food here is inexpensive and best shared, so bring as many friends as possible. Chopsticks are the norm as you begin with spring rolls served with mint and a spicy dipping sauce. The Vietnamese use a lot of vegetables in their food. Two chef's specials are fried stuffed chicken wings and beef with rice noodles. The wine list is short and moderately priced. The restaurant has a terrace for dining.

AT LOS ALAMOS

Frutos, carretera de Cádiz, Km 235. ☎ **238-14-50.**

Cuisine: SPANISH. **Reservations:** Recommended.
Prices: Appetizers 600–1,200 ptas. ($4.30–$8.50); main courses 1,000–2,100 ptas. ($7.10–$14.90); fixed-price menu 1,200 ptas. ($8.50). AE, MC, V.
Open: Lunch daily 1–4:30pm; dinner Mon–Sat 8pm–midnight.

Frutos stands next to the Los Alamos service station about 1¼ miles from the center of Torremolinos. Malagueños frequent the place in droves, as they like its old-style cooking. Here the food is Spanish with a vengeance; nothing is made fancy for the occasional tourist who might wander in. The portions are large, and the food is good—if you don't mind a bit of a wait on crowded days. Service can be hectic at times, but chances are you'll be pleased.

Many diners like to begin with ham and melon, followed by fresh seafood, likely to be something from the day's catch. Perhaps rape (angler fish) will be served, or mero (grouper), which rarely appears fresh on any menu along the coast. Maybe you'll be in for a garlic-studded leg of lamb or oxtail prepared with a savory ragoût. It's wise to reserve a table and hope that it will be available upon your arrival.

AT BENALMÁDENA

 Mar de Alborán, avenida de Alay 5. ☎ **244-64-27.**

Cuisine: BASQUE/ANDALUSIAN. **Reservations:** Recommended.
Prices: Appetizers 750–1,850 ptas. ($5.30–$13.10); main courses 1,600–2,350 ptas. ($11.40–$16.70); *menus del día* 3,500–4,000 ptas. ($24.90–$28.40). AE, DC, MC, V.
Open: Lunch Sun and Tues–Fri 1:30–3:30pm; dinner Tues–Sun 8:30–11:30pm. **Closed:** Dec 22–Jan 22.

Stylishly decorated in themes of yellow and white, this restaurant offers an elegantly airy decor that seems appropriate for its open-windowed location near the sea. Located a short walk from the resort's Puerto Marina, it offers a tempting combination of the regional specialties of both Andalusia and the Basque region of northern Spain. Menu items change with the seasons but might include cold terrine of leeks; crabmeat salads; Basque *piperadda* in puff pastry; *piquillos rellenos* (red peppers stuffed with pulverized fish in sweet-pepper sauce); *bacalao* (salted cod) "Club Ranero," served with garlic and red-pepper cream sauce; *kokotxas*, the Basque national dish of hake cheeks in a green sauce with clams; anglerfish with prawns; pork filet with béarnaise sauce; duck with apples; and foie gras served with sweet Málaga wine and raisins. In season, the restaurant's game dishes are renowned. Dessert might be a frothy version of peach mousse served with purée of fruit and dark-chocolate sauce.

Marrakech, carretera de Benalmádena 7. ☎ 238-21-69.

Cuisine: MOROCCAN. **Reservations:** Recommended.

Prices: Appetizers 650–850 ptas. ($4.60–$6); main courses 1,200–2,000 ptas. ($8.50–$14.20). AE.

Open: Lunch Wed–Sat 12:30–4:30pm: dinner Mon and Wed–Sat 7:30pm–midnight.

Marrakech offers an excellent Moroccan cuisine in the midst of a rather garish decor. Some of the more famous dishes of the Maghreb are served here, including couscous, tagine (meat pies), and various kebabs, usually made with lamb. The stuffed pastries make a fitting dessert if you like them on the sweet side.

Evening Entertainment

Torremolinos has more nightlife activity than any other spot along the Costa del Sol. The earliest action is always at the bars, which are lively most of the night, serving drinks and *tapas* (Spanish hors d'oeuvres). Sometimes it seems there are more bars in Torremolinos than people, so you shouldn't have trouble finding one you like. **Note:** Some of the bars are open during the day as well.

DRINKS & TAPAS

Bar Central, Plaza Andalucía, Bloque 1. ☎ 238-27-60.

Bar Central offers coffee, brandy, beer, cocktails, limited sandwiches, and pastries, served on a large, French-style covered terrace if you prefer. It's a good spot to meet congenial people. Drinks begin at 125 ptas. (90 ¢) for a beer or 350 ptas. ($2.50) for a hard drink. Open Monday through Saturday from 9am to 2am.

Bar El Toro, calle San Miguel 32. ☎ 238-65-04.

Bar El Toro, in the very center of Torremolinos, is for bullfight aficionados. Kegs of beer, stools, and the terrace in the main shopping street make it perfect for drinking a before-dinner sherry or an after-dinner beer. As a special attraction, the staff prepares a bullfight poster, with your name between those of two famous matadors, for 550 ptas. ($3.90). Drinks at your table begin at 175 ptas. ($1.20) for beer or 380 ptas. ($2.70) for a pitcher of sangría. Open daily from 8am to midnight.

La Bodega, calle San Miguel 38. ☎ 238-73-37.

La Bodega relies on its colorful clientele and the quality of its *tapas* to draw customers, who seem to seek this place out above the dozens of other tascas in this very popular tourist zone. You'll be fortunate to find space at one of the small tables, since many clients consider the bar food plentiful enough for a satisfying lunch or dinner. Once you begin to order one of the platters of fried squid, pungent tuna, grilled shrimp, or tiny brochettes of sole, you might not be able to stop. Most *tapas* cost 175 to 650 ptas. ($1.20 to $4.60). A beer costs 125 ptas. (90 ¢). Open daily from noon to midnight.

DANCE CLUBS & DISCOS

New Piper's Club, Plaza Costa del Sol. ☎ **238-29-94.**

The leading disco in town resembles a subterranean world; the decor is tongue-in-cheek and suggests the caves at Nerja. Spread over many levels, with connecting ramps and tunnels, it has several dance floors, splashing water in reflecting pools, strobe lightning, and an aggressive set of international records to amuse its packed audience. It's very much the 1960s in aura and ambience. After your first drink, a beer costs 300 ptas. ($2.10). Open daily from 6 to 10:30pm and 11pm to 4:30am.

Admission (including first drink): Before 10pm, 800 ptas. ($5.70); Sun–Thurs after 11pm, 1,100 ptas. ($7.80); Fri–Sat after 11pm, 1,300 ptas. ($9.20).

El Palladium, avenida Montemar 68. ☎ **238-42-89.**

Set close to the Hotel Sol Palomas, within a 10-minute walk south of the town center, this well-designed nightclub is one of the most convivial in Torremolinos. The illumination contains strobes and spotlights accompanying a sound system described as loud and distortion-free. It's open daily from 6pm to 4am, with disco music beginning around 10pm. Expect to pay from 350 ptas. ($2.50) for a drink.

Admission: 800 ptas. ($5.70) after 10pm.

THE GAY LIFE

Torremolinos has the largest cluster of gay life, including bars and restaurants, of any resort along the coast of southern Spain. Gay men (and, to a lesser degree, lesbians) flock here from England, Germany, and Scandinavia. Gay bars seem to huddle together in clusters. The most outstanding of these is in **Pueblo Blanco,** which is like a little village of its own. Young men bar-hop here with "gay" abandon.

Much gay life sprawls across the development of **La Nogalera,** which is like a village within a village, with a wide scattering of restaurants, bars, souvenir shops, and apartment complexes. The restaurants here—even those that draw a large gay clientele—tend to be mixed.

Bronx, Edificio Centro Jardín. ☎ **238-73-60.**

This is the leading gay disco, with beer going for 350 ptas. ($2.50). Open daily from 10pm to 6am.

Admission: 1,000 ptas. ($7.10).

Men's Bar, La Nogalera 714. ☎ **238-42-05.**

One of the most popular gay bars in La Nogalera, this place is crowded most nights and charges 300 ptas. ($2.10) for beer. Open daily from 9pm to 5am.

A CASINO

Casino Torrequebrada, carretera de Cádiz 266, Benalmádena-Costa. ☎ **244-25-45.**

Considered one of the major casinos along the Costa del Sol, this establishment is located on the lobby level of the previously recommended Hotel Torrequebrada. The Torrequebrada combines a nightclub/cabaret; a restaurant; and an array of tables devoted to blackjack, chemin de fer, punto y banco, and two kinds of roulette.

The nightclub year round offers a flamenco show presented at 11pm on Thursday, Friday, and Saturday nights; in midsummer, there might be more glitz and frequent shows (ask when you get there or call). The casino is open daily from 9am to 4am. Nightclub acts begin at 10:30pm (Spanish revue) and midnight (Las Vegas revue). The restaurant is open nightly from 9:30pm to 2am.

Admission: Casino, 600 ptas. ($4.30). Cabaret/nightclub, 3,500 ptas. ($24.90), which includes two drinks, admission to both shows, and admission to the casino.

4 Fuengirola & Los Boliches

20 miles (32 km) W of Málaga, 64$^1/_2$ miles (104 km) E of Algeciras, 356 miles (573 km) S of Madrid

GETTING THERE • By Train From Torremolinos, take the Metro at the Nogalera station (under the RENFE sign). Trains depart every 30 minutes.

• By Bus Fuengirola is on the main Costa del Sol bus route between Algeciras in the west and Málaga in the east.

• By Car Take the N-340 east from Marbella.

ESSENTIALS The **telephone area code** for Fuengirola and Los Boliches is 95. The **Tourist Information Office** is at avenida Jesús Santos Rein 6 (☎ **95/246-74-57**).

The twin fishing towns of Fuengirola and Los Boliches lie halfway between the more famous resorts of Marbella and Torremolinos. The promenade along the water stretches some 2$^1/_2$ miles, with the less-developed Los Boliches just half a mile from Fuengirola.

The towns don't have the facilities or drama of Torremolinos and Marbella. Except for two major luxury hotels, Fuengirola and Los Boliches are cheaper, though, and that has attracted a horde of budget-conscious European tourists.

On a promontory overlooking the sea are the ruins of **San Isidro Castle.** The Santa Amalja, Carvajal, and Las Gaviotas **beaches** are broad, clean, and sandy. Everybody goes to the big **flea market** at Fuengirola on Tuesday.

Where to Stay

⭐ **Byblos Andalus,** Urbanización Mijas Golf, 29640 Fuengirola. ☎ **95/246-30-50.** Fax 95/247-67-83. 144 rms, 3 suites. A/C MINIBAR TV TEL

Rates: 20,000–24,000 ptas. ($142–$170.40) single; 25,000–33,500 ptas. ($177.50–$237.90) double; from 47,000 ptas. ($333.70) suite. Buffet breakfast 1,800 ptas. ($12.80) extra. AE, DC, MC, V. **Parking:** Free.

This luxurious resort, which has a health spa and lavish rooms, is in a magnificent setting. It's 3 miles from Fuengirola and 6 miles from the beach. The grounds contain shrubbery, a white minaret, Moorish arches, tile-adorned walls, and an orange-tree patio inspired by the Alhambra grounds, 97 miles away. Two 18-hole golf courses designed by Robert Trent Jones, tennis courts, spa facilities, a gymnasium, and five pools bask in the Andalusian sunshine. The spa is a handsome classic structure, Mijas Thalasso Palace.

The rooms and suites are elegantly and individually designed and furnished in the Roman, Arabic, Andalusian, and rustic styles. Private sun terraces and lavish baths add to the comfort.

Dining/Entertainment: Dining choices include Le Nailhac, with its French gastronomic offerings; El Andaluz, with its regional and Spanish specialties, and La Fuente, with its dietetic cuisine. The San Tropez Bar opens onto a poolside terrace, and live entertainment is often presented.

Services: Room service, laundry/valet, babysitting.

Facilities: Health club, sauna, solarium, two outdoor pools, three indoor pools, golf courses, tennis.

Florida, paseo Marítimo s/n, 29640 Fuengirola. ☎ **95/247-61-00.** Fax 95/258-15-29. 116 rms. TV TEL

Rates: 3,600–5,700 ptas. ($25.60–$40.50) single; 6,200–8,600 ptas. ($44–$61.10) double. Breakfast 575 ptas. ($4.10) extra. AE, DC, MC, V. **Parking:** Free.

There's a semitropical garden in front of the Florida, and guests can enjoy refreshments under a wide vine-covered pergola. Most of the comfortable rooms have balconies overlooking the sea or mountains. The floors are of tile, and the furnishings, particularly in the lounge, have been renewed. It's a 10-minute walk from the train station.

$ **Hostal Sedeño,** Don Jacinto 1, 29640 Fuengirola. ☎ **95/247-47-88.** 30 rms.

Rates: 2,225–3,200 ptas. ($15.80–$22.70) single; 3,180–3,750 ptas. ($22.60–$26.60) double. No credit cards.

The Sedeño is three minutes from the beach, in the heart of town. Its modest lobby leads to a larger lounge furnished with antiques and reproductions. You pass a small open courtyard where stairs go up to the second- and third-floor balconied guest rooms. These overlook a small garden with fig and palm trees, plus a glassed-in room with a terrace. No breakfast is served here, but there are several cafes nearby.

Las Piramides, paseo Marítimo s/n, 29640 Fuengirola. ☎ **95/247-06-00.** Fax 95/258-32-97. 280 rms, 40 suites.

Rates (including breakfast): 7,925–10,475 ptas. ($56.30–$74.40) single; 10,450–13,650 ptas. ($74.20–$96.90) double; 13,950–16,050 ptas. ($99–$114) suite. AE, MC, V. **Parking:** 1,000 ptas. ($7.10).

This resort, much favored by northern European travel groups, is divided into two 10-story towers capped with pyramid-shaped roofs, from which the complex takes its name. It's a citylike compound, set about 50 yards from the beach, with seemingly every kind of divertissement: flamenco shows on the large patio, a cozy bar/lounge, traditionally furnished sitting rooms, a coffee shop, a poolside bar, and a gallery of boutiques and tourist facilities, such as car-rental agencies. All rooms have slick modern styling, as well as private bath and terrace. Room service is provided, as are laundry/valet services and babysitting.

Where to Dine

Casa Vieja, avenida Los Boliches 27, Los Boliches. ☎ **258-38-30.**

Cuisine: FRENCH. **Reservations:** Recommended.

Prices: Fixed-price three-course lunch (Sat–Sun only) 1,550 ptas. ($11); dinner appetizers 555–1,650 ptas. ($3.90–$11.70); main dinner courses 1,175–2,350 ptas. ($8.30–$16.70). AE, MC, V.

Open: Lunch Sat–Sun 12:30–3pm; dinner Tues–Sun 7:30–11pm.

Set inside the thick stone walls of a cottage built in the 1870s for a local fisherman, this restaurant lies on the main street of Los Boliches, a short walk east of the center of Fuengirola. Owned and managed by London-born Jon Adams, the establishment is a favorite of the British expatriate community living among the nearby hills. A flowering patio is available, weather permitting, for outdoor dining, and there's a cozy bar available for dialogues with the owner. Menu items include a subtly flavored terrine of oxtail; fresh vegetable soup; king prawns; tournedos with béarnaise sauce; suprême of salmon; gratin of sole in puff pastry; guinea fowl with cumin and honey-glazed turnips; duck breast with creamy foie-gras sauce; and turbot in white-wine sauce. The house's special dessert is a *tarte tatin,* an upside-down tart served with fresh cream and ice cream.

Don Pe', calle de la Cruz 19, Fuengirola. ☎ **247-83-51.**

Cuisine: CONTINENTAL. **Reservations:** Recommended for dinner.

Prices: Appetizers 325–800 ptas. ($2.30–$5.70); main courses 750–2,100 ptas. ($5.30–$14.90). AE, DC, MC, V.

Open: Dinner only, Mon–Sat 7pm–midnight. **Closed:** Lunch July–Sept.

Don Pe' lies amid a cluster of less desirable restaurants in the center of Fuengirola. Because of its quality, it seems to get more repeat business than most of its competitors. During hot weather many visitors prefer to dine in the courtyard, whose roof can be mechanically retracted to allow in the air and light. During cold weather, the staff builds a fire in a hearth.

The menu lists specialties in three different languages and includes a selection of game dishes, such as medallion of venison in wine sauce accompanied with red cabbage, roast filet of wild boar, and duck with orange sauce. The ingredients are imported especially for the restaurant from the forests and plains of nearby Andalusia. Less powerful dishes include peppers stuffed with prawns, fresh salmon covered with an herb sauce, and even an alpine version of fondue bourguignonne.

Monopol, Palangreros 7, Fuengirola. ☎ **247-44-48.**

Cuisine: INTERNATIONAL. **Reservations:** Recommended.
Prices: Appetizers 390–1,100 ptas. ($2.80–$7.80); main courses 990–1,550 ptas ($7–$18.10); fixed-price menus 1,150–1,990 ptas. ($8.20–$28.30). AE, MC, V.
Open: Dinner only, Mon–Sat 7pm–midnight. **Closed:** Aug.

Set in the heart of town, near both the beach and Fuengirola's post office, this cozy restaurant is the domain of German-born Paul Wartman and his wife, Barbal. Since 1981, Monopol has catered to a varied European clientele, many of whom appreciate the culinary specialties of their respective homelands. The building was constructed about a century ago, and although it's not graced with an open-air courtyard, the restaurant offers a quartet of rustically decorated dining rooms and a wine list that includes a fine assortment of Riojas. House specialties include ragoût of chicken with mango and curry cream, filets of lamb saddle with rosemary, magret of duck with lentils, and filet strips in fines herbes sauce.

El Paso, calle Francisco Cano 39, Los Boliches. ☎ **247-50-94.**

Cuisine: MEXICAN. **Reservations:** Recommended.
Prices: Appetizers 375–850 ptas. ($2.70–$6); main courses 1,000–1,950 ptas. ($7.10–$13.80). MC, V.
Open: Dinner only, daily 7pm–midnight.

The building was built a century ago as a canning factory for sardines, with a row of fishermen's cottages set close nearby. Today this is one of the neighborhood's busiest Mexican restaurants, where a splashing fountain enlivens an outdoor patio rich with blooming flowers. (There are additional tables set up inside.) By far the most popular drink here is a frothy Margarita, which might be followed by your choice of tacos, burritos, frijoles, fajitas, and guacamoles. Be alert to the numbers of drinks you consume, however, since the bill, once you begin, seems to mount quickly.

Restaurant Tomate, El Troncon 19, Fuengirola. ☎ **246-35-59.**

Cuisine: INTERNATIONAL. **Reservations:** Recommended.
Prices: Appetizers 350–725 ptas. ($2.50–$5.10); main courses 650–1,990 ptas. ($4.60–$14.10). AE, MC, V.
Open: Dinner only, Tues–Sun 7pm–midnight.

One of the most gastronomically sophisticated restaurants in town presents the best culinary traditions of northern and southern Europe. Set in the heart of Fuengirola, in a century-old town house with dining space in the back, the restaurant is the creative statement of German-born Michael Lienhoop. Meals might include dishes from Spain (gazpacho, filet of hake floating on a lake of mustard-flavored cream-and-herb sauce); France (*langoustines provençales*); Germany (sauerkraut with an assortment of smoked meats, or pork in a red wine–and–mushroom sauce); and Scandinavia (a selection of marinated herring and marinated salmon with dill sauce).

5   Mijas

18¹/₂ miles (30 km) W of Málaga, 363 miles (584 km) S of Madrid

GETTING THERE • By Bus   There's frequent bus service from the terminal at Fuengirola.

• **By Car**   At Fuengirola, take the Mijas road north.

ESSENTIALS   The **telephone area code** for Mijas is 95.

It's called "White Mijas" because of its bone-white Andalusian houses. Just 5 miles from Fuengirola above the Costa del Sol, the village is a gem, standing at the foot of a sierra. From its lofty perches 1,400 feet above sea level, a panoramic vista of the Mediterranean unfolds. Along its narrow, cobblestone streets have walked Celts, Phoenicians, and Moors. You'll do better hiring a "burro-taxi." In a park at the top of Cuesta de la Villa, you see remnants of a Moorish citadel dating from 833. Shops threaten to inundate the village and sell everything from original art to olive-wood jewelry. Incidentally, Mijas possesses the only square bullring in Spain.

Where to Stay

⭐ **Hotel Mijas**, Urbanización Tamisa 2, 29650 Mijas.
☎ **95/248-58-00.** Fax 95/248-58-25. 100 rms, 3 suites. TV TEL
Rates: 8,000–10,000 ptas. ($56.80–$71) single; 10,000–12,000 ptas. ($71–$85.20) double; 20,000–24,000 ptas. ($142–$170.40) suite. Breakfast 1,200 ptas. ($8.50) extra. AE, DC, MC, V. **Parking:** Free.

One of the most charming hotels on the Costa del Sol was built in the 1970s on steeply sloping land in the town center. Designed in an Andalusian-inspired four-story block of white walls, wrought-iron accents, and flowering terraces, it features sweeping views over the Mediterranean from most of its public areas and accommodations. Throughout, the style is sunflooded and comfortable, and the staff is tactful and hardworking. The in-house tavern is accented with enormous kegs of wine, while the lounge is the setting for live music on some evenings, performed amid Iberian antiques and a collection of unusual fans. A fixed-price meal in the restaurant costs 2,500 ptas. ($17.80). The hotel's facilities include tennis courts, a pool, a sauna, a gymnasium, a boutique, facilities for games of lawn bowling, a hairdresser, and a barber. If you have an aversion to climbing stairs, ask for a room on one of the lower floors, because there is no elevator.

Where to Dine

Club El Padrastro, paseo del Compás. ☎ **248-50-00.**
Cuisine: INTERNATIONAL. **Reservations:** Recommended.

$ Prices: Appetizers 450–1,475 ptas. ($3.20–$10.50); main courses 975–2,400 ptas. 6.90–$17); fixed-price menus 1,175–2,215 ptas. ($8.30–$15.70). AE, DC, MC, V.
Open: Lunch daily 12:30–4pm; dinner daily 7–11pm.

In Spanish, *padrastro* is a curious word, for it means both "stepfather" and "hangnail." However, it also suggests height, a commanding position—which you'll appreciate after climbing the 77 steps to reach the restaurant, although it's more sensible to take the elevator from the town parking lot. The restaurant is in the center of Mijas. After you've scaled the heights, a pool and an artfully decorated restaurant await you. Before dinner, order a drink under pine trees by the pool and enjoy the view. Inside, picture windows on two levels also open onto the panorama, and soft music plays. The food is quite good. Specialties include fish soup Padrastro, bass with fennel, and a special flambé Padrastro.

Restaurante El Capricho, calle los Caños 5. ☎ 248-51-11.
Cuisine: INTERNATIONAL. **Reservations:** Recommended.
Prices: Appetizers 400–875 ptas. ($2.80–$6.20); main courses 1,400–2,100 ptas. (9.90–$14.90); fixed-price lunch 1,000 ptas. ($7.10). AE, DC, MC, V.
Open: Lunch Thurs–Tues 12:30–4pm; dinner Thurs–Tues 7–11:30pm.
Closed: Nov 15–Dec 15.

El Capricho, located in what was an 1850s private home in the town center, draws a large English-speaking clientele, and the varied menu is geared to their tastes. Appetizers include prawn cocktail, Serrano ham, omelets, corn on the cob, soups, and salads. Among the main dishes are sole and trout, grilled swordfish, chicken Kiev, shish kebab, steak Diane, chicken Hawaii, and pheasant Capricho. You might prefer the paella Mijena, which is excellent. Desserts range from flambéed concoctions to baked Alaska. The wine list offers good choices, including the house Valdepeñas.

6 Marbella

37 miles (60 km) W of Málaga, 28 miles (45 km) W of Torremolinos, 47 miles (76 km) E of Algeciras, 373 miles (601 km) S of Madrid

GETTING THERE • By Bus   Twenty buses run between Málaga and Marbella daily, plus three buses coming in from Madrid and another three buses from Barcelona.

• By Car   Marbella is the first major resort as you head east on the N-340 from Algeciras.

ESSENTIALS   The **telephone area code** for Marbella is 95. The **Tourist Information Office** is at Glorieta de la Fontanilla s/n (☎ 95/277-14-42).

In the shadow of what was once an Arab fortress, Marbella is definitely chic and attracts a fashionable crowd of movie people and socialites. Many mansions and villas are found hereabouts.

About halfway between Málaga and Gibraltar, Marbella is at the foot of the Sierra Blanca, which keeps the climate mild. Its best beaches are the 600-yard-long El Fuerte and the 800-yard-long Fontanilla. But actually Marbella is one long beach, taking in about 17 miles of sand from Guadalmina to Cabopino. Some 60 beachfront complexes and hotel clusters line this stretch. The beach resorts have elaborate swimming pools and all the trappings; the beachfronts are open to the public. From national highway N-340, you'll see different roads signposted leading to the various beaches.

You don't need to get dressed to go to lunch either, as many of these beaches have bar/restaurants called *chiringuitos*. Right on the beach, these places sell cold beer throughout the day and often grill freshly caught fish for your lunch. Women often go topless on these beaches, but total nudity is prohibited. However, nudists still disrobe at some of the more isolated places at the eastern stretch of beach. Sports, such as waterskiing, shark fishing, and tennis, are popular. The even more athletically inclined dance until dawn.

Traces of Marbella's past are found in its palatial town hall, its medieval ruins, and its ancient Moorish walls. Marbella's most charming area is the **old quarter,** with narrow cobblestone streets and Arab houses, centering around the Plaza de los Naranjos.

Where to Stay

Since the setting is so ideal—pure Mediterranean sun, sea, and sky, plus the scent of Andalusian orange blossoms in the air—some of the best hotels along the Costa del Sol are found in Marbella.

EXPENSIVE

Andalucía Plaza, Urbanización Nueva Andalucía, Apdo. 21, 29660 Nueva Andalucía Marbella. ☎ **95/281-20-00.** Fax 95/281-47-92. 289 rms, 20 suites. A/C MINIBAR TV TEL

Rates (including American breakfast): 9,000–15,000 ptas. ($63.90–$106.50) single; 13,000–20,000 ptas. ($92.30–$142) double; 17,500–27,000 ptas. ($124.30–$191.70) suite. AE, DC, MC, V. **Parking:** Free.

Built in 1972, the Andalucía Plaza is a resort complex on a grand scale. On the mountain side of the coastal road between Marbella and Torremolinos, twin five-story buildings are linked by a reception lounge and formal gardens. On the sea side is the hotel's beach club. The public rooms in the hotel buildings are spacious and lavishly decorated. Equally luxurious are the guest rooms furnished with reproductions in the classic Castilian manner. The hotel is on more than a 300-foot strip of sand, 4 miles west of the center of Marbella.

Dining/Entertainment: The restaurant Córdova serves upscale international meals, a fixed-price menu costing 3,850 ptas. ($27.30). The Bar Toledo, primarily a watering hole, offers light snacks and suppers. There's also an in-house casino (see "Evening Entertainment," below).

Services: 24-hour room service, concierge, babysitting, laundry.

Facilities: The hotel's beach club includes a 300-foot strip of sand, with adjacent sunbathing terraces, tennis courts, two saunas, a gymnasium, an open-air pool, and an enclosed all-weather pool. About half a mile away there's a 1,000-berth marina, where the hotel will arrange the rental of a vessel for deep-sea fishing.

Hotel Don Carlos, Jardines de las Goldondrinas, carretera de Cádiz, Km 192, 29600 Marbella. ☎ **95/283-11-40,** or toll free **800/223-5652** in the U.S. and Canada. Fax 95/283-34-29. 223 rms, 15 suites. A/C MINIBAR TV TEL
Rates: 9,000–21,100 ptas. ($63.90–$149.80) single; 12,000–26,000 ptas. ($85.20–$184.60) double; 29,000–96,500 ptas. ($205.90–$685.20) suite. Breakfast 1,200 ptas. ($8.50) extra. AE, DC, MC, V.
Parking: Free

One of the most dramatically alluring hotels along the coastline, the Don Carlos rises on a set of angled stilts above a forest of pines. Between it and its manicured beach, considered the best in Marbella, are 130 acres of award-winning gardens replete with cascades of water, a full-time staff of 22 gardeners, and thousands of subtropical plants. There's far more to this hotel than the modern tower that rises above the eastern edge of Marbella. Its low-lying terraces and elegant eating and drinking facilities attract high-powered conferences from throughout Europe, as well as individual nonresident diners from along the Mediterranean coast.

Each guest room has its own panoramic balcony, lacquered furniture, a bath done in honey-colored marble, and satellite TV.

Dining/Entertainment: You can dine amid splashes of bougainvillea beside an oversize pool bordered with begonias and geraniums or in La Pergola, where ficus and potted palms decorate the hundreds of lattices. A hideaway, Los Naranjos, has a sun-flooded atrium with mosses and orange trees. A grand piano on the marble dais provides diverting music. Fixed-price meals here go for 4,800 ptas. ($34.10). Meals in the other restaurants, including grills or elaborate buffets in the semioutdoor beachfront cabana, cost about half as much.

Among the bars scattered around the various terraces and marble-lined hideaways of the public rooms, the most popular offers an English-inspired decor of exposed hardwoods, a panoramic view of the sea, plenty of sofas, a dance floor, and a musical trio.

Services: 24-hour room service, laundry, babysitting.

Facilities: Three pools, use of five golf courses nearby, saunas, gym, tennis courts; water sports cost extra.

⭐ **Hotel Puente Romano,** carretera de Cádiz, Km 167, 29600 Marbella. ☎ **95/227-01-00.** Fax 95/277-57-66. 142 rms, 67 suites. A/C MINIBAR TV TEL
Rates: 27,500 ptas. ($195.30) single; 34,700 ptas. ($246.40) double; from 40,500 ptas. ($287.60) suite. Breakfast 1,700 ptas. ($12.10) extra. AE, DC, MC, V. **Parking:** Free.

This hotel was built as a cluster of vacation apartments, a fact that influenced the attention to detail and the landscaping that surrounds it. In the early 1970s a group of entrepreneurs transformed it into one of the most unusual hotels in the south of Spain, sitting close to the frenetic coastal highway, 2¹/₂ miles west of Marbella midway between Marbella and Puerto Banús.

If you're wondering who your fellow guests might be, the King of Spain, Barbra Streisand, Björn Borg, Stevie Wonder, Julio Iglesias, the Kennedys, and the President of Ireland have all enjoyed the pleasures of this establishment.

Once inside the complex, guests wander through a maze of arbor-covered walkways. Along the route, they pass cascades of water, masses of vines, and a subtropical garden. The Andalusian/Mediterranean–style accommodations are a showcase of fabrics, accessories, and furniture. Each of the guest rooms has a semisheltered balcony with flowers, private bath, and electronic safe.

Dining/Entertainment: Nestled amid the lushness are well-upholstered indoor/outdoor bars and restaurants. Three of these overlook a terra-cotta patio, bordered at one end by the stones of a reconstructed Roman bridge, the only one of its kind in southern Spain. There's also a nightclub.

Services: 24-hour room service, laundry/valet, babysitting.

Facilities: The edges of the free-form swimming pool are bordered by trees and vines and a drain-away waterfall, which makes it look something like a Tahitian lagoon. There's also a sandy beach with water sports, tennis courts, a cluster of boutiques, a gym, a sauna, and a solarium.

⭐ **Marbella Club,** carretera de Cádiz, Km 178, 29600 Marbella. ☎ **95/277-13-00.** Fax 95/282-98-84. 76 rms, 24 suites, 10 bungalows. A/C MINIBAR TV TEL

Rates: 27,000 ptas. ($191.70) single; 35,000–38,000 ptas. ($248.50–$269.80) double; 45,000–84,000 ptas. ($319.50–$596.40) suite; 97,000–240,000 ptas. ($688.70–$1,704) bungalow. Breakfast 1,600–2,100 ptas. ($11.40–$14.90) extra. AE, DC, MC, V. **Parking:** Free.

Until a handful of equally chic hotels were built along the Costa del Sol, the Marbella Club reigned almost without equal as the exclusive hangout of the world's commercial and genealogical aristocracy. Among its first guests when it opened in 1954 were actress Merle Oberon and novelist Leon Uris, and since then the names and titles on its roster of famous guests could have kept a society columnist busy for months. Established on land originally owned by the father of Prince Alfonso von Hohenlohe, the resort sprawls over a landscaped property that slopes from its roadside reception area down to the beach. Composed of small, ecologically conscious clusters of garden pavilions, bungalows, and small-scale annexes (none of which is higher than two stories), the Marbella basks amid some of the most well conceived gardens along the coast. Rooms have private balconies or terraces. Today, its clientele is discreet, international, elegant, and appreciative of the resort's small scale and superb service.

Dining/Entertainment: The Marbella Club Restaurant moves from indoor shelter to an outdoor terrace according to the season. (For more information, see "Where to Dine," below.) A bar is located in the garden nearby.

Services: 24-hour room service, babysitting, laundry/valet, massage, concierge well-versed in the arrangement of almost anything.

Facilities: There are two pools and a beach with a lunch restaurant. Golf can be arranged nearby. Tennis courts are available within a two-minute walk at the Marbella Club's twin resort, Puente Romano.

Melía Don Pepe, Finca Las Merinas, 29600 Marbella.

☎ **95/277-03-00,** or toll free in the U.S. **800/336-3542.**
Fax 95/277-99-54. 204 rms, 18 suites. A/C MINIBAR TV TEL
Rates: 22,200–25,900 ptas. ($157.60–$183.90) single; 32,800 ptas. ($232.90) double; from 55,000 ptas. ($390.50) suite. Breakfast 1,500 ptas. ($10.70) extra. AE, DC, MC, V. **Parking:** Free.

The Melía Don Pepe occupies 6 acres of tropical gardens and lawns between the coastal road and the sea. Its well-furnished bedrooms, with private baths and wall-to-wall carpeting, face either the sea or the Sierra Blanca mountains. The facilities are so vast you could spend a week here and not use them all.

Dining/Entertainment: The hotel has lounges, bars, and restaurants. La Farola grill provides international à la carte cuisine, with meals costing from 5,500 ptas. ($39.10).

Services: 24-hour room service, laundry/valet, babysitting.

Facilities: Four pools, tennis courts, Swedish sauna, bridge clubroom, boutiques, yacht harbor along the beach, golf course.

★ **Los Monteros,** carretera de Cádiz, Km 187, 29600 Marbella.
☎ **95/277-17-00.** Fax 95/282-58-46. 169 rms, 10 suites.
A/C MINIBAR TV TEL
Rates (including breakfast): 25,000 ptas. ($177.50) single; 32,000 ptas. ($227.20) double; from 55,000 ptas. ($390.50) suite. AE, DC, MC, V. **Parking:** Free.

Los Monteros, 400 yards from a beach and 4 miles (6 km) east of Marbella, is one of the most tasteful resort complexes along the Costa del Sol. Situated between the coastal road and its own private beach, it attracts those seeking intimacy and luxury. No cavernous lounges exist here; instead, many small public rooms, Andalusian/Japanese in concept, are the style. The hotel offers various salons with open fireplaces, a library, and terraces. The guest rooms are brightly decorated, with light-colored lacquered furniture and terraces.

Dining/Entertainment: The hotel has a bar and four restaurants on different levels that open onto flower-filled patios, gardens, and fountains. Within the precincts, Grill El Corzo is one of the finest grill rooms along the coast. The grill, done up in Toledo red, is on the first floor. Wall-size scenic murals are in the background, and tables are bedecked with bright cloths and silver candlesticks. Soft, romantic music is played nightly. Meals begin at 6,000 ptas. ($42.60). The cuisine is a pleasing combination of French and Spanish.

Services: 24-hour room service, babysitting, laundry/valet.

Facilities: Free use of Río Real, nearby 18-hole golf course; several pools; beach club with heated indoor pool; 10 tennis courts; 5 squash courts; riding club/school; fully equipped gym with sauna, massage, and Jacuzzi.

MODERATE

Hotel El Fuerte, El Fuerte s/n, 29600 Marbella. ☎ **95/286-15-00.**
Fax 95/282-44-11. 261 rms, 2 suites. A/C MINIBAR TV TEL

Rates: 8,400–9,200 ptas. ($59.60–$65.30) single; 11,400–17,200 ptas.
($80.90–$122.10) double; 27,900–33,400 ptas. ($198.10–$237.10)
suite. Breakfast 1,200 ptas. ($8.50) extra. AE, DC, MC, V. **Parking:** 600
ptas. ($4.30).

The largest and most recommendable hotel in the center of Marbella,
with a balconied and angular facade divided into two separate six-
story towers, El Fuerte is set directly on the waterfront. Built in 1957,
it added a wing in 1987 and was last renovated in 1994. Catering to
a sedate clientele of conservative northern Europeans, it offers a palm-
fringed pool set across from a sheltered lagoon and a wide-open beach.
The hotel offers a handful of terraces, some shaded by flowering
arbors, that provide hideaways for quiet drinks. Inside, the public
rooms contain a wide variety of tilework, certain sections of which
were culled from much older buildings. The guest rooms are contemporary, with piped-in music and terraces.

The hotel offers a coffee shop plus a restaurant serving a *menu del
día* for 3,392 ptas. ($24.10). The facilities for leisure activities include
the above-mentioned pool, a floodlit tennis court, a health club, and
two squash courts.

Hotel Guadalpín, carretera Cádiz-Málaga 340, Km 179, 29600
Marbella. ☎ **95/277-11-00.** Fax 95/277-33-34. 110 rms. TEL
Rates: 4,450–6,550 ptas. ($31.60–$46.50) single; 6,300–9,400 ptas.
($44.70–$66.70) double. Breakfast 455 ptas. ($3.20). AE, DC, MC, V.
Parking: Free.

This three-star 1960s hotel is right on the coast, only 300 yards from
the beach and a mile from the center of Marbella. Guests spend hours
relaxing around one of the two pools or can walk along a private
pathway lined with fir trees to the Mediterranean. The dining room
has large windows overlooking the patio and pool, and the main
lounge has been designed in a ranch style with round marble tables
and occasional leather armchairs arranged for conversational groups.
A *menu del día* in the hotel restaurant costs 1,850 ptas. ($13.10). The
bar area of the spacious lounge is brick and natural wood, which
makes it warm and attractive.

Each guest room has not only two terraces, but also a living room
and bedroom combined. Most of the rooms are furnished in "new
ranch" style. Only 10 single rooms are available.

INEXPENSIVE

 Residencia Finlandia, Finlandia 12, 29600 Marbella.
☎ 95/277-07-00. 11 rms. TEL

Rates: 3,000–3,500 ptas. ($21.30–$24.90) single; 3,500–6,360 ptas.
($24.90–$45.20) double. Breakfast 400 ptas. ($2.80) extra. AE, DC, MC,
V.

Situated in the Huerta Grande, a peaceful residential section, the
1970s Finlandia is only a five-minute walk from the center of the

old quarter and 200 yards from the beach. It's clean and well run, with spacious guest rooms and contemporary furnishings. Your bed will be turned down at night.

$ Residencia Lima, avenida Antonio Belón 2, 29600 Marbella. ☎ **95/277-05-00.** Fax 95/286-30-91. 64 rms. TEL

Rates: 6,360 ptas. ($45.20) single; 7,950 ptas. ($56.40) double. Breakfast 425 ptas. ($3) extra. AE, DC, MC, V.

Tucked away in a residential section of Marbella, right off the N-340 and near the sea, this hotel is more secluded than the others nearby. The modern eight-story structure features bedrooms with Spanish provincial furnishings and private balconies.

Residencia San Cristóbal, Ramón y Cajal 3, 29600 Marbella. ☎ **95/277-12-50.** Fax 95/286-20-44. 96 rms. A/C TV TEL

Rates: 3,675–6,250 ptas. ($26.10–$44.40) single; 5,400–8,600 ptas. ($38.30–$61.10) double. Breakfast 450 ptas. ($3.20) extra. AE, MC, V.

In the heart of Marbella, 200 yards from the beach, this 1960s five-story hotel has long, wide terraces and flower-filled windowboxes. The guest rooms have walnut headboards, individual overhead reading lamps, and room dividers separating the comfortable beds from the small living-room areas. An added plus is the private terrace attached to each room—just right for a continental breakfast, the only meal served here.

El Rodeo, Victor de la Serna s/n, 29600 Marbella. ☎ **95/277-51-00.** Fax 95/282-33-20. 100 rms. TEL

Rates: 3,800–5,500 ptas. ($27–$39.10) single; 5,000–7,750 ptas. ($35.50–$55) double. Breakfast 475 ptas. ($3.40) extra. AE, DC, MC, V.

Even though this modern hotel stands just off the main coastal road of Marbella—within walking distance of the bus station, the beach, and the old quarter—it's quiet and secluded. Facilities in the seven-story structure include a pool, terrace, sunbathing area, solarium, and piano bar. Two elevators whisk you to the sunny, spacious second-floor lounges with country furnishings; there's also a bar with tropical bamboo chairs and tables. Continental breakfast is the only meal served in the cheerful breakfast room. The guest rooms are functional, with several shuttered closets, lounge chairs, and white desks.

BUDGET

$ Hostal El Castillo, Plaza San Bernabé 2, 29600 Marbella. ☎ **95/277-17-39.** 26 rms.

Rates: 1,700 ptas. ($12.10) single; 3,500 ptas. ($24.90) double. No credit cards.

At the foot of the castle in the narrow streets of the old town, this small but choice budget hotel opens onto a minuscule triangular square used by the adjoining convent and school as a playground. There's a small covered courtyard, and the second-floor guest rooms have only inner windows. The spartan rooms are scrubbed clean and contain white-tile baths. No morning meal is served, and not one word of English is spoken.

$ **Hostal Munich,** calle Virgen del Pilar 5, 29600 Marbella. ☎ **952/77-24-61.** 18 rms. TEL

Rates: 2,995 ptas. ($21.30) single; 4,275 ptas. ($30.40) double. No credit cards.

Set back from the street and shielded by banana and palm trees, this unassuming three-story hostal is just a short walk from the water and the bus station. Some rooms have balconies; all are simply furnished and well kept. A continental breakfast is the only meal served. The homey lounge/breakfast room is warm and inviting.

Where to Dine

EXPENSIVE

★ **La Fonda,** Plaza Santo Cristo 9–10. ☎ **277/25-12.**
Cuisine: INTERNATIONAL. **Reservations:** Required.
Prices: Appetizers 1,300–1,800 ptas. ($9.20–$12.80); main courses 1,700–2,900 ptas. ($12.10–$20.60). AE, DC, MC, V.
Open: Dinner only, Mon–Sat 8–11:30pm.

Considered both a gem of 18th-century Andalusian architecture and a gastronomic citadel of renown, La Fonda is the Costa del Sol extension of one of the most famous restaurants in Europe, the Madrid-based Horcher's (for more information, see Chapter 5). The restaurant was the outgrowth of a simple inn that had been created by interconnecting a trio of town houses in Old Marbella. Today a central patio with a murmuring fountain, a series of colonnaded loggias, carefully chosen Andalusian *azulejos* (glazed tiles), beamed ceilings, open fireplaces, grill-covered windows, and checkerboard-patterned marble floors have been respectfully maintained.

Some of the most beautiful (and richest) faces come here regularly for long and languid dinners. The cuisine is international, and so is the crowd. Menu specialties change every four months or so but might include fish terrine with herb sauce; avocado pancakes with prawns; guinea fowl or partridge; coq au vin; blanquette de veau; and chicken Kiev.

★ **La Hacienda,** Urbanización Hacienda Las Chapas, carretera de Cádiz, Km 193. ☎ **283-11-16.**
Cuisine: INTERNATIONAL. **Reservations:** Recommended.
Prices: Appetizers 1,200–1,800 ptas. ($8.50–$12.80); main courses 2,200–3,200 ptas. ($15.60–$22.70); fixed-price menu 6,500 ptas. ($46.20). AE, DC, MC, V.
Open: Summer, dinner only, Wed–Sun (plus Mon in Aug) 8:30–11:30pm. Winter, lunch Wed–Sun 1–3:30pm, dinner Wed–Sun 8:30–11:30pm. **Closed:** Nov 15–Dec 20.

La Hacienda, a tranquil choice 8 miles east of Marbella, enjoys a reputation for serving some of the best food along the Costa del Sol. In cooler months you can dine inside in the rustic tavern before an open fireplace. However, in fair weather, meals are al fresco, served on a patio partially encircled by open Romanesque arches. The chef is likely to offer foie gras with lentils; lobster croquettes (as an appetizer); and roast guinea hen with cream, minced raisins, and port. An iced soufflé finishes the repast quite nicely.

⭐ **Marbella Club Restaurant,** in the Marbella Club, carretera de Cádiz, Km 178. ☎ **277-13-00.**

Cuisine: INTERNATIONAL. **Reservations:** Recommended.

Prices: Lunch buffet 5,300 ptas. ($37.60) per person; dinner appetizers 1,100–2,500 ptas. ($7.80–$17.80); dinner main courses 1,900–4,500 ptas. ($13.50–$32). AE, DC, MC, V.

Open: Lunch daily 1–3:30pm; dinner 9pm–12:30am in summer, 7:30–11:30pm in winter.

Much of this establishment's charm derives from the willingness of the staff to move its venue outdoors onto a flowering terrace whenever the weather justifies it. Lunch is traditionally a buffet served under an open-sided pavilion. Teams of formally dressed waiters frequently replenish a groaning table best described as tastefully elaborate for a clientele that has often been a *Who's Who* of the discreetly rich and famous. Dinners are served amid blooming flowers, flickering candles, and the strains of live music that might include a Spanish classical guitarist, a small chamber orchestra playing 19th-century classics, or perhaps the soothing tones of a South American vocalist. Menu items change with the season, but include an international array of foods inspired by the cuisines of the European continent.

Villa Tiberio, carretera de Cádiz, Km 178.5. ☎ **277-17-99.**

Cuisine: ITALIAN. **Reservations:** Recommended.

Prices: Appetizers 750–2,000 ptas. ($5.30–$14.20); main courses 1,200–2,300 ptas. ($8.50–$16.30). AE, MC, V.

Open: Dinner only, Mon–Sat 7:30pm–midnight.

Villa Tiberio's nearness to the upscale Marbella Club, about a five-minute walk away, ensures a flow of visitors from that hotel's elite confines. Set in what was built as a private villa during the 1960s, it serves what might be the most innovative Italian food in the region. Owned by the Morelli brothers, gregarious proprietors of restaurants as far away as London, it was established in 1990 and today is considered a venue for important events in the lives of the many northern European expatriates living nearby.

Appetizers include grilled eggplant stuffed with onions, mushrooms, and tomatoes; slices of thinly sliced smoked beef with fresh avocadoes and oil-and-lemon dressing; prawn crêpes au gratin; and *funghi fantasia,* composed of a large wild mushroom stuffed with seafood-and-lobster sauce and any of a wide array of pastas. Especially tempting is the *pappardelle alla Sandro,* large flat noodles studded with chunks of lobster, tomato, and garlic. Other versions come with cream, caviar, and smoked salmon. Main dishes include grilled monkfish with prawns and garlic butter, grilled filets of pork or veal with mushroom-cream sauce, and osso buco. Live music sometimes accompanies a meal here.

MODERATE

Hostería del Mar, avenida Cánovas del Castillo 1. ☎ 277-02-18.

Cuisine: MEDITERRANEAN. **Reservations:** Recommended.
Prices: Appetizers 700–875 ptas. ($5–$6.20); main courses 1,700–2,100 ptas. ($12.10–$14.90). AE, MC, V.
Open: Lunch Mon–Sat 1–4pm; dinner Mon–Sat 7:30pm–midnight.

Hostería del Mar lies at the beginning of the bypass road that runs beside the Hotel Meliá Don Pepe. Its cuisine is known throughout the region as being both delicious and highly unusual. The Hostería has been called the most consistently good restaurant in the region—a judgment with which many loyal clients agree.

You'll be seated in a dining room decorated in shades of fern green and cream, accented with wooden columns, a blue–and–terra-cotta floor, decorative ceiling beams, and hand-painted porcelain. In summer, a tree-shaded patio is set with tables for additional seating. Meals might include calves' sweetbreads in mustard sauce; clams stuffed with ratatouille; roast duck with a sauce made from roasted figs and cassis; Catalán-style shrimp with chicken; and quail stuffed with spinach, mushrooms, and pâté. Desserts are appropriately sumptuous and include a selection of cold soufflés.

$ Mesón del Museo, Plaza de Los Naranjos 11. ☎ 282-3332.

Cuisine: SWEDISH/INTERNATIONAL. **Reservations:** Recommended.
Prices: Appetizers 800–1,200 ptas. ($5.70–$8.50); main courses 1,000–2,800 ptas. ($7.10–$19.90). AE, MC, V.
Open: Dinner only, Mon–Sat 7:30–11:30pm. **Closed:** Two weeks in Aug.

Mesón del Museo bears its name because of its location on the upper floor of an 18th-century building that contains one of the oldest art and antiques galleries in Marbella. Although its dining room contains Iberian accessories and Andalusian antiques, its menu is pure Swedish—the inspired result of the partnership of Stockholm-born Hans Jöhncke and his Chilean wife, Valeska. Menu items include smoked or marinated salmon served with mustard sauce and creamed spinach; beef Stroganoff; succulent versions of Swedish meatballs with gravy and mashed potatoes; and top-quality sirloin filet prepared in at least five versions (variations on the theme include versions served with béarnaise, green pepper, madeira, or *cabrales* [a Spanish blue cheese] sauce, as well as filets stuffed with truffles and/or foie gras). Desserts might include a very succulent homemade pear tart with vanilla sauce. The restaurant lies in the oldest and most historic core of Marbella.

Santiago, avenida Duque de Ahumada 5. ☎ 277-43-39.

Cuisine: SEAFOOD. **Reservations:** Required.
Prices: Appetizers 750–3,000 ptas. ($5.30–$21.30); main courses 1,200–3,200 ptas. ($8.50–$22.70). AE, DC, MC, V.
Open: Lunch daily 12:30–5pm; dinner daily 7pm–midnight.

As soon as you enter Santiago, the bubbling lobster tanks give you an idea of the kinds of dishes available. The decor, the stand-up *tapas* bar near the entrance, and the summertime patio join together with fresh fish dishes to make this one of the most popular eating places in town.

On my most recent visit I arrived so early for lunch that the mussels for my mussels marinara were just being delivered. The fish soup is well prepared, well spiced, and savory. The sole in champagne comes in a large serving, and the turbot can be grilled or sautéed. On a hot day, the seafood salad—garnished with lobster, shrimp, and crabmeat, served with a sharp sauce—is especially recommended. For dessert I suggest a serving of Manchego cheese.

INEXPENSIVE

La Gitana, calle Buitrago 2. ☎ 277-66-74.
   Cuisine: INTERNATIONAL. **Reservations:** Recommended.
   Prices: Appetizers 500–900 ptas. ($3.60–$6.40); main courses 1,100–2,100 ptas. ($7.80–$14.90). AE, MC, V.
   Open: Dinner only, daily 8–11:45pm.

La Gitana offers popular rooftop dining on a narrow street in the old pueblo off the Plaza de los Naranjos. It specializes in barbecued meats, including honey-glazed chicken, spareribs, sirloin steak, and even lamb. Other dishes, such as fresh fish, are also available.

$ Mesón del Pasaje, Pasaje 5. ☎ 277-12-61.
   Cuisine: CONTINENTAL. **Reservations:** Required.
   Prices: Appetizers 550–650 ptas. ($3.90–$4.60); main courses 1,100–1,700 ptas. ($7.80–$12.10). AE, MC, V.
   Open: Dinner only, Mon–Sat 7:30–11:30pm. **Closed:** Nov to mid-Dec.

A well-run restaurant in an old house in the ancient quarter, just off the Plaza de los Naranjos, this *mesón* is a maze of little dining rooms. Since word is out that the food is the best in the old town—for the price—the place invariably fills up. You can fill up on one of the excellent pastas, which are most reasonable, or try the well-prepared but more expensive seafood and meat selections. The place has charm and is a good value.

$ La Tricyclette, calle Buitrago 14. ☎ 277-78-00.
   Cuisine: INTERNATIONAL. **Reservations:** Not required.
   Prices: Appetizers 400–1,350 ptas. ($2.80–$9.60); main courses 750–1,800 ptas. ($5.30–$12.80); fixed-price menu (Oct–May only) 1,500 ptas. ($10.70). AE, MC, V.
   Open: Dinner only, Mon–Sat 7:30pm–midnight.

One of the more popular dining spots in Marbella, this restaurant is in a converted 18th-century home—courtyard and all—located on a narrow street in the old quarter near the Plaza de los Naranjos. Sofas in the bar area provide a living-room ambience, and a stairway leads to an intimate dining room with an open patio that's delightful in the warmer months. Start with crêpes with a soft cream-cheese filling, or with grilled giant prawns, then move on to a delectable main dish such as roast duck in beer; filet steak with a green-pepper sauce; or calves' liver cooked in sage and white wine. The wine list is extensive and reasonable.

NEARBY DINING

El Refugio, carretera de Ojén (C337). ☎ 288-10-00.

Cuisine: SPANISH. **Reservations:** Not required.

Prices: Appetizers 550–750 ptas. ($3.90–$5.30); main courses 1,400–2,000 ptas. ($9.90–$14.20); fixed-price menu 2,550 ptas. ($18.10). AE, DC, MC, V.

Open: Lunch Tues–Sun 1–4pm; dinner Tues–Sat 8–11pm.

If the summer heat has you down, retreat to the Sierra Blanca, just outside Ojén, where motorists come to enjoy both the mountain scenery and the cuisine at El Refugio, lying 12^1/$_2$ miles up in the hills north of Marbella. Meals are served in a rustic dining room, with an open terrace for drinks. Specialties include local versions of various spicy regional sausages, roast pork, roast chicken, grilled steaks, and local pheasant in season. The lounge has an open fireplace and comfortable armchairs, along with a few antiques and Oriental rugs.

Evening Entertainment

No doubt about it—the best way to keep food costs low in Marbella is to do what the Spaniards do: Eat your meals in the *tapas* bars. You get plenty of atmosphere, lots of fun, good food, and low costs. On a **Marbella *tasca* crawl** you can order a first course in one bar with a glass of wine or beer, a second course in another, and on and on as your stamina and appetite dictate. You can eat well in most places for around 600 ptas. ($4.30)—and *tascas* are found all over town.

A DANCE CLUB

Ana María, Plaza del Santo Cristo 4–5. ☎ 268-07-04.

The elongated *tapas* bar here is often crowded with locals, and a frequently changing collection of singers, dancers, and musicians performs everything from flamenco to popular songs. Open daily from 11pm to 4am; closed November and Monday from December to March. Drinks cost 1,000 ptas. ($7.10).

Admission: 2,200 ptas. ($15.60).

A CASINO

Casino Nueva Andalucía Marbella, in the Andalucía Plaza Hotel, Urbanización Nueva Andalucía. ☎ 281-40-00.

Set 6 miles west of Marbella, close to Puerto Banús, this casino lies on the lobby level of the Andalucía Plaza Hotel (see "Where to Stay," above). The designers carefully incorporated graceful traffic flows between the facilities of the hotel and the jangle and clatter of the casino it contains. Unlike the region's competing casino at the Hotel Torrequebrada, the Nueva Anadalucía does not offer cabaret or nightclub shows. The focus instead is on gambling, which the mobs of visitors from northern Europe perform with abandon. Individual games include French and American roulette, blackjack, punto y banco, craps, and chemin de fer. You can dine before or after gambling in the Casino Restaurant, which is raised a few steps above the gaming floor, for about 4,000 ptas. ($28.40) per person, excluding wine. Jackets are not required for men, but shorts and T-shirts will probably be frowned on. The casino is open daily from 8pm to either 4 or 5am. La Caseta Bar offers flamenco shows at 11pm on Friday and Saturday. Entrance is free, but drinks cost from 1,500 pesetas ($10.70).

Admission: Casino 600 ptas. ($4.30) and presentation of a valid passport.

7 San Pedro de Alcántara

43 miles (69 km) W of Málaga, 42¹/₂ miles (68 km) E of Algeciras

GETTING THERE • By Bus   Service is every 30 minutes from Marbella.

• By Car   Take the N-340 west from Marbella.

ESSENTIALS   The **telephone area code** for San Pedro de Alcántara is 95.

Between Marbella and Estepona, this interesting village contains Roman remains that have been officially classified as a national monument. Since the 1960s it has been extensively developed as a resort suburb of Marbella and now offers some good hotel selections.

Where to Stay

Cortijo Blanco, carretera de Cádiz, Km 172, 29670 San Pedro de Alcántara. ☎ **95/278-09-00.** Fax 95/278-09-16. 327 rms. A/C TEL
Rates (including half board): 4,400–9,400 ptas. ($31.20–$66.70) single; 6,600–16,600 ptas. ($46.90–$117.90) double. V. **Parking:** Free.

The design of this landscaped hotel emulates that of an extended Anadalusian village. Accommodations are contained in a compound of white-sided *pueblos*, groups of which are clustered around courtyards with fountains and banks of flowers. Linking them into a coherent unit are views of a soaring bell tower, and tangled masses of subtropical vines and vegetation that entwine themselves through wrought-iron balustrades. Many guest rooms face the main garden, which is dominated by a generously sized pool.

Built during the early 1960s, the hotel was renovated and doubled in size in 1991. The dining room has a decor inspired by Old Spain, with copies of Valencian antiques and attentive service. Lunch is usually served around the garden's covered pergola which, like the rest of the hotel, lies 600 yards from the beach.

Golf Hotel Guadalmina, Hacienda Guadalmina, carretera N-340, 29670 San Pedro de Alcántara. ☎ **95/288-22-11.**
Fax 95/288-54-48. 80 rms. A/C MINIBAR TV TEL
Rates: 15,600 ptas. ($110.80) single; 19,990 ptas. ($141.90) double. Breakfast 1,100 ptas. ($7.80) extra. **Parking:** Free.

At this moderately priced, large country club–type resort, the first tee and 18th green are right next to the hotel. The golf course is open to both residents and nonresidents. An informal place, it's really a private world on the shores of the Mediterranean. You reach it by a long driveway from the coastal road; the location is 50 yards from the beach, 8 miles east of Marbella, and 1¼ miles from the center of San Pedro de Alcántara. Two seawater pools attract those seeking the lazy life; the tennis courts appeal to the athletic. The guest rooms—most opening onto the pool/recreation area and the sea—are attractive in their traditional Spanish style.

The hotel offers two dining choices—one a luncheon-only reed-covered poolside terrace overlooking the golf course and the sea; the other an interior room in the main building, with a sedate clubhouse aura. Informality and good food reign.

8   Puerto Banús

5 miles (8 km) E of Marbella, 486 miles (782 km) S of Madrid

GETTING THERE • **By Bus**   Fifteen buses a day connect Marbella to Puerto Banús.

• **By Car**   Drive east from Marbella along the 340.

ESSENTIALS   The **telephone area code** for Puerto Banús is 95.

This marine village is a favorite resort of celebrities from all over the world. Almost overnight the village was created in the traditional Mediterranean style. There is no sameness here—each building appears different in design—yet everything blends into a harmonious whole. Yachts can be moored at your doorstep. Along the harborfront is an array of bars and restaurants—all expensive.

Try, if you can, to wander through the back streets as well, past elegant archways and grilled patios. The rich and elegant rent apartments in this village for the winter season. In all, Puerto Banús is like a Disney World concoction of what a Costa del Sol fishing village should look like.

Where to Stay

Hotel Marbella-Dinamar, Urbanización Nueva Andalucía, carretera de Cádiz, Km 175, 29660 Puerto Banús. ☎ **95/281-05-00.** Fax 95/281-23-46. 112 rms, 5 suites. A/C TV TEL

Rates: 9,350–14,550 ptas. ($66.40–$103.30) single; 11,855–18,150 ptas. ($84.20–$128.90) double; 35,750 ptas. ($253.80) suite. Breakfast 1,200 ptas. ($8.50) extra. AE, DC, MC, V. **Parking:** Free.

Distinctly Moorish in flavor and feeling, this striking and exotic resort celebrates the Arab domination of what is today Spanish Andalusia. Set on the seafront, just 400 yards from both the beach and the borders of Puerto Banús's congested center, it was built around 1980 with stark-white walls, soaring arches, and a central courtyard contains a large abstractly shaped swimming pool. Bedrooms offer views of the palm trees beside the pool or of the sea, and each contains two large beds and a simple and airy collection of furniture. The resort offers tennis courts (floodlit at night), easy access to both the casino at the neighboring Plaza Andalucía Hotel, and one of the best all-around golf courses along the Costa del Sol. There's also an additional indoor pool suitable for year-round use. Perhaps best of all, the diversions and facilities of Puerto Banús lie within a three-minute walk.

Where to Dine

$ Dalli's Pasta Factory, Muelle de Rivera. ☎ **281-24-90.**

Cuisine: PASTA. **Reservations:** Not accepted.
Prices: Pastas 650–1,050 ptas. ($4.60–$7.50); meat platters 1,300–1,650 ptas. ($9.20–$11.70). No credit cards.
Open: Dinner only, daily 7pm–1am.

Its lighthearted, California-inspired philosophy has added a new way to save pesetas in high-priced Puerto Banús. Its specialty is pasta, pasta, and more pasta, which, served with a portion of garlic bread and a carafe of house wine, is amply adequate for the gastronomic needs of many budget travelers. In a setting inspired either by high-tech or art deco (even the owners aren't absolutely certain of how to define it), you can order nutmeg-flavored ravioli with spinach filling, penne all arrabiata, lasagne, and several kinds of spaghetti. More filling are the chicken cacciatore and the scalloppine of chicken and veal. These are served with—guess what?—pasta as a side dish. The establishment's owners, incidentally, are a trio of Roman-born brothers who were reared in England and educated in California.

Don Leone, Muelle Ribera 45. ☎ **281-17-16.**

Cuisine: INTERNATIONAL. **Reservations:** Recommended.
Prices: Appetizers 750–1,500 ptas. ($5.30–$10.70); main courses 1,950–3,800 ptas. ($13.80–$27). AE, DC, MC, V.
Open: Lunch daily 1–4pm; dinner daily 8pm–1am. **Closed:** Nov 21–Dec 21 and lunch mid-June to mid-Sept.

Consistently popular, with a hard-working and polite staff, Don Leone has built up a loyal clientele scattered along the Costa del Sol. Featuring Italian specialties based on seasonal ingredients, it sits in Puerto Banús's center, at the edge of the dock. Tables are scattered along the wharfside, in emulation perhaps of a chic restaurant on Italy's Amalfi peninsula. A broad-based array of wines can accompany your meal, which might include consistently popular versions of spinach salad and Caesar salad, minestrone, osso buco, veal or chicken parmigiana, fish, and roast baby lamb. Pasta addicts will appreciate the choice of homemade pastas, made on the premises and served in an array of savory sauces.

Red Pepper, Muelle Ribera s/n. ☎ **281-21-48.**

Cuisine: GREEK/INTERNATIONAL. **Reservations:** Recommended.
Prices: Appetizers 550–750 ptas. ($3.90–$5.30); main courses 1,500–4,000 ptas. ($10.70–$28.40). AE, DC, MC, V.
Open: Daily 11am–1 or 3am.

Run by an exuberant band of Cypriot expatriates, Red Pepper offers an array of Greek and international food in a sparsely furnished sunny dining room. Selections include Hellenic chicken soup; moussaka; a variety of well-seasoned grilled meats; lots of fish; calf's liver; lamb on a skewer in the Greek fashion; and especially king prawns and lobster, which are the most expensive main courses because they are priced by the gram. Full meals are usually accompanied by a selection of Greek and Spanish wines. You'll find the place in the center of the paseo Marítimo.

La Taberna del Alabardero, Muelle Benabola A2. ☎ **281-27-94.**

Cuisine: INTERNATIONAL. **Reservations:** Required.
Prices: Appetizers 1,500–1,800 ptas. ($10.70–$12.80); main courses 2,000–3,200 ptas. ($14.20–$22.70). AE, DC, MC, V.
Open: Lunch daily 1–4pm; dinner daily 8pm–2am. **Closed:** Sun in winter; Jan 15–Feb 15.

This restaurant lies directly on the harborfront, within full view of the hundreds of strolling pedestrians whose numbers seem to ebb and flow like the tides. You can dine inside its big-windowed interior, but you might have more fun at one of the dozens of outdoor tables, where the only clues to the upper-crust status are the immaculate napery, well-disciplined waiters, and discreet twinkle of some very expensive jewelry among the blue jeans or formal attire of the prosperous and fashionable clientele. An armada of private yachts bobs at anchor a few feet away. Meals might include crêpes stuffed with chunks of lobster and crayfish; hake and small clams served in Basque-inspired green sauce; filet of duck's breast with green peppercorns or orange sauce; and a wide array of desserts.

Evening Entertainment

Hollywood Bar, Muelle Ribera 14. ☎ **281-68-12.**

Hollywood Bar offers a place to sit and examine the yachts bobbing a few feet away and the pedestrians who may be admiring the boats as much as you are. The establishment contains a green-and-white decor of arched awnings and terra-cotta tiles focused around a series of collages of the best shots of the Hollywood stars of yesteryear. Monroe and Chaplin mark the entrance to the toilets. Beer starts at 300 ptas. ($2.10), with hard drinks going for 600 ptas. ($4.30) and up. Open daily from 9:30am to 2am.

Sinatra Bar, Muelle Ribera 2. No phone.

The Sinatra Bar is a center for people-watching. Residents of the nearby apartments meet here for drinks late in the evening. The preferred spot, if the weather is right, is on one of the chairs set out on the sidewalk. Only a few feet away, rows of luxury yachts await your inspection. Tables are usually shared, and piped-in music lets you hear Sinatra's voice. Snacks such as the "Mama-burger" are served throughout the night. Hard drinks begin at 500 ptas. ($3.60); burgers start at 450 ptas. ($3.20). Open daily from 9pm to 4am.

Appendix

A Basic Phrases & Vocabulary

English	Spanish	Pronunciation
Hello	**Buenos días**	*bway*-noss *dee*-ahss
How are you?	**Como está usted?**	koh-moh ess-*tah* oo-*steth*
Very well	**Muy bien**	mwee byen
Thank you	**Gracias**	*gra*-thee-ahss
Good-bye	**Adiós**	ad-*dyohss*
Please	**Por favór**	pohr fah-*bohr*
Yes	**Sí**	see
No	**No**	noh
Excuse me	**Perdóneme**	pehr-*doh*-neh-may
Give me	**Deme**	*day*-may
Where is . . . ?	**Donde está . . . ?**	*dohn*-day ess-*tah*
the station	**la estación**	la ess-tah-*thyohn*
a hotel	**un hotel**	oon-oh-*tel*
a restaurant	**un restaurante**	oon-res-tow-*rahn*-tay
the toilet	**el servicio**	el ser-*vee*-the-o
To the right	**A la derecha**	ah lah day-*ray*-chuh
To the left	**A la izquierda**	ah lah eeth-*kyayr*-duh
Straight ahead	**Adelante**	ah-day-*lahn*-tay
I would like	**Quiero**	kyehr-oh
to eat	**comer**	ko-*mayr*
a room	**una habitación**	oo-nah ah-bee-tah-*thyon*
How much is it?	**Cuánto?**	*kwahn*-toh
The check	**La cuenta**	la *kwen*-tah
When	**Cuándo?**	*kwan*-doh
Yesterday	**Ayer**	ah-yayr
Today	**Hoy**	oy
Tomorrow	**Mañana**	mahn-*yah*-nah
Breakfast	**Desayuno**	deh-sai-*yoo*-noh
Lunch	**Comida**	co-*mee*-dah
Dinner	**Cena**	*thay*-nah

Numbers

1	**uno** (*oo*-noh)	15	**quince** (*keen*-thay)
2	**dos** (dose)	16	**dieciseis** (dyeth-ee-*sayss*)
3	**tres** (trayss)	17	**diecisiete** (dyeth-ee-*sye*-tay)
4	**cuatro** (*kwah*-troh)	18	**dieciocho** (dyeth-ee-*oh*-choh)
5	**cinco** (*theen*-koh)	19	**diecinueve** (dyeth-ee-*nyway*-bay)
6	**seis** (sayss)	20	**veinte** (*bayn*-tay)
7	**siete** (*syeh*-tay)	30	**trienta** (*trayn*-tah)
8	**ocho** (*oh*-choh)	40	**cuarenta** (kwah-*ren*-tah)
9	**nueve** (*nway*-bay)	50	**cincuenta** (theen-*kween*-tah)
10	**diez** (dyeth)	60	**sesenta** (say-*sen*-tah)
11	**once** (*ohn*-thay)	70	**setenta** (say-*ten*-tah)
12	**doce** (*doh*-thay)	80	**ochenta** (oh-*chen*-tah)
13	**trece** (*tray*-thay)	90	**noventa** (noh-*ben*-tah)
14	**catorce** (kah-*tor*-thay)	100	**cien** (thyen)

B Menu Savvy

Alliolo Sauce made from garlic and olive oil

Arroz con costra Rice dish of chicken, rabbit, sausages, black pudding, chickpeas, spices, and pork meatballs—everything "hidden" under a layer of beaten egg crust

Arroz empedrado Rice cooked with tomatoes and cod and a top layer of white beans

Bacalao al ajo arriero Cod-and-garlic dish named after Leonese mule drivers

Bacalao al pil-pil Cod with garlic and chili peppers

Bacalao a la vizcaína Cod with dried peppers and onion

Bajoques farcides Peppers stuffed with rice, pork, tomatoes, and spices

Butifarra Catalonian sausage made with blood, spices, and eggs

Caldereta Stew or a stew pot

Caldereta extremeña Kid or goat stew

Caldo gallego Soup made with cabbage, potatoes, beans, and various meat flavorings (ham, chorizo, spareribs)

Chanfaina salmantina Rice, giblets, lamb sweetbreads, and pieces of chorizo

Chilindrón Sauce made from tomatoes, peppers, garlic, chorizo, and spicy sausage

Cochifrito navarro Small pieces of fried lamb

Cocido español Spanish stew

Cocido de pelotas Stew of minced meat wrapped in cabbage leaves and cooked with poultry, bacon, chickpeas, potatoes, and spices

El arroz amb fessois i nape Rice with beans and turnips

El caldillo de perro "Dog soup," made with onions, fresh fish, and orange juice

El cocido madrileña Chickpea stew of Madrid, with potatoes, cabbage, turnips, beef, marrow, bacon, chorizo, and black pudding

El pato a la naranja Duck with orange, an old Valencian dish

Empanada Crusted pie of Galicia, with a variety of fillings

Escudella Catalan version of chickpea stew

Fabada White bean stew of Asturias

Habas a la catalana Stew of broad beans, herbs, and spices

Judías blancas Haricot beans

Judias negras Runner beans

Lacón con grelos Salted ham with turnip tops

La cassolada Potato-and-vegetable stew with bacon and ribs

La salsa verde Green sauce to accompany fish

Las magras con tomate Slices of slightly fried ham dipped in tomato sauce

La trucha a la navarra Trout fried with a piece of ham

La pericana Cod, olive oil, dry peppers, and garlic

Mar y cielo "Sea and heaven," made with sausages, rabbit, shrimp, and fish

Merluza a la gallega Galician hake with onions, potatoes, and herbs

Merluza a la sidra Hake cooked with cider

Morcilla Black sausage akin to black pudding

Paella alicantina Rice dish with chicken and rabbit

Picada Sauce made from nuts, parsley, garlic, saffron, and cinnamon

Pilota Ball made of meat, parsley, bread crumbs, and eggs

Pinchito Small kebab

Pisto manchego Vegetable stew from La Mancha

Pollos a la chilindron Chicken cooked in a tomato, onion, and pepper sauce

Romesco Mediterranean sauce, with olive oil, red pepper, bread, garlic, and maybe cognac

Samfaina Sauce made from tomatoes, eggplant, onions, and zucchini

Sangría Drink made with fruit, brandy, and wine

Sofrito Sauce made from peppers, onions, garlic, tomatoes, and olive oil

Sopas castellanas Bread, broth, ham, and sometimes a poached egg and garlic

Sopa de ajo castellana Garlic soup with ham, bread, eggs, and spices

Tapas Small dishes or appetizers served with drinks at a tavern

Tortilla de patatas Spanish omelet with potatoes

Turrón Almond paste

Zarzuela Fish stew

C   Glossary of Architectural Terms

Alcazaba Moorish fortress

Alcázar Moorish fortified palace

Ayuntamiento Town hall

Azulejo Painted glazed tiles, popular in Mudéjar work and later architecture, especially in Andalusia, Valencia, and Portugal

Barrio (Barri in Catalán) City neighborhood or district

Churrigueresque Floridly ornate baroque style of the late 17th and early 18th centuries in the style of Spanish sculptor and architect José Churriguera (1650–1725)

Ciudadela Citadel

Cortijo Andalusian country house or villa

Granja Farm or farmhouse

Isabelline Gothic Architectural style popular in the late 15th century, roughly corresponding to the English perpendicular

Judería Jewish quarter

Lonja Merchants' exchange or marketplace

Medina Walled center of a Moorish city, traditionally centered around a mosque

Mezquita Mosque

Mirhab Prayer niche in a mosque, by Koranic law facing Mecca

Mirador Scenic overlook or belvedere, or a glassed-in panoramic balcony sheltering its occupants from the wind

Mudéjar Moorish-influenced architecture, usually "Christianized" and adopted as Spain's most prevalent architectural style from the 12th to the 16th century

Plateresque Heavily ornamented Gothic style widely used in Spain and Portugal during the 16th century. Its name derives from the repoussé floral patterns hammered into silver (*la plata*), which were imitated in low-relief carvings in stone

Plaza de Toros Bullring

Plaza Mayor Square at the center of many Spanish cities, often enclosed, arcaded, and enhanced with cafes and fountains

Puerta Portal or gate

Reja Iron grilles, either those covering the exterior windows of buildings or the decorative dividers in churches

Retablo Carved and/or painted altarpiece

D The Metric System

Length

1 millimeter (mm)	=	.04 inches (*or* less than $1/16$ in.)
1 centimeter (cm)	=	.39 inches (*or* just under $1/2$ in.)
1 meter (m)	=	39 inches (*or* about 1.1 yards)
1 kilometer (km)	=	.62 miles (*or* about $2/3$ of a mile)

To convert kilometers to miles, multiply the number of kilometers by .62. Also use to convert kilometers per hour (kmph) to miles per hour (m.p.h.).

To convert miles to kilometers, multiply the number of miles by 1.61. Also use to convert from m.p.h. to kmph.

Capacity

1 liter (l)	=	33.92 fluid ounces	=	2.1 pints
	=	1.06 quarts		
	=	.26 U.S. gallons		
1 Imperial gallon	=	1.2 U.S. gallons		

To convert liters to U.S. gallons, multiply the number of liters by .26.

To convert U.S. gallons to liters, multiply the number of gallons by 3.79.

To convert Imperial gallons to U.S. gallons, multiply the number of Imperial gallons by 1.2.

To convert U.S. gallons to Imperial gallons, multiply the number of U.S. gallons by .83.

Weight

1 gram (g)	=	.035 ounces (*or* about a paperclip's weight)
1 kilogram (kg)	=	35.2 ounces
	=	2.2 pounds
1 metric ton	=	2,205 pounds (1.1 short ton)

To convert kilograms to pounds, multiply the number of kilograms by 2.2.

To convert pounds to kilograms, multiply the number of pounds by .45.

Area

1 hectare (ha)	=	2.47 acres		
1 square kilometer (km²)	=	247 acres	=	.39 square miles

To convert hectares to acres, multiply the number of hectares by 2.47.

To convert acres to hectares, multiply the number of acres by .41.

To convert square kilometers to square miles, multiply the number of square kilometers by .39.

To convert square miles to square kilometers, multiply the number of square miles by 2.6.

Temperature

To convert degrees Celsius to degrees Fahrenheit, multiply °C by 9, divide by 5, and add 32 (example: 20°C × 9/5 + 32 = 68°F).

To convert degrees Fahrenheit to degrees Celsius, subtract 32 from °F, multiply by 5, then divide by 9 (example: 85°F − 32 × 5/9 = 29.4°C).

Index

ACCOMMODATIONS

Key to abbreviations: *B* = Budget; *E* = Expensive; *I* = Inexpensive; *M* = Moderate; *VE* = Very expensive

Excursion Areas

RESTAURANTS

Costa del Sol ——————

ACCOMMODATIONS

Key to abbreviations: *B* = Budget; *E* = Expensive; *I* = Inexpensive; *M* = Moderate;
VE = Very expensive

RESTAURANTS

Now Save Money On All Your Travels By Joining FROMMER'S™ TRAVEL BOOK CLUB The World's Best Travel Guides At Membership Prices!

Frommer's Travel Book Club is your ticket to successful travel! Open up a world of travel information and simplify your travel planning when you join ranks with thousands of value-conscious travelers who are members of the *Frommer's Travel Book Club*. Join today and you'll be entitled to all the privileges that come from belonging to the club that offers you travel guides for less to more than 100 destinations worldwide. **Annual membership is only $25.00 (U.S.) or $35.00 (Canada/Foreign).**

The Advantages of Membership:
1. Your choice of **three free** books (any **two** *Frommer's Comprehensive Guides, Frommer's $-A-Day Guides, Frommer's Walking Tours* or *Frommer's Family Guides*—plus **one** *Frommer's City Guide, Frommer's City $-A-Day Guide* or *Frommer's Touring Guide*).
2. Your own subscription to the **TRIPS & TRAVEL** quarterly newsletter.
3. You're entitled to a **30% discount** on your order of any additional books offered by the club.
4. You're offered (at a small additional fee) our **Domestic Trip-Routing Kits.**

Our **Trips & Travel** quarterly newsletter offers practical information on the best buys in travel, the "hottest" vacation spots, the latest travel trends, world-class events and much, much more.

Our **Domestic Trip-Routing Kits** are available for any North American destination. We'll send you a detailed map highlighting the best route to take to your destination—you can request direct or scenic routes.

Here's all you have to do to join:
Send in your membership fee of $25.00 ($35.00 Canada/Foreign) with your name and address on the form below along with your selections as part of your membership package to the address listed below. Remember to check off your three free books.

If you would like to order additional books, please select the books you would like and send a check for the total amount (please add sales tax in the states noted below), plus $2.00 per book for shipping and handling ($3.00 Canada/Foreign) to the address listed below.

FROMMER'S TRAVEL BOOK CLUB
P.O. Box 473
Mt. Morris, IL 61054-0473.
(815) 734-1104

[ ] **YES!** I want to take advantage of this opportunity to join Frommer's Travel Book Club.
[ ] My check is enclosed. Dollar amount enclosed   *
(all payments in U.S. funds only)

Name _____

Address _____

City _____ State _____ Zip _____

All orders must be prepaid.

To ensure that all orders are processed efficiently, please apply sales tax in the following areas: CA, CT, FL, IL, IN, NJ, NY, PA, TN, WA and CANADA.

*With membership, shipping & handling will be paid by Frommer's Travel Book Club for the three free books you select as part of your membership. Please add $2.00 per book for shipping & handling for any additional books purchased ($3.00 Canada/Foreign).

Allow 4-6 weeks for delivery. Prices of books, membership fee, and publication dates are subject to change without notice. Orders are subject to acceptance and availability.

Please send me the books checked below:

FROMMER'S COMPREHENSIVE GUIDES

(Guides listing facilities from budget to deluxe,
with emphasis on the medium-priced)

	Retail Price	Code		Retail Price	Code
☐ Acapulco/Ixtapa/Taxco, 2nd Edition	$13.95	C157	☐ Jamaica/Barbados, 2nd Edition	$15.00	C149
☐ Alaska '94–'95	$17.00	C131	☐ Japan '94–'95	$19.00	C144
☐ Arizona '95 (Avail. 3/95)	$14.95	C166	☐ Maui, 1st Edition	$13.95	C153
☐ Australia '94–'95	$18.00	C147	☐ Nepal, 2nd Edition	$18.00	C126
☐ Austria, 6th Edition	$16.95	C162	☐ New England '95	$16.95	C165
☐ Bahamas '94–'95	$17.00	C121	☐ New Mexico, 3rd Edition (Avail. 3/95)	$14.95	C167
☐ Belgium/Holland/ Luxembourg '93–'94	$18.00	C106	☐ New York State, 4th Edition	$19.00	C133
☐ Bermuda '94–'95	$15.00	C122	☐ Northwest, 5th Edition	$17.00	C140
☐ Brazil, 3rd Edition	$20.00	C111	☐ Portugal '94–'95	$17.00	C141
☐ California '95	$16.95	C164	☐ Puerto Rico '95–'96	$14.00	C151
☐ Canada '94–'95	$19.00	C145	☐ Puerto Vallarta/ Manzanillo/ Guadalajara '94–'95	$14.00	C028
☐ Caribbean '95	$18.00	C148			
☐ Carolinas/Georgia, 2nd Edition	$17.00	C128	☐ Scandinavia, 16th Edition (Avail. 3/95)	$19.95	C169
☐ Colorado, 2nd Edition	$16.00	C143	☐ Scotland '94–'95	$17.00	C146
☐ Costa Rica '95	$13.95	C161	☐ South Pacific '94–'95	$20.00	C138
☐ Cruises '95–'96	$19.00	C150	☐ Spain, 16th Edition	$16.95	C163
☐ Delaware/Maryland '94–'95	$15.00	C136	☐ Switzerland/ Liechtenstein '94–'95	$19.00	C139
☐ England '95	$17.95	C159	☐ Thailand, 2nd Edition	$17.95	C154
☐ Florida '95	$18.00	C152	☐ U.S.A., 4th Edition	$18.95	C156
☐ France '94–'95	$20.00	C132	☐ Virgin Islands '94–'95	$13.00	C127
☐ Germany '95	$18.95	C158	☐ Virginia '94–'95	$14.00	C142
☐ Ireland, 1st Edition (Avail. 3/95)	$16.95	C168	☐ Yucatan, 2nd Edition	$13.95	C155
☐ Italy '95	$18.95	C160			

FROMMER'S $-A-DAY GUIDES

(Guides to low-cost tourist accommodations and facilities)

	Retail Price	Code		Retail Price	Code
☐ Australia on $45 '95–'96	$18.00	D122	☐ Israel on $45, 15th Edition	$16.95	D130
☐ Costa Rica/Guatemala/ Belize on $35, 3rd Edition	$15.95	D126	☐ Mexico on $45 '95	$16.95	D125
			☐ New York on $70 '94–'95	$16.00	D121
☐ Eastern Europe on $30, 5th Edition	$16.95	D129	☐ New Zealand on $45 '93–'94	$18.00	D103
☐ England on $60 '95	$17.95	D128			
☐ Europe on $50 '95	$17.95	D127	☐ South America on $40, 16th Edition	$18.95	D123
☐ Greece on $45 '93–'94	$19.00	D100			
☐ Hawaii on $75 '95	$16.95	D124	☐ Washington, D.C. on $50 '94–'95	$17.00	D120
☐ Ireland on $45 '94–'95	$17.00	D118			

FROMMER'S CITY $-A-DAY GUIDES

	Retail Price	Code		Retail Price	Code
☐ Berlin on $40 '94-'95	$12.00	D111	☐ Madrid on $50 '94-'95	$13.00	D119
☐ London on $45 '94-'95	$12.00	D114	☐ Paris on $45 '94-'95	$12.00	D117

FROMMER'S FAMILY GUIDES

	Retail Price	Code		Retail Price	Code
☐ California with Kids	$18.00	F100	☐ San Francisco with Kids	$17.00	F104
☐ Los Angeles with Kids	$17.00	F103	☐ Washington, D.C. with Kids	$17.00	F102
☐ New York City with Kids	$18.00	F101			

FROMMER'S CITY GUIDES

(Pocket-size guides to sightseeing and tourist
accommodations and facilities in all price ranges)

	Retail Price	Code		Retail Price	Code
☐ Amsterdam '93-'94	$13.00	S110	☐ Nashville/Memphis, 1st Edition	$13.00	S141
☐ Athens, 10th Edition (Avail. 3/95)	$12.95	S174	☐ New Orleans '95	$12.95	S148
☐ Atlanta '95	$12.95	S161	☐ New York '95	$12.95	S152
☐ Atlantic City/Cape May, 5th Edition	$13.00	S130	☐ Orlando '95	$13.00	S145
☐ Bangkok, 2nd Edition	$12.95	S147	☐ Paris '95	$12.95	S150
☐ Barcelona '93-'94	$13.00	S115	☐ Philadelphia, 8th Edition	$12.95	S167
☐ Berlin, 3rd Edition	$12.95	S162	☐ Prague '94-'95	$13.00	S143
☐ Boston '95	$12.95	S160	☐ Rome, 10th Edition	$12.95	S168
☐ Budapest, 1st Edition	$13.00	S139	☐ San Diego '95	$12.95	S158
☐ Chicago '95	$12.95	S169	☐ San Francisco '95	$12.95	S155
☐ Denver/Boulder/Colorado Springs, 3rd Edition	$12.95	S154	☐ Santa Fe/Taos/ Albuquerque '95	$12.95	S172
☐ Dublin, 2nd Edition	$12.95	S157	☐ Seattle/Portland '94-'95	$13.00	S137
☐ Hong Kong '94-'95	$13.00	S140	☐ St. Louis/Kansas City, 2nd Edition	$13.00	S127
☐ Honolulu/Oahu '95	$12.95	S151	☐ Sydney, 4th Edition	$12.95	S171
☐ Las Vegas '95	$12.95	S163	☐ Tampa/St. Petersburg, 3rd Edition	$13.00	S146
☐ London '95	$12.95	S156	☐ Tokyo '94-'95	$13.00	S144
☐ Los Angeles '95	$12.95	S164	☐ Toronto '95 (Avail. 3/95)	$12.95	S173
☐ Madrid/Costa del Sol, 2nd Edition	$12.95	S165	☐ Vancouver/Victoria '94-'95	$13.00	S142
☐ Mexico City, 1st Edition	$12.95	S170	☐ Washington, D.C. '95	$12.95	S153
☐ Miami '95-'96	$12.95	S149			
☐ Minneapolis/St. Paul, 4th Edition	$12.95	S159			
☐ Montreal/ Quebec City '95	$11.95	S166			

SPECIAL EDITIONS

	Retail Price	Code		Retail Price	Code
☐ Bed & Breakfast Southwest	$16.00	P100	☐ National Park Guide, 29th Edition	$17.00	P106
☐ Bed & Breakfast Great American Cities	$16.00	P104	☐ Where to Stay U.S.A., 11th Edition	$15.00	P102
☐ Caribbean Hideaways	$16.00	P103			

FROMMER'S WALKING TOURS

(With routes and detailed maps, these companion guides point out the places and pleasures that make a city unique)

	Retail Price	Code		Retail Price	Code
☐ Berlin	$12.00	W100	☐ New York	$12.00	W102
☐ Chicago	$12.00	W107	☐ Paris	$12.00	W103
☐ England's Favorite Cities	$12.00	W108	☐ San Francisco	$12.00	W104
☐ London	$12.00	W101	☐ Washington, D.C.	$12.00	W105
☐ Montreal/Quebec City	$12.00	W106			

FROMMER'S TOURING GUIDES

(Color-illustrated guides that include walking tours, cultural and historic sites, and practical information)

	Retail Price	Code		Retail Price	Code
☐ Amsterdam	$11.00	T001	☐ New York	$11.00	T008
☐ Barcelona	$14.00	T015	☐ Rome	$11.00	T010
☐ Brazil	$11.00	T003	☐ Scotland	$10.00	T011
☐ Hong Kong/Singapore/ Macau	$11.00	T006	☐ Sicily	$15.00	T017
			☐ Tokyo	$15.00	T016
☐ Kenya	$14.00	T018	☐ Turkey	$11.00	T013
☐ London	$13.00	T007	☐ Venice	$9.00	T014

Please note: If the availability of a book is several months away, we may have back issues of guides to that particular destination. Call customer service at (815) 734-1104.